D1552176

THE PAIN AND THE PRIVILEGE

Joseph Gallagher

Joseph Gallagher

THE PAIN AND THE PRIVILEGE

Diary of a City Priest

IMAGE BOOKS

A Division of
Doubleday & Company, Inc.
Garden City, New York
1983

"The Living Room of Belva Thomas": Reprinted with permission of the America Press, Inc., 106 West 56 Street, New York, N.Y. 10019, Copyright © 1976, all rights reserved.

"A Long Night of Waiting to See a President," "Reliving Memories 'Vividly Personal,'" "An Open Letter to Mr. Mahoney," and "Cardinal Shehan's Pastoral on the Vietnam War": Reprinted in whole or in part with permission of the *Catholic Review,* Baltimore.

"An Open Letter to the U.S. Catholic Bishops": Reprinted by permission of the *National Catholic Reporter,* P.O. Box 281, Kansas City, Mo. 64141.

Items reprinted in whole or in part from the *Evening Sun,* Baltimore, appear with the permission of that newspaper.

"Vacillation" Stanza IV: Reprinted with permission of Macmillan Publishing Co., Inc., from *Collected Poems* by William Butler Yeats, Copyright 1933 by Macmillan Publishing Co., Inc., renewed 1961 by Bertha Georgie Yeats.

Lines from "The Municipal Gallery Revisited": Reprinted with permission of Macmillan Publishing Co., Inc., from *Collected Poems* by William Butler Yeats, Copyright 1940 by Georgie Yeats, renewed 1968 by Bertha Georgie Yeats, Michael Butler Yeats, and Anne Yeats.

Lines from "Breaking and Entering": Reprinted with permission of the University of Pennsylvania Press from *The Chinese Insomniacs* by Josephine Jacobsen, Philadelphia, 1981.

Lyrics excerpted from "Show Me," Copyright © 1956 by Alan Jay Lerner & Frederick Loewe. Chappell & Co., Inc., owner of publication and allied rights throughout the world. International Copyright Secured. ALL RIGHTS RESERVED. Used by permission.

Library of Congress Cataloging in Publication Data

Gallagher, Joseph.
    The pain and the privilege.

    1. Gallagher, Joseph. 2. Catholic Church—Clergy—United States—Biography. 3. Catholic Church—History—1965- . 4. United States—Social conditions—1960- . 5. United States—Politics and government—1945- . I. Title.
BX4705.G146A36 1983   282'.092'4 [B]
ISBN: 0-385-19019-0
Library of Congress Catalog Card Number 82-1766

Copyright © 1983 by Joseph Gallagher
All Rights Reserved
Printed in the United States of America
First Edition

DEDICATION

TO J.C., STRONG AND GENTLE CARPENTER,
AND ALL THE CARPENTERS OF THE STORIED YEARS
WHO HELPED ME BUILD AND HELPED BUILD ME.

EPIGRAPH

Half the glooms that grieve me sad come from joys
I wish I had;
While half my happy moods consist of miseries
I know I've missed.

CONTENTS

Preface

> "Like golden apples in silver settings are words spoken at the
> proper time."
>
> Proverbs 25:11

In 1979 I celebrated my fiftieth birthday and began my twenty-fifth
year as a Catholic priest working in Baltimore, one of the oldest,
largest, and most colorful of U.S. cities. "It was a very good year,"
then, a golden and silver occasion for looking back and taking stock.
So I decided to keep a daily journal full of flashbacks, a kind of calendar in 3-D. That turned out to be the year of Three Mile Island,
Skylab's return, the first papal tour of the U.S., the seizure of the
U.S. Embassy in Teheran, and Baltimore's 250th birthday.

While noting external events, I wanted to record what was happening privately in the life of one fifty-year-old clergyman, and what
his memories were like. I wanted to recall some of the peaks and valleys of my first half century. Some of these I shared with millions of
others: Pearl Harbor, V-J Day, the deaths of FDR and JFK. Others
were intensely personal.

I wanted to put on record some of my favorite stories and rarest
experiences: as a human being in the twentieth century; as a white
American male caught up in the storms of Civil Rights, Vietnam,
and urban riots; and as a Catholic priest reverberating to the slow
earthquake of the Second Vatican Council and the fast one of Pope
Paul VI's encyclical against contraception.

As a graduate of the "old" seminary and a teacher in the "new,"
as an editor of a diocesan newspaper before, during, and after Vatican II, and as a translator of Council documents, I had the privilege
and the pain of some close-up views of Catholicism at home, in
Rome, and elsewhere during the past three historic decades. As an
urbanite, traveler, occasional picketer and protester, I witnessed at
firsthand some of the symptomatic disturbances which have rocked

the U.S. and the world scene in the latter half of this vertiginous century.

My journal, which was temporarily interrupted toward the end by a sudden, "catastrophic" illness, came to 1,100 typewritten pages and a third of a million words. That's what you get when you compose an average of three pages a day for a year. This present volume contains excerpts from the full diary.

As in some calendars, each day is decorated with a quote. I have always been intoxicated by long thoughts in short spaces, brevity in wit, and beauty in brief. The quotes I cite are those which, during years of reading and listening, have struck me as especially revealing or provocative. I've initialed the few that are my own. Where no author is given credit I am either ignorant or unsure of who deserves it.

☘

It is perhaps as difficult to write a good life as to live one.
                                              Lytton Strachey

January 1, 1979

It was my fiftieth New Year to heaven (as Dylan Thomas would say), and I woke in the capital of the Confederacy—in the Richmond rectory of young priest-friend Mike Schmied. I had arrived there on New Year's Eve with another young friend, John Corcoran, a carpenter from Pittsburgh. John and I had just spent the final two days of 1978 visiting colonial Williamsburg.

Today we two left Richmond before noon and drove 365 appropriate miles to John's home in Wexford, fifteen miles north of "the Steel City." Shortly before 6 P.M. we arrived at his Tudor-frame house on the side of a hill. There his wife, Nanci, and their two youngsters, Jason (five) and Brenda (two), were waiting for us.

Though twenty-nine-year-old John had been a seminarian for five teen-age years, I met him only four years ago through his younger brother, Pat, who was at the time a student of mine at St. Mary's Seminary in Baltimore. From the start I was struck by John's quiet and his gentleness. Last year he designed his new home, let me officiate at the ground-breaking on Easter Monday, began building in early April, accepted my help during the summer, and moved in on September 16.

Last year also, after twenty-three years in the priesthood, I had begun the process of dismantling my clerical self and returning to the lay state. There were physical, psychological, and theological reasons for this decision—which I had come close to twice before, in 1969 and 1974. (During one of these periods of soul-searching I was strolling near a friend's home in Detroit and came upon a street corner where two street signs and a traffic sign combined to declare: "Lehmann/Gallagher/Stop." I chuckled and recalled the Irish warning: "Don't be superstitious; it's bad luck.")

At the heart of my decision were the tensions and contradictions I felt in my role as a religious answer man at a time of agonizing confusion within Catholicism and within myself. My family has a history of emotional collapses, and I felt I had overdosed on problems and on people with problems.

Getting away from my native Baltimore and doing physical work for fifty days on a friend's house seemed good therapy as the resignation process got under way after my visit to Archbishop Borders last June. Later, just as I was about to send my decisive letter to Pope Paul VI, he died. Until I sent that letter I would still enjoy my priestly faculties, and I had been waiting until I helped celebrate a friend's wedding in early August.

Like many another, I was captivated by Pope John Paul I and feeling a new sense of hopefulness in the church, when suddenly he, too, died. The subsequent election of a pope from behind the Iron Curtain exhilarated me, though I didn't expect him to make any immediate changes in matters that had troubled me—the ban on contraception and the law of clerical celibacy, for instance.

My original decision to resign was not easy, and I was still torn inside. Then, less than a month ago, one of the human beings I loved the most in this world died in Rhode Island. She was the mother of a close seminary friend who had himself died as a deacon in 1954. "Ma" Nunes was my idea of a saint, and seeing her look so lovely and loving even in death, and thinking of her self-giving life, I felt myself being pulled back into a willingness to try to live again with the stress and strain of ministry.

Tonight as John and Nanci went to a wake, I minded the children. I sat before the fireplace which John and I had built in the heat of last July. Imbedded in it and arranged in the form of a cross are stones from Jerusalem, Jericho, Bethlehem, Nazareth, and the Dead Sea. I had collected them during my trip to Israel last May.

On the Mount of Olives an old man named Hassim led me by candlelight down numerous steps into the Tomb of the Prophets. "Watch your step, Father," he warned. Startled and reassuring myself that I was wearing ordinary tourist's clothing, I asked him how he knew I was a priest. "My heart," he replied, "is pushing me to call you that." It was an uncanny conversation in that particular setting.

Once before, when I was similarly dressed, I gave a lift to a hitchhiking sailor near Los Angeles. I asked him if he was a native of L.A. "No—I'm from up north, Father." I was so stunned I almost drove off the road. "How did you know I was a priest?" He gave me a quizzical look. "I said I'm from up north farther."

After John and Nanci went to bed, and as the fire died out and the outside temperature dipped, I listened alone to Jane Olivor's first album, *First Night*, with its hit rendition of "Some Enchanted Evening." It was an apt ending to the year's first night.

I reminisced about my father's father, born this day in 1862 at the other end of Pennsylvania. And about the ailing Dr. Alexander Schaffer, born in Baltimore seventy-seven years ago—who may well have saved my nephew's life. And of Jule Williams, married to a Philadelphia cousin. Seventeen years ago this morning he woke, leaned over to kiss his wife, and died.

Finally I went to bed. The long brass bed was my gift to the room, as it had been a gift to me from an old poet and friend who had gone last summer to England to die. Elliott Coleman had presumably lived into 1979, however, in a nursing home near Oxford. Across the Irish Sea from him was that County Wexford where my mother's mother had been born more than a century ago. Now I was falling asleep in a small Pennsylvania town named after her native Wexford.

Ghosts are everywhere.

🌳

The present is the past, struggling to become the future;
the future is the past returning through another door.

January 2

Planning to make my exit for Baltimore tomorrow, I spent a leisurely day with this young family. John went off to the funeral of the first man to hire him as a carpenter. Feisty Nanci was busy being a post-holiday mother and housekeeper. Serious Brenda wandered about, looking like a pigment of Renoir's imagination. Jason went off to his noon session of kindergarten.

Once I was trying to dissuade the boy from playing with a fragile toy motorcycle given to his Uncle Pat by a girl friend. After providing Jason with several arguments that failed to impress him, I invoked several solemn polysyllables: "It has incalculable emotional significance." "Yeah," replied Jason, "but does it have a motor?"

Today I phoned a prison near Greensburg to see whether a Pittsburgh priest-friend of mine was still an inmate there, and whether I could visit him tomorrow. Dick, a gifted writer and musician, is sixty-five, and was sent to jail about two months ago on "corruption of youth" charges. He taught me English in first high, my first year in the seminary. I was in awe, knowing him to be a published writer. Through the years he has always encouraged me in my own writing.

Some years ago he was put on a medicine which turned out to be addictive for him. Since then he has been having trouble with drink and drugs and other problems they cause—though he tells me the current charges are false. I believe he tells me what his memory tells him, but I'm not sure about his memory. He has always been a loner, and feels that his church superiors worked at frustrating his gifts and needs. His original bishop, for example, encouraged him to study the organ as a seminarian and then assigned him to a parish without an organ.

He was on the "Phil Donahue Show" a few years ago discussing his book about the church's repression of sex. (On most other subjects Dick is notoriously conservative.) Donahue later said he never before received so many violent phone calls about a guest. He soon featured another priest to refute Dick.

The prison guard took my phone number, and Dick called me back, in apparent good spirits. He said his tablemates had never heard of Rasputin. He had no memory of my visit to him in a Greensburg hospital last Thanksgiving time. He said that on the day he entered jail he had taken thirty or forty Elavils and a pint of vodka. On an earlier occasion severe depression had led him to the brink of hanging himself. But at the last minute there came a knock at the door and curiosity got the best of him. In his darkest times he flares wittily. In a sunnier 1943, one of my classmates asked him if it was true that you can't become a priest if you're illegitimate. Dick eyed him for a few seconds and replied: "Worried?"

Though once painfully idealistic and naïve, I now know what T. S. Eliot meant by "the wounded healer." Human weakness in clergymen no longer scandalizes me. As with other professionals, such as doctors and lawyers, the wounding often results from the very attempt to heal, and from learning too much about human nature. It has been said that to get a person out of hell, you have to go there yourself.

✤

For such a man, a man both weak and cowardly, to bear the burden of his weakness and struggle valiantly to live a beautiful life—that's what I call great.

Shusaku Endo

January 3

History is a series of exaggerated reactions.

January 4

History is philosophy teaching by examples.

January 5

Life is a silent film about snow, with white subtitles.

J.G.

January 6

Driving in a wind-chill index of minus thirty degrees, my VW Dasher broke down on the Pennsylvania Turnpike three days ago. I was told my cylinder head had "freezed up," and total repairs would cost $1,300. That frustrating car had already bled me of $3,000 in repairs in less than four years, so I decided to trade it in for a 1975 Pacer. With my dashed Dasher thrown in, the secondhand car cost me $1,500 and got me home from Pittsburgh about eighty hours after I had left for Baltimore.

My home is a three-story brick row house at 1807 Park Avenue. The park in question is Baltimore's largest, Druid Hill, into which my street dead-ends a few blocks north of me. It was laid out by the Olmstead who designed New York's Central Park. My home is two houses north of North Avenue, which was once the northern boundary of the city, but which is now in about mid-city.

Baltimore is shaped roughly like a rectangle measuring ninety-two square miles. Like a few other U.S. cities, it is in no county—though it is surrounded by Baltimore County. It is the nation's ninth largest city, with a population around 786,000.

I'm also about six blocks west of the street which divides Baltimore east and west—Charles Street. When I entered the seminary in 1943, my family lived about a mile east of here. Noxzema (which "knocks eczema") was invented in a drugstore once located at a nearby North Avenue address.

My current house address goes back to one day in the late 1950s when I was hearing confessions in the city's old cathedral. Speaking in the faceless dark, an elderly woman told me of her distress that the brother who lived with her was house-bound and never saw a priest. I asked her where she lived, and she gave the address which is now my own. Realizing that her residence was not far, I volunteered to visit her brother.

His name was Sothoron, and she was Victorine Key Robertson. They were the children of a Confederate soldier who had fought at the Battle of Berryville (Virginia) and who moved to this house in the early 1900s. (The house was at the time perhaps ten years old.) She was a relative of Francis Scott Key and of F. Scott Fitzgerald.

I discovered this latter connection in a deflating way. I had just read a book about the author of *The Great Gatsby* and learned that he once lived at 1307 Park Avenue. One afternoon, as I was driving Victorine to lunch, I asked her if I might take a brief detour. Knowing her to be an unworldly person, I thought I had better explain that at this address had onced lived "the novelist, F. Scott Fitzgerald." "Oh, you mean Scotty," she responded. "You know of him?" "Indeed; he was my cousin—a lovely fellow, though he drank too much."

Victorine had been born on May 15, 1885, exactly a year before Emily Dickinson's death. She never married, though she spoke of a fiancé who died young. Victorine's last brother, who was also her last close relative, died shortly after she returned from a European pilgrimage which I chaplained in 1961.

Though the neighborhood turned rough, Victorine refused to leave her home. She closed off the second and third floors, and locked herself in her bedroom at night, fortified by a telephone and a gun given her by a distant relative. She was mugged once or twice on the street. It was her custom to walk the seven blocks or so to daily Mass. In winter she wore all black; in summer, all white.

She was found dead in her bed a few days after Christmas, 1974—her ninetieth year. She had been on a trip to Washington the previous day. In her will, of which I was the executor, I was left the furnishings (some pre-Revolutionary) of the three-story house and 10 percent of her estate. Her brother had apparently been a compulsive collector: I found the seventeen rooms crammed full of boxes and jars; closets and drawers were filled to overflowing. Burned matches were stored in matchboxes, partially smoked cigars in cigar boxes. I found hundreds of streetcar transfers dating from the teens, the twenties, and the thirties—all arranged chronologically.

Even with the help of many students it took me four or five months to go through everything in the house. We found a Chippendale chair in the jam-packed garage. We found a 1770 A.D. letter from one relative to another, and several front pages of old Baltimore newspapers dating from 1907 to 1924. Among the preserved headlines: "Hungry German Dies in Satisfying Ravenous Stomach"; "Boy Climbs into Gun and Is Shot Up in Air"; "Woodrow Wilson Dies in His Washington Home."

On Good Friday I unearthed $20,000 worth of savings books. Underneath the kitchen floor a bucketful of silverware lay hiding, some from the eighteenth century. One old knife had "Bread" carved into its handle, and on its blade were engraved the words "Cutler to Her Majesty the Queen."

(The phrase reminded me of the two London bakeries, side by side, which had been competing for the business of Buckingham Palace. The winning bakery put up a sign: "We bake for the Queen." The losing neighbor put up a sign: "God save the Queen.")

The value of the house was about the same as my share of the estate. So, I took the house instead of the money, and sold most of the furnishings to a competitive auctioneer. I used the money to renovate the house and moved in on September 20, 1975.

A youthful picture of Victorine hangs on the parlor wall, gazing benignly down on my various relatives and friends of all ages who have enjoyed the hospitality of her once hushed, darkened, and lonely house.

Tonight my nephew Frank arrived with five college friends. We all sat relaxing around the newly activated fireplace in the first-floor back. On the mantelpiece stands a bronze statue of Joan of Arc which I purchased when Victorine and I were pilgrims in France. As the flames rose toward the statue, I recalled that today was St. Joan's birthday.

Mention of the saint recalls a scholar who was on his deathbed. Had he actually expired? "Feel his feet," someone suggested. "No one ever died with warm feet." The scholar opened his eyes, said, "Joan of Arc did," and died.

☘

Life is what happens to you while you're making other plans.

January 7

One clock stopped and learned the meaning of time.

January 8

I had supper with my older brother's family at their home in northeast Baltimore, near the new cathedral. I hadn't seen any but Frank since Christmas Day. Ever since my brother died nearly seven years ago I've tried to have supper with them at least once a week.

Mary, the mother, is three months younger than I. For about four years she has been working part-time in a downtown travel agency. Recent rumors whisper that I have married Mary or am about to do so. Even my archbishop has been making discreet inquiries. It is educational to be the object of a rumor, sometimes quite detailed, which is altogether false. Nephew Frank thinks the rumor is absurd, though I had to wonder why he was so emphatic about it.

Niece Mary Ellen is twenty-four and has worked in a downtown bank for several years. She is attractive and petite. I'm her godfather. Born during my last months in the seminary, she made me an uncle for the first time.

While she was being born my brother slipped into the unlit chapel at Mercy Hospital. When his eyes grew accustomed to the dark he realized that next to him in the aisle was a nun in her coffin. She was to be buried the following morning. In the old days we would have said this was a sign that Mary Ellen should be a nun.

Frank you already met with his college friends around my bedroom fireplace. Once I asked Frank if he realized that we spend a third of our lives sleeping. "Yes; it's wonderful, isn't it?" That's his attitude toward life in a nutshell.

John J., my namesake, is fifteen and a sophomore at Loyola High, from which his father and older brother graduated. He is studious and introspective, though more humorous and outgoing of late. He has a fabulous memory and darkly handsome looks. One day he came upon me sitting quietly in a yoga position. He gazed at me for a few seconds and then said, "That doesn't work, does it?" That is John in a nutshell.

Pat and Jim are twelve-year-old identical twins. They are in the sixth grade at the new cathedral school. The twins get along very well with each other. Once, when Mary Ellen gave Pat a crack for misbehavior, Jim gallantly objected, "You don't hit me that hard when I'm bad."

❧

To whom God sends no sons the devil sends nephews.
Spanish proverb (arguable)

January 9

Even a stopped clock is right twice a day.

January 10

Through some sleuthing contacts in the telephone company, I learned today that my out-of-touch younger brother Tommy is still living in Long Beach, California. Seventeen months my junior, he was a more typical youngster and student than our older brother Francis and I. I've often wondered whether he was damaged by teachers and others who compared him unfavorably to his more studious and docile older brothers.

Tommy quit high school and joined the Navy, but soon received a medical discharge. Later he joined the Baltimore police force and was a hero in a 1955 downtown fire which killed half a dozen firemen. (I have a newspaper photo showing him at the rescue.)

The incident must have shaken him, tender-hearted as he is. He simply disappeared a few days later, leaving his pistol and badge at

our mother's apartment, where he had been living. When I was ordained three months afterward we still didn't know where Tommy
was.

He eventually wrote to me from California, where he married an
older divorcée. I visited them in 1957. In 1964 he returned, divorced,
to Baltimore for a year or so, but finally drifted back to California.

He has a genuine talent for writing and once composed a poem
about my family coming to the minor seminary on the monthly visiting Sunday:

> Here's to Joe seeking in youth
> The source of a thousand resurrections,
> Beckoning from atop that windy hill
> A family eager with ice-cream.

In his younger days he worked in a downtown meat market whose
personnel manager was one Spiro T. Agnew. My older brother
taught speech writing at Johns Hopkins to that same gentleman
even before he was known enough to be referred to as Spiro Who?

Did I unwittingly help Agnew become Maryland Governor and
U.S. Vice-President? More about that melancholy possibility in its
proper place.

❦

Dear Brother Thomas: I have been brave but wicked—pray for
me.

Note scribbled by a dying Union soldier

January 11

Josephine and Eric Jacobsen invited me to supper at their apartment tonight. It was just eighteen years ago this month that I gave a
particular sermon at Baltimore's old cathedral at an afternoon Mass
—a rarity in those days. I stressed the folly of automatically identi-
fying anyone who is concerned with social problems as a Marxist. I
cited the senator who quoted some anonymous pro-labor statements
to a self-proclaimed Marxist expert. "That's a Commie talking,"
affirmed the expert. The quotes were from Popes Leo XIII and Pius
XI.

A few days after my sermon a letter arrived at the rectory for the

"priest who had the 4 P.M. Mass." It was a supportive letter from
Josephine Jacobsen, whose poetry reviews I had read and admired in
the *Evening Sun*. (She never showed off and always seemed to find
something to praise.) I replied by letter, we arranged a chat, and we
have been close friends ever since then.

To know Josephine closely means coming to know and admire her
courtly husband, Eric, a gentleman of the old school. They have
been married now for more than forty-five years, a fact which as-
tonishes many of her much-married literary friends. He is an avid
reader himself, and Josephine once cited him in a speech she gave
about the delights of rereading old favorites: "Last winter, for
example, my husband took a Trollope with him to the Caribbean."
Eric has handled gallantly his wife's increasing celebrity over the past
decade.

Following in the footsteps of poets like Frost, Robert Lowell, and
Stephen Spender, she was poetry consultant at the Library of Congress, and for an unusual two terms (1971–73). Her fifth book of
poems, *The Shade Seller*, was nominated for the 1974 National Book
Award. Just this week her first book of short stories, *A Walk with
Raschid*, was chosen by the American Library Association for its
small list of Notable Books of 1978.

Over the years I have visited the Jacobsen home in New Hampshire quite a few summers. Supposedly haunted, it is featured in
Yankee Ghosts by Hans Holzer; Sibyl Leak performed a séance
there. In 1967 and 1975 I spent some winter weeks with them on
the paradisiac island of Grenada, their favorite Caribbean haunt.
But even in Baltimore, when you're with the Jacobsens, you travel.

She turns from the priest
potent and humble:
between her teeth
God breaks and crumbles.
Fair enough. God eats her slowly.
　　　　　　Josephine Jacobsen, "Breaking and Entering"

January 12

Freshly falling snow provided an ideal backdrop for the birds who
have gotten wind of the new feeder that John Corcoran built for

me, and are now frequenting my yard as never before. Most of the birds look like sparrows to me, but I've seen one cardinal and one bluejay, and a goodly number of blackbirds, glossy and bossy. As a novice bird watcher, I'm struck by the way these birds steal from one another, how they erupt into wing-wild, fistless furies, how they push away intruders, and how they come and go in groups.

When I spent such leisurely moments watching nature and tasting a sudden refreshment, I recall a critical moment that occurred in my life back in the sixties. At the time I was an editor on the archdiocesan newspaper, archdiocesan director of radio, TV, and the bureau of information, and chaplain at a motherhouse of nuns. One morning as I was rushing around getting ready to leave my chaplain's quarters and head downtown to interview someone at a radio station, I happened to look out at the sky.

It hit me hard: I hadn't taken the time to look at the sky for what seemed like months. I wondered just why I was doing all this rushing, and I revolted against my excess of activity. I made a phone call or two, canceling the interview. I put some favorite music on the stereo and stretched out on the carpet, totally dedicated to looking through the window at the puffy clouds blowing across a bright blue sky.

I think I made a fundamental decision that morning, one which gradually unfolded itself over the intervening years—despite frequent lapses into more activity than I could properly digest. Even though I realize how restorative contemplation is, rushing around is habit-forming, and the withdrawal pains can be fearsome. I know—don't we all?—what is meant by the agony of sitting still.

Meantime, despite good intentions, my mind and my body are not as harmonious as I think they should be, as occasional colon spasms attest. So today I phoned a Sister of Mercy, a nurse whom I've met off and on over the past decade. In recent years she studied at Oxford to become an acupuncturist and is now working at an acupuncture center in Columbia, Maryland. I'm due to give lectures in Columbia during February and March, so I thought it might be timely and convenient for me to discover for myself what acupuncture has to offer to this Westerner.

Sister Charlotte was encouraging. We decided it might be best for me to deal with Robert Duggan, the director of the center, who is a resigned priest. I'll try to make an appointment sometime next week.

Tonight I was able to share the relative quiet of my home with a priest-friend who has been an auxiliary bishop of Baltimore for the last three years. Frank Murphy was consecrated a bishop on February 29, 1976, so he can celebrate his anniversary only once every four years. That's just as well—so busy has he become.

Frank's master gift is his chief problem: he's pastoral, personable, and wants to be available. So everyone is after him and he has to fight for breathing space. Very few people, I think, have a grasp of the draining demands made on a pastoral priest or bishop during these years of upheaval and challenge. The danger is that such shepherds will be worn down too soon by the very openness which is so promising. I remember a statement which Pope Paul VI made early in his pontificate: "Everything moves; everything is a problem."

But this night at least, Frank Murphy was nourished, not by Mrs. Murphy's chowder, but by my Dinty Moore stew, and by a restful hour or two watching my fireplace blaze while nobody knew where to interrupt him.

❦

What is this life if, full of care,
We have no time to stand and stare?
William Henry Davies

January 13

The most important gift a father
can give his children is his choice of their mother.

January 14

About 11 A.M. I said Mass in the parlor of the Gallaghers. Four years ago today the boys' paternal grandmother, my mother, died of cancer at the age of seventy-four in the Good Samaritan Hospital. She had been hospitalized for fifty-two days; on December 7 the disease was diagnosed. At that time she was in Union Memorial Hospital, a few blocks from her small apartment near Johns Hopkins University campus. She had lost her voice, and eventually had to be given a tracheotomy. (So much for those final conversations about which I had fantasized.) At first she wrote me notes, then slipped into a placid coma. As she lingered I arranged to have her transferred just before Christmas to "Good Sam," an extended-care hospital.

That following January 14 my older brother's third anniversary of death was less than a month away. I left my mother's side to have a quick supper with my deceased brother's family. Before I finished, the nearby hospital phoned me to return at once to my mother's room. I had been away less than an hour. Nephew Frank came with me. Mother was dead when we got there. It wasn't so much that hot tears welled up, as that I sank down into them after my long vigil, like a spent swimmer consenting to drown. Frank put his arm around me.

There was a nun in the room who normally did not nurse on that floor. She happened to be in my mother's room when she was obviously dying. She prayed for her and stayed until I arrived. Later she wrote to me that while she does not fear the dying she had always had a dread of the dead. This time, to her surprise, she felt no fear. My mother, whose long and troubled life had ended, was always good at putting people at ease.

Sitting by her side on her last day of life, I tried to capture her spirit in these words for her memorial card.

Though life withheld or withdrew many
gifts from her, it failed ever to rob
loveliness from her face, dignity from
her manner, or sympathy from her heart.
As daughter, sister, wife, mother,
widow, and steady friend, she was a
womanly woman of gentle simplicity.
Life found her vulnerable and left her
more wounded than most, but failed in
all its hardness to make her hard.
Selfless and defenseless to a rare degree,
she preserved to the end her valiant will
to cheerfulness, and kept surprising us
with her hidden strengths. She was not a
Christian with many answers, but she
spent herself her whole life long as
though kindliness must surely be one of
them—as she herself was surely one of
the kindliest of creatures. This was her

best, and she gave her best, and the
memory of her plucky tenderness may well
persuade us that such indeed is the best
there is.

🌱

You have dropped your dusty cloak and taken your wondrous
wings to another sphere where no pain is.

Thomas Hardy

January 15

Martin Luther King's fiftieth birthday. We were born the same
year. I heard him give his "I have a dream" talk at the Lincoln Memorial during the famous March on Washington of 1963. I was in
the march, but because of the crowds I went to the Washington
Press Club with reporter Charlie Whiteford of the Baltimore *Sun*
and watched the speech on TV.

Some years later, protesting the Vietnam War, I was in Arlington
National Cemetery when Dr. King and other religious leaders arrived to lead us in a prayer which had to be silent because some
official had decided that it was against the rules for a "political"
prayer to be said aloud there.

I learned of King's death while I was discussing the problem of
evil in a philosophy class with a small group of students at old St.
Mary's Seminary. In the group was our only black student, George
Quickley. We watched Robert Kennedy on TV, comforting a group
of Negroes at an airport with his favorite lines from the poet
Aeschylus. Two months later these awesome lines (which conclude
this entry) appeared on Kennedy's own memorial card.

Two months ago I visited Atlanta for the first time, went to
King's church there (where his mother was killed), and viewed his
marble tomb nearby. It struck me as ironic tonight when I heard a
radio reporter refer to his "white" marble tomb. I wonder if anyone
thought of using black marble. (In Paris, with similar irony, Napoleon is entombed in porphyry, which came from the Russia which
defeated him.)

For over three years now, by my own choice, I have been living in a poor black neighborhood. At times I have been the only white in this block. Last September I rented the top floors to two black women. When Kathy, the student on the third floor, fell behind in her rent, she told me resentfully that she spends her time working and then giving all of her money to white men. Just before Christmas she moved out owing me three weeks rent and taking the keys with her.

Beverly, the other black tenant, has been no trouble. The neighbors have been generally quite friendly—they know I am a clergyman. I was impressed with the man up the street who always waves at me. Then I learned he waves at everybody.

Some of the local teen-age boys are quite frosty with me. When I first moved into the neighborhood I passed a teen-age girl who was sweeping the pavement. "How you doing?" I asked as I passed. "How do you *think* I'm doing?" she retorted.

About the same time, I was putting some bricks around my tree out front. An elderly black woman walked slowly by and glanced my way; then, looking ahead somewhat resignedly, she said softly, "I hope they stays nice, if you knows what I mean." Apart from two stones thrown through my front windows during the first couple of months I lived here, things have remained generally "nice."

Last May, outside a neighborhood McDonald's, a man claiming to be a lost Nigerian lifted my wallet in the process of graphically describing the seductive behavior of the bad kind of girls he didn't want to meet. Unsuspecting, I drove him downtown, where he planned to meet a good girl. He said I was the nicest white man he had ever met. He also said he was a Moslem and prayed five times a day. (On whom? I later wondered.)

Two doors from me lives one of the kindliest, best-natured people I have ever met, Georgie—the black working mother of a handful of youngsters. Last summer her teen-aged Michael was shot in the back not far from here as he tried to escape some black youths who were out to rob him. The doctors say he will never be able to walk on his own again.

While blacks were rioting in Baltimore after Dr. King's assassination, I watched fires burning in the neighborhood of old St. Mary's. A young black woman was walking down an alley near the window at which I stood. "Hello," I said when she looked up at me. "How come you never said hello *before?*" she responded menacingly. No use to say I lived on the other side of the building and couldn't recall ever having had the pleasure of seeing her before. I just had to laugh. . . .

I had supper tonight at the home of my doctor-friend, Hiltgunt Zassenhaus. She is an anti-Nazi German heroine to the hundreds of Scandinavian prisoners she helped save during the war. At war's end, the Gestapo was after her. She told of her experiences in her much translated book, *Walls*, which was published in 1974, the year she was nominated for the Nobel Peace Prize. When the Japanese prime minister won the award, she joked, "Well, I didn't get the prize, but I got the peace." She served me a savory combination of potato, carrot, and turnip. (Did she learn this dish in the war?) She is one of the brightest, liveliest people I have ever met—and an extraordinarily devoted doctor.

❧

> Even in our sleep, pain that cannot forget falls drop by drop
> upon the heart, until in our despair, and against our will, comes
> wisdom by the awful grace of God.
>
> *Aeschylus*

January 16

"Choose your friends—your relatives are thrust upon you." So Mark Twain advised. I'm especially glad that some of my relatives were thrust upon me, but I don't mean to thrust very many on the reader. My father's only sister, however, has become a model of determination for me. She had to be institutionalized in her latter years, and when her daughter took her home for Christmas, my aunt insisted that she wasn't going back to that place. She repeated her intention over the next few days. Pretending to be taking her for a ride, her family drove her back to the hospital. When she realized the strategy, my aunt grew enraged. As she was being escorted across the threshold, she collapsed. Shortly afterward my aunt was pronounced dead.

My mother's sister, Stasia, is good-hearted to a fault. One Christmastime she and I were visiting her brother Joe at a Veterans Hospital, where he was a patient for more than half a century. While waiting for Joe, we noticed a spastic patient sitting in a wheelchair with a can in his hand. I assumed it was beer. Stasia

thought otherwise. She opened her heart and her purse, walked over
to the man, and dropped a quarter into his suds. Startled, he made
the perfect comment: "You didn't have to do that!"

Another relative and her husband had season tickets to the symphony. On one occasion, her husband said he had to be out of town
so they would have to miss a certain concert. The morning of the
concert, however, my cousin accidentally discovered that the tickets
were missing. She went to the symphony alone, purchased another
seat, and saw her husband and another woman using their regular
places. She left the concert early and went straight to bed, leaving
her ticket stub on the table for her husband to see. The next day,
while her husband was out on business, she had everything removed
from the apartment. Aware of what was going on, the mover made
her pay for special insurance for his workers. Movers have been shot
on such occasions.

Today I visited my mother's two sisters, Stasia and Margaret, who
share an apartment in northeast Baltimore. Then I drove west of
Baltimore, to Ellicott City, where my mother's brother Tony lives.
The old Yankee saying, "Don't speak unless you can improve upon
the silence," is his (unspoken) motto. His eldest son, also Tony,
lives near his parents and it was for young Tony's home I was
heading. For twelve years now, cousin Tony and his wife Mary
Ellen have known that their firstborn son Michael has cystic fibrosis.
Three or four times a day, since he was eighteen months old, they
have had to help Mike do his "tricks"—cough up while they angle
him and pound on his back.

Once, when this son's illness was getting Tony down, he spoke of
"watching Michael die all these years." A counselor gently suggested
that he could just as correctly say that he had been watching Michael
live.

Talking on one occasion with Michael about abortion, Tony told
him that some parents with CF genes abort their children. "Knowing all that you've had to go through, would you have wanted your
mother and me to have had an abortion?" Mike looked directly at
his father with those probing, adult eyes of his: "No, I would rather
have lived."

❧

Life is a tragedy that is full of joy.
                    Bernard Malamud

January 17

Last year was the year of the three popes. In the last three days my native state has had three governors. More than that, we've had two governors for each of these three days. Explanation: last week Governor Marvin Mandel's conviction for political corruption was upset by an appeals court. Two days ago he decided to take over the reins that day from acting-Governor Blair Lee. Yesterday he let Mr. Lee be governor again for an hour so that he could swear in a certain judge. Then at noon today Harry Hughes took over from Mandel as our fifty-seventh governor.

Neither Marvin Mandel nor his predecessor, Spiro T. Agnew, were invited to the Hughes inaugural. When Governor Agnew became Vice-President, the Maryland Assembly had to elect a successor. It seemed inevitable that they would choose one of their own, and most probably the speaker of the house, Marvin Mandel. Some political friends of my older brother persuaded him to spearhead at least some token resistance from outside the Assembly. So he threw his hat into the ring and garnered fifteen votes.

A friend sent him one of those humorous greeting cards which was almost perfect for the occasion. The cover said: "It isn't whether you win or lose that counts." Inside were the words "But 112 to 11 is ridiculous!" As with everything else, Francis X. Gallagher took the card in good humor.

We'll double-cross that bridge when we get to it.

January 18

I drove today to a high-rise near the University of Maryland campus in College Park. I was about to pay my sixteenth visit to author Katherine Anne Porter, now eighty-eight and partially paralyzed by a stroke. She lives in a three-sided apartment on the fifteenth floor. In the distance you can see the Washington Monument, the Catholic National Shrine, and the Episcopal National Cathedral.

Just a year ago this coming Sunday I paid my first visit there. Sister Kathleen Feeley, the president of Baltimore's Notre Dame College, had come to know Miss Porter through their mutual admiration for Flannery O'Connor. Knowing of Miss Porter's Catholic background, Sister Kathleen asked her if she would like to be visited by a priest. A positive response led the nun to contact me last January, and we went out together, along with Notre Dame poet Sister Maura.

Katherine Anne, of *Ship of Fools* and short-story fame, proved to be a tiny woman with beautiful white hair, bright welcoming eyes, and a lively spirit—occasionally mischievous, occasionally fiery. Despite the stroke which occurred several years ago and which afflicts her right side (and her writing hand), her mind is quick, though from time to time she cannot speak the words which she says are in her mind. Such frustrations are understandably vexing to her—a woman who always took her lifelong vocation of wordsmith very seriously.

I hadn't seen her since just before Christmas, when she seemed to have failed noticeably. (She has nurses around the clock; one of them said she might have to be hospitalized soon.) Today she wanted to be wheeled into the sitting room, elegant with its collection of books, photographs, and antique furniture. In a nearby closet was the wooden, brightly colored coffin she ordered some years ago. She wants to be cremated and buried in it near her mother in Texas.

Dressed in a dark red robe, she talked awhile about the book on her lap—*Published in Paris* by Hugh Ford. The volume deals with American and British writers who resided in Paris from 1920 to 1939. It speaks of Katherine Anne and many of her friends. I noted a picture of her from the thirties. "You look serious." "I was." Tears came to her eyes as she recalled one friend who died before she could get to his side.

As usual, when I asked her how she was, she answered intently, "I'm going to die, you know. But I'm not afraid of it." We recited the Lord's Prayer, and I read some of my favorite prayers for the dying. Her head rested on my hand, which held the arm of her wheelchair. When I finished, she said, "Now you know why I'm not afraid to die—because that's what I believe."

I gave her Holy Communion. (I had gone to Corpus Christi Church near my house to get the Host. I carried it in a small golden container given to me as a memorial by the cousin whose husband had suddenly kissed her and died on New Year's Day, 1962.)

I told Miss Porter that her *Ship of Fools* was in the news these days. The stories about actor Lee Marvin and the suit against him by his former lover mentioned that they had met while he was being filmed in the Hollywood version of her Pulitzer Prize novel. She told me again that she had never liked the movie.

As I left I invited her again to phone me anytime she wants—as she occasionally does. I never know when I have spoken for the last time with that gifted and rightfully celebrated human being, who claims kinship with Daniel Boone, Cole Porter, and William Sydney Porter (alias O. Henry). But it is enough that she is related to her writings.

❦

Only the work of saints and artists give us any reason to believe the human race is worth belonging to.

Katherine Anne Porter

January 19

At eighteen, a man's convictions are a mount from which he looks out; at forty-five they are a cave in which he hides.

F. Scott Fitzgerald

January 20

Those who cannot remember the past are condemned to repeat it.

George Santayana

January 21

Those who remember what Santayana said about the past are condemned to repeat it.

J.G.

January 22

I drove to Mercy Hospital (where I was born) to keep an appointment with Dr. Nelson Sun, a relatively young Filipino whom I've consulted for several years. Some time ago he put me on a blood pressure pill, but switched me to another brand when I began developing breasts—a complication I didn't need. (I reminded myself of a Caribbean priest who reportedly presented his bishop with a theological problem by having a sex-change operation in the mid-sixties.)

He thinks I am suffering from depression and prescribed a pill called Triavil. I'm not to expect immediate improvement. He graciously allowed that we all have neuroses; he described himself as a workaholic and perfectionist.

In response to my mention of heart palpitations he said I could take a Holter Monitor heart test, one that extends over many hours. He thinks it would reveal nothing, but he will prescribe it if it would reassure me. I'll have to find out whether my insurance covers this expensive test.

People should rejoice in their neurotic suffering, for this is a
sign of the availability of energy to transform their characters.

Rollo May

January 23

Is this pill going to cause flashbacks of the six drug sessions I underwent in 1973–74 at the Maryland Psychiatric Research Center? A form of LSD was used (DPT—dipropiltriptomine), and I went from injections of 30 mgs. to 150 mgs. A fellow faculty member at St. Mary's Seminary had undergone the program and spoke highly of William Richards, the psychologist who worked with him. Having run low on funds, I had just terminated nearly two years of psychoanalysis (thrice a week, usually), but still felt the desire to explore my unconscious more deeply. The research program was free.

I had about forty-five sessions with Bill Richards; most of these involved just conversation or practicing "Guided Affective Imagery" with the use of music. A nurse was always on hand for the drug sessions, which lasted from about nine in the morning until mid- or late afternoon. At the lengthiest, I was in the deepest part of the drug experience for about three hours, during which I was totally immersed in the fantastic, isolated world of a waking dream.

I'm not sure just what I gained from the experiences, apart from the memory of having had the "courage" to undergo something that terrified me, and also discovering that no hidden kegs of psychic dynamite exploded. Unlike a priest-friend who succeeded me in the program, I had no really "bad trips"—which are said to occur when you resist what's happening under the drug.

At the end of each session I would feel reassuringly compact, "put together." I thought of myself as a man walking the tightrope of sanity. For balance I carried a bamboo rod, which represented the whole spectrum of experience, from the most internal to the most external. The side representing the impact of external experiences on my life had begun to grow dangerously top-heavy. The drug experience taught me how much power churned in the depths of my internal world. This felt discovery tipped the bamboo rod back into balance and allowed me to proceed more trustingly on the tightrope.

I've spoken of flashbacks. This might be a convenient place to recall some highlights of my first drug session. The day before that session I had a meeting with Bill Richards. He said that under the influence of the drug I might feel that I was going crazy forever, or that my heart was bursting, but that I should just "be, accept and trust." When he asked me to sign a form saying that I realized that the drug could bring about major personality changes, I asked him about that word "major." "You wouldn't want your experience to be merely minor, would you?"

My friend Dr. Zassenhaus was against what I was doing, as was Dr. Riva Novey, my psychoanalyst. My regular doctor, Edwin Mueller, who had to certify that I didn't have certain medical problems, said something biblical and discouraging about the last state being worse than the first.

But I trusted Bill Richards and was ardent enough about wanting to improve my self-mastery. The most terrifying time of the whole experience was that dull afternoon when Bill told me about the sensations I might feel. I turned into a block of ice.

On the morning of November 2, 1973, I arrived at the Spring Grove Research Center just before nine.

Went to therapy room . . . long, comfortable couch made up as bed . . . clock on the wall near my head . . . a table with a rose in a vase . . . I removed my shoes and sweater, got under the sheets. Bill Richards put the blinders and the earphones on me: Rachmaninoff's *Second Symphony*. . . . Nurse Janet Flaherty injected the needle into my left arm . . . fairly painless . . . I gave her an "A" for Addiction . . . (thirty mgs of DPT) . . .

At first nothing seemed to happen . . . then I noticed my heart beating somewhat faster. . . . Suddenly on my left I saw something like a white palm frond with crimson spots on it. Then to the bottom of the far right, a sort of orange lightning . . . to the right of center I saw a well-formed spider web . . . an intensely white light seemed to leak upward from the bottom left—like an atomic explosion in slow motion. . . .

Here I may have begun deep, deep breathing and perhaps some enjoyable moaning. . . . I began to sense time moving very slowly, like a languid giant. It seemed I would fall asleep between moments of awareness, and I was afraid I would forget what had happened previously. . . . I felt I was slowly falling through foam-rubber clouds which could hold me awhile but eventually had to let me slip through to a lower cloud. I had some worry that I might run out of clouds. . . .

Music was playing during all the two and a half hours, but at times I was totally oblivious of it; at other times I was acutely aware of it and wanted to hum along . . . my feelings now became much more visceral, possessive, glutinous, adhesive. It was not so much that I had the feelings as that they had me.

Maybe it was about this time that I grew aware of considerable bodily twitching and spasms—arms, hands, legs. The movements seemed fairly intense and jerky but didn't frighten me.

While thinking of my mother I wanted to feel Janet's hand and fingers, smell her skin, eventually to stroke her

hair and press her close to my chest. I reveled in her soft-
ness, yet I worried that I might somehow be endangering
myself, making myself vulnerable if I surrendered to the
delight of reposing in her tender, relaxed mothering.

Between those gestures of tenderness, during which I
said how good it felt to hug her and how good it felt to be
able to say how good it felt, I worried about who would
take care of Janet/mother. Was I a small boy in a crib, in a
room with white walls and a patch of sunlight?

I said I wished my mother and father would love each
other and not fight. Bill and Janet put their hands together
and placed them over my hands. Here I think I had my
first explosion of tears. I couldn't stand the happiness of
my father and mother loving each other. I yelled and
sobbed, "It would be too easy; it would be too easy." Here
my bodily, physical involvement seemed total.

It would be heaven if my parents loved each other. It
couldn't be earth. And how could it be morning, as I felt it
was. Heaven is at the end, and morning is just the beginning. It was all confusing.

In the final main episode I said how much I loved other
people, and how much I wanted to tell people this, but
how hard it is, or how you are not supposed to. Here I felt
I was yelling and crying violently. I spend my whole life
not telling people, especially men, how much I love them.
I was shouting—"Who made things this way?"

Deep sighs, moans, breath sucked in, absolute emotional
involvement here. It felt plenty good.

I wondered what time it was. In one way it seemed that
only fifteen or twenty minutes had elapsed. In another, it
seemed that dozens of years and thousands of sleeps had
intervened. (It was 11:30 A.M.) I felt good, though very
tired—as though I had just had a series of wrestling
matches. . . . I was relieved that the trip had not really
been horrible. I was astonished to find that Bill and Janet
had taken twelve pages of notes on long yellow paper—
recording what I did and said and what music was being
played. I was impressed by how really different from what
I expected were the trancelike, thoroughly involved, visceral
feelings that came—and how inadequate the preliminary
descriptions were.

The drug experience left me with a sense of strength. As I noted the next day, after I had driven to Ocean City, Maryland: "I did feel an unusually abundant sense of power, fearlessness, interior cushioning. I thought of airplanes and my fluctuating fear of riding them. Now I felt I could fly without fear, and if the plane was crashing I would not merely accept the crashing but would positively assert it, with a kind of defiant willfulness."

In entering into the abyss of himself, a man may show as reckless a courage as those that die upon the field of battle.

W. B. Yeats

January 24

I caught the 8:54 A.M. train to Philadelphia in order to visit my sixty-eight-year-old cousin Anne Williams, who is due to undergo surgery tomorrow. I was returning to the city where my father was born in 1897. He was drafted literally on Armistice Day, 1918, and sent south.

As I heard the story, he was discharged from the army not long afterward. On his way back to Philly, he stopped off to see his married sister in Baltimore. Aunt Marguerite was in Baltimore because that was the home of her husband, Tom Oldham. She had met him when he played cricket at the Merion Cricket Club near Grandfather Gallagher's home.

Dad never really left Baltimore. He worked as a mechanic and salesman, met my mother, and married her in 1926. (So I could be called a 1929 war baby.) Dad's mother died of Bright's disease when he was about nine. She had been a Gallagher before she married John J. Gallagher. Later my cousin Rita Gallagher married an Eddie Gallagher. There was a local saying: "Never criticize a Gallagher— you are probably talking to one of their relatives." In the current Philadelphia phone book, there are seventy-eight John Gallaghers, thirty-one Joseph Gallaghers, and twenty-one John Josephs.

Granddad G. died at eighty-four, and all my memories of him are patriarchal. I remember him as a pleasantly detached man whose head shook, who was fond of whistling, and who thought that wearing a belt gave you cancer. "Oh, for God's sake, Georgie, leave me alone," he would say when his second wife fussed with him.

In addition to my father (the youngest) and Aunt Marguerite, there were two older boys: Uncle Joe and Uncle Jack. It was Jack's daughter Anne I was about to visit in the Lankenau Hospital.

Anne is one of the saintliest souls I have ever known. She is full of compassion and remembrance. She remembers everyone's birthday. She spent years cataloging the birth, marriage, and death dates of every reasonably close relative. When you visit her, she says "It's so good to see you" about every ten minutes, with incontestable sincerity.

A few hours after her husband's burial she fainted. I helped carry her to her bedroom. When she recovered she looked smilingly at me and said: "Jule will be so glad to know you are here." I realized that she had forgotten that he was dead. . . .

I arrived at the Thirtieth Street Station on time and caught a local train to Merion Station, near the home of Anne's elder daughter, Judy McGinn.

I've made a point of growing closer to Judy in the past few years. An artist and a searcher, an ardent reader and a journal-keeper, Judy has a passionate interest in nature. In high school she fell down a metal stairway, cracked her head, and was not expected to live. Since then she has always been in delicate health. She is exquisitely sensitive to nature, and in some mystical way she becomes the thing she sees. Tensions arise because this kind of entrancement is not practical for a mother of five.

She can be practical in emergencies, though. Once she was comforting a small boy who had just been hit by a car. "Is it true? Is it true?" he asked in disbelief. "Yes," answered Judy, ingeniously changing the subject, "it's true that help is on its way."

She met me at the local station and drove me to the nearby hospital. On "grandmother" Anne's wall was a beautiful sign painted and scripted by Judy: "In our family, wisdom and love are measured by Grams." With Anne (Grams), whose kindly face is fittingly crowned with what looks like Christmas-tree angel hair, was her other child, Marita Podder.

Marita is another gem. She has a singing voice of professional calibre and is an esteemed amateur actress. If Judy is the Mary, Marita is the busy, practical Martha—though you won't hear her complain of her sister. Marita, her husband, and two children live with Anne in the home that belonged to Anne's parents before it was her own. Last fall the home was broken into, and the indignity of this violation sickened Anne in her reverence for the dead and for sacred associations.

Back to Judy's house (just across the street from St. Charles Borromeo Seminary) where all the Podders had supper with all the McGinns. En route, Judy showed me an apartment complex where naturalist Loren Eiseley once lived. Not long ago she planted a seed nearby in his honor.

That reminded me of the post-midnight hour just about seven years ago when, as the finale of many errands, Judy drove me to the dark and deserted cemetery where her Aunt Rita had been buried six months earlier. Judy placed a corsage on the grave. Later that day Rita's eldest child was to be married.

After supper we paid a second visit to Anne. She waved a final good-bye to us from the fifth-floor window after we exited the hospital and headed for the parking garage. [One year later, at that very hour, I would be waving good-bye to Anne as I preached her funeral sermon.]

I caught the 11 P.M. train to Baltimore. (As I left her, Judy slipped $10 into my hand where earlier Anne had slipped $10 and Marita had slipped $10. Protests were fruitfully fruitless.) Riding on the rocky Amtrak, crossing the Susquehanna River, which I used to fear crossing in my youth, I wondered again how blessedly different my life would have been, how many pains avoided or eased, had I grown up around the Gallaghers in the city of brotherly love.

❦

> But I do love the world. . . . I love its small ones, the things beaten in the strangling surf; the bird, singing, which flies and falls and is not seen again. . . . I love the lost ones, the failures of the world.
>
> *Loren Eiseley*

January 25

Twenty years ago today Pope John XXIII announced his intention to convene an Ecumenical Council. I heard the news on a car radio outside New York City. I was driving to Boston to confer with the architect of Baltimore's new cathedral, whose guidebook I was preparing. When I heard the flash I hadn't the slightest notion that seven years later I would end up as the author of perhaps the most widespread translation of the Council documents in the world, certainly in the English-speaking world.

This afternoon Pope John Paul II, molded by that Council and carrying out its ideals, arrived in Santo Domingo and kissed the ground where the first Mass was offered in the western hemisphere. I enjoy watching this vigorous, self-possessed man in action.

Someone less self-possessed stopped by this evening, a former seminarian who is seeing a therapist regularly. As we sat before the fire I tried to tell him that he shouldn't be expecting a trouble-free life as a sign that he is getting stronger. "The goal is not an absence of struggle, but a psychic ship which is more seaworthy and trusting of itself and of the laws of buoyancy. We get rid of the imaginary Moby Dicks so that we can deal more successfully with the real ones."

I told my young friend that he should fall asleep at night counting not sheep but all the things that are not wrong with him. I should try that myself.

🌳

> The serious problems of life are never solved, and if it seems that they are, something important has been lost.
>
> *Carl Jung*

January 26

> There are two unnatural things: a woman who is vulgar and a man who isn't.
>
> *G. K. Chesterton*

January 27

The big news today was the death, in curious circumstances, of Nelson Rockefeller. When Mr. Rockefeller divorced his wife and married the divorced "Happy" Murphy, I editorialized in the *Catholic Review*, vis-à-vis his presidential aspirations, that I thought the First Lady should be first in every respect. I cited the politician who said that people like to see a wife standing at a candidate's side. Someone asked him, "But whose?" This story was picked up by *Time* magazine that week.

My editorial was also mentioned on the local radio news. Soon afterward, my phone rang. A woman stated that she had canceled her subscription to the *Catholic Review* some time ago, but now regretted doing so. "Why?" I inquired, with preparatory pride. "*Because I'd like to cancel it again,*" she shouted in my ear.

In the office we joked about a new slogan: Take out several subscriptions. Don't be caught short when you want to cancel.

I told the story to Price Day, a *Sunpaper* editor. He countered with the story of a man who apparently enjoyed the sports section but disagreed with *Sunpaper* editorials, so he phoned to ask whether he could cancel the front part of the newspaper.

I caught the 7 and 11 P.M. news about the pope's thronged visit to Mexico City and Guadalupe. What courage, to stand up and out so visibly and vulnerably in an era of assassins.

🌳

A thought for Mozart's birthday:

Whether the angels play only Bach in praising God I am not quite sure; I am sure, however, that *en famille* they play Mozart.

Karl Barth

January 28

Father Eugene Walsh, who was sixty-eight last week, has had the longest, steadiest, and most fatherly influence on me of any man dead or alive. When I was attending St. Ann's grammar school in Baltimore, his family home was one block from mine, while he himself taught in a local seminary.

I can remember oversleeping one Sunday, missing the children's Mass but then attending a breakfast for the parish drum corps to which I belonged. (I carried a rifle, then I played the Scotch drum, graduated to the snare drum, and had a brief career as drum major before I gave up worldly renown and joined the seminary high school.)

After the breakfast I was passing the sacristy and wondering whether I was obliged to attend a grown-ups Mass about to begin. I spotted Father Walsh, who was going to celebrate that Mass. I told him of my dilemma. He said, "Why put it on the basis of obligation? Maybe you'd like to make the sacrifice as a free gift." I did, and never forgot his approach to such questions.

There was a joke in the seminary that Gene Walsh's penitents usually quit the seminary. The point was that he took the time to help students discover their own motivations and realize that God wouldn't be angry or depressed if they didn't really have a priestly vocation.

Gene's father was a quiet man whom I didn't know well. His mother woke one morning to find him dead beside her. In her grief she kept saying, "You didn't say good-bye." She was the inspiration of a poem of mine called *The Circumstances*. Mamie was benevolence incarnate. She always knew just when to disappear when a troubled person stopped by her house to see her priest son. In her eighty-fifth year they found her dead in her writing chair, Christmas cards in front of her, some signed, some blank.

Tonight I joined about twenty-five other guests who came to an Ellicott City rectory from various locations to sing "Happy Birthday" to Gene. He and I were both "St. Ann's" men, members of a once vibrant, closely knit parish. There used to be a jocular prayer for the ladies: "Good St. Ann, get me a man." Two blocks from her church and a block from his own home, a needful youngster found a man who has been a faithful father all these years since.

When the student is ready, the master will appear.
                                                    Zen saying

January 29

I spent the heart of the day composing and retyping an article about Pope Pius XII and Hitler and dropped it off at the *Sunday Sun*. I hope their "Perspective Section" will use it next month, the fortieth anniversary of the death of Pius XI. This February is also the sixteenth anniversary of the premier of Rolf Hochhuth's play attacking Pius XI's successor for not openly denouncing Hitler during World War II (which also started forty years ago this year).

I was still editor of the *Catholic Review* when Hochhuth's play was making the headlines. I never saw the play, but I did read the text and wrote several editorials on the subject. While doing some research I made one of the most instructive finds of my editorial career.

After *The Deputy* opened on Broadway in February 1964, the New York *Times* editorialized on it under the title of "Silence." Admitting that the play's indictment of Pius XII may have been too severe, the editorialist went on to condemn the silence of religious leaders during the Hitler years.

Meantime I wondered how the world press reacted to Pius XII's 1942 Christmas message, in which he passionately lamented that "hundreds of thousands of persons, through no fault of their own, have been condemned to death or to progressive extinction." I checked the *Catholic Review* of the time and found a reprint of a New York *Times* editorial entitled "The Pope's Verdict" and commenting on this very Christmas message.

Said the *Times* at the time: "This Christmas more than ever the Pope is a lonely voice crying out of the silence [!] of a continent . . . when he assails the exile and persecution of human beings 'for no other reason than their race' . . . the 'impartial' judgment is like a verdict in a high court of justice."

Later that same year the *Review* carried the text of a prayer for Pius XII composed by one of Baltimore's most eminent rabbis. Calling him "the prisoner of the Vatican," Rabbi Lazaron said that the pope had bravely condemned anti-Semitism and all its works.

Whatever the ultimate judgment of history on that pope's decision as to the best way to handle the maniacal Hitler—and after all there were thousands of priests in the same concentration camps with Jews—I learned a memorable lesson in shifting historical perspectives.

The unhistorical are usually, without knowing it, enslaved to a very recent past.

                                                    C. S. Lewis

January 30

> Television lives and makes things thrive,
> And even brings you funerals "live."
>
> J.G.

January 31

And so the last January of the seventies comes to an end—a month that brought death to Nelson Rockefeller, a commutation to the imprisoned Patty Hearst, exile to the Shah of Iran, and a U.S. tour to China's Vice-Premier Teng.

Carl Jung wrote about synchronicity—the seemingly related way that certain seemingly unrelated events take place simultaneously. How he would have been struck by the two clergymen who are capturing the headlines and drawing vast crowds as this month concludes.

The one is pope, dressed all in white. He leaves Europe through the airport of Rome and travels westward; there he preaches love and tells his clergymen to stay out of politics.

The other is the Ayatollah Khomeini, dressed all in black. He leaves Europe through the airport of Rome and travels eastward. There he warns of chopped-off hands and urges his clergymen to enter politics and lead the revolution.

There are many ironies in the fire.

⁂

A coincidence is a minor miracle for which God wishes to remain anonymous.

Anonymous

February 1, 1979

Only the passionate heart is pure.
St. Augustine

February 2

A neighborhood stroll in the brisk weather took me past Phil Berrigan's home, a block from my own. Burly, gentle, and warm-hearted Phil was a Josephite priest before his marriage to Elizabeth McAllister, a former nun and fellow anti-Vietnam War activist. They and their two children live in a commune called Jonah House. Phil and Liz were supper guests of mine late last year. More recently they paid a visit to meet Dr. Zassenhaus, whose book *Walls* I had lent them.

Phil lost a good bit of backing when his marriage was revealed, and not merely because he had not sought a dispensation from his vow of celibacy. Many honorable priests marry without a dispensation—either because they have come to regard obligatory celibacy as an inhuman and unscriptural prerequisite for ordination or because they view the dispensation process as demeaning. You practically have to depict yourself as a hopelessly sex-hungry creature who is throwing himself on the mercy of the Holy Father. Unless you specifically do so (as I refused to do), your dispensation may relieve you of all other priestly duties but not of celibacy. In that case, according to church law, you must live as a celibate layman!

No, Phil's problem was that he had been accusing the government of deception and dishonesty, and then underwent a clandestine marriage. Moreover, according to some of his one-time seminarian admirers, he had been telling them that celibacy is the ideal option for a genuine revolutionary, who for the sake of the cause should be glad to give up the trifling creature comfort of sex.

In many ways I admire Phil and his Jesuit brother, Dan. (This priest-poet once forwarded me a letter from Phil which had been smuggled out of a federal penitentiary. "Don't mention this letter when you write to me," Phil warned.) I don't agree with a relative of mine who thinks they are publicity hounds. I suspect that the glamor of a jail cell wears thin rather quickly. But I can't go along with some of the tactics they employ in their antiwar, antigovernment, antinuclear protests.

But, in any case, I was glad to be a witness for the defense at Phil's first trial, in April 1968. And when my older brother died he was acting as one of the defense lawyers for the Harrisburg Seven, which included Phil and Dan. While he was waiting for his second Baltimore trial, Phil wrote me from the Baltimore County Jail urging me to become more actively involved in antiwar protests. "As protests mount . . . you will approve in time—you may even join really serious dissent. Or you will allow events to pass you by, to retire before your time. This may sound cruel, but I venture it in light of the fact that the institutions of power are under their first serious challenge in our history." (Letter of October 2, 1968.)

❦

As life is action and passion, it is required of a man that he should share in the passion and action of his time, at the peril of being judged not to have lived.

Oliver Wendell Holmes, Jr.

February 3

To act from passion lessens both praise and blame. To act with passion increases both.

St. Thomas Aquinas

February 4

Passions, because most living, are most holy . . . and a man shall enter eternity borne upon their wings.

W. B. Yeats

February 5

Today was my final day of preparation for the Dante course I
start teaching tomorrow at Notre Dame College. Scandalously
enough, I was never formally exposed to the world's greatest Catholic classic during my twenty years of Catholic education. Out of
shame I tackled the whole of Dante's *Divine Comedy* while I was
staying at the Trappist Monastery in Berryville, Virginia, in the
summer of 1970. I was by then well beyond "the midpoint of our
life's journey," at which Dante begins his story.

As I have grown to know and love and teach the book during the
seventies, I have come to see why it is said to be the most written-
about book in the world—if you consider the Bible as a collection of
books. I don't think, though, that I'll ever be able to match the enthusiasm of one of my faculty confreres at old St. Mary's Seminary.
Father Alvin Burnhardt treated every new book he encountered the
same way: he checked the index to see if Dante was mentioned. No
matter if the volume was about athlete's foot or Alaskan sled dogs!

But it has not been only Dante and in seminaries that I've taught.
I've been a teacher in elementary schools, high schools, colleges,
universities, night schools, summer schools, in adult education, and
in lecture series. (There's a Baltimore priest, Joe Muth, whom I
taught in high school, college, and university.)

I've taught religion, poetry, poetry writing, preaching, English,
philosophy, and the practical psychology of living. Most of these
subjects were just hobbies. My only degrees are a B.A. in philosophy
and an M.A. in creative writing. My lack of a more extensive background has at times weakened my self-confidence and my success, especially with brighter students.

But discipline has never been a major problem for me in the classroom. I do recall a boisterous third-grader whom I finally ejected
from a catechism class at the old cathedral. His regular teacher ordered him to write me a letter of apology. I still have it. It reads: "I
am sorry I was bad. It will not happen a third time."

A highlight of my teaching career occurred one day while I was
teaching English at St. Paul's Latin High School. I wove a quotation
into my remarks and paused to ask, "What play is that from?"
"Shakespeare's," came a chorus of answers. "Of course," I countered,
"but *which one?*" "William!" somebody shouted.

✣

Education is quite costly. Only the lack of it is more so.

February 6

The latest *Time* arrived with a wrap-up article on the pope's Mexico visit. I'm still not clear about the full impact of what he said or didn't say. I was interested to note that the current issue of *America*, a Jesuit journal, criticized his remark about "the joys of the poor" and his failure to mention the people who have been tortured and killed in Latin America this past decade in the name of social justice and human rights. . . .

Mary Jo, my only sister, phoned and was in high spirits. She, her husband Bill Burdell, and their two children live in southeast Baltimore, near the Bethlehem Steel shipyard where Bill works. My eleven-year-old niece Mary Beth got on the phone. She is personality plus. After she heard a little girl do some swearing in the movie *The Goodbye Girl*, she asked me whether God realized that the girl was just acting.

When my mother died, I tried to explain to Mary Beth what it meant to say that her soul "went up to heaven."

"If you let go of a balloon, what will happen?"

"It would go up. But did she burst?"

Hmm. I'd better change the imagery. "If you opened a birdcage, what would the bird do?"

"It would get out and fly away," she replied. Then she added with a smile of discovery, "And it would *sing*."

✣

Children are a consolation in your old age, and help you to get there sooner.

February 7

In the middle of winter, I learned at last that I carried within myself an invincible summer.

Albert Camus

February 8

Fifteen years ago this time I began a weekend retreat known as a *cursillo*—a "little course" in Christianity. Held in a parish hall in Bradshaw, Maryland, this intense and (at that time in the U.S.) new approach to soul-searching has revolutionized the lives of many retreatants through its emotional, highly affectionate approach to Christian community. In many ways it heralded the charismatic movement which blossomed later. Among my fellow retreatants that weekend was Michigan's outstanding senator, Philip Hart.

The retreat talk which moved me the most was given by a young man who told of the day he signed up for the Korean war and went home to tell his family. His mother was quite upset, his brothers were excited, but his undemonstrative father didn't say much. The enlistee fell asleep that night thinking that he might never see his family again. In a deep sleep he gradually became aware of drops falling on his chest, and of someone sitting beside him, sobbing. Before even opening his eyes he reached out and said: "Don't worry, Mom." He opened his eyes, and even in the darkness he could see that it was his father. . . .

One of the morning *Sun*'s columnists, Isaac Rehert, is a neighbor and friend of mine. We were both past our prime when we were classmates in Elliott Coleman's poetry-writing course at Hopkins. We used to console each other over a cup of coffee when we couldn't understand or appreciate the more experimental, less syntactical poems of our more youthful classmates.

Ike phoned me tonight to tell me that his home had just been burglarized for the second time in recent months. The police say there has been a rash of break-ins lately in this area. Often the burglars gain entry through a fire escape. I wonder how vulnerable my house is—though I have no fire escape.

Through the years cars of mine have been broken into on several occasions, and suitcases stolen from them. I had an apartment in Washington from which were stolen a new suit, an old gold watch, a slide projector, and 432 irreplaceable slides of Rome during the Second Vatican Council. I've had my pockets picked, once while I was wearing them, and once while I was swimming at a health club. I've had an overnight guest whose car was stolen. Four times in one year I ran into bomb threats: on a plane refueling in Puerto Rico, in the lobby of our local Mercy Hospital, at a jubilee Mass for Cardinal Shehan, and at a reunion of old cathedral parishioners and priests.

During my first trip to Europe, French peasants blocked the paths of trains and buses I was on; in Florence I saw riot police spraying hard-to-remove red dye on strikers; Tyrolean separatists bombed the railroad tracks leading me out of Italy; I left Germany just before the infamous Berlin Wall was built. That was the summer when a busload of U.S. teachers plunged into a Swiss lake after I had visited it, and a train full of tourists crashed in England just before I arrived.

I think I can boast that I have been a man of my time.

> Any twentieth-century man who wants peace and quiet has chosen the wrong century to be born in.
>
> *Leon Trotsky*

February 9

On the radio tonight I heard songs from Gilbert and Sullivan's *Mikado*. When in 1949 I was finishing my sixth and last year at St. Charles Seminary, our class presented the *Mikado* and I had the relatively small role of the emperor himself. Twenty years later, when I was on the faculty of St. Mary's, Roland Park, I learned that our music director was producing the *Mikado* at a nearby parish. I casually mentioned to him one day that I had been the Mikado half a lifetime previously.

About a week later I received a desperate phone call from my confrere: the Mikado in his production had fallen and broken a leg. The play was scheduled to open about a week later. The cast had been practicing all summer. Could I step in as a last-minute substitute? Well, of course, the show must go on, so I accepted and had a lot of fun refreshing my old lines and my old song about letting the punishment fit the crime.

My older brother came to the matinee, armed with two pocket radios so he could hear the World Series and a Colt football game. That reminded me of the time I was doing a TV show about the liturgy one Saturday afternoon and discovered that during the live filming the cameramen for my show were watching a football game on another channel.

We have so little time to be born to this moment.
                                        St. John Perse

February 10

I phoned local cousin Patsy Doyle to wish her a happy birthday. She's the one who told me once that she pictures God as staying up all night to figure out what you couldn't possibly live without, and then taking it away from you. Odd how some people with good luck don't believe in God, while others keep believing despite their bad luck. I recall the ancient pagan who said he knew that the gods existed because he had felt their wrath.

When this same cousin once gave shelter to a homeless school girl I told her that a blessing would surely descend on her house. Some months later she reminded me of my remark and told me that in the intervening months she had broken her ankle, developed rheumatoid arthritis and a lump in each breast (which proved benign). She begged me to invoke no further blessings.

I was taken to lunch today by a woman whom I knew only by letter and telephone. Her son told her last year that he is homosexual; then she read an *Evening Sun* article I wrote last June pleading for a compassionate understanding of the emotional plight of the homosexual.

I asked this mother if she had shown the article to her son. "Yes," she answered. "What did he think?" "He said you must be gay yourself." His comment reminded me of a humorous twist that came with the check paying me for that article. The editor had chosen the title "Human Rights for U.S. Homosexuals." The voucher which came with the money spelled out the title in capitals and without punctuation, so that it read "HUMAN RIGHTS FOR US HOMOSEXUALS." . . .

Earlier today I phoned Bishop Frank Murphy, who had planned to have a day of leisure tomorrow. But suddenly there were two deaths he had to reckon with: that of a local rabbi who died yesterday and who had asked in his will that the local Catholic bishops share in his funeral procession; and that of the father of a mutual priest-friend.

It used to be said of any newly appointed Catholic bishop, "He'll never hear the truth, read a book, or have a bad meal again." But despite what many people may think, a bishop's lot today is not an easy one. "It's no fun being a bishop anymore"—such are the words attributed to the now retired bishop of Richmond, who as a younger priest was kind to me in the confessional as I was discovering the fearful fascination of sex. After being involved in some controversy this same Bishop Russell was once complaining to Washington's crusty Cardinal O'Boyle about letters calling him an s.o.b. "I've been getting letters like that for years" responded the cardinal. "Yes," said the genial bishop, "but in my case it's not true."

Sometimes I think God was not entirely serious when he gave man the sexual instinct.

Graham Greene

February 11

My older brother died seven years ago today. I made arrangements to offer Mass in his home this morning. Along with my brother's widow, all the children were there except Frank, who is a student at Georgetown.

John, the oldest son present, read an excerpt from the *Book of Wisdom* about people who die young but who have lived a full life of goodness. I read the Gospel of the Beatitudes, with its words "Blessed are those that mourn." I pointed out that none of us can do much about the length of our lives, only about the depth and height and width of them.

At the kiss of peace Mary gave her children strong hugs. She has done a valiant job raising her five children alone these past seven years. During the Mass the fine portrait of my brother gazed down upon his family from above the fireplace. Sixteen months apart in age, I can't recall a single argument that we two ever had. I did send him a letter once severely chastising him for his perilous overactivity, but he never mentioned it to me. When he landed in the hospital a week or so later, he told a mutual friend that my letter had been right on target.

My brother, Francis Xavier Gallagher, was born on February 25, 1928. My jubilant father, himself already over thirty, proclaimed that this son was going to be a priest. At the time of his baptism, Catholic churches in Baltimore were observing an annual novena in honor of St. Francis Xavier. This fact and my father's name being Frank seem to have produced this saint's name for my brother.

From childhood he suffered from migraine headaches. During the summer between high school and college he had sixty consecutive days of headaches. Studious, self-starting, quick-witted, and energetic, he earned a law degree from the University of Maryland at the same time he was gaining a master's in speech, writing, and drama at Johns Hopkins. After one oral exam he could recall about forty of the forty-five questions that had been asked him.

Just as he obtained these two degrees he married a neighborhood girl, Mary Kelly, and began his law practice at twenty-three. He served as assistant city solicitor, was elected a member of Maryland's House of Delegates, and appointed people's counsel for the Public Service Commission.

He started his own law firm and became the lawyer for the Archdiocese of Baltimore. (One day, when his regular lawyer was ill and failing, Archbishop Keough met me in the hallway of the old cathedral rectory and said, "I understand your brother is a lawyer; do you have his phone number?")

He was elected to Maryland's Constitutional Convention, was twice a campaign official for Senator Joe Tydings, and was state chairman for Robert Kennedy's ill-fated presidential campaign. My brother then switched to the Gene McCarthy camp and was one of his delegates at the turbulent 1968 Democratic Convention in Chicago. While strolling in that city filled with protesters, he encountered some of Mayor Daley's tear gas.

Meantime he worked long and hard hours, said yes to almost every opportunity to help others, neglected his heath and exercise, and grew overweight—though he never smoked and almost never drank alcohol. Handling his problems by "a flight into reality," he was a perfect candidate for the so-called executive heart attack. He had a number of episodes such as dizzy spells which put him in the hospital. He told me one day that he had appointed me guardian for his five children.

On February 9, 1972, his secretary phoned me to say that he had been admitted to the cardiac intensive care unit at Johns Hopkins. I visited him at once and found him fretful that this hospitalization was occurring at a time when he was critically engaged in some major legal work, including the conspiracy trial of the Harrisburg Seven.

Though visitors were severely restricted, I saw my brother again the next day. Expecting to leave the intensive care unit shortly, he urged me not to bother visiting him on the following day. On that third day his wife phoned that he was better and was soon going to be moved to a regular room. So I decided to stay put at the seminary, where a sticky fatigue had overtaken me. (I had nearly passed out as the doctor was repeating his evaluation to my sister-in-law.)

In the late evening I spent some time in the recreation hall, conversing and listening to music. As I reentered my room, the phone rang. "I've been trying to get you." It was our switchboard operator. "There's been an emergency at the hospital. Your sister-in-law said to phone her there."

It was shortly before midnight. Mary came to the phone. "Frank just died," she said. It was two weeks before his forty-fourth birthday. With midnight came Abraham Lincoln's birthday—another able and compassionate lawyer who died early. A few years before, I had bought Francis a bust of Lincoln in Gettysburg. It was pictured behind him in an article on prominent Baltimoreans that had recently run in a national magazine. There would be no more pictures now.

❦

Hands

My fruitful brother
is six years gone
and childless I
these years between
have woven my love
around his children
saving at least
myself from freezing.

Last night he came
to me in sleep,
sitting beside me
in the car I drove.
An infant child
divided us
and as I braked
to a sudden stop
my responsible hand
flung down fearful
to hold it safe.

And there, before
those brittle bones,
because he rushed
to do the caring
same, I felt
again my brother's
warm and living
hand.

J.G.

February 12

I woke to a snowing that lasted all day. The radio was announcing cancellations and closings. There's a nursery school called The Open Bible, and I chuckled at the news that "The Open Bible will be closed today."

A London postcard came from friend Ed Wall, a globe-trotting executive of the International Catholic Press Association. Thanks to Father Thurston Davis, who was at the time editor of the Jesuit weekly *America,* I was instrumental in having Ed become the managing editor of Baltimore's *Catholic Review* in 1965. A good-hearted, droll, and steady person, Ed went on to become the head of the national Catholic news service in Washington. For several years now he has edited the Chicago Catholic paper, with Cardinal Cody as his boss.

Faithful Ed is the one who sent me from Rome last October the only picture I have of John Paul I. (According to an inscription found in a Chicago bar, John Paul has become the patron of temporary employees.)

Pictured on Ed's postcard today was a timely photo of the fine Saint-Gaudens statue of Lincoln near the Houses of Parliament. The evening news tonight showed protesting farmers in D.C. driving their tractors to the Lincoln Memorial. The sculptor of that marvelous seated Abe said that the best tribute he ever received was from a little boy who said that the statue makes you want to sit on his lap.

As a Baltimorean, of course, I've found it easy to visit that Memorial as well as Ford's Theatre and the nearby Petersen House in which Lincoln began to belong to the ages. Earlier in this decade I visited his birthplace in Kentucky, and his mother's in West Virginia. One of my chief tourist intentions is to visit his home and grave in Springfield.

Lincoln is one of my supremely favorite human beings. It angers me when people try to debunk him by measuring him against today's standards of totally correct thinking on the race question. I relish his saying that a man's legs should be long enough to reach the ground, and that most people are about as happy as they make up their minds to be. At scenes of parting I love to recall his farewell to the people of Springfield: "I commend you to Him who can go with me and remain with you and be everywhere for good." . . .

A doctor-friend was with my sister-in-law at the hospital the night my brother died. This Dr. John Harvey picked me up at the seminary about 1 A.M. as he was driving Mary home. She said to me, "I'll have to lean on you." I said, "I'll be there." (Later on I came across these words in the Old Testament Book of Sirach 4:10: "To the fatherless be as a father, and help their mother as a husband would, and thus you will be a son to the Most High, and He will be more tender to you than a mother.")

Friends were waiting at the house when we arrived. Young Frank, suspecting that something was wrong, came down the steps in his pajamas. As his mother broke the news, she embraced him and said, "You are good and kind, like your father." Mary Ellen, then seventeen, was worried about the impact of this loss on the three youngest boys. "It isn't fair," she said.

I slept in young Frank's room. On the floor was a game called "Stay Alive." (A few days later I saw on my brother's office desk a holy card with the words of Christ: "Come, follow me.") During the night this sleeping firstborn son called out, "Daddy!"

Living alone in her apartment near Hopkins University, my mother often listened to the early morning news. I wanted to get to her before she heard anything. So I knocked on her door not long after 7 A.M. "Don't tell me something's wrong," she said, startled to see me. I told her. It was probably the worst moment in my life, as I'm sure it was in hers. I thought she wasn't going to be able to catch her breath and I had to slap her. Children always want their parents to be parents, to be the strong ones, no matter how worn-out and old they get to be.

I had phoned earlier and asked her sisters Margaret and Stasia and my brother's secretary Fran to come early to the apartment and stay with my mother after I had to leave for the undertaker's. They arrived shortly after I told her.

I returned to the Gallaghers' where I told John, who was eight and already too pensive. He said, "He was so nice . . . I'm afraid I'll forget him." Later he wondered, "How will we eat?" and "Will we still be able to go to Ocean City in the summer?"

The twins were five and, in a way, the hardest to tell. Mary and I took them to her bedroom. When I told them their father had died, they reached out playfully to poke my face. I had to make it clear: "Your father won't be coming home anymore." They looked at

Mary and me, read our expressions, and probably deduced that they ought to lower their heads on our chests and sob—which they did.

Later they asked whether you can get Coca-Cola in heaven, and said they hated God and hospitals. Young Frank said it was a rotten thing for God to do.

The new cathedral was packed for his funeral. Cardinal Shehan preached, calling my brother "his own man," and likening him to St. Thomas More. All three local dailies eulogized him. One said he had the gifts to take him to the top of American politics.

Mother stayed with her two sisters, too upset to visit the funeral parlor or attend the funeral. "Give him a kiss for me," she asked.

My brother was buried in the New Cathedral Cemetery, where an elegant Celtic cross is carved on his large, shiny-gray stone. Our mother had to endure only two of his anniversaries. A month before the third, she was buried up the hill from her firstborn, next to my long-dead father and two of their baby grandchildren.

At my brother's funeral I tried to sketch his character in these few words:

> The profoundest wellspring in my brother
> was a passionate love for life—despite
> all its aches and shadows, with which he
> was not unacquainted, and of which I
> never heard him complain.
>
> What he loved most about life was people,
> people as people, in all their wonderfully
> wild variety—black and white, Protestant,
> Catholic and Jew, believer and unbeliever,
> "important" people and just plain people,
> Democrats and, as he would probably say,
> "even" Republicans.
>
> What he loved most about people was the
> chance to befriend them in their need,
> to ease their pain even though it
> magnified his own—that pain which he
> never outwitted, but which he held in
> heroic contempt. By the alchemy of his
> boundless drive, resourcefulness,
> generosity, and availability, he transmuted
> his own sufferings into a soothing medicine
> for countless others.

The truest comfort to be found in our
present pain is the astonishing and blazing
witness of the healing use to which he
always cheerfully put his own.

We are none of us surprised that his great
heart gave out, for his heart was giving
out all his short life long, and that was
the part of himself he used the most.

After big holiday meals, my brother loved
to quote the words: "We thank you, Lord,
for this brief repast; many a man would
have called it a meal." Grateful for the
feast of him, we might aptly say today as
our Grace After Him: "We thank you, Lord,
for his brief sojourn; many a man would
have called it a lifetime."

Perhaps one of his beautiful children spoke
most simply and eloquently for us all.
Learning of his father's death, he said in
a tone of measureless loss, "He was so
nice." So indeed he was.

There are in the heart of every man places which do not yet
exist. Pain must enter in before these places can come to be.

Léon Bloy

February 13

We don't go on as though nothing had happened. We just go
on.

February 14

After the fifth consecutive night of record low temperatures,
bundled against the cold and carrying a piping hot mug of tea to the
car with me, I left the house about 8 A.M. and drove the twenty

miles or so to the Center for Traditional Chinese Acupuncture at Columbia, Maryland.

Before bed last night I read some literature which the Center had sent me: it said that a patient should continue taking whatever medicine has already been prescribed; that sometimes there occurs after acupuncture a temporary aggravation or return of symptoms; that the insertion of the needles (of about two hairs' thickness) is generally not painful. The presumption that it would be painful has long been in my mind—though I clearly recalled that acupuncture had been the anaesthetic used on James Reston of the New York *Times* when he had his emergency appendectomy in China.

At fifty I feel more in control of my life than I was at twenty, thirty, or forty; certainly I have stripped from myself and had stripped from me many of the dependencies on sources outside of myself that I once had. Yet, I feel that I still have a major mid-life project to finish on myself as a human being; I think I am ripe for the benefits which acupuncture is said to offer.

After arriving at the Center I filled out a somewhat lengthy medical questionnaire. I also signed a statement saying I realized that acupuncture is still viewed as an experimental technique in the U.S., and that it can occasionally have side effects such as bleeding, and that I freely and knowingly enter the program.

By about 9:30 a large, gray-bearded man invited me to his office. He turned out to be Bob Duggan, the director of the Center and (I was told some time ago) a Catholic priest no longer in church ministry. He was warm and friendly as he listened and took notes for two hours while I gave him background on my life, family, friends, etc.

Then the "Western" doctor, Haig Ignatius, gave me a one-hour physical. He detected signs of a sinus infection, noted a rash on my left shoulder and considerable wax in my left ear, and, asking me whether I felt edgy, said that my pressure was on the high side— 150–160 over 100–110. I didn't feel particularly edgy.

Bob Duggan returned and gave me a "Chinese" exam: he gently felt for the six pulses in each wrist, pressed down on several places around my abdomen, inspected my feet, and asked me if they were usually cold. Then he lit a sweet-smelling stick, brought its burning end close to quite a few places on my hands and feet, and asked me to tell him as soon as I felt any heat. This probing was a trifle unpleasant, though quite tolerable.

He asked whether a gall-bladder test I had referred to on my med-

THE PAIN AND THE PRIVILEGE

ical questionnaire had revealed any problem. When I said, "No," he answered quietly, "I thought not." He said I should go easy on salt and flush out my kidneys by taking more liquid.

He said he felt he was getting a fairly clear picture of what was going on in my life. Pointing to a chart entitled "The Law of the Five Elements," he said that he detected a major blockage of energy between what he termed "the wood" and "the fire." I was, he said, giving off quite a quantity of heat, but taking in very little. In other words, my wood was not getting to my fire. He referred to a statement I had made earlier, that I felt as though I was a fireplace for many people, but had no fireplace of my own. I then cited a statement I had once made to another therapist—that I felt my joys were not talking to my sorrows.

We made an appointment for next week, on a day when I could relax after my first needle treatment. Bob said that he felt some mending was already going on within me and that I would probably not need to be seen twice a week. In three months or so, acting out of a genuine center and not having to crash back and forth between contrary magnets, I would (he felt) see clearly whatever major decisions awaited me. (I felt calm and confident with my therapist—not least of all because he was the only person ever to have mentioned a darkening spot on my upper right cheek. I've been wondering about that spot myself, knowing how prone the Irish are to skin cancer.)

Only when we are sick of our sickness shall we cease to be sick.

Lao Tzu

February 15

Fourteen years ago today I flew to Rome with my brother, sister-in-law, and two planeloads of other people accompanying Baltimore's Cardinal-elect Shehan to the ceremony at which the red hat was conferred on him by Pope Paul VI. When I became aware that not a single Negro was in his entourage, Shehan readily accepted my suggestion that he invite as his personal guest Anita Williams, a saintly woman who had worked long and devotedly for Catholic charities. She arrived on time for the highlights of the occasion.

On the night of our arrival I went with my brother and his wife to

St. Peter's Square in Vatican City and saw the light burning in the pope's apartment in the Vatican Palace. A few hours later a bomb exploded at one of the gates to Vatican City. Emotions were running high in Rome as efforts were being made and being resisted to present Hochhuth's play, *The Deputy*, with its defamatory view of Pope Pius XII.

Altogether I visited Rome six times during the sixties. I've probably spent more time in the Eternal City than in any other locale outside of my native country. (Try to get a papal dispensation in a hurry and you'll find out one reason why Rome is called the Eternal City.) Lovers of that magnetic city, among whom I count myself, are quick to point out that *Roma* spelled backward is *Amor*, and that every Westerner who returns to Rome is returning home.

During my first visit I saw and heard Pope John XXIII during a general audience in St. Peter's Basilica. He was fatherly and cheerful, stirring emotions quite contrary to the fresh news of Ernest Hemingway's self-inflicted death. In each of the other four years I saw Paul VI, the man to whom I had given a tour of Baltimore's new cathedral in 1960.

In 1963, as he opened the second session of Vatican II, I sat with other journalists to the right of the high altar—that's where the bishops sat during Vatican I. At the Vatican Palace I saw him twice again that visit: during an audience for journalists (he addressed us as "gentlemen of the press," offending some lady journalists) and at an audience for Americans on the occasion of the beatification of Bishop Neumann of Philadelphia. In 1965, as a very reverend monsignor, I watched him from my "official" position on the steps of St. Peter's high altar as he celebrated the final indoor Mass of Vatican II.

In 1967 I saw him in the new audience hall in the hill town of Castel Gandolfo, where he was to die. (On the previous day I had eaten breakfast in the capital of Ireland, lunch in the capital of England, and supper in the capital of Italy. That sequence of events was reminiscent of the joke about the wonders of aviation, which allow you to have breakfast in London, indigestion in New York, and your baggage in Calcutta.)

It was almost a year later when I saw the Rome of Paul VI for the last time. On this occasion I attended a midday audience in the inner court of his summer residence at Castel Gandolfo. He had issued his detonating encyclical against contraception just two weeks earlier. That same morning my statement reluctantly disagreeing with the encyclical was appearing on the front page of the *Sunday Sun*. Now I would hear its author say, "We bless those who accept Our encyclical and We bless those who do not."

✤

Life is a blessing, even when we cannot bless it.
                                                    W. H. Auden

February 16

Twenty-five years ago today my lawyer brother succeeded in keeping a prisoner from hanging. Just forty-eight hours before the scheduled execution, Governor McKeldin issued a staying order. As a seminarian I had visited the Maryland Penitentiary and talked with Sylvester Madison, a soft-spoken Negro who had already been on death row for two years. He had been convicted of the holdup murder of a grocer—on the testimony of a single eyewitness, who gave evidence of having been pressured into testifying as she did.

Without prospect of a fee, my older brother interested himself in the case and began trying to track down the eyewitness. He combed various rough back alleys and left his calling card with anyone who admitted knowing her. Then one day the witness and a companion knocked at the door of my brother's apartment. He was at his office, but his wife invited the callers to wait in her parlor while she phoned her husband to come home at once.

(While waiting for my brother his wife overheard this exchange in the parlor: "Why are you flicking your ashes on the rug?" "I don't want to mess up that lady's clean ashtrays.")

In short order my brother obtained from the eyewitness a repudiation of her original testimony. He scheduled an appointment with the governor virtually on the eve of the execution. But when he arrived in Annapolis the appointment was suddenly canceled without explanation. My brother said he would not budge until he had seen the governor. Eventually he was told to file his affidavits and a stay of execution would be granted.

In a two-to-one decision the original judges declared that the court was powerless to grant a new trial after such a time lapse. All three agreed, though, on the "unreliability of the witness," who had in the meantime retracted her retraction.

After the Court of Appeals upheld the majority opinion, the governor commuted the sentence to life imprisonment in January 1955. By that time Sylvester Madison had endured the longest stay in the death house in Maryland's history: three years and three months.

I've lost track of Sylvester. I should try to get in touch with him. I'll never forget the double-meaning headline in the local *Afro-American*: "Seminary Student Held Up Hanging."

♣

For the crime of having been born, we are all under sentence of death . . . with an indefinite stay of execution.
                                        Calderón de la Barca (plus addendum)

February 17

Five years ago this time I returned to Baltimore's Spring Grove Hospital for another drug session. It was actually my fifth session, but this seems a convenient place to summarize what happened in the second session, after the beginnings I recalled last month.

Shortly after the nurse, Janet, arrived, I removed my shoes, got on the couch, lay on my stomach to receive two needles, one in each buttock (75 mgs this time). I had just turned on my back and let Bill put the earphones on me when the drug took effect with what seemed like furious speed. I felt my heartbeat quicken at once, and to ward off panic I made myself think of that beat as the heartbeat of the universe—a strong, dependable beat which was friendly toward me.

Nevertheless, at the start of my instant plunge into engulfing explosions of color (or their instant appropriation of me) and into the sense of being at the mercy of a whirlpool of energy, of being out of control, I thought how perilous all this was, and I regretted submitting to it. I surely would not do so again.

I called out to Bill and Janet. They seemed far away—as though in another time zone, on the other side of some psychic international date line.

I felt I was so much deeper into myself than during the first session. Indeed I realized that this *was* my first session. . . . I felt far beyond the mother-and-father kinds of concerns and remembrances. Affairs now seemed more lonely, more impersonal, more archetypal. Beyond tears, in a way.

I was thrust into delirious eruptions of color: purples and greens, diamonds, jewels. They shimmered and quivered. They melted snakily. The beauty was so absolute, so stark, so merciless, that it intimidated me, almost petrified me. I didn't know what to do with it.

But the scene kept changing with breakneck speed. Later I thought it was like going through a whole year of the New York *Times* on microfilm in about five minutes—and going through it physically, reliving every story emotionally.

Relatively early in the trip I had the sense that I should be letting go more than I was, but that if I did I might become divine in some terrifying way, and not be able to return to a specific place and belong to a specific time. I would just swirl endlessly and lose my identity. Would this mean being like God? And is our temptation *not* to be like Him?

How simple it would be, this letting go; but what audacity it would require—that's why it is a secret, despite its being so obvious a step. Being God would mean not having a father, not being able to look at some antecedent and recognize that you came from there and could measure or localize yourself in terms of that superior fixity, that comforting priority. Being God means having no such place to come home to.

I saw images of Aztec warrior-gods carved on a temple wall. I found myself thinking that if I were the official outcast of the tribe, then being an "outcast" would be my way of being "in," of belonging. . . . I had the feeling of a great trembling. I had a fear that I might find out that at the heart of things God himself is nervous and trembling, and I didn't want to discover that.

As all these various things were happening, as scenes shifted rapidly, I had the sensation that some great force was swinging me by my feet and catapulting me through weird scenarios, making me pass through various epochs of civilization. . . .

My thinking drifted toward the idea that God has no father, and that I can empathize with him because my father did not love me, and so I was emotionally fatherless. I keep God company by that feeling. To die would mean to join God and soften his loneliness.

Tears came as I thought how beautiful and tender and loving it would be if a human person agreed to the experience of "never having a father" so that he could keep God company in this feeling. What if the person also agreed to suffer forgetfulness about this arrangement so that his sense of loss could be more real?

If I let myself feel that God loves me, if I really relax in Him, I would be giving up my sense of being unfathered and could no longer keep Him company in His fatherlessness. And if I directly befriend Him, would I not be fathering Him and thereby making us lose our equal status as unfathered? An unstable relationship, ours.

> For Beauty's nothing
> but beginning of Terror we're still just able to bear
> and why we adore it so is because it serenely
> disdains to destroy us.
>
> *Rainer Maria Rilke*

February 18

I went to Loyola College to say a 10:30 Mass for a group that meets weekly near the Loyola chapel. It includes a number of resigned priests. Today three such were in attendance, along with wives and children and others, totaling about twenty-five.

During the dialogue homily, several mentioned a sense of despair at the world condition. Author Garry Wills was there (along with son Garry); he spoke of the Christian's belief that the worst is already over and that only mopping-up operations remain. ("The dreadful has already happened," wrote the philosopher Heidegger.) I thought of the Battle of New Orleans, which took place after the War of 1812 had already officially ended.

On my tape machine when I returned was a phone call from priest-friend John Auer. When I last spoke with him a few weeks ago, he mentioned that he was going skiing with a mutual priest-friend, Jack Hooper, who is about my age, though he was ordained two years after me. John's message was that Jack had dropped dead last night after playing tennis at a racquet club. Jack was extremely athletic and active. He has been a chaplain in the national guard for many years. He plays soccer, swims, hikes, skis.

One day in Jack's seminary career his theology professor was about to discuss diabolical possession, obsession, poltergeists, and related phenomena. This Father Dukehart never used the podium chair, but always set it aside and leaned over the desk and the textbook.

Before this particular class Jack tied one end of a string to the podium chair and the other to his own seat in the front row. As Father Dukehart began to talk about occult happenings, Jack slowly pulled the chair of theology across the podium until it tumbled to the floor. The teacher and many of the unsuspecting students sustained a preternatural jolt. I was in a classroom at the far opposite end of the building, and we could hear plainly the uproar shattering the customary class-time silence.

Jack was always keen for getting his fellow priests together for New Year's parties and such. He went out of his way to think of priests who might have some special need of camaraderie.

When I made my statement opposing the encyclical *Humanae Vitae*, Jack wrote to me: "Although I agree in most part with your issues, I do disagree with your method . . . I realize you are following your conscience and must speak out—even at the cost of losing some friends . . . So may I go on record, in these trying times, as being counted among your friends."

Jack was a man's man and a priest's priest. Never much interested in theory, he was a people's priest, too, with a genius for the common touch. When you'd tell him a touching or dramatic tale, his pet response was "It kind of breaks you up." The phrase is apt tonight at the thought that the life of this life-loving, steady, good-natured, and faithful friend has come to a sudden end.

The man who has one good friend has more than his share.

February 19

If in the dead world they forget the dead, I say that there too I shall remember him, my friend.

Achilles of Patroclus, Iliad 22:389

February 20

Looked back on, life will seem like one night spent in a bad hotel.

St. Theresa of Ávila

February 21

A friend is someone who knows the song in your heart and sings it back to you when you forget how it goes.

February 22

For nearly a decade (1957–66) I was in charge of the archives of the Baltimore Archdiocese, the richest storehouse of U.S. Catholic history. Washington's birthday reminds me of one of the treasures of that storehouse: a letter from the Founding Father to a committee of eminent U.S. Roman Catholics who upon his election sent him congratulations on behalf of their co-religionists. In his reply of March 12, 1790, the man who had banned the celebration of the anti-Catholic Guy Fawkes Day in the Continental Army went out of his way to cite the decisive help given the colonies by Catholic France and to voice the hope that non-Catholic Americans "will not forget the patriotic part which you took in the accomplishment of their Revolution."

I was able to scrutinize more than one hundred other letters from fourteen other presidents—though none, alas, from Lincoln. Reflecting his low opinion of clergy in general, there's a rather humorous one from Thomas Jefferson. Writing to Baltimore's Archbishop Marechal, he refers to a papal nuncio he had met in Paris and says that their encounters "taught me to value his pure and sincere heart, his correct and dignified deportment and a most amiable modesty, rare endowments in his high station."

Earlier, Baltimore's first archbishop wrote to Jefferson to sound out his feelings about the priest whom Carroll was thinking of putting in charge of the Catholic church in the new Louisiana Territory. As Secretary of State, James Madison replied for Jefferson: ". . . as the case is entirely ecclesiastical, it is deemed most congenial with the scrupulous policy of the constitution in guarding against a political interference with religious affairs, to decline. . . ." Nevertheless, Madison enclosed a second letter, marked *private*: ". . . an official answer to your enquiries has not been given. The reason for declining it does not however forbid my saying in a private letter that . . . no objection can lie against the use you propose to make of Mr. L'Espinasse [the aforementioned clergyman]."

In a more recent letter President Franklin Delano Roosevelt wrote proudly of his distant kin, Elizabeth Ann Seton, who at that time was buried next to their common kinsman, James Roosevelt Bayley, eighth archbishop of Baltimore.

As I made my way through numerous Vatican documents I discovered that the very first one to bear the actual signature of a pope was signed by Pius VII in 1817 and condemned a Father Gallagher— a controversial priest of Charleston, South Carolina, who bore the name Simon Felix and the reputation of a popular preacher and a hyperactive imbiber of alcoholic spirits.

❧

Drinking doesn't drown your sorrows, it only irrigates them.

February 23

I arrived at the Acupuncture Center by 9:45. I was taken to a different room this time. There I stripped to my shorts and lay on the table, a pillow under my head, a yellow sheet over me.

Bob came in, asked if I wanted to add anything to my remarks of last week. He felt my pulses again. Then, after smearing on a bit of alcohol, he inserted a needle into the outside of my left calf, and the inside of my left ankle. I felt only the slightest tingling sensation. In a minute or so, I noticed a slight numbing inside my left forearm and then my right. I also had the sense that my torso was filling up with a moderate, pleasant warmth. I said I felt like an empty bag filling up with warm cement.

Bob left the room for five minutes or so. When he returned, I mentioned a slight aching sense where he had left the needles. "I

took the needles out," he said, to my surprise. Then he inserted a
needle below my middle right toe, and let it stay put for a few minutes. "I don't want you to have too strong a reaction," he confided.

He warned me to stay away from alcohol for the rest of the day,
and to try to endure any symptoms for which I might take occasional medicine. He said he wanted the treatment to get to a deep
organ, but that by trying through medicine to maintain my customary balance of energy, I could offset the new and better balance that
would be trying to assert itself. He said he would tell me next week
what precisely he has been doing. Meantime I should phone if I
have any questions about handling any symptoms.

I went back to my Ellicott City cousins' for a nap, and underwent
an energetic bowel movement, accompanied by an unusual quantity
of gas. Was this a reaction to the acupuncture?

I phoned my senior nephew at the Capitol, where he works for
Senator Sarbanes. We agreed to have dinner in Georgetown this evening. He was out of his university room when I arrived, but my
priest-friend Bob, a graduate student, was in his apartment. So I
paid him a visit and accepted his offer of overnight accommodations.

After the school newspaper told of his admitted homosexuality,
one of his windows had been broken by a stone. Some students say
that outsiders did it, and the timing was just a coincidence. In any
case, for a while Bob received many obscene phone calls at all hours.
People he knew snubbed him on campus. As many as 150 students
had been coming to the Sunday liturgy which he conducted; on the
Sunday after the newspaper article, only five showed up.

Bob told me that he had befriended a gay organization on campus
and had been telling its members not to succumb to self-hatred because of their sexual orientation. So, when the campus newspaper interviewed him about his work and asked him whether he was gay, he
felt he would be betraying those he had counseled if he said no.

He's not sure what his bishop will do, although he was friendly
enough when Bob told him of his orientation last summer, before
any publicity. He wasn't sure for a while whether the university
would allow him to continue as residence director, but he has been
guiding thirteen assistant directors and his record is fine. It now
seems he will stay on as R.D. while doing his dissertation.

He has decided to write about an ethics for homosexuality, based
on the laws of friendship. He gave me a copy of a D.C. magazine

which had interviewed him, and said there was due to be an article about him in next Monday's Washington *Star*.

Frank phoned from his room. We went to a Georgetown restaurant for a late supper, returning just before midnight.

The students were holding a carnival party in Bob's building. Despite his recent back operation, Bob insisted on sleeping on the couch. As I slipped into his bed, next to a great plate of glass, I thought of Josephine Jacobsen's most celebrated story, about a man in the wrong bed who gets himself beheaded by mistake.

We atone for the sins that we're inclined to
By condemning those that we have no mind to.

February 24

Bob doesn't usually eat breakfast, but he could offer me a welcome cup of coffee. Then he escorted me to a nearby chapel so that I could obtain a Communion Host for Katherine Anne Porter, whom I was due to visit later today. She was inhaling oxygen when I arrived.

Katherine Anne said that this time she was really dying. She has been telling her friends good-bye for keeps, urging them not to bother to return. One of those friends, Robert Penn Warren, had been there the other day with his wife. Katherine Anne said she introduced "Red" to writer Eleanor Clark, and is godmother for their first child.

We talked a bit about Allen Tate, who died a few weeks ago. She knew him well and gave me a brief outline of his life and his wives. Then she said, "That's all there is to it."

She said she was at peace, despite her lingering sickness and pain. I read again for her the prayers for the dying. Her eyes moistened. "How could anybody hear such lovely words and not want to have lived a life worthy of them?" Once again, I gave her Holy Communion.

She apologized for the lack of tea in the kitchen, but insisted that I drink her orange juice. We kissed good-bye. I noted that Ash Wednesday was near. She replied that spring too would soon be here, and she just might wait for it. Earlier she had said she still reads the newspaper. "I try to keep up with the world as long as I'm still in it."

❦

We are all in the Departure Lounge.

February 25

There are three kinds of people: those who make things happen; those who watch things happen; and those who have no idea what happened.

February 26

Cloudy skies kept me and other Baltimoreans from seeing any of today's eclipse of the sun. My next Baltimore chance won't be for thirty-five years; in that case, I've probably had my last local chance. I read somewhere that scientists have learned most of what they know about the sun by studying its corona during eclipses. That's a parable about how much we learn about ourselves during the dark times in our lives.

Jim Redding, a former seminarian, dropped by for lunch and a chat. I taught Jim philosophy at old St. Mary's. A native of Gettysburg, he served in Brazil in the Peace Corps after he left the seminary. Quite a few of my students entered the Corps in the late sixties.

Steve Herrick, who went to Paraguay, married a Peace Corps girl and adopted an orphaned Paraguayan Indian of the Tupi-Guarani tribe. (They gave us the word "tapioca.") The youngster was named Chebugi, i.e., "tapir-person," after the animal that his father killed ritualistically just before the son's birth. These people never eat an animal that they kill, but give it to someone else.

In Chebugi's language the phrase for a large number is "as many as trees." After Steve and Sandy took him to a large city, he spontaneously changed the expression to "as many as cars."

Gus Bamat, another former student, went to Chile as a Maryknoll missionary. He told me that once he was staying overnight in a

THE PAIN AND THE PRIVILEGE

remote village and heard someone shouting *"Bashu, Bashu"* through
the midnight dark. The next morning, when he asked about the
repeated cry, he was told a marvelous story: originally the rainbow
was married to God, but she was seduced by the devil (*Bashu*).
Human beings are the children of that second union. Ever since the
seduction, God has been hunting down the devil, calling his name.

When an illness hits a village, the devil is considered to be the
cause. So a holy man repeatedly calls out the devil's name at night.
The villagers hope the devil will think God is closing in on him, and
so he'll leave and take his sickness with him.

Back to Jim, who does social work outside of Philadelphia: he
took me to lunch at a nearby downstairs restaurant called The Soup
Cellar. Normally, it is a quiet place, and I once took a cousin there
who had heart trouble. Here, at least, I thought, we could have a
peaceful meal. But in the middle of our lunch, violent shouts and
the sound of crashing dishes and pots and pans erupted from the
kitchen. One of the cooks had gone berserk, and she had to be
dragged out past us by the police. So much for my careful planning!

This evening John Standafer arrived from Iowa. He is one of my
favorite "sons" from the Children's Village. He will stay with me for
two days while he is taking the Maryland bar exam.

🌳

The devil knows more from being old than from being the
devil.

February 27

John and I rose early enough so that we could have breakfast and
I could deliver him by 9:15 to the downtown Civic Center for the
first half of his bar exam. He took me to supper at Jimmy Wu's,
where I introduced him to beef lo mein; in honor of my acupuncture
and belief in yin and yang, I ordered sweet and sour pork.

The Wus once lived near my older brother's home. I have a poem
about the time my niece and little Susie Wu were playing in the
backyard. Mary Ellen pointed to a rosebush and said, "Look at that
Japanese beetle." Susie replied, "We're Chinese, you know."

Passing by the Children's Village today, where I was chaplain
from 1962 to 1963, I thought of Joe, another youngster I grew close

to. Like John, he went to Boys Town. He too went into the service, but was killed in Vietnam shortly before the end of his tour of duty there. I had his funeral service and visit his grave occasionally at the National Cemetery in southwest Baltimore.

Once, while visiting Baltimore, Joe had been beaten up by some older relatives. He went to another relative's house and was talking to me on the phone when the abusive relatives pulled up in a car. Joe, who was tough, told me he had a knife in his hand and was going to kill anyone who tried to touch him. Luckily, I had two lines on my phone at that time. I told him to hang on while I called the police on the other line. I kept telling him to stay calm, and the police arrived before any tragedy occurred.

I took one of Joe's buddies to the undertaker's the night before the funeral. Harold didn't talk much on our way back. As he got out of the car, he said, "Well, at least Joe will be at peace . . . for the rest of his life."

Go to the gods, Alexander. May the River of Ordeal be as mild as milk to you, and bathe you in light, not fire. May your dead forgive you. . . . You were never without love; and where you go, may you find it waiting.

Mary Renault

February 28

When we're young we want to change the world; when we're old we want to change the young.

March 1, 1979

A law of courage to clip and save: the fearless breast cannot be brave.

J.G.

March 2

Toward the end of my acupuncture session today Bob knelt down beside me and addressed me at eye level. He said there was a major disconnection between my right and my left pulses. The situation, he said, was serious—on this side of critical. He felt, though, that there had been no irreparable tearing, and that healing forces were already at work. Though spoken gently, Bob's words have triggered some anxiety in me.

I should have no peace for a moment if I thought I lacked anxiety.

Christopher Fry

March 3

Show me a sane man and I'll cure him.
Carl Jung

March 4

I splurged tonight and treated three of my Gallagher nephews to supper at McDonald's. As I drove them home we passed a small parish cemetery where six of our relatives are buried, including their great- and great-great grandparents. One of these, my mother's mother, died two dozen years ago today—on the ninetieth birthday of the grandmother I never knew and who died when my father was nine.

Grandma Doyle had been living with my mother for some months when on this day in 1955 my mother went to call her for supper and found her dead. (My policeman brother had disappeared about two weeks earlier.) I was ordained a deacon the following day, and at her funeral I performed as a deacon for the first time by singing the Gospel.

Grandma Doyle had been born Anastasia Maloney in County Wexford, Ireland, on St. Patrick's Day, 1869. The youngest of thirteen, she came to America as a young woman and finally settled and married in Baltimore. Granddad Doyle was Baltimore-born, but had parents from the same County Wexford.

I remember Grandma as a kind, witty woman who wore long, faded dresses and her gray hair in a bun. She suffered from "the catarrh," as I did too in my younger days. When you asked her how she felt, she'd reply, "Well, outside of being no good, I'm fine." She often responded to radio commercials by saying, "You don't say so!"

There was always a pot of soupy lamb stew on her kitchen stove. (My mother hated soup in her grown years and would never order it when we ate out.) When I was taken out of the first grade for several months because of a supposed heart murmur, Grandma gave me many an afternoon dime to buy myself a cup of vanilla ice cream with the face of a movie star under the lid.

We Gallaghers lived with our grandparents for several extended periods. It was there that my father had met my mother when he crashed a Halloween party given by Aunt Stasia. Though located across the street from a convent of Negro nuns whose early morning chanting seemed a benediction, the Brentwood Avenue house seemed adhesively gloomy to me, even before I realized that the state penitentiary with its death house was just down the street.

Once when we were staying there, Granddad, who was gentle and soft-spoken and given to long stays in bed, commented to my music-loving mother, "Nellie, you sure are hep on that radio." On another occasion someone sent him a dollar for his birthday. Phoning to thank his benefactor, he was overheard saying—in all innocence, I'm sure—that prices were so high these days you couldn't get a decent pair of shoestrings for a dollar. One of my prized remembrances of that crippled man with a cane is watching him walking slowly in his backyard when I was a young boy, and envying him all the memories he had to keep him company.

When Grandma was found to be suffering from an aneurysm, the gloomy house had to be sold and Granddad Doyle was sent to a nursing home. There, two weeks later, he died unexpectedly.

Mom had a twin sister who died in infancy. ("I've inherited her sorrows," she used to say.) Two years earlier a brother had also died young. Grandma said she thought she'd never live through that loss. Two other brothers would spend long years in mental hospitals. My mother and one of her sisters married turbulent alcoholics who died young and poor. Unmarried Aunt Stasia would endure a long and cheerless life of ill health.

So there was many a sorrow in the Doyle family, that family of "dark strangers," as their name means. Once, commenting on her tribulations, Grandma said that Christ had to bear a crown of thorns, so why shouldn't she. Your heart has to kneel in silence before a remark like that.

🌳

We can pay our debt to the past only by putting the future in debt to us.

John Buchan

March 5

A dozen years ago today I attended Mass at old St. Mary's Seminary and had my first exposure to the new seminary and to modern seminarians. In that lovely little gem of a chapel I heard the choir and community sing "You Are My People." That was the first modern religious folk song I ever heard, and I was enchanted. I didn't realize it that day of a casual visit, but I would return a month later and for eight years thereafter seminarians would be "my people" in a special way.

One of those students, now married and the father of two, phoned me today from South Carolina. Joe Walker, tough and athletic, was one of the most philosophic students I ever knew. He relished metaphysics, and lived what he loved. One Thanksgiving eve he sat in my rocking chair in the seminary and talked for about four hours, using the chair and its motions as an extension of body language.

He told of a watch he inherited from his esteemed and deceased father. Once Joe had to make a critical personal decision. He was winding the watch, and just as he made the key decision, he broke the spring of the watch. The watch still tells the decisive moment, since he deliberately refused to get it fixed.

Philosophy is the disease of which it ought to be the cure.
Ludwig Wittgenstein

March 6

The kind of philosophy a man chooses depends on the kind of man he is.

J. G. Fichte

March 7

As one who several times taught a survey course in Thomism, I couldn't forget that today used to be the feast of St. Thomas Aquinas, and a seminary holiday. The feast has been moved to January 28, and I doubt that it is still a holiday in many seminaries, for the philosophy of Aquinas no longer holds monopolistic sway over the seminary curriculum, as it did in my day.

At the Council of Trent in the sixteenth century, the *Summa Theologica* of St. Thomas was given a place on the high altar alongside the Bible itself. In the documents of Vatican II, by way of contrast, Aquinas is mentioned but twice in the body of the text. Whence the conciliar joke: "Should auld Aquinas be forgot?"

When I began teaching in the seminary in 1967, the administration asked me to conduct the course in Thomism. I soon discovered how professionally unprepared I was for that assignment. The new breed of seminarians were ready, willing, and able to question everything, skeptical of "old thoughts," and pressured personally by life problems which made Thomism as usually taught seem aggressively irrelevant.

(There's a story about a pilot who bailed out over unknown territory and landed in a tree. Seeing two monks walking nearby, he yelled to them and asked where he was. One of them replied: "You're in a tree." "Oh," countered the pilot, "you must be Thomists. What you say is true, but it's not very helpful.")

I could empathize with the attitude of my students, since I myself had rather despised Thomism as it was taught to me. My attitude was improved by the books of Joseph Pieper. His essay, "The Negative Element in the Philosophy of St. Thomas," hit me like a bombshell. He made clear to me the vital role which mystery plays in the world view of Aquinas. In the sense of a close-minded know-it-all, Thomas was no Thomist. "All the effort of human thought," he wrote, "has not been able to exhaust the essence of a single fly."

Just such a creature was the focus of a startling experience I had in my second year of high school. As I sat studying one afternoon, a shaft of sunlight cut across my desk. Suddenly a fly landed in the light "with Blue—uncertain stumbling Buzz." As I stared at the sunlit fly I was powerfully struck by the fact that the fly was its own independent source of energy—that it wasn't "plugged in." There was a unique flash of perceptiveness to this very commonplace occurrence. It was as though every previous fly I had ever seen had been a tiny neon sign, but this was the first one which had ever "turned on."

One brisk autumn morning six years earlier I was walking to school across a sun-drenched, dew-drenched field when I was seized by an enrapturing sense of peace and fulfillment, and communion was all that was. Only years later did I realize that that ecstatic moment remained as a kind of touchstone of beauty and happiness in a youth which was often ugly and besieged.

A third and even earlier memory is of a simple but somehow indelible encounter with a buttercup in a field across from my childhood home. It was as though one golden flower in all the multiple world had taken a fancy to me and stamped my virginal vision with its blazing signature. When in later years I heard Tennyson speak of the flower in the crannied wall which somehow locked into the meaning of absolutely everything, when I heard Wordsworth speak of the inward eye and of moments when we seem to see into the heart of things, I felt as though I knew exactly what they were talking about, thanks to these existential experiences which remained inexplicably precious in my memory.

My philosophy teachers had said very little about existentialism.

One day, though, a fellow seminarian asked me to return a book for
him to the city library. (He is now the bishop of Raleigh.) It was a
treatise on existentialism by Paul Foulquié. I started reading it and
was spellbound. With a sudden shift of focus I was in the world of
Kierkegaard, Marcel, Sartre, Unamuno, and kindred spirits. For years
I had been looking into the mirror of philosophy and felt like an
alien because I saw little that was mine. Now, all at once, I was seeing my own face and my own heart. Not every existentialist could
provide me with my answer, but most of them asked my kind of
question. Confirmed in my own way of seeing, I was now ready to
see even the existentialist in Aquinas, for whom the supreme form
of being is One Whose essence it is to exist.

It is a great advantage for a system of philosophy to be substan-
tially true.

George Santayana

March 8

Twenty-five years ago I knew Walter Sullivan as an upperclass-
man at St. Mary's Seminary; he was a good-natured clerk in our
bookstore, where you could also buy items like soap and toothpaste.
Now he's the bishop of Richmond.

Seven years ago I attended the first Mass of one of my poetry students. Though a New Yorker, Bob had been adopted by the Richmond diocese and held his reception in the city's Jefferson Hotel,
whose staircase was reputedly featured in *Gone With the Wind*.

Today Bob and Bishop Sullivan appeared together on page three
of the *Sun* under the headline "Gay Va. Priest Unfrocked." I've already mentioned how, when I visited Georgetown recently, Bob told
me that the Washington *Star* was due to publish an interview with
him. It now seems that the interview appeared last Sunday. The
bishop is reported as saying that Bob "knew the consequences of his
action when he made his public announcement. Today I am notify-
ing him that he may no longer function in his priestly ministry."

Bob is quoted as saying that his homosexual orientation does not
mean that he has broken his vow of celibacy, though the article may
have led the bishop to jump to that conclusion.

Downtown I was able to buy a copy of the *Star* article. It began on the front page of the metropolitan section, and included a large picture of Bob in casual clothing with a Georgetown University background. Entitled "Gay Priest Copes with Harassment, Uncertainty," the article is well-done and quite moving at times. This evening I tried to phone Bob and offer him the support of friendship, but I received no answer. . . .

Around noon I went shopping for some basics to put into the Jacobsens' refrigerator; they are due to return today from the Caribbean. The last time I did such an errand, nephew Jimmy was with me. "Are the Jacobsens rich?" he asked, noting a statue or two and some paintings in their apartment. With sage avuncularity I replied, "There are many ways to be rich, you know." "Yeah," the eleven-year-old answered, "but I mean the *good* way."

Jimmy took a more spiritual interest in my other poet-friend, Elliott Coleman. "Does he still write poetry," the youngster asked me one day, "or has he had all his thoughts?"

Jimmy's own thoughts don't always quite match his words. He spoke recently of an important event as a "handmark." He has also noted that the pope is against "divortion." He was pleased when his mother visited Israel and brought him back a "yamaha" for his head. He spoke lately of someone who is suffering a "priority complex" and occasionally refers to my benefactress Victorine as "Listerine."

The trouble with most of world's opinions is that they are held by people who have never really been in trouble.

March 9

I phoned Bob at Georgetown this morning. He said the past few days have been exceedingly hectic. Reporters, photographers, and TV cameramen have swooped down on him. The New York *Times* is due to have an article on him. The university has indicated that it wants to stay out of the dispute between Bob and Bishop Sullivan. Before announcing Bob's suspension, the bishop had not told him of his decision. Bob phoned him yesterday to ask just why he was being suspended. "For making that public statement," answered the bishop.

A letter came today from one of Bob's seminary classmates, Loren Hoffman of Detroit. Gentle and thoughtful "Guz" is one of my all-time favorite students and was part of one of my all-time treasured days. It was April of 1967, and I was spending some time in a kind of retreat at St. Mary's on Paca Street. The previous several months had been harrowing and lonely ones for me after my resignation from the archdiocesan newspaper.

Guz and three other seminarians whom I scarcely knew invited me on a gloomy day to go with them on a day trip to western Maryland. On our way to Harpers Ferry the sky turned cheerful. We had lunch at the spot which Thomas Jefferson said was worth a trip across the Atlantic. From an overhanging rock you can see the states of Maryland, Virginia, and West Virginia; you can also see the Shenandoah River merge with the Potomac on its way to Washington.

There was something massively healing and incandescent about those hours I spent in the company of those friendly and idealistic seminarians. It was a feast after a long fast, and not to be forgotten. . . .

A lunch with a different tone marked my noontime today, when I went to The Soup Cellar with Roxie Powell. His delicately lovely wife, Kathleen, died of cancer last year after four months of marriage. They were both graduates of Elliott Coleman's seminars at Hopkins. In Kathy's memory Roxie gave me a gold-leafed icon that she smuggled out of Russia.

Now in his forties, Roxie is a benignly frenetic man. He writes "a poem a day," and just had a collection of them published. He spent part of his Christmas vacation in San Francisco trying to persuade his mother that the poem about her on page eleven is not obscene. He's not sure he succeeded.

After lunch we walked around, talking for an hour in the congenial sunshine. He said Kathy told him her greatest wish was to have been a saint.

❧

There is really only one tragedy in life, not to have been a saint.

Léon Bloy

March 10

Twenty-two years ago today I first met Monsignor Louis Stickney, who had been Cardinal Gibbons' secretary and had personally known the father of St. Thérèse of Lisieux ("He's the one they should have canonized") as well as Leo XIII and Pius X. Once he accompanied Gibbons' successor, Archbishop Curley, to Rome.

In an audience, Pius XI asked Curley what he was doing for the Italians in the United States. The outspoken Curley, vexed at poorly instructed immigrants, asked the pope what he was doing for the Italians in Italy. Afterward the monsignor asked the archbishop if he had ever thought he might get the red hat of a cardinal. "Well, yes," Curley replied. "Well," advised Stickney, "drop it!" (He never did get it.)

Michael Curley, the first prelate to bear the burden of being my archbishop, confirmed me at St. Ann's church on April 7, 1940. In those days bishops gave you fair warning by slapping your cheek during the ceremony. Like tenor John McCormack, he was born in Athlone, Ireland. Once when Curley's mother was singing the praises of McCormack, the archbishop pointed out that her own son hadn't done so poorly himself. "Ah," she said, "there's many an archbishop, but only one John McCormack."

When he first came to Baltimore, Curley said that if he had a choice he would build a school rather than a church. Some years later he was questioning a girl whom he was about to confirm. She showed such a mastery of the catechism that he called her up to the front of the church and pointed with pride at this youngster who splendidly vindicated his school policy. "But, Archbishop," she announced, "I go to public school."

Many a priest was more afraid of Curley than that girl was. Once a nervous master of ceremonies put the mitre backward on Curley's head, so that the wide, long flaps fell down over the prelate's face. "Stand back," Curley is said to have commanded, "and let everyone see what a nincompoop you are!" Perhaps it was this same ill-fated cleric who on another occasion forgot to put the mitre on Curley. "Put the mitre on! Put the mitre on!" barked the archbishop. The priest was so rattled that he obeyed by putting the mitre on his own head.

Even outside of church this archbishop was not free from frustration. Once when he was taking a stroll he saw a little boy stretching hard to ring a doorbell. Indulging a paternal impulse, the archbishop went over and lifted the boy so he could reach the button. "Now," advised the youngster, "run like hell!"

"Would you care for some grace, Your Gravy?"
                                        Nervous curate to visiting prelate

March 11

Local newspapers and TV newscasters have been focusing these days on the mercy-killing trial of a nurse who worked at Maryland General Hospital. For the first seven years of my priesthood I took my turn being on call by day and night for chaplain duties at that hospital, which is in the old cathedral parish.

Once an anxious grandmother phoned from the hospital for a priest to come give a blessing to her ailing grandchild. She hadn't told the child's father that she had summoned a priest. When I walked into the room, the father angrily shouted, "Who called for him? He gives me the creeps!"

I received a warmer welcome on another, tragic occasion. A fire on Eutaw Place brought a whole family to the hospital in critical condition. Eyewitnesses said that the mother had tossed her children out of a window like blazing Christmas trees. The doctors didn't even bother to bandage the grandfather. When I walked into his room the nurse said, "Thank God you've come, Father. I've been standing here praying." The children were so thoroughly bandaged that I couldn't tell their age or their sex. Eventually the entire family died.

A priest never knows when he is going to be pitched into the heart of such a happening. He needs to be able to shift his emotional gears swiftly. I can recall one afternoon in my life when: I absolved penitents in the confessional, baptized a premature baby at Maryland General, anointed a ninety-year-old woman dying in her dingy room, celebrated the Eucharist, and joined in holy wedlock two starry-eyed lovers.

To the extent of my power, precisely because I am a priest, I wish from now on to become conscious of all that the world loves, pursues and suffers. . . . I want to become more widely human than any of the world's servants.

Teilhard de Chardin, S.J.

March 12

I went for a noonday stroll and within a hundred steps of my home I saw a willow tree exuding its first golden fuzz, and a smaller tree erupting into tiny red buds. Is there any kinder treat from nature than just this gradual return of color after winter's bleakness? I thought of A. E. Housman's lines: "Give me a land of boughs in leaf . . . I love no leafless land."

Down by the entrance to the Jones Falls Expressway, I saw the brown, marcescent leaves of a sizable tree. (I love that word "marcescent"—"dying but not falling off." My problem is, what happens next? Do green leaves push off the old brown ones?)

It was thirty-five years ago tonight, at our home about eleven blocks east of here, that my forty-six-year-old father died. I was then in my first year of high school in the seminary. On a cold Wednesday morning during a study-hall period, while I was learning in Latin the passive of the verb "love," the prefect called me to his office, said that my father had been taken ill, and I should go home at once.

At home I learned that my father had caught a chill three days earlier. The doctor said he had lobar pneumonia, and his general physical condition was not encouraging. I found my father in bed in the first-floor back room. I don't recall that we conversed very much. Though an irregular churchgoer, he was fond of making the annual "novena of grace," held in honor of St. Francis Xavier from March 4 to March 12. He had begun it before the pneumonia set in, and now my mother was helping him to say the prescribed prayers for each day.

My older brother Francis was going to be master of ceremonies for a parish St. Patrick's Day show. On Sunday night he was attending a rehearsal. A rainstorm delayed him, but when he finally arrived home shortly after eleven, our father had just died.

My mother, my younger brother, and I were in the room at the awesome moment of death. My father had been breathing irregularly, with lengthening pauses. One pause protracted itself into not being a pause at all. So this is what the end is: a pause that never ends. That's how I knew my turbulent, opaque father was dead and that I was now officially fatherless. It was the last night of the novena.

Embarrassingly, the owners of our house had nailed a metal "For Sale" sign next to our front door. As soon as he realized our father had died, Francis went out in the rain and ripped the sign off the wall.

My sister was only six. We let her view our father briefly in the coffin in the front parlor. The bottom half of the coffin was closed; a crucifix adorned its lid. Mary Jo looked awhile and asked only two questions: "Can we keep the cross?" and "Where's his legs?"

Thomas Wolfe said, "Every man's life is a search for a father." If he dies when you're fourteen, he's even harder to find.

Those few months that he lived after I left home for the seminary, he sent me a number of newsy letters in his strong, fine script. Mom would usually write only about such dull things as my health. Dad talked about Mussolini and the war. I saved those letters for a year or two, then, in a fit of holy detachment, I destroyed the only letters he ever sent me.

That was one of the most regrettable things I ever did. Now, I'm older than both my older brother and my father. Reading those letters now, I might find more of our father than I knew was in them at the time.

Childhood is the kingdom where nobody dies—nobody that matters, that is.

Edna St. Vincent Millay

March 13

Like most Americans, I suppose, I went to bed thinking that President Carter's trip to the Middle East had ended up a failure. I woke to find that by some intervening miracle, peace might actually be on the verge of breaking out between Egypt and Israel.

I bought an early edition of the *Evening Sun*, which carried the first article I've done for the new Op Ed page. Entitled "Posters and Imposters," it deals with wall posters that cite wrong sources for their quotes. How embarrassing to find eighteen typos in this fault-finding article!

At dinner last night Josephine Jacobsen spoke of her recent stay on the Caribbean island of Grenada and of rumors that guns were being smuggled onto the island. She wondered whether any such activity could escape the secret police of the island's dictator, Eric Gairy. Today's paper brought word that a revolutionary group had overthrown the Gairy government while he was out of the country.

When I was last in Grenada, in 1975, I saw a slogan on one of its walls: "Gairy is the best." Someone had altered the "best" into "pest." I looked around carefully before I snapped a picture of that slogan.

For the record let it be said that in all my considerable travels I have never been more geographically gratified than when I was sitting on my cliff-edge cabin at Grenada's Ross Point, looking out past the antlered frangipani tree and the purple bougainvillea to the aquamarine Caribbean, down at the crashing surf, up to the jungled mountains, and over to the quaint, up-sloping capital city of St. George's, "the most picturesque and photographed harbor in the Caribbean."

In search of spice islands, Columbus sighted Grenada but made no landing. Too bad. Grenada is now known as "the Spice Island of the West."

On this, the eve of Einstein's centenary, a friend of his cited on TV an example that this genius once gave of relativity: "If my theory proves true the Germans will call me a German, and the French a Jew; if it proves false, the Germans will call me a Jew and the French a German."

March 14

Down from the north, up from the south, in from the west. It was a conspiracy of friends on this, the one hundredth birthday of Einstein. Before 9 A.M., I picked up Theresa Lester and her two small children and drove them to the Baltimore-Washington International Airport to meet Tom Lester, who was flying in from Oregon. Theresa is visiting her expectant Baltimore sister.

Tom was on time, his slim, bearded face beaming quietly on the wife and two children from whom he has been separated for two weeks. Tom met Theresa when he was a seminarian and she was his dentist's secretary. I like to say she extracted him from the seminary.

After I dropped off all the Lesters I went to St. Mary's Seminary, Roland Park, where I first met Tom. A meeting was held there today for vocation directors from various dioceses; one of them, Father Griswold, was a former student of mine. We went to lunch at nearby Thompson's, which has the world's best clam chowder. Ed was ordained in 1973 and had been a classmate of my suspended priest-friend at Georgetown.

A few years ago Ed had me give a poetry reading to his parishioners near New Brunswick, New Jersey. When I finished creating an hour of deathless beauty, I asked, "Are there any questions?" A man raised his hand. "Yes?" "Did you get those shoes in Baltimore?" "Why, yes," I replied. "Well," he said, "I designed them." In a flash we had traveled from poetic feet to mine. You never know who is out there listening.

I returned Ed to the seminary, then headed for a two-day visit to Washington. I stayed at a home which my nephew Frank is baby-sitting. Seven of his nervous classmates had slept there on Sunday night, the evening a Georgetown student had been assaulted, and the day after another had been murdered. After supper tonight with two priest-friends who had journeyed up from Virginia for the day, I was ready to turn in for my first night of sleeping on Capitol Hill.

Reviewing the day, I reflected that in Baltimore I had seen my first flowers of the year—purple and golden crocuses. Back to mind came that day over thirty-five years ago when I served a funeral Mass during Lent. Since in those days flowers weren't kept on the altar during Lent, the nun in charge of the sacristy gave me a clutch of carnations—my first bouquet ever. I was exalted. But on my way home I stopped by to see an ailing classmate, Charlie Zimmerman. When his mother opened the door and saw the flowers, she praised my thoughtfulness, took the flowers from my hand, and went off scurrying for a vase. She never knew.

There is an old Baltimore tradition that spring has truly arrived when the first crocus blooms on the grounds of the old Catholic Ca-

thedral. These crocuses have a habit of blooming before any nearby
Protestant crocuses. I once heard of a rumor that we Catholics
achieve our annual victory thanks to hot-water pipes secretly in-
stalled underground.

☙

"My roses," said the king—and his gardener smiled.

March 15

I had a restless night in a strange bed with my nephew, and with
an even more restless giant sheepdog roaming around the rooms.

Shortly after ten, I drove my nephew to Georgetown University,
and then went to Harbin Hall to see my suspended priest-friend,
Bob. He looked a bit haggard, and spoke of the vicious phone calls
he had received on a radio talk show last night. He pointed to a
stack of mail he had received, much of it abusive. He showed me a
blunt letter to his bishop he had been composing.

Last Saturday he was driving away for a day in the mountains
when he realized he had left his sunglasses in his office. He returned
to get them and the phone rang. It was the police telling him one of
his students had been murdered. Friends of the student said she had
liked Bob; they wanted him to offer the school memorial Mass and
the funeral Mass. Because of his suspension, he had to turn them
down.

The next evening, while a memorial Mass was being offered for
the slain Maureen McCarthy, a strange man with a knife accosted a
girl who lived on the same floor as the dead girl. He was probably a
thief who had read in the papers that the ninth-floor students had
all gone home after the murder. He was hiding in the showers.

He let the girl go unharmed, but panic seized the campus when
the rumor went out that the killer was stalking the university. Police
flooded the campus and once again Bob was up all night. He told
me he scarcely slept from Saturday morning until Monday night.

I left Bob and drove to Columbia, where I saw Bob Duggan from
3:30 to 4:30. I felt headachey and keyed up and told him so. He inserted pins in the outside bottom of my thumbs and the inside
crook of my elbows. He left them in for about half an hour, to
sedate me. After about twenty minutes, I did feel the headache and

tension drain away. This was the first time I felt any significant change during a session.

I asked him what precisely the needles did. He said the best imagery is to think of the quick in-and-out needles as acting like magnets to pull sluggish energy currents along. A needle that remains inserted pulls energy to itself and slows down an energy stream.

🌳

One is distressed by the failure of reasonable men to perceive the depth of evil in the world or the depths of the holy.

Dietrich Bonhoeffer

March 16

Today I paid my eighteenth visit to Katherine Anne Porter. She was using her oxygen tube again and I found her quite hard to understand about a third of the time. She talked about a favorite theme: how she almost died three times before. She said so many of her friends had died; the remaining ones were "about my age" she said, then corrected herself by saying "—that's impossible."

I reminded her that she said she would try to live until spring, which was now only a week away. "I think I can hang on that long." She smiled. I gave her Holy Communion again. She wept at this, saying that she doesn't usually weep, "but this touches me so."

I made my final trip to Capitol Hill for a while and took the big dog, Chester, for his evening walk. That may have been the first time in my half century that I ever walked a dog. I let him do most of the leading and I wondered whether he would get me in trouble as he made his multiple nature stops.

Frank and I headed for Baltimore about 6:30. At home a sad letter awaited me from my brother Tommy. The envelope was dated March 12—our father's anniversary and the same day I sent him my letter. He is now in the Patton State Hospital in California: "I love you and wish we could get closer. I sense for me death at any time." His handwriting and spelling indicated severe agitation. . . .

Twenty-two years ago today, at a St. Patrick's Day luncheon given by the Baltimore Friendly Sons of St. Patrick, I heard the young Senator John Kennedy give an address. He had been sick and just about made the dinner. As I shook his hands I could see how swollen his jaws were. I saw him once or twice during his presidential campaign, and I have a picture I took of him from outside the White House fence when he was entertaining Britain's Prime Minister Macmillan. Finally, I have a letter he sent me in grateful response to an editorial I wrote when he announced his candidacy for President. I was counterattacking some argument which claimed that a Catholic could not be a dutiful President. "You can be sure," he wrote, "that your editorial had a heavy readership in my office."

❧

I know you are all eager to hear the dope from Washington, but there seems to be a screw loose in the speaker.

March 17

Pages facing each other in the morning *Sun* carried two stories about the 800 block of North Avenue, which is a block away from me. A man from that block is serving a life term for the death of a hostage he took while trying to commit a robbery. The Maryland Court of Special Appeals ruled that he and his companion were responsible for the hostage's death, even though a police bullet killed him.

The other story told of a woman from the same block who died yesterday of a heart attack after being robbed and stabbed outside her apartment.

Beneath one of the stories was a smiling ad for the new Walt Disney movie, *North Avenue Irregulars*. "What these ladies do to organized crime is outrageous," says the ad.

Nephew Frank has to be at the nearby train station early tomorrow, so he is staying overnight with me. We hit the hay about 2:45 A.M.—that's about the latest I've stayed up for a long time.

I was too sleepy to reminisce about my 1967 visit to St. Patrick's reputed grave in Downpatrick, Ireland. Surprisingly, there isn't any memorial inscription on the huge stone above it. I read somewhere the reason for the omission: the Catholics and the Protestants could never agree on the wording.

⚜

Far away from where I am now, there is a gap in the hills, and beyond it, the sea: and 'tis there I do be looking the whole day long, for it's the nearest thing to yourself that I can see.

From the letter of an Irish shepherd boy to his sweetheart

March 18

The most beautiful thing that we can experience is the mysterious . . . He to whom this emotion is a stranger, who can no longer pause to wonder and stand rapt in awe, is as good as dead.

Albert Einstein

March 19

Today is the feast of St. Joseph, my chief patron saint. In grammar school we learned a prayer, "Sweet Heart of Mary, be my salvation." This prayer we playfully turned into a romantic one to her spouse: "Sweetheart of Mary . . ."

As I grew older I was also happy to learn good things about the patriarch Joseph—him the dreamer, him of the many-colored cloak. Last summer I visited his grave at Hebron, as well as the traditional site of the other Joseph's carpenter shop in Nazareth. In the latter city, on a Thursday, an Arab boy named Joseph Thursday helped me find a medal of St. Joseph the Carpenter, and wouldn't take a tip.

I was glad that Pope John XXIII's given name was Joseph and that he once greeted a group of visiting Jews with the words of the patriarch: "I am Joseph your brother."

On the subject of dreamers: I awoke this morning remembering a richly symbolic dream. I was in a room where two tables were afloat on water: the smaller one was mine; the larger one, not far away, was a kind of altar, like the table of the Last Supper. A number of people were at that table, including my present archbishop. I had to get my food from that table and swim back with it to my own table. The question was, could I get the food there without losing it in the intervening water. As I recall, I sensed that I had a problem, but I didn't feel overwhelmed by it.

I heard a timely Irish joke today about a man visiting Ireland. Suddenly he felt a gun in his back. "Catholic or Protestant?" demanded a menacing voice. "If I say Catholic he'll surely be Protestant . . . and vice versa," thought the tourist. So he summoned all his shrewdness and answered, "I'm Jewish." The voice exulted, "I must be the luckiest Arab in all of Ireland!"

Gazing down from outer space, Dante describes the earth as "the little threshing-floor that makes us so fierce."

Paradiso 22:151

March 20

Today is the last day of winter. Eleven years ago I published a rather plainspoken expression of the winter of discontent which was then afflicting American Catholicism and was clearly not about to give way to a second spring of any sort.

In early 1968, as turbulence grew in the U.S. over the Vietnam War and racial problems, and as it increased in post-Vatican-II U.S. Catholicism, the U.S. bishops issued a collective pastoral which many people found quite disappointing, as usual. (It referred to resigned priests, for example, as "derelicts.") As Jesuit sociologist Joseph Fichter wrote of the bishops, "Do they really know what is going on in the Church in the U.S.? Nowhere is there any indication that they did their homework."

The pastoral did, however, invite dialogue. Since I had been listening closely to seminarians for almost a year, I decided to write an open letter in their name to the U.S. bishops. I tried to summarize the negative view which many of the most gifted seminarians and many other U.S. Catholics held of the hierarchy in general.

The article appeared in the March 20 issue of the *National Catholic Reporter*. I was amazed by the passionate backing I received. Letters poured in from about twenty-three states, as well as from Canada, South America, Central Africa (in French), and New Guinea in distant Asia. Two publishers invited me to write a book on the subject.

I heard from about forty-three priests: religious superiors, rectors, and deans of seminaries, university faculty members, pastors, young priests, old priests, Jesuits, Carmelites, Franciscans, Vincentians, Sulpicians, Holy Cross Fathers, Assumptionists.

I heard from nuns: Notre Dame, Mercy, Immaculate Heart of Mary, Filippini, and others. I heard from former priests, former nuns, parents of former priests, from seminarians and former seminarians. I heard from laymen: respected writers and editors and artists; also from simple parishioners, including one who was a "registered nurse, mother of five."

The well-known priest-author John A. O'Brien of Notre Dame University mailed a copy of the article to every bishop in the U.S. who did not subscribe to the NCR. Another volunteered to pay for the sending of a copy to every bishop in America. I was told later that the "Open Letter" came up at the April Bishops' Meeting in St. Louis.

A number of correspondents wondered whether reprisals would be taken against me. (None were.) Another asked for my forwarding address; a third humorously asked to be told when the excommunication hearings would be held. A fourth simply asked, "Guess who will never ever be appointed a bishop of anywhere?" Touchingly, many strangers expressed love and affection.

I received only three negative letters. A bishop from Kansas whom I had met and liked in Rome sent a mostly good-natured letter, though he spoke of "your angry bit of prose," which he ascribed to my perhaps having had "a drink or something angry" under my belt.

A Chicago mother spoke of the liberal theologians who were subverting the church and making parents of large Catholic families feel betrayed. "Holy Mother Church was worth dying for a short while ago—but what you and people like you have done to it makes it not even worth living in."

An Oregon priest wrote of his wish to get away from a "Disneyland Christianity of toy prophets like yourself. . . . You may be a 'Monday morning hero' in your philosophy classes for having 'told off' the Bishops . . . but don't kid yourself. Any young men you turn against the Bishops will turn against the Church and even against Monsignor Gallagher another day."

It was interesting to me that quite a few correspondents noted that my article was written "without bitterness or rancor"; one even noted its respectful tone. Yet in awarding it a prize for the "Best Single Column of the Year," the Catholic Press Association judges stated, "This clearly angry dissertation might fairly be regarded as too general in its denunciation. But . . . the writer is pleading from the depths of his soul." And so I was, perhaps too needfully asking father figures to be knowing and caring, and to show that they are so.

The year 1968 was, of course, critical in numerous ways—the death of King and Kennedy, the riots, the presidential conventions, the war, the encyclical *Humanae Vitae*. I think we have many more pastoral bishops now in America, though I don't think we have much national leadership. And many of the most expectant, most caring Catholics of the late sixties simply stopped caring about the bishops or the church. (There are recent signs, however, that a notable number of the sixties dropouts are on their way back to the church, finding reconciliation, perhaps, in the recognition that the bishops and the church are not the same thing.)

But it is a measure of what ten years have done to us all that today I wouldn't bother to write such an open letter, and very few readers (I suspect) would bother reacting to it with letters of their own.

(For the text of the "An Open Letter to the U.S. Catholic Bishops," see Appendix A.)

❧

What the world expects of Christians is that they speak out . . . that they get out of their abstractions and stand face to face with the bloody mess that is our history today.

Albert Camus

March 21

Spring arrived at 12:22 A.M. today and found that a perfect day was on hand to greet it. The temperature reached almost seventy. If you said something about the plants now *springing* out of the earth, many people would think you were punning. The same goes for the leaves *falling* in the fall of the year. But apparently it is exactly from these two natural motions that these seasons take their names.

Thirteen years ago today I received in the mail my first paperback copies of *The Document of Vatican II*. It was published jointly and ecumenically by the Jesuit America Press, the YMCA Association Press and the Guild Press of the Western Publishing Co. In 1966 it sold for ninety-five cents; now it costs $4.50 in its thirteenth edition. (In 1966 Association Press and Herder and Herder also issued a hardback version for ten dollars.)

I was translation editor for the eight-hundred-page volume, which has in the meantime sold probably more than two million copies. It has also provided me with about $30,000 in royalties—America Press splits with me what it gets—and the federal and state governments with quite a bit of taxes. (Things have changed since I reported a total income of $720 in my first 1040 form as a priest.)

I was working with the *Catholic Review* when the first documents were released in late 1963. Like many another I was appalled at the English translations, which in 1964 included such items as: "Having sinned in Adam, God the Father decreed the redemption of the human race"; "Conceived by the Holy Spirit, Mary brought forth Christ"; "Opinions of the laity should be expressed by organs erected by the church." I was told that these translations were made in a hurry for the U.S. bishops by seminarians studying in Rome.

In April 1965, I was visiting *America* magazine in New York and talked about the bad translations. Father Thurston Davis, S.J., who was editor in chief at that time, told me that *America* had been approached about getting out a book of commentaries on the documents, but that he too worried about the translations. Would I be willing to make or get adequate translations? I knew that I could not do worse, so I agreed, and thus began the story I tell in greater detail on December 9.

For my part, I either translated or retranslated most of the sixteen documents. In a few cases, e.g., the document on religious liberty and the document on the Scriptures, special translators did a fine job, so I needed to make only a few changes for the sake of consistency in the whole volume.

I worked closely with Father Walter Abbott, S.J., who wrote one commentary himself and supervised the work of one Catholic and one non-Catholic commentator for each document. Appearing side by side and alphabetically on the book's spine, his last name and mine make it look as though I have entered a monastery and seized power.

✣

I said to the almond tree, "Sister, speak to me of God." And it
blossomed.

Nikos Kazantzakis

March 22

The tragedy of life lies not in how much we suffer, but in how
much we miss.

Thomas Carlyle

March 23

The mail brought an announcement from one of my old seminary
students that his wife had delivered their first child. (The stamp
honored the International Year of the Child.) Wrote Frank Gor-
bett, "When we bend over the cradle of our own child, God throws
back the temple door, and reveals to us the sacredness and the mystery of a parent's love."

Similar thoughts were part of a long lunch I had this afternoon
with my friends the Lesters at Jimmy Wu's restaurant. Tom is a former student who after his devout mother's death searched his soul
and decided he didn't have enough faith to be a priest. This decision was one he regretted, and he pursued theological studies even
after he married the devout Theresa. They recently attended a marriage encounter and were asked to become a team couple. Tom wondered whether his agnosticism would be a barrier, and he received
conflicting replies.

Finally, Theresa asked him to distinguish between his thoughts
and his feelings—a practice stressed by the encounter program.
Recalling the transcendent feeling of a sacred presence which
often strikes him as he looks with love at his wife and children, Tom
"felt" that there had to be a God. Shortly afterward, in church by
himself, he received Holy Communion and felt a great sense of
peace. He said to God, "Well, what is there to say?" and decided
that nothing had to be said. . . .

Fourteen years ago today a document was signed in Rome naming me a monsignor with the (lesser) rank of domestic prelate (very reverend). This honor, requested by Cardinal Shehan, was an overflow of his having been named a cardinal that year.

Twelve years ago today I paid my first visit to a Baltimore psychiatrist, Dr. James Whedbee. A former woman penitent recommended this extraordinary man to me. My need to see him was an overflow of a clash I had with Cardinal Shehan and which led to my resignation from the *Catholic Review* and my leaving the archdiocese.

✤

After Henri Matisse had finished laboriously painting a chapel, he stood back, looked at his work, and said, "Now I know I believe in God."

March 24

I hadn't realized before now how much this was a publication anniversary week in my life. Nine years ago today I received the first hardback copies of my book of essays, *The Christian Under Pressure*, which sold about 20,000 copies before it went out of print.

The previous year Father John Reedy of the *Ave Maria* Press had phoned me to ask whether I could do a series of articles on the generation gap for *Ave Maria* magazine. I told him that I didn't feel competent, but that I had available a series of talks on "survival" techniques. These I had prepared for a retreat I had recently given at a seminary in San Antonio, Texas.

This particular seminary had been going through serious upheavals in the aftermath of Vatican II. Faculty and students were fired. One deacon had attempted suicide. My job seemed like giving a retreat at Pearl Harbor during the Japanese attack. The issues were tension and survival. Since I had just turned forty, I decided to look back over my life and try to pick out some fundamental insights or rules of thumb which had helped me to deal creatively with pressure.

I sent the talks to John Reedy, who liked them and asked only that introductory and concluding chapters be added, making ten altogether. One of his staff made the comment that some of my "quotes" were a bit dated. So, for revenge, I included in my introductory chapter two quotes from books which hadn't even been published yet. I had read advance reviews and had already picked out two striking remarks.

The articles appeared in the fall issues of the 1969 *Ave Maria*. They were then chosen to be a book club selection for the Spiritual Book Associates, directed by the same Father Reedy. This meant an automatic sale of 5,500 hardbacks, which was an excellent start. Father Reedy chose the somewhat sectarian title (*The Christian Under Pressure*) so it would sell better in church magazine and book racks. I tell my non-Christian friends that there is a special edition for them: *The Christian Under Pressure: How to Keep Him There.*

Shortly after my articles appeared in *Ave Maria*, the magazine underwent its *hora mortis* and was replaced by another, entitled A.D. 70. (It was going to alter its name yearly.) But soon after an ad for my book appeared in it, it too "died out." You can get a reputation for such coincidences.

❧

"Let's talk about *you* awhile. Have you read my last book?"
"I certainly hope so."

March 25

After the most careful examination, neither as an adversary nor as a friend, of the influences of Catholicism for good and evil, I am persuaded that its devotion to the Madonna has been one of its noblest and most vital graces, and has never been otherwise than productive of true holiness of life and purity of character.

John Ruskin

March 26

A few days ago the forsythia bushes on nearby Druid Hill Park broke out into their lemony blossoms. And now this morning, snow flurries hit the Baltimore area!

I was still eating breakfast when Katherine Anne Porter phoned. She is convinced she is going to die today. She seemed indignant that her nurse was trying to force breakfast on her on such a special day. "I know you can't say anything new," she allowed, "but I want to hear the old things again." I told her I would try to see her later today, but after checking with her nurse this evening I decided I would wait until after my Dante class tomorrow.

By noon I arrived at the Golden Dragon Restaurant on Liberty Road where I was to talk to a sorority of Jewish women about my trip to Israel last May. I began to talk exactly at two o'clock, just when the Egyptian-Israeli Peace Treaty ceremony was due to begin on the White House lawn.

The evening news interviewed a widow in Cairo who lost two sons in the 1967 war and a Jewish couple who lost two sons in the same war. It was poignant indeed to hear the Jewish father say that his wife had been more afraid that their sons might have had to kill someone than that they might be killed.

Sometimes these interviews uncover human beings of extraordinary goodness. The other night a Vietnam veteran was asked about a U.S. prisoner who had gone over to the enemy and who was now returning to the U.S. after fourteen years. Did he want to see this man punished, who had once punched him in the stomach? "No," he said, "I don't think the fellow soldiers who died in my arms would have wanted this confused young man to be severely punished."

An older congressman, though, was worried that if we didn't punish those who broke military laws in the last war, soldiers might not be obedient in the next war. That's not what worries *me* about the next war!

Thirteen years ago tonight I returned to my chaplain's quarters at the Mission Helpers of the Sacred Heart. Unsuspectingly, the sisters had let into my apartment a man whom I had been instrumental in having committed to a mental hospital. He had a glazed look, refused to leave, and said he would sleep on the sofa. I had no lock on my bedroom door and was not about to try to sleep while he was in the next room.

Around midnight I managed to phone the police, and soon two ambulances and five or six squad cars with blinking blue lights converged on the convent. Knowing of my visitor's propensity for slugging policemen, I warned the officers, who replied that they could handle such matters. Just as my visitor was being escorted through the front door, he delivered a hefty punch to one of the policemen. For peace and quiet, get thee to a nunnery.

✣

If your heart does not want a world of moral reality, your head will assuredly never make you believe in one.

William James

March 27

The roots of the eyes are in the heart.

March 28

An event: having lunch for the first time in fifty years with a cousin who was married before I was born. That's what happened at the Hopkins Faculty Club today. Henry J. Knott, an eminently successful Baltimore builder and financier, is my second cousin: my maternal grandmother and his were Irish-born sisters. I like to say that his side of the family belongs to the Knotts and ours to the Have-Knotts. A generous benefactor, Henry likes to tell of the millionaire who died. "How much did he leave?" "Everything."

Among other points of interest, Henry told me of the time he came to the rescue of a friend of my brother by investing a million dollars in a particular stock. That sent its price up and thereby discouraged outsiders from buying sufficient stock to take control away from the friend.

On another occasion a desperate man came to Henry insanely wanting him to influence a grand jury. Said my cousin, "The last time you said your prayers you were talking to the only person who is going to fix that jury."

Later in the afternoon, I picked up my friends the Lesters and their two children to pay a visit to Dr. Schaffer. When their first child Joe was born, there was some worry about brain damage. I arranged for Dr. Schaffer to see him, and he reassured the parents immeasurably. Joe has grown perfectly and this was an occasion for showing "Buck" how right his diagnosis was. We bought a bouquet of spring flowers for little Joe to give the doctor.

We returned to the home of Theresa Lester's sister, who was back from the hospital with her new baby. I held infant Christine Julia for a while; she seemed to be gazing studiously at my beard. Looking at her delicate features, I recalled Whitaker Chamber's remark that he became a believer while pondering the delicacy of his infant's ear. And Christine's hand—one of them could just about encircle a finger of mine and cover half its length.

I had to wonder about this child's future: the big news tonight was about a radiation leak today from a nuclear power plant near Harrisburg; the radioactivity penetrated a wall four feet thick and was found as far as a mile away.

I neglected to mention yesterday that it was the eleventh anniversary of the death of Atlanta's Archbishop Paul Hallinan. When I was archdiocesan archivist, he came here as a monsignor to do some research for a doctorate in history. All of us at the old cathedral were smitten by his genial personality and that sunburst of a smile which distinguished him. Not long afterward he was named bishop of Charleston. He invited me to spend a week there training two of his seminarians to organize Charleston's archives in the Baltimore fashion. I stayed in the home where the bishop lived with his personable young chancellor, Father Joseph Bernardin. During that sweltering week in June 1958, I noticed that the bishop had no air-conditioner in his room, just a fan.

The *National Catholic Directory* used to list the archdioceses by seniority, so that Baltimore came first. When the archdiocese of Atlanta was created in 1962, and Hallinan named its first archbishop, the *Directory* decided to list by alphabetical order, so that the youngest archdiocese took pride of place from the oldest.

I wrote an editorial in our diocesan paper suggesting that Baltimore always be kept first for historical reasons. Archbishop Hallinan sent us and the *Directory* a magnanimous letter offering to yield Atlanta's place to Baltimore. A typical gesture, even though the *Directory* now, without distinction, lists dioceses and archdioceses in simple alphabetical arrangement.

During the Second Vatican Council the archbishop contracted a severe case of hepatitis, and while still in his fifties died in 1968. In many ways he was the brightest promise of the U.S. hierarchy. His loss was a prime example of what a priest-friend of mine calls the maldistribution of early demises.

A man does not fight merely to win.
Cyrano de Bergerac

March 29

Tonight I concluded a weekly lecture series in Columbia, Maryland. I talked about "the repression of the sublime"—a phrase coined by some psychotherapists to describe what makes some patients sick: they ignore their deeply rooted impulse to devote themselves generously to the pursuit of the true, the beautiful, or the good. These therapists believe that such an impulse is fundamental to human nature and causes trouble when it is unsatisfied.

After class one of my women students spoke about her fourteen-year-old retarded child and his boundless, infectious sense of wonder. "He is the worst and the best thing that has ever happened to us."

The heroism we recite
Would be a daily thing
Did not ourselves the cubits warp
For fear to be a king.
Emily Dickinson

March 30

Today the thermometer hit eighty-seven around Baltimore—a record for this month, for this day, and the highest reading today anywhere in the U.S. Things are blooming all over the place—though not yet the horse chestnut tree in my backyard.

My sister-in-law Mary went to D.C. overnight, so I took John and the twins to the Rustler's for supper. Later we watched the TV news, which was full of the nuclear reactor accident near Harrisburg. The Pennsylvania governor has urged that pregnant women and pre-school children leave a five-mile area around the Three Mile Island site.

For the first time the dreaded word "meltdown" was officially mentioned as a possibility. The newsmen pointed out how confusing and at times contradictory was the information being given out by various authorities. Is doomsday nearer than anyone thought? Later tonight each network had a special program about the incident and its potential consequences.

I love this poor earth, because I have not seen another.
Osip Mandelstam

March 31

As baby-sitter for the Gallaghers I got less sleep than my Saturday usual because I had to deliver Jimmy to lacrosse practice by 9:15. Before leaving the house I noted that the mail brought the latest issue of *National Geographic*. With spine-tingling timeliness it contains an article about nuclear energy and the problem of safety. I read the article and, with continued bad news in my ear from Three Mile Island, I found myself growing terrified at what man hath wrought.

I headed down to Dundalk to pick up from my sister forty-six pages of transcript she had typed from Monsignor Tom Whelan's taped memoirs. I then had lunch with Tom and eight other priests at their retirement home in Towson. I sat next to Monsignor Dan McGrath, who "sent" me to the seminary from St. Ann's thirty-six years ago.

Dan told a mirthful story about the physical exam he took when he entered the chaplains corps in 1943. "Bend over and spread your cheeks," the doctor said. Dan thought his teeth were going to be examined, so he grabbed his face and leaned toward the doctor.

"No," said the embarrassed doctor, "I mean with your hands behind your back." Marveling at the strange way of army doctors, Dan leaned toward him again, crisscrossed his hands behind his head, and pulled at his cheeks as best he could.

✤

Quiet minds cannot be perplexed or frightened, but go on in fortune or misfortune at their own private pace, like a clock during a thunderstorm.

Robert Louis Stevenson

April 1, 1979

Scholars seem uncertain about the origin of April Fool's Day. I recall that for many centuries in England, March 25 was New Year's Day. April 1 would then have been the octave day of New Year's and as such would have climaxed a week of festivities and high spirits. Some historians explain April Fool's in the light of these facts.

In any case, I heard of a seminarian who took an out-of-town classmate home for this day. He told the student that his father was hard of hearing, so he would have to shout. In the meantime he had phoned the father to tell him that the student was hard of hearing. The result was a shouting match, hilarious to those who knew the secret.

A few years ago there were only two doctors of canon law in the archdiocese. (Their J.C.D. was said to mean "Just Can't Decide.") Both of our doctors, Joe Gosman and Porter White, were born on All Fool's Day, and much was made of that. Jesuit Gustave Weigel used to say that canon lawyers are the warts on the Mystical Body. Another saying declares that "canon law is the bad news about the good news." Understandable both: the need for law and resentment of it.

Church laws and practices must sometimes be carried out in strange settings. In one instance I heard of, a priest was called to an operating room to anoint a patient who was undergoing emergency surgery. Leaning close to the man's ear to speak words of comfort, the priest breathed in too much ether, and fell unconscious to the floor. Since all the doctors and nurses were busy, they proceeded with the operation and let the priest lie where he fell.

On another occasion, a priest-classmate of mine was being initiated into the Knights of Columbus. He was on his guard for tricks, so when he was suddenly asked to attend to another member who seemed to be suffering a heart attack, Jim went along with the gag and consoled the man with great calm and confidence. It turned out that this was no trick. The man survived and gave great credit to the tranquilizing impact of Jim's manner.

A final April Fool's item: another priest-classmate answered the rectory door one cold, snowy night and found that a young couple had arrived to undergo the customary "prenuptial investigation," which is mostly paper work based on separate interviews. Luke said he would show the girl to the parlor, and that meanwhile the bundled-up boy should go to his office "and take your things off." Luke chatted with the girl for a moment to calm her nervousness, and when he arrived at his office—well, you guessed it.

❧

You can fool most of the people most of the time, and that's all that's necessary.

April 2

I was luckily on hand for the sole performance of today.
Steve Herrick

April 3

Eleven years ago today I paid a visit to Cardinal Shehan's office. Reacting to my "An Open Letter to the U.S. Bishops" in the *National Catholic Reporter,* he said he felt it was unfair and that it would hurt St. Mary's Seminary, where I was then teaching. He also said that he was due to attend the upcoming graduation at the seminary, but would probably cancel. He considered that my article was mostly a criticism of him and that the students would demonstrate against him.

I tried to assure him that, like myself, the students felt an unusual degree of respect for him. The cardinal had learned that I was composing a second article, about the silence of the U.S. hierarchy on the Vietnam War. My point was that as a group they had not followed up Pope Paul's plea for peace during his 1965 visit to the UN. I suddenly realized that the cardinal had arranged this meeting

partly to dissuade me from publishing the second article. I told
him that I had already submitted it to the *National Catholic Reporter*.

As I was leaving his office I made some reference to the fact that
my seminary training had not prepared me to wrestle nicely with ecclesiastical elephants. "Well," replied this five-foot-four gentleman,
"I'm not a very big elephant."

❦

Life is a stage, and most of us are desperately underrehearsed.

April 4

May God deny you peace but grant you glory.
                Miguel de Unamuno

April 5

Look your last on all things lovely every hour.
                Walter de la Mare

April 6

Thirteen years ago today I gave a tour of Baltimore's old cathedral
to the Jesuit general from Rome, Father Pedro Arrupe. This only
Basque successor to the Basque Ignatius of Loyola was in Hiroshima
when the atom bomb fell, and made urgent use of his medical training.

Once a fellow diocesan priest and I were accused of being Jesuits
by an unknown woman in a restaurant because we had "that well-
scrubbed look." When people ask me if I am a Jesuit, I like to joke
by saying, "No, but my father was one."

On another occasion I was talking with a polite young man who
mentioned that he lived in a certain parish staffed by ordinary diocesan priests. I asked him whether he knew this or that priest who was
stationed there. In each case he answered, "No," somewhat apolo-
getically. Finally he tried to explain by saying, "Actually I have

stayed close to the Jesuit priests who taught me in high school and college, so I don't know many *lay* priests."

My friend the historian Monsignor John Tracy Ellis was once asked by a group of Jesuits to make candid criticisms of U.S. Jesuits in a talk he was to give them. In his usual courteous manner he suggested that the Jesuit habit of referring so often to other scholarly Jesuits can generate a negative impression on outsiders. As a sample he noted how often Jesuits and Jesuit publications refer only to Jesuit Walter Abbott when they cite the U.S. translation of *The Documents of Vatican II*, omitting mention of Walter's fellow editor on the project, and the actual translator, yours truly.

All religious orders are equal in My sight.
(*Signed*) God, S.J.

April 7

Eleven years ago today I had one of the scariest experiences of my life. It was Palm Sunday. On the previous Thursday, Martin Luther King had been assassinated. The next night at midnight a Molotov cocktail was thrown into the lumberyard adjacent to old St. Mary's Seminary, where I was then a teacher. That perilous fire was quickly extinguished.

But on the next evening riots began to break out in Baltimore and an 11 P.M. curfew was imposed. About 9:30 P.M., I walked alone to a nearby fire which was visible from the seminary. I decided to leave as a crowd of angry blacks started stoning the firemen. I hailed a cab and, because of complicated one-way streets, I wanted to get out a few blocks from the seminary. "I'm taking you to the door," said the black driver, worried about my safety.

The next morning I said two Masses at St. Gregory's, a black parish. As usual I stood in the back of the church to greet the parishioners as they left. One black woman said, "Don't you feel bad; you are not to blame." Returning to the seminary, I gave a lift to a white policeman who has just gone off duty. "They had no right to shoot that man," he said, without naming the victim.

A curfew had been announced for that night, but it kept being advanced until it reached 4 P.M. Meantime, I could see great clouds of smoke billowing up in the vicinity of Johns Hopkins hospital. I drove over to the site, and found National Guardsmen protecting the firemen. An old black woman sat on her steps, weeping. "This didn't have to happen," she kept repeating.

The curfew hour was approaching, so I began to head for the seminary. I stopped for a red light not far from the fire. A group of young blacks who were standing on the corner suddenly sent rocks crashing through the windshield of a white driver's car. He gunned his accelerator and sped off to the sound of falling glass.

Then the group began to move toward me, heavy rocks in their hands. Sheer terror rippled through me. I couldn't believe what was going on. One of the youths saw my clerical collar. "He's a priest— let him go." And go I went!

Back at the seminary a faculty meeting was held. Since we had been officially maintaining that we were part of the neighborhood, and since most of our neighbors had nowhere to flee, we and some student representatives decided that we would stay put, though we were in an old, largely wooden building full of whites in the heart of a black and burning district.

A few students, pleading unshakable terror, were permitted to go home. Some bricks were later lobbed into the prayer hall and into the biology lab, but no one was injured. Day and night, students took turns keeping an eye on every part of the hulking building.

When federal troops were dispatched to Baltimore they advanced up the rainy street in front of the seminary and headed for the nearby armory. Fires had broken out all over our neighborhood; people young and old could be seen carrying loot down the streets and alleys.

Good Friday of that week there was an eclipse of the moon. Along with some students, I sat watching the eclipse on the wall of the small seminary cemetery. All of a sudden we found ourselves the object of army guns and spotlights and the demand to know what we were doing "up there."

For many Baltimoreans and Americans, black and white, that was one April which proved itself to be the cruelest month.

❧

Violence is the italics of the desperate.

J.G.

April 8

Today was the start of Holy Week, and I replaced the old palm behind my parlor crucifix. Overcoming inertia and the knowledge that the *Evening Sun* has several articles of mine which it hasn't yet published, I composed and delivered a piece for Good Friday. It dealt with the struggle between life and death, and focused on two towns which have become famous since last Easter: Jonestown and its mass suicide-massacre, and Middletown across from the atomic reactor on Three Mile Island.

I cited two astounding life/death statistics: that every two seconds some human being dies of starvation, and that the total world cost for armaments last year alone exceeded what it would have cost Jesus had He spent $500,000 per day on charity since his birth and up to the present day. That means that if guns had been turned into groceries, each of the 45,000 people who starved to death every day last year could have been given in excess of $10 worth of food.

The supreme greatness of Christianity derives from the fact that it does not seek a supernatural remedy against suffering, but a supernatural use for suffering.

Simone Weil

April 9

Eight years ago this time I was on the high seas, serving as chaplain for an eight-day cruise to the Caribbean. I had done this once before; due to some mix-up there were this time two Catholic chaplains aboard, so we had to share our rather small quarters.

One night the purser asked if he could talk with me. Seated comfortably in his suite, I heard him remark that almost everybody on a trip of this sort is there for a special, dramatic reason: trying to forget something, to run away from someone, to make a major decision. He proceeded to tell me about a crisis in his own life.

In discussing the crisis, I used the phrase "sexual intercourse." "I hate that phrase!" he said. I wondered what substitute I could use. Finally I suggested "sexual communion." He leaped with delight and said that was the phrase he had been searching for all his life. I was a bit startled at his enthusiasm.

That 1971 trip was a bit of a bust for the would-be shoppers in our group. We stopped at San Juan on Good Friday, and all the stores were closed. We stopped at Nassau on Easter Monday, and once again all the stores were closed. The Caribbeans have the humane custom of observing a "recovery day" after each major holiday.

On that same Easter Monday I arrived at the ship's small chapel, and found no one waiting for Mass. So I indulged my nostalgia by offering Mass in the old Latin way, with all the gestures I had learned so meticulously in the seminary. When I tried to get breakfast afterward, I discovered that the ship had crossed a time zone, so I was an hour early. I raced back to the chapel and found people waiting for me to celebrate an "English" Mass. . . .

An invitation arrived today to the upcoming ordination of one of the students I taught in my seminary preaching class. Once I gave them an assignment to talk about what they would do if they were pope for a day. One whimsical student joked that he would canonize himself and then commit suicide.

The one about to be ordained began his talk fully vested as a bishop. His theme was that he would rid the church of its earthly wealth. As he talked he gradually stripped himself, à la St. Francis of Assisi, and ended up in his tennis shorts and a T-shirt. We were all wondering how far he would go. But there was no doubt that he had stripped us of any inattention.

If I had God's power, I'd change a lot of things; if I had His wisdom, maybe I wouldn't.

April 10

Pain and suffering, they are a secret. Kindness and love, they are a secret. But I have found that kindness and love can pay for pain and suffering.

Alan Paton in Cry, the Beloved Country

April 11

A religion which would be small enough for our understanding
would not be large enough for our needs.

Arthur Balfour

April 12

My mother, I think, had little interest in or knowledge of politics.
My father was somewhat more politically minded, I would guess.
But, in any case, he was a Democrat and was for FDR, as I presume
my mother was. By 1945 Franklin Roosevelt had been President
for as long as I could remember and it was a solemn thrill to hear
his resonant, cultivated voice over the radio when he gave one of his
fireside chats.

I knew he shattered tradition when he ran for and won a third
term. Then came World War II and the necessity of "not swapping
horses in the middle of a stream." So there had to be even a fourth
term for this peerless leader. I can recall hearing Walter Winchell
sign off a Sunday night news broadcast just before the Fourth of
July in 1944. He wished all Americans, especially FDR, "a happy
Fourth." I was pleased to have caught the double meaning.

I remember also a cartoon showing a Democratic father with his
baby son. A friend prophesied, "I'll bet he grows up to be President." "Why, what's wrong with Roosevelt?" retorted the offended
Democrat.

By April 12, 1945, I was a high school sophomore at the seminary.
We had our usual period of recreation after supper, and then
gathered in the study hall for a spiritual conference from the seminary rector, Father Gleason. I must have spent my recreation in the
library or some other solitary place, because I settled down to listen
to Father Gleason without any suspicion that this was an historic
day.

"Well," began the priest, "I suppose you all have heard the news
by now, that our President died suddenly this afternoon." My physical father had died the previous year. Now my spiritual father was
telling me of the death of the father of my *patria*.

The next morning after breakfast I joined my seminary mates
around the one radio we had access to—in the senior auditorium.

We heard bells tolling, and Winston Churchill addressing Parliament. Then our class bells rang, and I resented the fact that we were having classes "as usual" at such a time.

I presumed that at least our history teacher, though he disliked Roosevelt, would solemnize the occasion. "All I can say," Father Tierney remarked after the opening prayer, "is that they are burying that man with indecent haste. Now, as I was saying about Charlemagne on page 256 . . ."

🌳

> History is lived forward but written in retrospect. We know the end before we consider the beginning, and we can never wholly recapture what it was to know the beginning only.
>
> C. V. Wedgewood

April 13

A curious coinciding: today is both Good Friday and Bad Friday the Thirteenth. The paper said this "contradiction" hasn't happened for seventy-three years. Those who believe in lucky days must be in a quandary.

Dramatizing the thin line between good and bad "luck," the paper earlier this week carried an account of the reaction of passengers in a jetliner which recently went into a whirl, broke the sound barrier, but "miraculously" survived. One wife simply kissed her husband and said, "Well, we've had a good life." Another, unaccompanied, woman wondered, "Did I kiss my husband good-bye?" A husband recalled that he hadn't told his wife he loved her when he phoned her that morning. One social worker was escorting four orphan girls from India to the U.S. "Come on, God," she prayed, "these kids have made it through so much, don't blow it now."

As for myself, assuming that the human mind can reason about the divine, I find it hard to believe that prayer can prompt God to do some goodness which He would otherwise neglect to do. Are finite, sinful human beings more interested in goodness than the Absolute Good? Prayer, I rather believe, changes people and people change things to the extent they can.

The front page of the morning paper showed Pope John Paul kissing the feet of a handicapped person in the Holy Thursday liturgy.

Such a picture in the midst of all the hateful and horrid news must have touched many a heart. I have no doubt about it: the Jesus who inspires such gestures is at the world's hidden heart. If a man is going to be wrong about life's meaning or the lack of it, this is the best way to be wrong, and better than being right.

> Those who have been uniquely close to God at any time are nearer to us than our contemporaries.
>
> *Wilbur Urban*

April 14

The trial of Jesus was relived liturgically by the church this week. Today marks the eleventh anniversary of the only trial for which I was ever a witness. Phil Berrigan, knowing of my problems with the Vietnam War, asked me to be a witness at his Baltimore trial in 1968. He and his lawyer wanted to show that "even respectable establishment figures" like my editorial self had moral doubts about the U.S. involvement in Vietnam. Phil and his partners had poured human and animal blood on draft files in protest against that involvement.

The Martin Luther King riots had caused the trial to go into recess. When it was resumed I was called to the stand. The prosecuting attorney was Steve Sachs, a close friend and eventual pallbearer of my lawyer brother. To every question that Phil's lawyer addressed to me, Steve raised an objection which the judge sustained. So, my appearance was futile.

But I did get to meet for the first time Dan Berrigan, who sat with the spectators. When he and Phil were arrested not long afterward for burning draft records in Catonsville, I visited both of them in the Towson jail.

I told Dan at that time that I had problems about the dangerous precedent of taking the law into one's own hands. What if they had burned the records of people who agreed with the war? Where do you draw the line in such invasions of privacy? Had not their own cause lost backing because of such tactics? Dan didn't try to answer me. It was as though he had decided that either you saw the matter as he did, or you didn't, so there was no use arguing.

The first trial allowed me to hear the astonishing answers of the Protestant minister James Mengel, who was one of Phil's co-defendants. When the prosecutor asked whether he had poured blood on the records, he answered gently, "I would rather say I anointed them."

"Well, you would at least admit that you made them harder to read."

"I would rather say that I made them easier to read."

His replies reminded me of Joan of Arc's inspired answers at her own trial. The prosecution planned to trap her by asking her whether she was in God's grace. If she said yes, she could be accused of presumption. If she said no, then how could she be God's agent in the war?

This defenseless teen-ager with no theological sophistication gave the perfect answer: "If I am in God's grace, may He keep me there. If I'm not, may He put me there." . . .

I went to dinner tonight with one of my first altar boys, Jimmy French, who was in town with his wife and two children. I told Jim that after I visited his home last fall, I stopped to see a Philadelphia cousin. While she and I were talking, the nearby house of her mother and sister was being robbed.

About 9 P.M. tonight Jim and his family returned to visit my inner-city house. As soon as I entered the parlor I saw desk drawers open. In the adjacent bedroom my clothes were thrown all about the floor. Burglars had been in my house. Were they *still* in the house?

I started up the stairs to my study, and saw a radio at the top of the steps, as though waiting to be heisted. I descended the steps at once, locked everyone in the parlor, and phoned the police. When they arrived one went upstairs with drawn gun; we found desk and bureau drawers overturned, the contents scattered on the floor. The same was true of the top floor and the basement.

The other officer had gone around the back alley and found my garage door open. The burglars had apparently entered through a basement kitchen window. As we stood in the backyard, one officer noticed someone descending a fire escape a few houses away. The policeman bolted through the garage and shouted, "Stop." Shortly afterward I heard gunfire. A crime lab technician who was standing in the yard ducked into my kitchen. "When the police go that way," he said, "I go this way."

The officers, meantime, captured two suspects, and found a cache of loot in a nearby yard. I was asked if I could identify any of it. As I investigated, I didn't realize that a few feet from me a third suspect was hiding on the ground, a knife in his hand. After I returned to my house, an officer caught sight of the hiding man. In the ensuing scuffle, the officer used my lantern flashlight to club the suspect. Blood was on it when he returned it to me.

The police were here for about two hours; several fresh squad cars and crime lab cars arrived; a helicopter circled above, looking for suspects or loot. I was exceedingly grateful that no one had been seriously injured, that my house had not been ravaged, and that any stolen items will probably be recovered.

I went to bed after midnight, but was too keyed up to fall asleep until several hours had passed. I recalled that this was the night in 1865 when Abraham Lincoln lay dying from a bullet wound. Few stories have moved me as deeply as that of the doctor, Charles Leale, who held Lincoln's hand until the end. He knew the President had been blinded by the bullet, and did not want him to feel alone if he should regain consciousness but know "that he was in touch with humanity and had a friend."

I thought, too, of Lincoln's assassin, John Wilkes Booth, who is buried about a mile from here. Theodore McKeldin, former Baltimore mayor and Maryland governor, once told me he used to place flowers on Booth's grave each year on his anniversary of death. In his kindness, he remembered this unhonored grave, hoping Booth had found forgiveness on the other side of it.

Love your crooked neighbor with your crooked heart.
                                        W. H. Auden

Easter

I drove to Loyola College chapel to offer a 10:30 A.M. Mass for my regular group. This time we used the chapel proper and had organ music. Mary Gallagher was there with her five children; also, by my invitation, Josephine and Eric Jacobsen.

In my brief homily I quoted Josephine's recently published poem, *There Is Good News.* It fantasized about someone who would, after a period of non-use, give us back the abused word "love" in all its force and in its power to unite "roots with heavenly bodies." Author Garry Wills attended with his family; after Mass I introduced the Jacobsens to the Willses.

In midafternoon, beneath a sky alternately bright and rainy, I drove to the New Cathedral Cemetery on Route 40. I bought flowers on the way, and placed them at the grave of my parents, my brother Francis, Miss Robertson (who died in this house), Dr. Whedbee, and his niece, Kathleen Cooper Powell.

Kathleen, a fellow graduate of the Johns Hopkins writing seminars, was buried last year from Sacred Heart Church in our Mount Washington suburb. That church is modeled on the church in Stokes-Poges, England, where Thomas Gray wrote his famous *Elegy*. When I visited that church cemetery in 1977, I caught sight of this inscription on one of the graves there: *"Remembrance: love's last gift."* I quoted that line in Kathy's funeral sermon, and was surprised today to see those words on her small gravestone.

Until my mother's death in 1975 there was no stone on the plot which holds the remains of my father and my sister's infant boy and girl. I arranged for a stone which commemorates all four: the front inscription reacts to the fact that my father's family name means "helping stranger," while my mother's (Doyle) means "dark stranger." The inscription (written before I visited Stokes-Poges) is "Love's last hope: Strangers no more."

On the back of the stone I placed a poem which combines several sources: an ancient Gaelic poem; an inscription found on the prison wall of some Irish patriots; my own alterations and additions. I worked hard on it, and continue to like its simple monosyllables, its swift architecture:

> Like the snow when spring is come,
> Like the lilac, like the plum,
> Such is man from seed to grass—
> In grief and joy he comes . . . to pass.
> Flakes may melt and petals fall,
> Fruit decay, as so must all;
> Hope undaunted pleads her theme:
> The lost have found their deathless dream.

I saw today that the stone-carver who prepared this memorial for me died shortly afterward and is buried nearby beneath a striking black marble stone.

The New Cathedral Cemetery is not connected with Baltimore's "new cathedral" but is the "newest" of the cemeteries connected with the "old cathedral." It is very large; today it was quite extensively adorned with flowers freshly placed by Easter rememberers. I felt at peace there, almost at home. Since childhood I have been fascinated by these cities of the dead, where the living intrude, but only prematurely.

There is a sense of quiet completeness about such places. They are full of forgotten dramas. The remains of the speaking animal of the cosmos lie there, and eventful life stories have been pared down to a few letters and numbers, which the weather is wearing away.

From the grave of her two dead children, I drove over the Key Bridge to Dundalk to see my sister and her two living children. There I consumed my only jelly beans of the day, and gave Pat his first ride in my "new" car. Next, I drove to the Gallaghers for an Easter buffet dinner.

I concluded the day with a brief visit to the Jacobsens at their apartment. Years ago, while looking for a home in New Hampshire, they spotted an old cemetery and discovered this inscription: *It is a fearful thing to love what death can touch.* Josephine tried to discover whether it was a quote from some great poet. She searched in vain.

A few years afterward, she read a play review in *Commonweal* which praised this very line. She wrote to William Alfred, the author of *Agamemnon*, the play in question. Did he know the origin of the words? He replied that apparently she had not yet received the copy of the play which he had sent her. In the front of the book, he acknowledged that he had indirectly received the quotation from her. The magic of those eleven words had captured a series of imaginations and come full circle.

I have told this story to several classes of students. One such student lost his mother not long afterward, and now that line graces her grave in Arlington National Cemetery. Another student told me of a line he would add to the original—"More fearful yet, never to have felt the touch of love."

In 1974 I tracked down Bernice Shallow, the granddaughter of the man on whose tombstone those words were carved. She lived alone in a trailer alongside a New Hampshire highway, and was nearly blind. She couldn't even recall the lines on the stone, but took from an old safe a scrapbook which had belonged to her grandfather and which was full of poems he had written—including one written in the aftermath of Lincoln's assassination.

He had become paralyzed a year after his marriage and wrote articles and verses for various local papers. I found the poem from which were taken the words on his baby daughter's gravestone. I suspect that the words on his own stone were taken from another of his poems. Although I found several poems which seemed to be leading up to those death-defying words, I didn't have time to read that bulging book thoroughly enough to locate them or to be sure that they weren't in the book.

The growing good of the world is partly dependent upon unhistoric acts; and that things are not so ill with you and me as they might have been, is half owing to the number who lived faithfully a hidden life, and rest in unvisited tombs.

George Eliot

April 16

Looking at what happened in Christ's life, Christians will expect to be saved, not from danger and suffering, but in danger and suffering.

Dorothy Sayers

April 17

It is dangerous to press upon a man the duty of getting beyond human love when his real difficulty lies in getting so far.

C. S. Lewis

April 18

The day which commemorates the midnight ride of Paul Revere afforded me a midday ride to Wexford, Pennsylvania, 260 miles to the northwest, and a visit with John Corcoran and his family. Before leaving town I talked with a neighbor whose apartment too was robbed last Saturday night, presumably by my burglars. He told me that the third suspect, who was hiding on the ground, had fallen asleep, and his snoring is what caught the attention of the police!

He who snores is always the first to fall asleep.

April 19

I drove another forty-five miles north of Wexford to Slippery Rock College, the butt of sports announcers, and located the off-campus apartment of John Corcoran's brother Tim. Tim's room-mate had decorated their room with so many and such centerfolds that I thought I was in some maternity ward at feeding time.

One of Tim's apartment-mates paid me the supreme compliment of stranger for stranger: he had memorized a loneliness poem I had written last May in Tel Aviv. Tim had passed it on to him from memory:

Lines from a Crowded Postcard

This magical city is brimming
with every enchantment but one,
as so I perceive it as empty—
by loneliness undone.

I needed you here to enjoy it,
to share every beauty in view,
to see what delights I would barter
for a tent in the desert and you.

It is better to write than to read; it is better to write poetry than to write; it is better to live than to write poetry.

Franz Rosenzweig

April 20

To be twenty and to be a poet is to be twenty; to be forty and to be a poet is to be a poet.

Eugène Delacroix

April 21

> I know not what evil lies in the heart of the basest criminal, but
> I have gazed into my own heart and I am appalled.

April 22

In the evening I joined John and Nanci Corcoran in watching a special three-hour TV movie entitled *Friendly Fire* and starring Carol Burnett. It was the true story of an Iowa couple who turned against the Vietnam War and our own government when their son was accidentally killed by his fellow soldiers. After a period of repression, that war seems to have erupted suddenly into American consciousness again.

Six years ago this time the U.S. had finally pulled its troops out of that tragic war, in which 2,800,000 Americans had served, 303,000 were wounded, and nearly 58,000 were killed—to mention the price paid by only one of the combatants. As an editor I was drawn into that conflict in a special way—a way that can be documented.

As far as I can determine, my first editorial on South Vietnam appeared on July 26, 1963—while President Kennedy and the Diem brothers were still alive and no U.S. combat troops had yet landed in that Georgia-sized nation. It dealt with the May 8 clash between Buddhists and government troops in Hue, and wondered whether Roman Catholics were persecuting Buddhists. Striking a motif which would persist, I spoke of "remarkable confusion" and "the complexity of the situation."

On August 16, I presented a background sketch of Buddhism and its founder Buddha—"that inconceivably sublime spirit," as Catholic theologian Romano Guardini called him.

On September 20, I commented on the continuing confusion about the conflicts within South Vietnam. While praising reporters like the *Herald Tribune*'s Marguerite Higgins, I cited *Time* magazine's claim that "the U.S. press corps in South Vietnam has been compounding the confusion because it has uncritically taken sides and is prone to distort the facts."

On November 8, after the death of the Diem brothers, I noted again all the contradictory statements in circulation about the Diem government. "We hope," I concluded, "that the truth was better served in what we were led to believe about the living Diem than in the official reports of his 'accidental suicide.'" Otherwise "that ingenious phrase may one day serve to describe our own American finale in Asia."

Reacting to the Gulf of Tonkin episode the following August, I wrote on August 7, 1964, "In view of the evidence available, this country was amply justified in its measured attack on North Vietnam." Still I allowed that "the motives for the provocative Communist behavior remain puzzling." Few Americans realized that the U.S. involvement in Vietnam had turned a decisive corner now that Lyndon Johnson had the permissive Gulf of Tonkin Resolution in his pocket.

My editorial of August 6, 1965 discussed an AP report that U.S. marines "showed little inclination to differentiate between civilians and enemy troops" in a village the marines were trying to save. "Certainly it does the American cause no good if 'protecting' the South Vietnamese means killing them recklessly." My Lai still lay ahead. In the meantime, a Vietnam vet, allowing that the war was immoral, said it was necessary and that antiwar protests were terrible. "America's moral sun will be setting," I wrote, "when brave men think it is a terrible thing to protest an immoral thing."

Antiwar sentiment in the U.S. now began to take organized form. In an editorial of October 22, 1965, I tried to point out the good and the bad side of such protests. "To the extent that they reflect a conscientious concern about the moral aspects of that bloody and brutal conflict, these exercises of the American right of protest have their good side." I concluded this way: "In the present situation, we do not believe that the basic American involvement in South Vietnam is immoral. If the situation changes and its immorality becomes evident, we hope to say so as clearly and courageously as the most sincere demonstrator."

On Christmas Eve of 1965, President Johnson ordered a pause in the intensive bombing of the North, which he had authorized the previous February. On January 28, 1966 my editorial was entitled "Don't Renew the Bombing Yet." Citing various arguments pro and con, I ended by saying, "If all hope of negotiations is permanently dashed, the eventual American casualties are going to be far, far worse than they have been." At this point U.S. fatalities were around 2,000. The final toll would be almost thirty times greater.

"Are We Wrong About Vietnam?" asked my editorial of March

11, 1966. "We admit that the Vietnam question is full of complex-ities, obscurities, and imponderables. . . . We state for the record our conviction that President Johnson's current policy is substan-tially right . . . because the ultimate aim of the Viet Cong and its sponsors in North Vietnam is to bring South Vietnam forcibly under Communist rule."

Conflict between Buddhists and Prime Minister Ky prompted a June 6, 1966, editorial entitled "South Vietnam Suicide," which ended this way: "If the recent chaos continues to prevail much longer, we think the U.S. will have only one reasonable choice: ar-range for the evacuation to friendly nations of all South Vietnamese who wish to leave their country, and withdraw American military power as soon as possible from what appears more and more to be an essentially hopeless and helpless situation."

This suggested evacuation may seem unrealistic. Still, 230,000 South Vietnamese left their land in 1975 to settle in North America. As for cost, it has been conservatively estimated that for the war the United States spent the equivalent of $7,500 for each of South Vietnam's 17 million citizens.

By September I knew that my days at the *Review* were numbered, so in a signed column dated September 23, I wrote a kind of over-view editorial called "*My* Vietnam Problems." I talked about the proven futility of the tactics of escalation, and the massive lack of world support for the drift of U.S. policy. Noting that escalation is often justified as an indirect fight against Red China, I confessed that "I'm not convinced of this argument" and pointed out that the Vietnamese are ancient enemies of China.

(I and my doubts were in good but secret company in late 1966. According to Adam Yarmolinsky, a chief aide to the Secretary of Defense, Robert McNamara was from 1966 on tormented by doubts and already believed that "this was not a war that could be won or not at a cost that could be justified. . . . It was a terrible mistake to have gotten into it.")

Two weeks later I agreed with James Reston that ex-President Ei-senhower had made a "mad proposal" when he recently said that America must win the war in Vietnam "at all costs"—including the use of nuclear weapons. I voiced my hope that at their upcoming meeting the U.S. Catholic bishops would corporately speak to their own people about the war in the same challenging and discrim-inating terms which Vatican II and Pope Paul had used.

In one of my final *Review* comments on Vietnam I was able to be glad that in the meantime the U.S. Catholic bishops had issued a statement which strikingly paralleled the wave-making pastoral which Cardinal Shehan had issued in late June of that year of 1966. I was able to report that Bishops Wright of Pittsburgh and Swanstrom of New York had publicly backed the UN's U Thant's appeal for the unconditional cessation of the bombing of North Vietnam.

The tide was slowly turning, though the war would continue for more than six years. Professor James Wright of the University of Massachusetts was convinced by his research that Catholics turned against the Vietnam War earlier than the rest of the American population. If so, they probably did so only after going through the kind of "agonizing reappraisals" reflected in these editorials of one American Catholic.

❦

There are two marks of salvation: candor and endless docility to the facts.

Baron von Hügel

April 23

Shakespeare and Cervantes (of *Don Quixote* fame) died on this day in 1616, though reference books give slightly different dates, since England and Spain were not then using the same calendar. Today is also generally reckoned as the Bard's birthday, though it is only known for sure that he was baptized a few days later in 1564. I have treasured memories of visiting Stratford in Canada and the original Stratford in England. I also treasure the memory of a man who kept one Shakespearean play purposely unread, so he could look forward to reading it fresh on his deathbed.

Some ingenious person has noted that in 1610, when the Psalms in the King James Bible were being translated, Shakespeare was forty-six. Rumor has it that the playwright had a hand in this translation. In any case, the forty-sixth word from the start of Psalm 46 is "shake"; the forty-sixth word from the end is "spear." . . .

I rose before seven today to breakfast with John Corcoran before he left for work. I was packed and on the road home by 9 A.M. My first stop was the State Regional Correctional Facility near Greensburg, some forty miles to the southeast. There I spent an hour or so visiting my priest-friend who since last September has been serving time on "corruption of youth" charges.

Ever the teacher, he said his fellow "residents" are poorly educated. "Hey Rev," one of them inquired, "do you spell sh— with one 't' or two?" "What do you miss the most?" I asked him. "My library and reference works."

My first prison experience occurred when I visited the Maryland Penitentiary during my last years as a seminarian. I recall these visits as dispiriting, especially when I talked with prisoners on death row. Though (as mentioned earlier) I was instrumental in having one death sentence commuted, I also talked with George Grammar, who was accused of killing his wife and making it look like a car accident. The police found a suspicious stone near the accelerator. And why did he get his mother-in-law to phone the morgue and try to speed up the autopsy?

When I conversed with Mr. Grammar, he was rather aggressively trying to disprove some point of Catholic doctrine by citing Bible texts. It seemed an odd preoccupation for a condemned man.

During the intervening years, like most clergymen, I have visited jails from time to time. My one effort to become jailed failed, as I will explain on May 1. My mother, the landlady, didn't try but succeeded when the police put her briefly in the clinker for neglecting to register a new roomer who was being shadowed by the law as a prostitute. . . .

Resuming the turnpike today, I drove another two hundred miles east to the state capital, Harrisburg. En route I heard that state's Governor Thornburg on the radio testifying about the nuclear accident at Three Mile Island. Arriving at New Cumberland, just outside the capital, I paid a visit to one of my favorite seminary classmates, Monsignor Tom Leitch, parish pastor and the bishop's right-hand man.

Last year, after a game of golf, Tom and a doctor were showering. Said the doctor, "Has that thing on your shoulder been bleeding long?" "What thing?" The doctor insisted that Tom visit his office the next day. A malignant melanoma was diagnosed, and Tom underwent an operation within days. He is still taking chemotherapy every two weeks in Hershey. [Tom died in February 1983.]

Tom was in a bright, playful mood; we had dinner in the rectory with two other priests. (The cook was a Laotian refugee.) Another one of my classmates is the only Catholic pastor in Middletown, just across from Three Mile Island. This George wasn't in when we tried to phone him, but in the company of one of my supper companions I drove to the floodlit site of the accident, viewing it from the nearby eastern shore of the Susquehanna. Blinking red lights identified the four giant water towers. It was hard to comprehend that the relatively small domed building in the midst of the towers had commanded world attention these past four weeks.

By 8 P.M., I was heading for Baltimore, seventy miles to the south. Tomorrow my students and I would accompany Dante and Beatrice on a journey to the moon, Venus, and Mercury. I fiddled with my radio dial. A voice caught my attention. "Tomorrow at dawn you can glimpse a rare sight. Above the crescent moon you will see Venus, the brightest 'star' in the sky. Beneath the moon you will see Mercury." Art and nature were coalescing.

If Francis Bacon didn't write the plays of Shakespeare, he lost the opportunity of a lifetime.

April 24

What we call non-existent is what we do not desire enough.
                                        Nikos Kazantzakis

April 25

On this day in 1968 I paid my first visit to St. Louis and stood beneath its giant arch on the west bank of the Mississippi. A National Committee of Concerned Catholics was holding its first meeting there. I had received an invitation to attend after my "Open Letter to the U.S. Catholic Bishops" appeared in the *National Catholic Reporter*. That hierarchy was also meeting in St. Louis at the same time. I was told that the "Open Letter" came up in their discussion. Of that meeting *Ave Maria* magazine's editor John Reedy told me, "The most disturbing thing is that the bishops don't seem disturbed."

🌲

He who does not rebuild the Temple in his lifetime, destroys it in his lifetime.

Ancient Jewish saying

April 26

God is not nice. He is not an uncle. He is an earthquake.

Hasidic saying

April 27

This was the day in 1963 when I first met Father Hans Küng, now possibly the world's most famous living Catholic theologian. In the midst of the Second Vatican Council this Swiss scholar had been touring the U.S. giving a speech about the need for reform in the church. He had one basic speech which he was to give a number of times, so he did not give a copy of his manuscript to the press. As a consequence, the papers were highlighting only the more "negative" aspects of his speech, and a lopsided impression of his thoughts grew prevalent.

When I heard him speak at Baltimore's Roland Park Seminary on this day, I was editor of our Catholic paper. He let me make notes from his text, and I was able to write an editorial which presented his ideas in a more balanced manner. Later, he wrote me from Tübingen, Germany, to thank me for my efforts: "It is certainly a great help to have this correction of false impressions."

This 1963 visit of his was connected with a famous scandal—the banning of four prominent Catholic theologians from speaking at the Catholic University in Washington. Hans Küng was one of them. I wrote an editorial entitled "The Very Idea of a University," attacking the school's decision, which was traced to its then rector, Bishop William J. McDonald, and to Monsignor John "Butch" Fenton, a notoriously conservative faculty member.

Another faculty member, reformist church historian John Tracy Ellis (and a friend of mine) quoted from my editorial in a statement issued by the university's Academic Senate and sent to the

U.S. hierarchy. As may be expected, the Senate condemned the banning.

There were two reasons why my editorial seemed especially knowledgeable about the university. I had just read the university's bylaws in a piece of promotion which came in the mail. Secondly, I had just finished reading a biography of the founding bishop of the university, John Lancaster Spalding.

Some weeks later, Archbishop Shehan asked me whether I had been in touch with Monsignor Ellis before writing my editorial. I told him the truth—no. All evening I wondered why he had asked me that question. Then it hit me—someone was claiming that the well-informed editorial was actually written by Monsignor Ellis. So he was then really quoting himself when he read the editorial into the record. A foul plot indeed, and one which imputed to me the dishonesty of pretending I had written it. For I had taken the unusual step of showing it to the archbishop before I published it.

Early the next morning I returned to the archbishop's office. "Is someone saying that Monsignor Ellis wrote that editorial?" "Yes," replied the archbishop. I had to blush at the thought of being thought so devious.

During the last session of the Council, Hans Küng stayed at the same Roman boarding house that I did. He had an audience with Pope Paul at the very end of the Council and presented a list of reforms he thought were urgent. I can hear Father Küng reporting to us the pope's reply: "Adagio, adagio [easy does it]."

In Rome I arranged to take a picture of the theologian, but I misunderstood where I was supposed to meet him. I finally located him, but am still embarrassed that I held up that busy man. (This and scores of other irreplaceable Council slides were later stolen.)

Once, in a misprint (which we caught), our newspaper referred to this controversial man as "Hang Küng." Hans Küng means "John King." So, ironically, does the name of Philadelphia's relatively conservative cardinal, John Krol.

When Father Küng's book, *The Church*, was first published I read a number of reviews which called special attention to his thoughts on the primacy of Peter and its relationship to the papacy. So, when I finally purchased the book, I at once checked the table of contents, and noted that his treatment of the primacy began on page 444. I instantly turned to that page and under the pertinent heading I read these words: "Readers who begin reading at this point are making a serious mistake."

I've often been smitten by a book, but that was the first and only time that I felt that I had been bitten by one.

If you're not a radical at twenty, something's wrong with your heart; if you're still one at thirty, something's wrong with your head.

April 28

Yesterday my youngest nephew, Jimmy, confided that he had a hard time lighting matches when he serves Mass. We practiced together, as I marveled how a grown-up can take certain skills for granted.

Serving Mass in the old days of Latin was even more of a challenge, so a brand-new server usually had a veteran altar boy for a partner. A priest-classmate of mine told me of a nervous neophyte who had to serve Mass alone on the second day of his first week of serving. The youngster seemed to have done well, and the priest congratulated him after Mass.

A minute or two later, however, a parishioner came to the sacristy and reported that at the Consecration of the Mass, when one altar boy usually rang the bell while the other lifted up the back of the vestment of the genuflecting priest, this youngster had done the lifting with his teeth. My friend summoned the boy and asked him why he had done so.

"But I had to, Father," he pleaded. "I needed one hand to ring the bell and the other hand to thump." (Vigorous thumping of the chest during the Consecration was a part of Catholic piety in those days.)

My priest-classmate, Ed Ginder, phoned from Laurel, Maryland, today. A practitioner of olden piety, he has been a federal prison chaplain for twenty years. This week the government wrote to tell him that since he is over fifty-five and involved in hazardous work, a new ruling requires him to retire at the end of June.

An army veteran, he recalled how he used to slip notes under my seminary door asking for help in translating Latin texts. Since his room was next to mine in our saintly prison, and since you needed permission to speak at anyone's door, we would at times discuss such matters from window to window a quarter of a century ago.

Even before he was a seminarian, Ed was a man of alarming faith. Once, when entering a church with an agnostic friend, he dipped his hand into a dish full of murky holy water. "You put your hand in that dirty water?" asked his doubly doubting companion. "My hand?" said Ed, sensing a challenge. Whereupon he lifted the dish and drank it dry.

🌱

They had always invited their pious neighbor to go with them on their picnic, but this year they forgot until the last minute. "It's too late," she said, "I've already prayed for rain."

April 29

We lay aside letters, never to read them again, and at last we destroy them out of discretion, and so disappears the most beautiful, the most immediate breath of life, irrecoverably for ourselves and for others.

Goethe

April 30

Lives of great men all remind us
As their pages o'er we turn,
That we're apt to leave behind us
Letters that we ought to burn.
                    A. S. W. *Rosenbach*

May 1, 1979

Four years ago today Saigon fell to the North Vietnamese, and that eminently barbaric and fratricidal war was at long last ended. Quite a few antiwar protests had been planned for our national capital on May Day 1971, and some of them sounded potentially violent. So, fellow faculty member Father Anselm Atkins (a former Trappist), myself, and about thirteen seminarians decided to conduct a peaceful prayer service starting at noon in front of the White House.

One of the seminarians was about to be ordained, and he looked forward to spending his priesthood retreat in jail. We all expected to be arrested, and made arrangements for Dean Bamberger of the Catholic University law school to bail most of us out after a day or two.

We converged on the White House from different directions and knelt in a semicircle, while each of us took turns leading the prayers or explaining our purpose to the passersby. (Some of these ignored us; others expressed disapproval.) After a policeman told us in vain that we would have to move, government officials arrived, dashed out of their cars, and began questioning us one by one, taking our answers on tape recorders.

When the hour was over, a member of the Department of the Interior asked us whether we were now going to leave. We said that some of us planned to stay longer. "You know, you need permission for this." "We didn't have time to get permission." "Well, if you wait here for an hour or so, I'll go get you emergency permission."

In our prayers and statements we had just been talking about reconciliation. It seemed provocative to frustrate this man's desire to legalize our protest. So, we had a sidewalk conference and decided to disband, since our main goal of an hour of prayer had been achieved. Frank Scollen was disappointed that he would have to make his retreat outside of jail.

(Not all seminarians were prepared for the protester's role. One especially absentminded student took part in the March on the Pentagon, was arrested, and gave an assumed name to the booking officer at the jail. He made his one permissible phone call to summon a classmate to bail him out. But he languished in jail longer than any of his confreres because he forgot to tell his friend what his prison name was.)

🌳

Emerson: "Why were you in jail?"
Thoreau: "Why were you out of jail?"

May 2

Man creates out of his mortal wounds.
                              Joost A. M. Meerloo

May 3

I was reading the morning paper before breakfast. Anatole Broyard was reviewing a new book by Lionel Tiger about the *Biology of Hope*. "Having children is what Mr. Tiger calls a 'dire' investment in life, one which exposes us to the cruelest possibilities of disappointment." The phone rang as I was reading that sentence. Gina was calling about her six-week-old baby, which I was due to baptize on Mother's Day. She told me little Christine Julia became ill yesterday, suddenly, mysteriously. She was on a respirator in the intensive care unit of the pediatric department at the University of Maryland Hospital.

When I arrived at the hospital, I joined a conference which the doctor was having with Gina and her husband, John. (I married them in the seminary chapel on June 22, 1975.) Dr. Steinschneider thinks a "crib death" was intercepted at the last minute, but he could make no hopeful promises. He talked compassionately about the guilty feelings which unjustly afflict mothers in such cases.

In December of 1961 my own sister lost her first child from this sudden infant death syndrome. Little Billie was also about six weeks old. John and Gina bravely took me into the room where their child was being closely and lovingly monitored by a special nurse. Gina placed her finger within the baby's miraculously tiny hand. Wonder clashed with wonder: life and the absurd interruption of it.

Gina said that the young priest who came to the hospital to baptize Christine was so upset that she found herself trying to be composed for his sake. "I never saw anything like this before," he explained.

☘

Something like a privilege is involved when a human being is not spared such monstrous torment, as if this ruthlessness were the expression of a kind of initiation, a sign of election to the extraordinary—as though this desperate suffering could happen only to a being from whom there were to be no secrets.

Rainer Maria Rilke

May 4

A quick glance at the morning paper apprised me that Margaret Thatcher will be England's first woman prime minister; she and the Queen are both fifty-three.

I drove to Columbia for a 9:45 acupuncture appointment. Bob inserted a needle quickly into the insides of each knee cap area and said he would be using less needles in future treatments. He gave me a chart listing the quaint names for various points on the body's energy pathways. Instant favorites of mine were: Grasping the Wind, Listening Palace, Jade Pillow, Walking on the Verandah, Amidst Elegance, Loathesome Jaws, Prostrate Hare, Abundant Splendor, Encircling Glory, Abdomen Sorrow, One Hundred Meetings, and Palace of Weariness.

I stopped at the Ellicott City Doyles' for lunch. Because of his cystic fibrosis, young Michael has been going to school only every other day for half a day. We were discussing crib death; Michael seemed quite interested, and commented that losing a child when it was older would be even rougher on the family.

I phoned the hospital from the Doyles' and learned from a sympathetic nurse that the baby has suffered brain death. She told me she was in awe at the courage of the parents.

🌲

To live is to suffer. To survive is to find meaning in the suffering.

Viktor Frankl

May 5

If childless people sneer—well, they have less sorrow. But what lonesome luck.

Euripides

May 6

The loneliness of great men is part of their ability to create. Character, like a photograph, develops in darkness.

Yousuf Karsh

May 7

Shortly before 5 P.M., Gina phoned to tell me that her six-week-old baby was officially dead. Earlier today she and John had held their baby a final time before the support system was removed. Later they were asked whether they wanted to hold the dead baby. At first Gina thought it would be too much to bear, but then she and John returned to cradle the blanket-wrapped infant. She said she felt sad to see the dead body, but she had a strong feeling that Christine was safe, wherever she was.

🌲

But the soul of her, the glowing, gorgeous, fervent soul of her, surely was flaming in eager joy upon some other dawn.

William Allen White, upon his daughter's death

May 8

I know of no one so entirely in harmony with life, recognizing
in what is gentlest and most terrible the one same force, a force
which conceals itself—but always, even when it kills, wants to
give.

Rainer Maria Rilke of Lou Andreas-Salome

May 9

At 12:15 I arrived downtown at Archbishop Borders' residence opposite the Central Pratt Library. His brother had lunch with us; he
is visiting from Indiana because his wife is getting therapy at a local
hospital. Later the archbishop and I talked for about thirty minutes.
I told him I would like an assignment as a convent or school chaplain, where I would have time to write and lecture and keep in close
touch with my family.

The Indiana-born archbishop is hard-working, plain-living, and pa-
tently sincere. The first time I lunched with him he ended our discussion with a spontaneous prayer. Somehow I can't imagine Cardinal Shehan or the typical pre-Vatican II bishop doing so under the
circumstances. It would have seemed an invasion of privacy and
vaguely Protestant.

Today the archbishop listened sympathetically and suggested that
I contact the personnel office. He thinks it bad for a priest to be as
isolated from priestly companionship as I am.

Before I left he spoke a little about a recent *Sun* column in which
Garry Wills accused him of having a list of forbidden speakers, such
as Phil Berrigan. He said he had no such list, and wasn't even aware
that Phil had been invited to speak at Loyola College. In any case,
the invitation was withdrawn.

In a *Harper's* article about a fund-raising scandal involving a
Pallotine priest based in Baltimore, Wills had already called Borders
a prelate "only slightly less ineffectual than his predecessor" (Cardinal Shehan). Such a judgment struck me as unduly harsh in both
directions. Shehan had already tangled with Wills, a Catholic, in
the *Sun*, after the latter had penned a critical article about Baltimore's new cathedral.

The morning paper told of the sudden death of Dr. Andre

Hellegers, whom I knew when he worked at Hopkins Hospital. A Dutchman by birth, he founded the Bio-Ethics Center at Georgetown and had been a member of Pope Paul's Birth Control Commission. His young daughter once announced to her classmates that her father was the pope's gynecologist. I'm sure he voted for a change in the church's official position, and helped persuade Cardinal Shehan to do the same. We had some lively discussions on the subject when I was writing editorials in the early and mid-sixties. He was only fifty-two—a great loss.

☘

Thou recallest me and I take my departure while thanking Thee without reservation for having admitted me to this great spectacle of the world.

Epictetus

May 10

I celebrated my first Mass as a priest twenty-four years ago this month at the Church of Saints Philip and James in mid-Baltimore. Four years ago I offered my mother's funeral Mass there. Today I went there a third time to offer a funeral Mass for the six-week-old baby of my friends the Woloszyns. The tiny casket was placed on a table just in front of the altar; it was scarcely as big as the spray of spring flowers covering it. The young parish priest, Father Bowen, assisted me and sang some hymns and psalms with his very melodious voice.

I found it difficult to preach. I stressed that we were celebrating the miracle of caring, which is so courageous because events like sudden death can overtake the objects of caring. I spoke my belief that "nothing dies but something's born."

Just before Holy Communion, as I spoke the prayer, Lamb of God, I glanced at the casket just in front of me and felt so deeply moved that I lost my voice awhile.

Christine Julia was buried in a country churchyard where Gina's grandparents have a lot. Her grandparents, in their eighties, were among the mourners. I noticed that a young child of theirs was buried near the freshly dug soil. When I asked the grandmother how old her baby was, I didn't realize that her memory had failed badly. "I don't remember," she answered with a gentle smile. Later I asked how the baby had died. She turned to her husband: "What did the baby die from?" This forgetting was almost as piercing as the many tears which Gina shed today.

✻

Every cradle asks us whence, and every coffin whither.

Irish saying

May 11

In 1975 this date was Mother's Day—the first after my own mother's death. I noticed on that day that the first signs of spring had appeared upon her grave. A haiku came from that sight: "From your winter grave, infant blades of grass have sprung. Green grief bathes them now."

I decided that afternoon to drive to my childhood home on Ridgewood Avenue in northwest Baltimore. The house was empty and a back door open. So, for the first time in forty years I roamed through the rooms that had housed me for the first six years of my life. My parents were buying this house, but lost it during the Depression.

I remembered certain features of the house, but was surprised how completely had flown all memories of my bedroom or the skylight in the upstairs bathroom. Gone but not forgotten were the tinkling Chinese chimes which used to enchant from the porch roof, and the nearby window sticker showing the blue eagle and my parents' endorsement of President Roosevelt's NRA (National Recovery Act). In the ghostly silence of that house with nobody in it I became again a bewildered boy, hearing my injured mother plead from the snowy steps outside, and seeing my father in pajamas racing down the inside steps to save her.

This is an all-black neighborhood now, and although I had driven past the house a number of times in recent years, I had never had the chance to walk through it. On my way from the cemetery to the old house on that sunny May afternoon I switched on my car radio and found waiting for me one of those gifts of synchronicity which life affords from time to time. A symphony orchestra was playing one of my favorite melodies from Dvořák's *New World Symphony*. In 1922, William Arms Fisher published words for the melody with the title "Goin' Home":

🌲

Goin' home, Goin' home, I'm a goin' home; Quiet like, some still day, I'm jes' goin' home. . . . Mother's there, 'spectin' me; Father's waitin' too; Lots o' folks gathered there; All the friends I knew.

May 12

She feels the giant agony of the world as a personal thing. There are not many who belong to this aristocracy of pain.

Said of Edith Hamilton

May 13

It tickleth me about my heart's root that I have seen the world as in my time.

Chaucer's Wife of Bath

May 14

A word is not the same with one writer as with another. One tears it from his guts; the other pulls it out of his overcoat pocket.

Charles Péguy

May 15

On the radio today I heard the National Press Club honoring this year's Pulitzer Prize winners. Katherine Anne Porter, who won such a prize in 1965, was eighty-nine today, and I paid her a visit at College Park. Three other friends were there, and we celebrated with devil's food cake and champagne. The honoree was in her wheel-chair; she said she was ready to die, but her bones had a terrific desire to stay above ground.

A year ago tonight I was falling asleep in Jerusalem for the last time during my second visit to Israel. It was Israel's thirtieth birthday by the Western calendar. Here's how I summed up the celebration which, according to Israel's lunar calendar, had occurred several days previously:

A card in my hotel room advised, "In Case of Air Raid Alarm, Go Straight to the Shelter." There was no alarm, but soldiers with M-16 rifles were plentifully in view, even in the hotel lobby. And no wonder. This was the capital city of a nation celebrating its thirtieth birthday, with terrorist attacks freshly in mind. At the end, the Jerusalem *Post* could breathe a sigh of relief—"Israel Free of Terror Attempts"—and cite a "giant security operation."

Our group of forty-three from the Baltimore area, including several survivors of Auschwitz, were staying at the Jerusalem Hilton, an apt name etymologically for a hill-town hotel, 2,500 feet above sea level. In the royal suite, two floors above my room, Egyptian and Israeli peace delegates had met earlier that year.

Looking north from my room, I could see the nearby Romema area where the Allenby Monument recalls that on December 9, 1917, "the Holy City was surrendered to the 60th London Division." Thus began thirty years of turbulent association with England—a link reflected by King George Street in the heart of Jerusalem.

Had I been able to look south I would have seen, at about the same distance, the two main sites of Israel's current celebration: Mount Herzl, where the father of Zionism is buried, and the Hebrew University Stadium, the gift of a couple from Michigan. (Ubiquitous plaques reveal that this is a gifted nation in that special sense too.)

Our group was lucky enough to get tickets to special events at each site. There could hardly have been a more moving way for an outsider to see and feel what this ancient and astonishing land means to the Jewish people.

At sundown May 10, as the air grew chilly, the speaker of the Knesset, Israel's Congress, arrived at Mount Herzl to preside at the conclusion of a Day of Remembrance for the nation's fallen defenders.

This is a young nation built on a dream and out of unspeakable sufferings. Since its birth it has known war on the average of once every seven years.

Now, from a flame at the tomb of its first dreamer, Theodor Herzl, twelve torches were lit by children and grandchildren of various national heroes. While a chorus sang softly, each youngster spoke briefly in Hebrew. Finally, everyone sang what to me is one of the world's most haunting anthems, the majestic "Hatikvah (Hope)." With freshly renewed images of the Holocaust in mind, I felt overwhelmingly the mystique of this tiny nation.

The next morning, with President Shamir and Prime Minister Begin presiding, more than two thousand soldiers paraded crisply in a score of units at the crowded stadium.

The soldiers, men and women, seemed depressingly young but high-spirited. Their features were strikingly various and confirmed the fact that the Israelis of today are a United Nations in themselves. One red-haired and freckle-skinned girl with a shy smile seemed straight from that other Holy Land, Ireland.

The weaponry aspect of the celebration seemed underplayed, though jets in formation flew by at the end, flawlessly forming a figure thirty. The ailing Mr. Begin, who had canceled two appearances on the previous day, spoke briefly here. Now he and the President were pelted with roses by a crowd so enthusiastic and pressing that the honor guard had to intervene. This they did with such finesse that the audience clapped.

A sour note was struck outside the stadium where a small group of American "Jews for Jesus" were trying to address the dispersing crowd. In the midst of some scuffling and pushing, a girl fell to the ground. A melancholy scene, laced with the irony of the Jewishness of Jesus. The best and the worst: that's what you get from religion.

A happier American note was the ecstatic response given to Leontyne Price that evening at an outdoor concert near the Jaffa Gate in Jerusalem. As this stately black woman sang Gershwin's "Summertime" the air seemed to grow warmer with hope—*hatikvah*. Someday soon the living would be easier, because—like the dove to the ark—shalom would return for good to this city of peace, this Jeru-Shalom, as the ancients interpreted it.

Here, in this most ancient and sacred of cities, people of all races, colors, creeds would discover and reveal once again how goodly and pleasant a thing it is when brethren dwell as one.

🌳

All day long, the search for the living and the dead went on in the ruins of Ben Yehuda Street. Someone had placed a cardboard sign: "Silence—so we can hear the wounded still under the rubble."

Collins and Lapierre in O Jerusalem

May 16

Give me your hand—I've taken a liking to you.
Johnson to Boswell

May 17

I drove to Georgetown to pick up my senior nephew. Planning to spend his junior year abroad in England, Frank had to pack all his belongings in my Pacer, attend to last-minute college business, and bid multiple farewells to many friends whom he isn't likely to see again for sixteen months.

Frank was mellow about this separation from buddies and sweethearts as he approached the end of his teens. As one who has been twenty (two and a half times), I thought of my own college farewells and how sincerely we thought we meant to keep in closer touch with each other than we actually did. A cynic (or perhaps a realist) would say that we keep in touch with absent friends until we find other friends who are more satisfying—if only because they are present. A romantic would say that we simply run out of time and/or energy to honor all our rosy-cheeked promises to keep in touch.

In any case, we do "spend our lives saying good-bye" and regardless of the outcome there is a poignancy to those promises and to those feelings that we are going to miss our schoolmates so much.

Some farewells are more devastating. Four years ago today a seminarian from St. Mary's was being ordained to the priesthood. As the bishop was about to enter the church to ordain him, Tom's mother was stricken with a heart attack. The bishop anointed her for death just before he set about ordaining her son for ministry.

During the Mass the bishop learned that the mother had died, and informed young Tom so that they could both offer the Mass for her repose. I can't imagine a more extreme clash of emotions.

Who has turned us around like this, so that always, do what we may, we assume the posture of one who is leaving?

Rainer Maria Rilke

May 18

I drove to College Park to hear Katherine Anne Porter's confession and give her Holy Communion. She said again that Holy Communion makes her weep. "I have a tenderness . . . for God—that's the only way I can say it." She has been in bed for two years and two months now with the stroke that has paralyzed her right side. "It's only my right hand," she says when she fondles the hand which wrote her great stories, and which she now playfully refers to as her kitten.

In her hallway I noted again three pictures she took of Hart Crane in her Mexican garden in the spring of 1931. I was two years old then! The following spring that restless poet who saw the Brooklyn Bridge as a mystical symbol of America's creativity jumped or fell from the bridge of a ship as he returned from Mexico. Of her many friends, Katherine Anne said they liked to kiss her because she liked to kiss them.

One of the friends who were visiting her on her birthday was there again today—Jane DeMouy, who has written a doctoral dissertation on the women in Miss Porter's writings. She finds in them a common conflict: the desire for the love and security inherent in the traditional roles of wife and mother, and the desire for the freedom to follow their art or their principles.

Life is easier to take than you think. All that is necessary is to accept the impossible, do without the indispensable, and bear the intolerable.

Kathleen Norris

May 19

I spoke by phone today with Father Jack Kinsella of the archdiocesan personnel office. He told me that Father Paul Cook of St. Joseph's parish in the Baltimore suburb known as Texas was looking for weekend help—two Masses on Saturday or Sunday. I phoned Paul and it is almost definite that we will become employer and employee starting the weekend after next.

❧

When your only tool is a hammer, you tend to approach every problem as though it were a nail.

Abraham Maslow

❧

Life is the art of getting along without what you couldn't possibly get along without.

J.G.

May 20

In the late afternoon I drove to the Woodlawn section of town to attend a party given by one of my Johns Hopkins classmates. After spending the 1971–72 school year together, and winning an M.A. in creative writing under Elliott Coleman, about thirty-five of us graduated just seven years ago this week. Eminently likable Kraft Rompf and wife, Shirley, gave the party because another classmate, Terry Porter, was going to be in town. Among the guests were two other local classmates, Roger and Maggie.

I brought along a class list and exchanged information about our far-flung mates. Duane Niatum, an American Indian, was being interviewed on the *Today* show when he was cut short by a special report on Frank McGee, the TV personality who had just died. Gil Scott Heron is still making news and music on the New York black scene. David and Betsy have split up, as have Tony and Sally.

On hand was also a turbulent poet who has just been divorced. I quoted Snodgrass: "Without love we die; with love we kill each other." Though not a Catholic, he told me he recently went to confession to a priest-friend, not to confess a sin or sins, but "my whole damned life." I respect these searching, aspiring, often tormented human beings. The divine voice at the end of Goethe's *Faust* spoke consoling words:

🌲

"*Wer immer strebend sich bemüht, Den können wir erlösen:* Whoever troubles himself with constant striving, him we can save."

May 21

Some of us don't have it hard—we just take it hard.

May 22

The mosquito is a small creature designed by the Creator to make us think better of flies.

May 23

Josephine Jacobsen and I were both friends of a remarkable crippled woman named Flossie McFee. Though confined to a wheelchair and afflicted with twisted hands, she not only wrote beautiful poetry, but she wrote poetry and everything else with a royally beautiful script. Nine years ago tonight I attended the opera *Rigoletto* as her guest at the Lyric Theatre. It had been quite an achievement to get her in and out of her chair, and in and out of my car. But we were finally safe in our box seats, enjoying *La Donna e Mobile* and the other music.

Before the final act I went to the men's lounge for a drink of water. There, for the first time in many years, I ran into George P. Mahoney, who two years earlier had been defeated in his race for the Maryland governorship. He gave me and my clerical collar an automatic, oleaginous smile, and then realized who I was. Yes, I was the former editor of the *Catholic Review* who in a pre-election "Open Letter" had stated that I could not vote for Mahoney because he was running a racist campaign.

It looked as though Mahoney were going to win—one network had even predicted him the winner on election night—but he was defeated. His aides said "his own people" had let him down. My "Open Letter" and the wide publicity given it were cited as factors in his loss.

Now he was looking the villain right in the eye. Mr. Mahoney lit into me, accused me of conniving with my lawyer brother to defeat him and take from him the thing he wanted most in life. I was a rotten priest and had flown to Rome expressly to throw my monsignorial robes in Pope Paul's face after his anti-birth control encyclical.

Everyone had left the lounge. I could hear that act four was under way, but on and on went Mr. Mahoney's flattering attack on my writer's pen. I thought I would give him the satisfaction of venting his rage, but he grew only increasingly angry. At length he grabbed my coat lapel and I was sure he would strike me if I made the wrong move. After about twenty minutes I told him I had to get back to the opera, where Rigoletto was unwittingly causing his own daughter's death. I explained briefly to Flossie what had kept me so long.

After the opera, I was wheeling Flossie down the ramp toward the exit. Up ahead I could see Mr. Mahoney pointing me out (in my clericals) to his statuesque second wife, decked out in a long white satin dress. Defying gravity, she flowed up the ramp, approached me, and in her thick southern drawl inquired, "Are *you* Monsignor Gallagher?" I confessed and did not deny. "Well," she continued, "Ah just want you to know that every night Ah pray that Ah'll see you burn in hale."

Trying to be a gentleman in the midst of the crowd that pressed all around us, I responded, "Well, I hope you won't *be* there to see it." At which point Flossie raised up her twisted head, eyed the regal lady, and affirmed, "You'll be there!" All in all it was quite a scene.

To get Flossie to my car, I had to cross a few dark streets, pushing her wheelchair slowly. In my paranoia I could imagine a big limousine suddenly bearing down on us. The irony was that patient, loving Flossie eventually moved to Mexico and had just found her first devoted sweetheart when she was killed in a car accident. If and when I get to heaven I fully expect that she'll be there.

"I taught you to love your brother."
"There is nothing left to love."
"There is always something left to love. And if you ain't
learned that, you ain't learned nothing."

Lorraine Hansberry, A Raisin in the Sun

May 24

Today I flew on Allegheny to Indianapolis, in the heart of Indiana. The flight took ninety minutes. Clearly in the air was the annual fever generated by the Indianapolis 500 car race scheduled to be held Sunday of this Memorial Day weekend. ("What do you think of the Indianapolis 500?" "They're all guilty!" said a gentleman weary of the antiwar protests of groups like the Catonsville Seven and the Harrisburg Nine.)

After a three-hour layover, I took an Ozark plane to Des Moines, Iowa, seventy minutes away, where Roberta MacDermott and John Standafer awaited me. They have asked me to preach at their wedding this Saturday.

We drove an hour farther west to Roberta's home in the tiny town of Jamaica (population 280). John later took me to the nearby house of Grandma Gannon, where I was to be lodged for the next few days.

You'd think I could remember incandescently the first time I ever flew. I *think* my maiden flight was just two dozen years ago and also took me to Iowa for the first Mass of my seminary classmate and roommate John Hynes of Davenport. Since then I have flown cross-country, across the Atlantic to Europe, and across the Mediterranean to Asia. Occasionally some fear of flying grips me, but I am generally rather matter-of-fact about the experience.

I think I am more afraid of falling out of a plane than of crashing in one. Does my (our) fear come from the guilty feeling that an earth-bound wingless creature has trespassed haughtily into forbidden heights?

On my cross-country bus trip last year I discovered in California that an airline exists which calls itself Icarus. The person who named that line was either ignorant of the ultimate fate of Icarus or had a macabre sense of humor. In any case, I think I would prefer to deprive that airline of my patronage.

❦

"So this was your first flight. Were you scared?"
"Well, to tell the truth, I never did put my full weight down on the seat."

May 25

Groom-to-be John came over at 7:30 for a hearty breakfast with me at Grandma Gannon's. Then back we drove to the Des Moines airport to pick up best-man Steve Chapelle, who had flown in from Maryland on American Airlines via Chicago's O'Hare airport.

Back in Jamaica we stopped at the tavern run by the bride's brother John and enjoyed a beer in a frosted mug. While we were there, a CBS bulletin came over the TV: an American Airlines jet plane had crashed just after takeoff at Chicago's O'Hare. We would later learn that the 271 resultant deaths made it the nation's worst single airline disaster. The equivalent of virtually the whole town of Jamaica was wiped out.

❦

This is the simple truth: that to live is to find oneself lost. He who accepts that has already begun to find himself, to be on firm ground.

Ortega y Gasset

May 26

Iowa artist Grant Wood ("Painter of the Soil") was on the verge of painting his classic *American Gothic* when I was born. This morning, after an early breakfast of bacon and eggs, I took a stroll around Jamaica, a city boy savoring the refreshment of grazing cattle, winging swallows, red barns, and white fences. The air was clean and coolish, the cerulean sky full of busy clouds.

Bridegroom and best man arrived for lunch around noon. Shortly after one, Father Tim and I drove again to St. Patrick's Church in

Bayard. The Nuptial Mass started at two, exactly on time—a rarity which does not invalidate the ceremony.

I then preached the homily, quoting the recipe for a happy marriage which a German priest gave to a woman I once met: "*Nicht fröhlich sein aber fröhlich machen* (Not to be happy but to make happy)." The German quote was a special touch for John, who served in the U.S. Air Force in Germany.

As a wedding gift for Roberta and John, I had given them a lovely silver tray which had belonged to Victorine Robertson. On the night of their engagement, the young couple had met at the house which I had inherited from Victorine.

It had just started to rain as I entered the church. As John in his black tuxedo and Roberta in her white satin walked down the aisle married, a thunderclap sounded to put a heavenly seal on the event.

For the reception we all drove to the community hall of another small town, Yale, another ten miles away.

Roberta's mother, Jeanne, invited me to dance, something I had never tried until a few years ago. She was gracious enough to detect good rhythm in my stammering steps. Probably because I have done so little dancing I am mesmerized by the sight of it. Last night at least I was only a little saddened by the thought of all the merry dancing my aging feet have never done. (I never saw my parents dance.) If Dante is right, there will be dancing galore on the heavenly floor. Meantime, according to Thomas Merton, we are invited to forget ourselves on purpose, cast our awful solemnity to the winds, and join in the general dance.

❦

Everything that touches us, you and me, brings us together as a bowstring does, drawing out of two strings a single voice.

Rainer Maria Rilke

May 27

I bought a Chicago *Tribune* at the Des Moines airport. Two large colored pictures of the Friday air disaster were featured on the front page, and related stories appeared on several other pages. One article spoke of a man who had generously surrendered his seat on the fatal plane to a young woman in a hurry. Another suggested that the passengers may have seen their own spinning and crashing on the closed-circuit TV.

I left Indianapolis before noon for the ninety-minute flight to Baltimore. There were two nuns in my row and a nun in front of me. One of the nuns was working her rosary. It seemed to be a nervous flight for the young girl beside me. I heard of a pilot who saw a clergyman on board his flight and told him that he now felt safer. Replied the clergyman, "Remember, I'm with personnel and not administration."

※

There are some things which not even the youngest curate can explain.

Leonard Merrick

May 28

Today is one of the days on which Memorial Day is being observed this week. What I am copiously remembering is my ordination as a priest in Baltimore's old cathedral twenty-four years ago this morning. I recall asking a classmate who had been ordained a few weeks earlier whether he had felt elevated by his ordination. "No," he answered, "I feel as though the priesthood has been lowered."

My day arrived after I had spent twelve years in four different seminaries. Today I attended Mass at the old cathedral. The rector, Father Paul Love, was the celebrant. In January of 1957 I had replaced him as archdiocesan archivist.

Things have obviously changed in two dozen years. He said the Mass in English, facing the people and using a portable altar near the sanctuary railing. (I, who had been in charge of the altar boys when I was assigned to the cathedral, noted that he had no altar boy.) The text of the Canon of the Mass has changed, and there are optional canons which did not exist in 1955. I could receive the sacred Host in my hands if I chose to.

Because of its beauty and historical associations, this church bears the honorary title of a Minor Basilica. Benjamin Henry Latrobe designed it in the early 1800s; Bishop John Carroll broke ground for it in 1806; it was opened for services in 1821. In a supplement to his 1936 book, *European Church Architecture,* expert Nicholas Pevsner called this edifice "the most beautiful church in North America." Next week it will be one of four buildings honored for their architecture by new U.S. stamps.

So some things have remained the same: the exterior is still marked by those columns, onion-shaped spires, and massive dome that I gazed at as a young boy while listening to music in the library across the street. The interior is still spacious and simple; the multiple circles induce a sense of serenity and fulfillment. Cardinal Gibbons' red hat still hangs crumbling from the arch above the Lady Altar.

There were about twenty people at Mass this morning: four nuns, fifteen other women (most elderly), another man, and myself. (I mused: maybe that's why priests must be males—so that at all Masses there will be at least one representative of that half of the human race.) After Mass, one lady recognized me and called out my name. Her companion, noting, no doubt, my beard, said, "Father Gallagher? I thought you were a pipe fitter."

Twenty-four years ago this building was crowded with the families and friends of myself and the nine other seminarians who were ordained that day. Among the other remembered dead on this Memorial Day: Archbishop Keough, who ordained me; my mother and older brother; "Ma" Nunes, the mother of my friend and classmate Joe, who was to have been ordained around this time but who died the previous October. Then, as now, my younger brother is in the far West.

I had entered the seminary when I was just over fourteen years of age. To this day I can clearly recall the moment when I decided I must be a priest. I was about nine years old, and living near Grandmother Doyle's. Somebody mentioned that a neighborhood boy had gone away "to become a priest." I was astonished at the thought that anyone could *become* a priest. I had encountered no relatives or family friends who were priests, but I had seen them doing their holy things at the awesome altar. I had thought these men were somehow always there, like God Himself. If you could become a priest, then surely you must want to—at least I had to. (No doubt I was also attracted to the church as a hospital and peacemaker. Oh the irony that it has lately become a battlefield and self-wounding sword!)

I doubt if I discussed this matter much with my parents, but at St. Ann's grammar school, well before I finished the eighth grade, I spoke my desire to the priest in charge of the drum corps, Father

Dan McGrath. In view of my firm resolve, it must have seemed proper to him that I enter the minor seminary for high school; and so I did, even though I had won a full scholarship to Loyola High School. I had won only a half scholarship to St. Charles Seminary; but this was actually worth more, since it covered six years and included room and board.

From the financial point of view (which was critical at home in those days) the seminary was a good place for me to attend high school and junior college. Within the year my father died, and my pastor at St. Ann's, Monsignor Harry Quinn, told my mother that the parish would take care of the balance of my annual tuition (which was $420 *in toto* in those days!).

I had taken a leave of absence from the seminary in the spring of 1950—as I was finishing my first year of philosophy at the Catholic University. The pressure of disliked studies joined with emotional depression and life confusion to make my situation intolerable. After some weeks at home I returned, completed the year as a lay student living in a private home, and happily rejoined most of my St. Charles classmates at Baltimore's old St. Mary's the following September.

Once again, three years later, I found seminary life and religious preoccupation insupportable. Once again theological gloom and confusion had produced a paralyzing depression in me. I had actually told the seminary rector that I was leaving, but as I was doing my farewell laundry, a surge of energy and rededication overtook me by surprise, and kept me at the new St. Mary's until ordination day.

I probably underwent ordination in a kind of numbness. As usual, I was not at all sure how well prepared I was—even for a church which was relatively tame and orderly. No doubt I was overly serious about all the serious things of life, despite my reputation for wit and humor.

Aspects of my personality such as wrath and sexuality were so well repressed that I didn't realize they were repressed. I mean that these instincts were not free to surface naturally and be rationally controlled.

It was vital for me to do everything perfectly. Unconsciously at least, I didn't believe that I could be loved for myself. At best I had to see to it that at least I was not rejected for failing to perform everything with prompt and flawless excellence.

Today I studied the composite picture of my ordination class. There were 108 of us from all over the States, and from China and

Japan as well. One of my Japanese classmates is now the Archbishop of Osaka; the Chinese priest has left the priesthood and is now married. Eighteen other classmates have left the ministry. The first to do so was rigidly anti-Communist and extravagantly pious. Another has a job playing a piano in a bar. A third was an outstanding chaplain in Vietnam. Some of the others were among the most serious and religious members of our class.

Five of my classmates have died: one of cancer, another of heart disease, a third of general complications. Two died in car crashes—one as he returned from delivering food to a needy family on Christmas Eve.

Of those eighty-four remaining in the ministry, I know four who have had serious nervous breakdowns. Three others have reputations as notorious conservatives. To my knowledge, only a few have gotten into "trouble" with women or altar boys.

All in all, I find myself keenly admiring my classmates now that I am twice as old as I was when I last saw many of them. I feel especially understanding of those who have left. I find in myself no need and even less right to criticize any of them.

We came to find ourselves as leaders in a church more turbulent and confusing than we could ever have imagined. The new liturgy required us to turn our backs on the sanctuary instead of facing it. The new church required us to turn our backs on much that we were rigorously prepared to explain and defend. (The heart's ivy of affection attaches itself—alas—even to nonessentials.) We knew the old church well; we felt the excitement of the Council years; we have tasted the disappointment and bitterness of the post-conciliar years.

The Old Testament Book of Sirach had advised us, "My son, when you come to serve the Lord, prepare yourself for trials." But we had no idea . . . and yet, we have seen gracious and heroic happenings—sometimes in ourselves—such as we could never have imagined.

"Without suffering," wrote the French writer Léon Bloy, "there can be no revelation." We had read those prophetic words which the old man Simeon spoke to the young mother of Jesus in the Temple of Jerusalem: "Thy own soul a sword shall pierce, that the thoughts of many hearts may be revealed" (Luke 2:35). These were mysterious words, weren't they, my scattered classmates, when we read them in our youth? Wherever you are tonight, in this world or in another, in the ministry, or with your wives and children, or with your lonely selves, as liberal or conservative Catholics or lapsed Catholics or former Catholics, do we not know better now what those words mean?

I like the freshness, the dedication, and the idealism I saw again in your photographs today. You have probably lost some of that glow along with your hair. I hope you have attained a better, more lasting beauty and that you feel some of the joy of it tonight.

> I understood how impossible it was for me to be religious up to a certain point.
>
> *Soren Kierkegaard*

May 29

Two dozen years have passed today since I offered my first Mass at the Church of Saints Philip and James. It had been my parish church for several years—since my mother moved from St. Ann's to Maryland and Twenty-seventh. It was at my new parish that I originally got to know the future Cardinal Shehan, who was its pastor at that time.

The church itself is spacious. Unlike the old cathedral, it is unimpeded by pillars; like the old cathedral, it is crowned with a large dome. When I attended noon Mass there today, a new side chapel was used. It was crowded with about twelve men and twenty-four women—most on the senior citizen side of life. The setting gave me a sense of cramp, and I longed for the generosity of the main church. Young and genial Father Bowen had the Mass; he was the priest who concelebrated the baby Woloszyn's funeral with me a few weeks ago.

The chalice I used for my first Mass was in part donated by the Nunes family in Rhode Island. The day my friend Joe Nunes died he was going to make his final decisions on the design of his chalice. My chalice was the one Joe was going to get, though the inscriptions were my own, and the few gems and gold decorations came from the rings of relatives of mine.

The inscription around the base—"*Oblatus Est Quia Voluit* (He was offered because He willed it)"—was taken from the inscription on front of the main altar of the seminary's new chapel, which opened up the week Joe died. On the underside of the chalice I quoted the words of Jesus about the dead Lazarus: "*Amicus Noster Dormit* (Our Friend Is Sleeping)." In his sermon at my first Mass my friend and seminary teacher Father Gene Walsh told the story of the chalice. As I mentioned, Joe Nunes' mother attended my ordination. It strikes me now more than ever how hard that must have been on her.

❈

Four archangels watched as God created the world. Each had a question: What are You doing? How are You doing it? Why are You doing it? Can I help?

May 30

As I begin my twenty-fifth year in the priesthood I'm doing plenty of recalling, some of which I plan to share in the coming days. For instance, I ran across a note recording the fact that in 1957 I heard 5,914 confessions at the old cathedral, where confessions were heard daily. In the past year I have heard scarcely fourteen.

I agree with the priest who said that whoever thought the confessional was the invention of priests as a way of keeping control over the people never sat in a dark, stuffy box for countless hours. There are some consoling and dramatic moments, but it is often sheer drudgery. For me personally, as I have grown older, the business of dealing with other people's consciences has become increasingly unpalatable.

One of my seminary teachers used to say that some people's consciences weigh in grams, and others' in tons. Scrupulous penitents can drive you mad—people who fret over how many distractions they may have had while they were saying their morning prayers, or how often they have missed their grace after meals. Hearing such confessions has been knowingly compared to being nibbled to death by ducks, or stoned to death by marshmallows. You even find (or used to find) penitents who return to make their tortured confession all over again because they are afraid they were distracted while saying their "penance" and hence invalidated their confession. (Speaking of penances: On one occasion I wanted to recommend a certain Gospel passage to a depressed lady. "Do you have a New Testament at home?" I asked. "No," she answered with apologetic tone, "I'm afraid ours is pretty old.")

Once, after hearing strange sounds, I discovered that a Catholic youngster had brought a non-Catholic buddy into the confessional with him, to give him a close-up view of the experience. On another occasion a little black boy brightened my day by confessing that he had told "a white lie."

Often a confessor has a penitent on either side of him, and uses a sliding door to maintain privacy. Once, after dealing at some length with a difficult penitent, I slid the door open for the opposite penitent: "I couldn't help overhearing that other penitent, Father," a voice in the dark announced, "and if I had been you I would have told him . . ."

I heard of a penitent who kept using the phrase "more or less" to indicate the number of times he had gone astray. He even said "Once, more or less." The confessor retaliated by saying, "For your penance say the Lord's Prayer once, more or less."

When a youngster was once told to say two Our Fathers for his penance, he pleaded, "But I only know one." Youngsters have long been the best brighteners of confessional darkness, especially with their well-intentioned variations on the traditional formulas for confessing and making the Act of Contrition. A composite of such variations might go like this:

Penitent: "Blast me, Father, for I have sins. This is my last confession . . since a month ago. I said 'Damn it' four times—three times before, and once just now. I ate meat on Friday."

Priest: "Anything else?"

Penitent: "Oh, yes: potatoes and gravy and corn. I am sorry for these and all the sins of my fast life."

Priest: "All right. Now make a good act of contrition."

Penitent: "A GOOD ACT OF CONTRITION—Oh my God I am hardly [heartily] sorry for having defended [offended] Thee, and I test [detest] all my sins because I dread the laws [loss] of heaven. . . . I firmly dissolve [resolve] to help Thy grace [with the help of Thy grace] to do the penance [to do penance] and to end [amend] my life. Amen."

These stories have reminded me of my own first confession, which I made when I was seven. I recall drawing up a list of my major offenses, and then wondering whether I was measuring up to expectations. "Mom," I inquired, "are thirty-four sins enough?"

At this point I can't recall the first confession I ever heard. But I did hear a story about an old pastor celebrating his silver anniversary at a banquet. In his speech he mentioned that he would never forget his first confession, since it involved a murder.

The town's mayor was an invited guest, but didn't arrive till after the speech. When the mayor rose to extend his congratulations, he said, "Father O'Flaherty probably never knew this, but I had the honor of being the very first person to enter his confessional."

Actually, I don't think a priest would have pinpointed a confession that specifically, lest he violate the seal of the confessional. I have never had trouble keeping silent about what I learned in the confessional, though I was once put on the spot by a wife who sent her husband to see me after he had promised her to tell me all. Shortly after he left, the phone rang and the wife inquired, "Did he tell you about the adultery?"

To be honest, I can't recall how I handled that one. I hope that by then I had learned a trick which someone else taught me. What you say when you don't want to say anything is "Well, of course, I never discuss anything like that over the telephone."

I wouldn't want to conclude these comments without stressing the fact that some of my most treasured priestly moments have occurred in the confessional. The whole subject of mercy and reconciliation touches the deepest roots of me. Once, at an airport, a man with a crushing weight on his conscience saw my collar, asked if I was truly a priest, and then trustingly confided a story which simultaneously melted my heart and caused my hair to stand on end. I'm not sure the man was even a Catholic.

In these privacy-violating times there aren't too many places besides the confessional where any man or woman of any faith or none at all can find, waiting and willing to listen, a human being who has placed himself forever under a vow of confidentiality.

And it must still be one of the most humbling and moving of human experiences for a man to have another human being approach him in absolute trust and, in the hope of healing, open up the most hidden recesses of his heart.

❧

You have no dirty hands because you have no hands at all.
                                                    Jean-Paul Sarte

May 31

Thinking back over my priesthood today, I recalled running into a young woman in New York's Grand Central Station. Obviously unhinged, she said she had been taking consecrated Hosts from her mouth at Communion time and storing them up in her purse. I asked to have them. She said no. So I left this walking tabernacle and ran for my train. The Roman collar is a magnet.

Today I looked over a list of marriages I have performed or preached at in the seventies. My all-time record was a total of three weddings and three receptions in two cities in one day. All three couples split up, but two have reunited. I wasn't in regular parish life this past decade, so most of my weddings involved relatives or personal friends, mostly former seminarians.

(I had dozens upon dozens of weddings during my seven years at the old cathedral, which is near the marriage license bureau. In those days Maryland law required that a clergyman preside at all marriages, even if the couple was agnostic or atheist. I wrote a *Catholic Review* editorial against these "Spiritual Shotgun Weddings," just as a bill repealing the law was defeated. I was later told that the legislators had thought "the Catholic Church" backed the old law, but my editorial indicated otherwise. The bill was revived and passed.)

As I calculate, I was involved in forty-three weddings in the seventies. In twenty-nine of these, former seminarians were being married; in five, relatives. As far as I know, eleven of the forty-three couples have split up—six involving seminarians and four involving relatives. As Judy Collins sings, "These Are Hard Times for Lovers."

My cousin Gene often takes pictures professionally at weddings. He says, only half jokingly, that he tries to develop the pictures fast enough to get them back to the couple before they break up. Samuel Johnson said that a second marriage is a triumph of hope over experience. That's getting to be true of first marriages.

When I taught preaching at the seminary I urged my students to use picturesque examples. One student wanted to show how a good marriage is more than the sum of its parts. Following my advice, he came up with an example which he meant to be serious but which divorced all his listeners from sobriety. Marriage, he said, is like the number "8"—it happens when two zeros get together.

Once a toastmaster asked me to suggest a toast for the bride and groom. "May you live as long as you want, and never want as long as you live" was the one he decided to use. But by adding one little word he brought down the house. Said he, "May you live together as long as you want . . ." (How short can long be? One of our Baltimore priests concluded a wedding by announcing: "Go in peace; the Mass and the marriage are ended.")

I like an experiment which is reportedly being tried in the French church. The sacrament of matrimony is reserved for those practicing and serious Catholics who wish their bond to mirror Christ's faithful love for His people. Catholics who do not feel ready for such a commitment can enter into another form of marriage recognized by the church but not considered sacramental (and unbreakable). . . .

Bishop Frank Murphy, our auxiliary, phoned tonight to see if I could give him some ideas and stories for graduation talks he has to give. I told him about the bishop who was visiting a small town which had a morning paper. The bishop was due to administer Confirmation two nights in a row, and wanted to tell the same few humorous stories at each service. When he saw a reporter covering the first night's event, the bishop requested that he not report the little pleasantries he was going to use. The reporter kept his word. As he said in his story: "The bishop told several stories that cannot be printed."

The power of the press was also impressed on Matt Shanley, one of my priest-classmates. He was stationed in a little Connecticut town and got involved with a local ballteam, though he suspected that the chancery office in Hartford might not like the idea. But surely, he thought, the officials there will never find out. As he pitched a championship game, snow started to fall, a photographer snapped the scene, and Matt's name and picture appeared on the front page of newspapers throughout the state.

✤

There are ecclesiastics, well-meaning, hard-working and, within their limits, capable men . . . who never yet expose the faith of their flock to such imminent peril as when they attempt to expound it.

Lewis May

June 1, 1979

June 1, 1963, was a Saturday. The police were waiting at the Senator Bar on Baltimore's Howard Street. At length a man dressed as a sailor walked in. He was arrested for murder.

The man had been coming there regularly on Saturday nights. He would sit alone, quietly drinking. Occasionally he would play the piano. Precisely at midnight he would say good night to the waitress and leave.

On the previous Saturday he had begun talking with another customer, who lived in the neighborhood. That man invited the sailor to his apartment. They sang awhile—a man in the next room remembered hearing "Get Me to the Church on Time." Then he heard what sounded like a tussle and a fall. The sailor left. The neighbor checked the room later and found the tenant unconscious from a crack on the head. A few days later he died.

Early the morning after the arrest, Archbishop Shehan phoned my lawyer brother. It turned out that the "sailor" was a priest from a neighboring diocese. My brother went at once to the jail to see him. Apparently the man who invited the priest to his apartment had made a sexual advance. The priest pushed him away angrily and left.

The police at the jail had been grilling the priest roughly, insulting and degrading him. The priest's own chancellor arrived, and to raise the self-respect of the dejected priest he humbly asked the prisoner to hear his confession.

The business of wearing a sailor suit—seemingly that was due to some mental quirk on the part of the priest, who did not have a regular parish assignment. Through my brother's efforts, he was transferred to a mental hospital.

That's all I heard of the story. Except for two comments: the priest's own bishop lamented, "I can see the headlines now—'Pope John XXIII Dies; Local Priest Arrested for Murder.'" A waitress at the bar told my brother she remembered that polite sailor, and how he played the piano, and how his favorite song was "Get Me to the Church on Time."

On this day in 1964, another priest was gotten to the church on time in an eerie way. He was William Kailer Dunn of the Baltimore archdiocese, and June 1, 1964, was the silver jubilee of his ordination. Since he was a college chaplain and had no parish of his own, he asked the rector of the new cathedral whether he might celebrate his anniversary Mass there with family and friends. Monsignor Whelan checked the schedule book, saw that the morning of June 1 was clear, and marked down 10 A.M. and the priest's name. This was early in February, so that the name, date, and hour lay waiting in the book for several months.

On June 1, 1964, at 10 A.M. the funeral of William Kailer Dunn was celebrated in the new cathedral.

If you were arrested for being a Christian, would there be any evidence against you?

June 2

A decade ago today old St. Mary's Seminary, my alma mater in the heart of downtown Baltimore, had its last graduation before closing down and being torn down. I had graduated from that senior college in 1951, and had returned as a teacher from 1967 to the end. So these were "my students" who were writing the finale to a history that had begun in 1791.

There was a spirit and an atmosphere about the giant old building that most students loved. Its wide wooden floors and high ceilings suggested a spaciousness and natural ruggedness that befitted the two years devoted to "philosophy" on that hallowed spot.

Its neo-Gothic chapel—the first such structure in the U.S.—is a gem that has been recognized as such by national landmark agencies. During one early morning Mass while I was a student at Paca Street, we were apparently singing our hymns rather languidly in that chapel. After the Gospel the rector turned around at the altar and chastised us for our dopey performance. "Sing out like men: Sing out!" he commanded. How could he have known that the next scheduled hymn was "Let All Mortal Flesh Keep Silence"?

At high Masses, faculty members sat in special pews at the far end of the chapel. The master of ceremonies was once instructing new students in liturgical etiquette. "Keep your birettas in your hands," he advised in his halting manner, "until the deacon . . . has returned . . . from giving the Kiss of Peace . . . to the Fathers . . . in the rear."

Paca Street had many a legend. One of the best pertained to an Irish student who at the beginning of supper was taking his turn reading to the community an excerpt from the Gospel. In so doing he pronounced the name of Mary Magdalen as Mary MacDillon. The French-born rector interrupted him to ask whether he was implying that the saint was Irish. "Well, I don't know for sure," the student replied, "but she certainly had French ways, didn't she?"

In my day there was an unworldly priest, Father Aycock, who had an unusual and much imitated way of talking. In the days of quiet seminaries, singing in the showers would have been against the holy rule. Well, one of my contemporaries was crooning away amid the suds one afternoon, when he heard a voice saying, *à la* Father Aycock: "Oh yeah, who's that singing in the showers?" Thinking it was a fellow student, my friend blithely replied, "It's Ingrid Bergman." "Well, then, please report to my room when you're finished, Mr. Bergman!"

This same priest taught biology, and the school catalogue straight-facedly announced that his course consisted of "a series of crosses." In one exam he asked the class to "compare the amoeba." "With what?" asked one student in the name of many. "Oh yeah," replied Father Aycock warily, "you want me to give away the answer?"

I heard of one Paca Street teacher who was writing on the blackboard when some student made a disruptive noise. The priest turned around and frowned, but said nothing. At the end of class, however, he stationed himself at the sole exit from the room. As each student went past, the teacher asked him whether he was the one who had made that noise. One by one the students denied being the culprit. So when the final student appeared, the priest didn't even question him, but simply and trustingly gave him a slap.

I myself was once sitting in on an oral exam and heard another seminary teacher ask a student to explain the concept of "theandric" actions as applied to Christ. The student looked confused, so the priest tried to be helpful.

"You know," he said, "actions which involve the human nature of Christ on the one hand, and His divine nature on the—"

"Other?" suggested the student.

"Very good. Very good."

This same priest had an ingenious way of trying to explain how the Psalmist in Psalm 136 could have wished to see the children of his enemies smashed against a wall. "You must remember, little Babylonians grew up to be big Babylonians."

One severe-looking rector grew up to be almost a divine figure in the eyes of the students. At least they gave him the nickname of Yahweh. One day a seminarian was passing by this Father Laubacher's door, and for the amusement of some nearby classmates he solemnly genuflected toward that awesome portal. Just at that point lo! and behold! the door opened and Yahweh, granting an epiphany, begged to be informed as to just what the student thought he was doing.

"Why, er, uh, I'm just tying my shoelaces."

"On loafers?" replied the all-seeing rector.

A special spring anthem of the old place was "Ball over," shouted by athletic students when somebody slugged one over the high wall, which was protectively covered with broken glass. In those days of friendlier race relations, the neighboring black kids could be relied upon to throw the ball back over into what they sometimes called "the priest factory."

There was something special about Paca Street and something special, too, I believe, about the last few years of seminarians to study there. They were still aglow with the memory of Pope John and John Kennedy, still stirred by the promise of Vatican II. To Paca Street and its last two years of students I dedicated my book *The Christian Under Pressure*. In my grateful fondness I may have slighted earlier generations. But I may be excused, I trust, for having had my own special reasons for saying, "Your best wine was last."

On a June day in 1951, I myself had graduated from old St. Mary's, one of a class of 115. Little did I suspect that eighteen years later, as a faculty member, I would attend its final graduation, and that in subsequent years I would drive by the site where my alma mater had been for so long so massively present but is now so massively gone.

✤

Consider that this day will never dawn again.

Vergil to Dante in the Purgatorio

June 3

It was emblematic of Pope John XXIII's courtesy that he died on a date which is so easy to remember: 6/3/63. Also, born in '81 he died at 81.

I had a special preoccupation with that pope's last days, for at the time I was an editor of the *Catholic Review* and my associate editor, Dave Maguire, was away on a trip to South America. Normally we would have gone to press on Thursday, May 30, but that was Memorial Day in 1963. At first we thought we'd go to press on Wednesday, but the pope's condition was critical and he could have been dead several days before our weekly paper reached some of our subscribers. In that event, it would be embarrassingly anticlimactic to have run the headline "Pope Ill."

So we decided to wait until Friday. On Thursday he was reported to have improved; then at 8:15 A.M. on Friday a bulletin flashed that he was much worse. We had prepared a special edition of the paper, with postmortem statements from Archbishop Shehan, the governor, the mayor of Baltimore, and others. If we went to press that day most of our subscribers wouldn't get the paper until Monday or Tuesday. Minute by minute we listened to the radio, trying to decide what to do.

Our press run was about 90,000 copies. By 1 P.M., I decided we couldn't wait any longer. Our main story dealt with the pope as gravely ill—something everyone knew already since the whole planet seemed to be engaged in a death watch. One week earlier, in his last public appearance at the window of his study, he had told the world that his bags were packed and he was ready to go.

We returned to the printer's on Saturday, sure that the pope would die any second. Omitting any date from the paper, we went ahead and printed the special six-page obituary issue. We delivered these to sixty parishes around the city, phoning the pastors and asking them to distribute the issue at Sunday Masses only if the pope had died. He didn't die, it may be recalled, until Monday afternoon; but at least one parish gave out the issue on Sunday anyway. That earned for us some indignant phone calls.

Looked back on now, the whole episode seems like much ado about nothing. But most newsmen hate to publish stale news on a major event, and we really wanted to do something special for that beloved man.

I had seen him in person only once, at a general audience in St. Peter's on July 5, 1961. The Basilica was jam-packed, and as we waited for the pope different national groups took turns singing native hymns. When the big back doors were closed we knew the moment was imminent. Like a sagebrush fire, applause swept up from the back of the world's largest church.

Held aloft in the portable chair that he detested, the sunny old man was everything I expected. There is an electric and "catholic" feeling at such papal moments that must be unique in all the world. You can almost believe that peace on earth is truly possible—almost easy.

The pope gave a talk in Italian which wasn't short. As his remarks were summarized in various languages, he looked about, smiling, swinging his feet above a white pillow. He had been taking English lessons, but he didn't speak it often in public. (He apologized to one U.S. group, saying that "In heaven we shall all speak American.")

I heard of a small audience which the pope gave not long before his death. In the group was a woman dying from cancer—her family had given her this trip as a final gift. Pope John came into the room, looked over the faces, and then walked to the ailing woman. Touching her arms, he whispered, "We shall meet soon again."

I never tire of remembering and repeating the genius of what this pope said to Khrushchev's son-in-law during the first audience of a pope with a Communist leader: "They tell me, sir, that you are an atheist; but surely you will not forbid an old man to send his blessing to your children."

In my editorial on Pope John's death, I cited from the talk he gave from his study window on the evening of the day he inaugurated the Second Vatican Council: "'Let us continue,' he begged, 'to love one another, emphasizing what unites us, and avoiding all that can keep us divided. And now when you return home I want you to embrace your children and to tell them that this is the embrace of the pope.' Then he stepped from view. But the light kept shining through the empty window."

It was because he said and meant such things that when he died the cartoonist Herblock drew a globe with a wreath around it, and inscribed five simple words. When I wrote to the Washington *Post* artist for permission to reprint the cartoon, he not only said yes, but sent me the original with its wording: "A Death in the Family."

When word of that death finally arrived amid a heavy downpour in Baltimore, I was in my office at the *Catholic Review*. I phoned Archbishop Shehan, who directed that the Basilica bells be tolled. Earlier that day, giving my final exam at St. Paul's Latin High School, I asked my students to comment on Christina Rossetti's poem *When I Am Dead, My Dearest, Sing No Sad Songs for Me*. One of my students, in a kind of awkward loveliness, wrote, "It places a peaceful feeling in you." Pope John's life—even his death—did just that for me and millions of others. On his eightieth birthday he had said, "Any day is a good day to be born on or a good day to die on." But June 3 will always be special.

🌳

Be noble, and the nobleness that lies/in other men, sleeping, but never dead,/will rise in majesty to meet thine own.

James R. Lowell

June 4

In my callow youth I was as uncritical an admirer of J. Edgar Hoover as most Americans were. I had special experiences, though, of the all-seeing eye of this director of the FBI. On April 11, 1958, I wrote a laudatory review for the *Catholic Review* of his *Masters of Deceit*. Six days later he sent me a letter of "sincere thanks," finding it "certainly encouraging that this book was so well received by you."

Three years later, concerned about self-appointed Communist hunters, I quoted in an editorial Mr. Hoover's warnings about the dangerous naïveté of such people. Within two weeks I had a second letter in which the director said he trusted "I will continue to merit your strong support."

That he didn't so continue might have been deduced from a packet which I received ten years ago yesterday. In it were 100 complimentary buttons from Personality Posters, Inc., New York. As more evidence surfaced of illegal bugging by the FBI, I thought the slogan "Hoover Bugs Me" would be timely. I phoned the idea to a New York button company and they adopted it. I have no idea how many buttons were sold, but to this day it remains the only button I ever begot.

As one who used to urge dubious young people to give the FBI the benefit of the doubt and not to underrate the subversive activities of Communists, I was certainly disillusioned and red-faced by the revelations of abuse by Mr. Hoover and the FBI. Senator Phil Hart spoke for many of us when he said he finally had to confess that his children were right and he was wrong—on this score and on others pertaining to dishonesty in the government and in the politics of the Vietnam War.

I thought again of this disillusionment when I saw a cartoon soon after the Three Mile Island incident. A straight-looking man, eyes bulging with fright, exclaims, "The weirdos were right again!"

🌳

Sincerity is believing your own propaganda.

June 5

Mary Lu, a nun friend of mine, was my guest for lunch. She teaches physics at Towson State University. Afterward, we drove down to the old cathedral, which was serving as a post-office-for-a-day because a new U.S. stamp featuring the Basilica was issued today, along with three others honoring "classical American architecture." In a few hours a total of 50,000 stamps were sold.

The date on the cancellation took me back eleven years to that day when a victorious Robert Kennedy was shot in a Los Angeles hotel. Three days later, at Ocean City, Maryland, I watched his funeral on TV and was unforgettably proud to be a Baltimorean when the train carrying his coffin reached our Pennsylvania Station. The large crowd of blacks and whites who waited to see the train pass spontaneously and gently began to sing "The Battle Hymn of the Republic."

Today was also the publication day in 1973 of my first book of poetry, *Painting on Silence*. A month earlier I had driven to Long Island to get my first advance copies, stopping to see Walt Whitman's birthplace and Theodore Roosevelt's tomb while I was in the vicinity. (I like to quote the inscription I read on his tomb that day:

something like, "Give me a man with his head in the stars and his feet on the ground.")

The eighty-seven poems in that book were mostly the result of my year in the creative writing seminars at Johns Hopkins. The title derived from a remark which the British conductor Thomas Beecham once made to a restless audience: "A painter paints on canvas; a musician paints on silence. We provide the music; you provide the silence."

Preparing this volume provided me with a needed distraction when in the same year as my brother's death his eldest son began a traumatic four-month stay in the hospital for a ruptured appendix. He now jokes with friends, "Get my uncle's book. It will become a collector's item since everybody else is burning theirs."

I gratefully dedicated that volume "to all the poems of my days, who came disguised as people and left a taste for song." One of the best of those poems was Josephine Jacobsen, who was bewitched enough by her friendliness to arrange for me to record the volume for the Library of Congress as she ended her term as poetry consultant there. . . .

I talked by phone tonight with Pat Corcoran, a favorite former student whose wife gave birth to their first child two days ago. He told me that as he held his daughter for the first time, he thought, "This is what life is all about, what makes it all worthwhile."

By last Sunday, though, life apparently seemed no longer worthwhile to the seminary doctor who was treating Pat for a persistent throat problem as he was preparing to quit the seminary. On the day Pat became a father, that doctor checked into a motel took an overdose of drugs, and died.

🌳

Do not seek death. Death will find you. But seek the road which makes death a fulfillment.

Dag Hammarskjöld

June 6

It's about 6:30 in the morning. Four hundred sleepy teen-agers kneel in the marble-walled chapel of the Baltimore junior seminary. Father White has just finished reading the meditation for the day and Mass is about to begin. For weeks he has been asking us to pray for our soldiers who are going to invade the European mainland. But drooped heads suddenly jerk up. He has just said, ". . . for our soldiers who invaded France this morning."

D-Day (1944) had arrived on our departure day—the summer vacation would begin that day. With my first year of high school completed, I would return for the first time to reside in a fatherless home. Some of my schoolmates may well have had fathers and brothers in that invasion, but no one close to me was in the service.

After breakfast we could hear newsboys in the neighborhood shouting their "Extra! Extra! Read all about it." Now we could go home and read the daily papers again—as we were not allowed to at St. Charles. (Sometimes the seminary unworldliness persisted even after ordination. When one parishioner who was interested in Portugal asked his pastor what he thought of Salazar, the pastor responded, "How long has he been in the parish?")

Available again, radios would play "When the Lights Go on Again (All Over the World)" and "(There'll Be Blue Birds Over) The White Cliffs of Dover" and "Johnny Doughboy Found a Rose in Ireland." President Roosevelt was getting ready to run for a fourth term, and Tom Dewey was getting ready to run against him. Shipbuilder Henry Kaiser was being dubbed "Sir Launch-a-lot," and giant convoys of merchant ships were plying the oceans. One such ship was wandering outside a protective smoke screen, so a destroyer signaled it, "Pardon me, but your ship is showing."

The government could use cooking grease in the war effort, and grocery stores were buying it from housewives. One busy store gained national attention with this sign: "Ladies: please don't bring your fat cans in here on Saturdays."

Another popular sign warned: "You can't spell victory with an absent-T."

There would be air-raid practices during the summer. Baltimore's famous gaslights had little wires hanging from them so that air-raid wardens could pull them and turn down the lights during the drills. On my way to Mass at St. Ann's on a morning after a drill I'd see shattered glass around some of those lampposts. If the wires didn't work the wardens simply sought out a stone or club and smashed the lamps.

Later on, June the sixth would mean the day of Robert Kennedy's death. When Kennedy broke with President Johnson over the war, I wrote the senator a letter of support. On March 25 of 1968 he replied. "Your views, along with those of thousands of other Americans who have been in touch with me, were a major factor in my decision to become a candidate for the Presidency."

One of the seminarians most active against the war is the Richmond priest in whose rectory this journal began. Gentle and genial Mike Schmied drove over today from a conference at Georgetown University and took me to supper in Little Italy for my upcoming birthday.

He talked about those many excellent classmates of his—the majority—who left the seminary partly because of the celibacy requirement, and of those numerous contemporaries in the priesthood who have left the ministry for the same reason. More pleasantly, we recalled our travels together to Rome, Athens, Constantinople, and Jerusalem. (Our Arab guide in the Holy City knew Robert Kennedy's assassin personally. "He was always crazy.")

Omaha Beach and My Lai seemed several lifetimes away.

✢

They shall not grow old as we that are left grow old; age shall not weary them nor the years condemn.

Inscription on a war memorial,
All Hallows Church, London

June 7

For the first time in a long time I saw in one day all my seven nieces and nephews (my "niblings," for short). The eldest of these took me to lunch at a new restaurant near the in-town bank where she is assistant manager. Then I took her brother, John, to the Motor Vehicles Administration to take the tests for a learner's permit. He passed. Next, we picked up his twin brothers and drove downtown to pick up their senior brother, Frank, outside his office. (He began working for the Maryland State's Attorney General Stephen Sachs this week.) From the back of the car, twelve-year-old Jimmy wanted to know if it was true that a Pope Leo died while committing adultery. His source was *The Book of Lists*. I told him everybody has his faults.

We all proceeded to my sister's house near Bethlehem Steel. Mary

Jo's eldest child, Patrick, was celebrating his fourteenth birthday with the assistance of his sister Mary Beth.

On my way back with the four Gallagher boys, we took the fairly new Francis Scott Key Bridge over the Patapsco River, not far from Fort McHenry. That put us in the vicinity of St. Charles Seminary, where I spent my last night as a student three decades ago tonight. We saw no sign of life and all the buildings were locked. But I showed them around the property—the domed chapel; the main building where the classrooms and the refectory were; the dormitory building in whose "attic" I spent a year—"pneumonia hall" we dubbed it; and the cemetery in the woods where lie buried a dozen or so faculty members from my day.

Near the tennis courts (which I was once put in charge of by a faculty benignly concerned by my lack of athleticism), I showed them the water fountain which our class donated when we graduated. The plaque is missing and the water gone dry.

I told the boys that their father attended my graduation from this school and took most of the photos I have of the event. I told them some of the stories I remembered: about the life-size statue of St. Joseph in one of the dorms. Occasionally when a boy returned to his bed in the middle of the night after using the lavatory he would find the saint in bed waiting for him.

Once, in "pneumonia hall," when some of the boys were making noises after the lights were out, the prefect sarcastically suggested that they chew celery, since it made more noise. The next day someone got to a store and purchased a large quantity of the recommended vegetable. That night they hid their stalks under their pillows until the count of twenty after the lights went out, and then began a massive corporate crunching. Trying to discourage such immaturities, our rector once reminded us, "You are men now, boys."

In November 1948, I slept in the dormitory proctored by Father "Buster" Cawley. A kindly man, he knew many of us were keenly interested in the outcome of the Truman-Dewey election. Since silence had to prevail until after Mass, he agreed to give us a signal: he would wear his biretta if Truman had won; he wouldn't if Dewey had. When he entered the dorm at 5:40 A.M., the outcome was still inconclusive, so he walked up and down the aisle tipping his cap.

Thinking back on nephew Pat Burdell's birth on this day in 1965, I recalled that Joe Feeley waited at the hospital with me. The child of a broken home, he was one of my altar boys at the Children's Vil-

lage. Catholic Charities had to turn him back to the state after he
became too old to stay at the Village. There was a danger that he
would be sent to a reform school, a prospect which terrified him.
Though he was sick of institutions, he agreed to go to Boys Town
but had nowhere to stay during a waiting period of a month or so.

I wanted to have him live at the faculty house where I was residing, but one of the officials there feared that he might be scandalized by hearing some priest say "hell" or "damn." But Archbishop
Shehan gave his approval, and Joe proved to be no trouble during
his stay. On his last night with me he told me the terrible, terrible
truth that he was illegitimate. "You know everything else about
me," he said, mustering his courage. I hope I told him there are no
illegitimate children—only illegitimate parents.

After Boys Town he went into the service and was killed in Vietnam in his early twenties. I presided at his burial in the National
Cemetery which adjoins the property of St. Charles.

I was in the last month of my teens when I graduated from this
seminary. It occurred to me tonight that my dead brother's eldest
son, walking with me around my "deceased" alma mater, will be
twenty this August, the same age that Joe was when he took on the
job that killed him.

> I didn't lose my life; I gave it.
> *A soldier's epitaph*

June 8

Two days ago I recalled the last day of my first year at St. Charles
Seminary. Thirty years ago today I spent the last day of my last year
there.

I lived the heavy bulk of my teen years at St. Charles; and every
adult knows how decisive those years can be. For better or worse, I
did no dating, dancing, smoking, or drinking in those years. (Baltimore seminarians had to take the pledge in those days: no intake of
alcohol until ten years after ordination.)

When my alma mater held her last graduation, on May 14, 1977,
I wrote an article of remembrance for the *Evening Sun*. After sum-

marizing some of the historical facts about the school's history, I continued:

Such bloodless data, of course, can't begin to capture the meaning of tomorrow's finale to an alumnus who spent six very impressionable years at that location. It was to its basement that I hurried when air-raid sirens shattered the suburban quiet during World War II. In its chapel, I learned that D-Day had arrived; in its senior study hall, that FDR had died; in its dining hall, that Germany had surrendered to the Allies. From its junior study hall, I was summoned home one cold March morning to my father's deathbed.

In those days, St. Charles meant rising at 5:40 A.M., visitors once a month, long periods of prayerful silence, six years of Latin, four of Greek, and an annual tuition of $420 for room, board and laundry. It meant no private radios, record players or TV, no cars, no school rings or yearbooks, no general access to newspapers, and only rare "walks" to Leeds or to Catonsville. It meant coats and ties most of the day, black coats and ties on Sunday.

It also meant plenty of companionship, the *esprit* of a common and lofty goal, concentration on education, and the example of dedicated teachers and domestic nuns. It meant unforgettable and irreplaceable religious experiences in a princely chapel donated by the prominent Jenkins family of Baltimore.

(Liturgical texts provided some humorist with titles for the three kinds of showers you took, depending on how much time you had between a game and supper: *lavabo* [I shall wash]; *asperges me* [You will sprinkle me]; *vidi aquam* [I saw the water].

There were funny moments, as when taxi drivers suddenly realized where they had taken you, and apologized for salty language; sad moments, as when Frenchie England was expelled for dancing in the parking lot with a classmate's sister on visiting day—he was drafted and later killed in Korea; exciting days, as when a monument was dedicated to John Banister Tabb, the priest-poet and faculty member who had helped another alumnus, James Cardinal Gibbons, write his famous book, *The Faith of Our Fathers*.

The brief Tabb poem on that monument still speaks of a lark which "rose, and, singing, passed from sight." As St. Charles College and the final embodiment of old St. Mary's pass from sight as living alma maters, cherished memories of them will be rising in the minds of thousands of alumni all over this nation. These memories will keep on singing in the hearts of men who were young there once, and perhaps learned there Cardinal Newman's words about mortal man: "He is young; he is old; he is never young again."

✵

Memory makes life beautiful; forgetfulness makes it bearable.
Enrico Cialdini

June 9

The past is as much a work of the imagination as is the future.

June 10

Today, Pope John Paul II ended his triumphal nine-day visit to Poland and returned to Rome. On this day in 1960, I first met his predecessor, who was also "on the road" that day. He was Cardinal Montini of Milan at that time, and three years away from being Pope John XXIII's successor. He had come to the United States to receive an honorary degree from Notre Dame University, and was on his way to South America.

Without much notice, Archbishop Keough was told that the cardinal would like to drive over from Washington to see our new Baltimore cathedral, which had opened the previous November. Since I had written a guidebook for the $7 million-gift church, I was asked to be on hand when the eminent churchman arrived. Already he was rumored as highly *papabile*.

After a wait of an hour or more at the new cathedral rectory, I saw several black limousines pulling into the driveway. Out of one of them popped Archbishop Vagnozzi, who was then apostolic delegate in the U.S. and widely disliked for his heavy-handed ways. (Some called him a papal bull in the china shop.) "We have ten minutes," he announced from behind his mafia-looking sunglasses. The future pope appeared thin, polite, and reserved. He put me in mind of Kierkegaard's "passionately inward man."

We dashed over to the cathedral—the cardinal and his companions escorted by our archbishop, his secretary, Monsignor White, and the cathedral rector, Monsignor Whelan. As we advanced down the long central aisle, I was invited to point out some salient features.

There is a niche in the far northwest corner of the edifice which contains a fine statue of St. Charles Borromeo, the cardinal's predecessor in the See of Milan. This the cardinal blessed; a nearby plaque now memorializes the event.

We were soon back out on the front steps of the cathedral, where several newsmen waited to question the visiting dignitary. (I can't recall how they learned of his visit.)

"How do you like the cathedral?" one journalist asked.

"*C'est très belle*," the cardinal replied, though he knew English.

"He says it's very lovely." Archbishop Vagnozzi assumed the role of translator.

"*C'est très grande*," the cardinal continued.

"He says it's very impressive," the archbishop continued.

"Fine taste," added the cardinal.

"Whatta you say?" barked the archbishop, puzzled at this unfamiliar French.

Some years later, during Vatican II, Archbishop Vagnozzi accosted Bishop Ernest Primeau (Manchester, New Hampshire) in St. Peter's Basilica and upbraided him about "that disgusting cartoon in your diocesan newspaper." A syndicated cartoon had recently appeared in several U.S. Catholic newspapers depicting the Roman Curia as a spaghetti curtain separating the pope from the faithful.

"What cartoon?" Bishop Primeau demanded.

"The one about the spaghetti curtain. It's an insult to the Holy Father, the Holy See, the Holy Church, and the Holy Spirit!"

"Archbishop, I don't even have a diocesan newspaper."

"Why do you not have a diocesan newspaper?"

I myself at least once had the honor of meriting this ecclesiastic's disapproval. In March of 1965, *Ave Maria* magazine published and *Time* magazine cited an article of mine, "The Crisis of Obedience." I showed the article to Cardinal Shehan before I sent it away, and he even added the words "curial officials" to my list of church authorities who might be less in step with church teaching than the people under them.

Not long afterward, in the presence of my brother, the apostolic delegate told the cardinal that he did not agree with this Father Gallagher's article. "A superior may listen, if he wants to, to the opinion of his subordinate, but he doesn't have to." Changing the subject, the cardinal introduced to him my brother as my brother. Later the cardinal said to Frank, "There's no use arguing with him."

Some priests at the National Catholic Welfare Conference, however, discovered otherwise. Growing tired of the delegate's frequent complaint that "the Holy Father" did not agree with various decisions or activities of theirs, they began to ask for copies of the documents in which such disagreements were expressed. The copies never came.

The great danger facing those who govern in the name of the Lord is that they themselves may become lordly. Bishops, for instance, may be God's "auxiliaries," but they do not have "the right to succession." Nevertheless I once heard of a lordly cardinal who was addressing his clergy on some matter where a dash of piety seemed appropriate. "The other night," he told them, "as I knelt in prayer, I fancied I heard our Lord speaking to me. And He said to me, 'Your Eminence . . .'"

The story goes that another priest was having trouble with titles. He had just been named a bishop, and he told a priest-friend that his biggest problem was what he was going to let his mother call him now that he was a successor to the apostles. "What the heck!" the bishop-elect blurted out after some moments of heavy thought. "After all, she *is* my mother. I'll just let her keep calling me Father."

❧

Complaining about the heavy hand of the Roman Curia, one of the speakers at today's session of the Council argued that bishops should be allowed to ruin their own dioceses.

My favorite misprint about Vatican II

June 11

Two dozen years ago yesterday I received a letter from Archbishop Keough. It read simply, "You are hereby appointed Assistant to Father Hopkins, Pastor of the Cathedral of the Assumption. You should report for duty on Saturday, June 11th. Praying God to bless you abundantly in your first assignment, I am with every good wish, sincerely yours in Christ, Francis P. Keough, Archbishop of Baltimore."

Situated between U.S. Route 40 going west and U.S. Route 40 going east, the Basilica rectory faces the Charles Street which divides Baltimore east and west, and is four blocks north of the Baltimore Street which divides it north and south. It has been the cathedral rectory for about 150 years. Cardinal Gibbons died there, and a few days after the Battle of Gettysburg, Archbishop Francis Patrick Kenrick was found dead in bed there.

When I rang the doorbell that June afternoon, I was greeted by an elderly black man who proved to be Wallace Carberry. Before his death in 1921, Cardinal Gibbons had added Wallace to the household staff. (Was he the one who called His Eminence "Your Remnants"?) More than thirty-five years later Wallace was telling me that my one room and shared bath were on the north end of the third floor facing Charles Street.

I shared the marble bathroom with Porter White, who was at that time Archbishop Keough's secretary and vice-chancellor. Porter had taught me Greek in college, and still has that same room in the Basilica rectory. Because we shared that bathroom, I probably saved his life some years later—a story I will tell in its proper place.

Wise old Wallace knew that all the older priests at the Basilica had all sorts of official jobs and would be apt to ask the fledgling priest to cover for them in such duties as hearing confessions and taking parlor calls. On one of my first days off at the Basilica, Wallace was casually crumbing the table after serving me breakfast.

"Is this your day off, Father Gallagher?"

"Yes, Wallace," I answered.

"Well," he said, pausing thoughtfully, "you ain't safe till you're past Center Street." (That was two blocks to the north.)

Father Tom Delea, a bear of a man with tender heart and avuncular concern, had already warned me soon after I arrived that I might be taken advantage of. His advice was "Play your cards close to your vest."

Once, a year or two later, the rector played his cards so close to the vest that I was locked out of the rectory when I came back late from my day off. Without telling me, the pastor had the locks changed that day. No one answered the doorbell and I didn't want to phone at that slumberous hour. I had the 6:30 Mass the next morning, so my only recourse was to take a room in the YMCA around the corner. There the elevator operator eyed my clerical outfit and asked, "Are you a Catholic priest?" When I owned up to the truth, he shook his head and said, "Shame on you."

☙

If the shoe fits . . . there must be some mistake.

June 12

For the first time in about a decade, I've been making a retreat this week with my fellow diocesan priests. The site this year is Mount St. Mary's Seminary in Emmitsburg, Maryland, near Camp David and Gettysburg. I have been worldly enough to watch television news and learn of the death of John Wayne.

Tonight as I went for a late stroll beneath the burnt-orange moon I encountered Archbishop Borders chatting amiably with some of the priests. His mention of theologian Karl Rahner put me in mind of a story about the brainy Rahner and his more clear-spoken priest-brother, Hugo. Once, when Karl was being introduced to a stranger, the latter asked whether he was the brother of the famous Rahner. "No," replied Karl, "that's my brother."

☙

. . . the little man is just as guilty of the war, otherwise the peoples of the world would have risen up in revolt long ago! . . . until all mankind, without exception, undergoes a great change, wars will be waged, and everything . . . destroyed.
May 3, 1944, entry of the Diary of Anne Frank, *born fifty years ago today*

June 13

During the past few weeks I have been mentioning a number of graduations and noticing how largely those events loom in the topography of my past. On this day in 1943, dressed in blue coat and white trousers, I had my first graduation as I completed the eighth grade at St. Ann's school.

My mother figures in two troubled grammar school memories. In the first grade at St. James's, the nun had us do an exercise in pointing while we chanted, "North and South and East and West; my mother is the sweetest and my daddy is the best." I, however, thought the text was ". . . but my father is the best," and I believed I was being asked to choose him over my mother. Only years later did it suddenly dawn on me that I had misheard the crucial conjunction.

Some years later, in religion class at St. Ann's, Father McGrath once wanted to stress how much Jesus loved us. He asked how many of us would die for our mothers. Nobody raised a hand. I knew I would die for mine, but I also knew the priest wanted us to prove his point by not raising our hands.

In those days I would write an occasional poem and then tell my classmate John Bauernfiend that I had done so. He could be relied upon to tell the teacher, who could be relied upon to ask me whether I would like to share it with the class. I would. Of these creations I can remember only the two lines which concluded one of them: "And if I try a little harder, I may grow up to be a martyr."

I may have tried to speed up that process in the seventh grade. A couple of students pulled a dishonest trick on the nun. During my lunch period I wrote her a note telling her of the trick (but not the names of the tricksters) and also commenting on the bad language in popular use among my classmates (all boys at that point). I must have signed the letter, for after reading it the nun lined us all up, asked us one by one if we were aware of the dishonesty, but skipped over me when my turn came. (Talk about betraying your informant!) Naturally enough a classmate soon came up to me and asked me if I had written the letter. "Yes," I answered, "go ahead and hit me." I don't recall that he did so, nor have I any memory of any other recriminations.

I can recall having had only one other extreme attack of righteous indignation in my early youth. There was a barbershop near my home which displayed a calendar with paintings of nudes. Too offended to remain silent, but too timid to complain openly, I sought out the barbershop quite early one morning and glued a disapproving note on the door. The calendar disappeared. Whenever I walked by, I wondered whether the barbers noticed me noticing.

I still have a few photos taken on my first graduation day. In one I have my arm around my sister; in another, around my mother. In still a third I am standing next to my father, whose curious pose turns him away from both me and the camera. There is no contact between us. Nor was there between him and my mother seventeen years earlier in the pictures taken after their wedding. Mother said he hated to have his picture taken. True, his large ears stood out a bit, but an arm around a son's shoulder would have redeemed a great many flaws. And it's the only picture taken of the two of us together.

That was in 1943. On this day in 1967 another Frank Gallagher was elected to Maryland's state constitutional convention. My brother chaired the committee on the governorship and worked hard on his part of a document which was widely praised as a model but ultimately rejected by the voters for a variety of reasons. It was called a magnificent failure.

Twenty years ago today I became "effective" as the consulting editor of the archdiocesan newspaper, the *Catholic Review*. Exactly four years after I arrived at my Basilica assignment Archbishop Keough sent me this letter: "You are hereby appointed Consulting Editor of the *Catholic Review*, effective as of Saturday, June 13th. Praying God to bless you abundantly in this field of work and with every good wish, I am . . ."

Thus began seven and one half years of work which had their moments of magnificence, I believe, as well as their moments of failure.

There are two classes of people: the righteous and the unrighteous; and the righteous do the classifying.

June 14

This college and seminary in Emmitsburg grew from the courage, genius, and vision of a French priest, John DuBois, who in 1791

came from the France to which I sailed on this day in 1961. He died
as the third bishop of New York. On this day in 1971 the auxiliary
bishop of Providence shocked many people by resigning his episcopate—largely in protest over the seeming indifference of his fellow
bishops to the brutality of the Vietnam War.

I had met Bishop Bernard Kelly in 1965 when I traveled to Rhode
Island to address a teachers' conference organized by my classmate
Father Ed Mullin. The bishop had an eminent reputation as a spiritual director and a holy priest. He reminded me of James Cagney
and seemed a man's man. His resignation marked a low point in the
morale of many of us priests at the start of this decade.

How his decision affected at least one fellow bishop is on rare
public record. My friend Joe Gossman was auxiliary bishop of Baltimore at the time and he spoke with unprecedented candor to a
Washington *Post* columnist: "I know how he feels. Bishops' meetings are very painful experiences. . . . It's not only that they don't
deal with some issues, but the way they do deal with other issues.
While everywhere else in the world there's a sense of urgency and
talk of morality on important issues, there seems to be a lack of a
sense of urgency when bishops meet."

When I read these blunt words I feared that Joe had now
sacrificed all hope of ever being given a diocese of his own. But to
my surprise he was named bishop of Raleigh a few years later. (One
wit suggested that this gift of the least Catholic diocese in the U.S.
was his punishment.) That was a sure sign that a new kind of
apostolic delegate was advising Rome from Washington, and that a
new kind of bishop was being sought out for the U.S. church.
Thanks to bishops like Joe, I'm certain that bishops' meetings are
now much more alive and searching. So perhaps the loss of a man
like Bishop Kelly was not a waste.

A similar shock had occurred a few years earlier with the resignation of one of the very brightest and most promising of U.S. Catholic bishops, James Shannon, auxiliary bishop of St. Paul/Min-
neapolis. I had first met him in San Francisco at a 1965 Catholic
Press Convention. Newly consecrated, he addressed us as assistant
episcopal moderator of the Catholic Press Department of the
National Catholic Welfare Conference. What a rising star he was:
open-minded, knowledgeable, well-spoken, sensitive to the concerns of thoughtful, world-serious Catholics.

We met, developed a speedy mutual respect, and corresponded
from time to time. Although the unprecedented news of his resigna-

tion focused on his marriage to a divorced woman, I can well imagine that his gifts and his convictions and his willingness to speak out alienated him from his brother bishops and produced an intolerable loneliness. . . .

Today is Flag Day and Baltimoreans proudly remember that the Star-Spangled Banner that flew over Fort McHenry and inspired our national anthem was made in Baltimore.

My favorite flag memories pertain to Maryland's handsome flag and the Maryland law requiring it to be topped on flagpoles by the kind of trefoil cross which appears on the coat of arms of the Calvert family, who founded our colony. Governor McKeldin loved to tell of the time he visited the West Point dining hall and was shown by the commandant how the flags of all the states decorated the walls. An eagle or a spear topped all the flagstaffs.

"But," said Governor McKeldin, "the law requires that a cross surmount the Free State flag."

"But," protested the officer, "that would make the Maryland staff different."

"The cross of Christ," replied McKeldin, "has always made a difference!"

On another occasion the devout McKeldin told me of a federal plaza in D.C. that displays all the state flags and rotates their positions daily. He pointed out to the man in charge that the Maryland flag must have a cross above it.

"But we can't be moving the cross each day as we move the flags!"

"The federal government has no right to violate state laws. If you can't display our flag correctly, I direct you to remove it!"

So, now one pole has a cross, with the Maryland flag beneath it, and all the other flags move around it.

The vibrant McKeldin was a very ecumenical Episcopalian. The story has it that when he was visiting Ireland he insisted on running his fingers through the river Shannon "because its water are as sacred to us Catholics as the Jordan's is to us Jews."

"Hey, take off your hat!" shouted a beery patriot as the national anthem was intoned at a ball game. He didn't know that the offending man had lost both his arms as a soldier.

June 15

Bishop Frank Murphy drove me home from Emmitsburg, stopping in Frederick for gas in order to avoid lines in Baltimore. The governor has issued a decree making it unlawful for cars with six cylinders or more to be given less than $7.00 worth of gas. The minimum is $5.00 for smaller cars. The idea is to weed out of the lines people who just want to keep their tanks full or near full all the time.

In mid-June 1955, I was settling in at Baltimore's old cathedral rectory. Ours was a downtown parish with many rooming houses and hotels. Our regular parishioners tended to be old and single. Many of our door callers were drifters or "knights of the road" looking for handouts.

Some of our handouts were quite elegant. One day, for example, Cardinal Gracias of Bombay visited the rectory. He needed another suitcase and I was told to buy one for him at an expensive store. It turned out that the store didn't have one to match. So, I phoned the cardinal, telling him I could get him one somewhat smaller or somewhat larger. "I'll take both," he said, getting me in Dutch with my superiors.

These are some of the more routine door calls I can readily recall:

* the intoxicated ex-marine with whom I talked for four hours. He returned the next day and had no recollection of meeting me before.

* the couple who said they were on their honeymoon, so they thought they would stop by to get married.

* the man who said he was really dead and this was purgatory. He confided to me that psychiatrists have a psychological need to be psychiatrists.

* the man who told me he was the grandson of Czar Nicholas, and that the only family member to escape Ekaterinburg was his mother, Tatiana. He said he was a hemophiliac, and invited me to go get a picture of the Czar and compare profiles. He was a brilliant talker and was widely read. He needed money.

* the poor family whom I invited to go through items we had collected in our basement during a clothing drive. Said one delighted youngster, "This is a swell coat, Mr. Priest!"

* the numerous shaky old men who said they used to be Cardinal Gibbons' altar boy, and could I spare a quarter. The cardinal died in 1921.

* the man who said he had escaped from Sing Sing and wanted to go back to give himself up, so I had better give him the bus fare or I would be responsible for what happened.

* the balmy young girl who tried to keep her orchid alive by massaging it with Noxzema. She slipped past me, invaded the butler's pantry, and tried to ride down to the kitchen on the dumb waiter.

* the thirteen-year-old girl who said she was an atheist and when I sneezed said "Gesundheit!"

Once a month after the last morning Mass I gave a special sermon to the few women who belonged to our sodality. I didn't so much mind the parishioners who would make the Stations of the Cross in the main aisle while I preached. The real distractors were those who lit candles at the altar rail while I spoke—and then dropped ten or twenty pennies in the box, one by clanking one.

Once, at a crowded Sunday Mass shortly after the liturgy was allowed to be said in English, an infant kept emitting blood-curdling screams all during Communion time. Imagine my delight when I approached the microphone shortly afterward to announce the Post-Communion verse from St. Matthew's Gospel: "Arise, take the child and his mother and flee into Egypt."

With similar double meaning, a curate I know (who didn't get along with his controversial pastor) used the pulpit each Sunday to ask prayers "for those sick of the parish." Once when the annual Indian and Negro missions collection was taken up at that same parish, racial tensions were reflected with the words scribbled across the special envelopes by one member of the congregation: "For Indians Only . . ."

At the old cathedral baptismal font, on the Feast of the Three Kings, I baptized my cousin Rickie King in the presence of his father, Dick King, and his godfather, Spencer King.

Also at that fountain I baptized a young woman who had expressed some doubts about the sufficiency of her faith. I had reassured her that her doubts were not essential ones. After pouring the water, I handed her a candle, telling her it stood for the light of faith. At once a breeze slipped through the nearby window and snuffed the candle out. We all laughed.

For quickie weddings we occasionally had to search the streets for a couple of witnesses, especially for out-of-towners. I can recall only one bride fainting on me during the ceremony itself. Like a parachutist, she just collapsed into her rustling gown. She exemplified the old pleasantry "I said wilt thou, and she wilted."

A few years ago, while giving a retreat in Philadelphia, I was approached by a woman whose name and face were vaguely familiar. "I was your first bride almost two dozen years ago. Do you remember what you told us?" I always quiver when I am asked a question like that, and as usual I couldn't remember. "You said, 'This is my first wedding, and I hope it's your last.'" So far my hope has been borne out.

On the sadder side: I once had the funeral of a man who had no visitors at the funeral parlor and no friends at the requiem Mass. Men who worked for the undertaker served as pallbearers. The words I read at his grave were achingly apt: "With Lazarus, who once was poor, may you now have rest."

One of the heaviest pastoral irritants—especially for those who can't easily fall back to sleep—are late-night phone calls of no urgent nature. I heard of a priest who hit on a good counterattack: he would tell the 2 A.M. caller that he was busy at the moment, but that if the caller would leave a phone number he would call back in an hour or so. "But I'll be in bed," was the hoped-for reply. Then the priest could inquire, "Where do you think I was?"

Hearing of this approach, another priest waited eagerly for the first foolish post-midnight call. Finally it came—at 1:45 A.M. The lady wanted to know how many sessions there were at the Second Vatican Council.

The priest reveled in his prepared answer. "I'm sorry, I'm busy right now. Would you give me your phone number so I can call back in an hour or so?"

"Oh, don't bother," replied the lady. "I'm in a phone booth. I'll call you."

I myself once had a call shortly after 6 A.M. An irate voice, obviously referring to the cathedral's 6 A.M. angelus bells, requested to know, "How the hell do *you* like being waked up so early? Why do you have to ring those damned bells?" I sputtered, "Why, ah, they're a call to prayer." "Oh, I didn't realize that. I'm sorry." He hung up.

※

The priesthood: "the sweet miracle of . . . empty hands."
Georges Bernanos in his The Diary of a Country Priest

June 16

President Carter is in Vienna for his first meeting with Russian President Brezhnev; they are due to sign the Salt II Treaty on Monday. The radio news said that gas in Vienna is going up to $3.00 a gallon. In Mexico it is about $.43 per gallon. The lines at gas stations are long and tempers are short around Baltimore where a gallon of regular costs $.85 (it's easy to remember that in '73 before the first oil embargo the price was $.37).

A dozen years ago today my temper grew short with one of the youngsters I got to know when I was chaplain at the Children's Village. (I passed the Village today, recalling that I had left there sixteen years ago this week.) Virgil had been arrested with a few buddies for roughing up an apartment in which they had been living. I got my busy brother to represent him in court, and the boy got away with a fine.

Later that day, Virgil called again from jail. He had decided to celebrate, was drinking a beer in public and arrested for being underage. Could I give him my brother's phone number? I promised to dismember him limb by limb if he bothered my brother.

I had paid his original fine, and he promised the judge to pay me back soon. (At that time, his salary exceeded my own.) When I ran into him months later and reminded him of his unpaid debt, he replied, "You aren't going to let money come between us, are you?"

I remember a similar episode with Joe, the Village boy who was later killed in Vietnam. He, too, was phoning me from jail. He had been frustrating me lately and I was very stern with him. Later he told me, "That was the day I realized that I really loved you—because even after you bawled me out I didn't want to tell you to go to hell."

"Go to hell" was a phrase that I heard the eminent German theologian Bernard Häring use on this day in 1964. The first national Ecumenical Workshop was being held at the Belvedere Hotel in Baltimore, and the saintly Redemptorist was a featured speaker. He was recalling the traditional church law against allowing non-Catholics to receive the sacraments. But a day came in World War II when as a German army chaplain he was celebrating Mass the night before a major battle. Many Protestants were in attendance, and when the time came to give Holy Communion, some of these rose from their pews and came forward.

"So," said Father Häring, "what was I to say?—'Go to hell, you goddamned Protestants!' No, I knew it was the Christian thing to give them the Sacrament."

(There's a story about a priest who was telling his bishop of a similar situation. "How did you handle it?" asked the bishop. "I asked myself what Jesus would have done." "You didn't!" gasped the bishop.)

It will be hard for younger Catholics to realize how bold this decision was in those days. "Let us rejoice," concluded the priest, "that we are living in a time when we must take risks in the name of charity." He took his own further risks in 1968 when he dissented from Pope Paul's encyclical *Humanae Vitae*. Not too many years before that he had been asked by the pope to give him and his staff their Lenten retreat.

🌲

Truth, the common patrimony of the race, always comes privately to each man through the prism of his own soul.
                                        Frederick D. Wilhelmsen

June 17

One score years ago this day I was working on the first issue of the archdiocesan newspaper to carry my name on its masthead. (Its date was my thirtieth birthday.) Since its founding in 1913, the Baltimore *Catholic Review* had generally had a priest on its staff, usually as the chief editor. By 1959, however, Mr. Gerry Sherry was the managing editor, and Father Ray Gribbin worked part-time as consulting editor. As Father Gribbin became increasingly involved in a busy parish, he found it growingly difficult to spend as much time on the archdiocesan paper as Mr. Sherry would have liked.

The *Review* office was then at 115 West Franklin Street, less than two blocks from my assignment at the old cathedral rectory. As far back as 1949 I had occasionally sent material to the *Review* and had it published. In the four years since my ordination I had written thirty-one items for the *Review*, including editorials, book reviews, and feature articles.

So, I had already been associated with the English-born and vivacious Gerry Sherry before my appointment as Father Gribbin's successor four years after my ordination. What was the sum total of my mandate from Archbishop Keough? "See Mr. Sherry." The vagueness of this order was to cause me considerable trouble in the years ahead, especially after Mr. Sherry left for newspaper work in a better climate because of his daughter's health problems.

As I now recall, he wanted me to help with the writing of editorials and occasional features, to act as a kind of in-house "censor" in the name of good taste and Catholic orthodoxy, and to help with such chores as proofreading and putting the paper to bed on Thursday mornings at the printer's on Gay Street near Route 40.

Since Mr. Sherry had been hired by the archbishop and enjoyed his confidence before I came on the scene, and since Mr. Sherry's rule of thumb was "when in doubt, leave it out," my role as "consulting" editor was fairly storm-free. Gerry's concern about social problems had already caused certain elements in the archdiocese to brand him as a "pinko" or outright "Commie." But Gerry relished a good fight and could defend himself quite capably. (One of the ironies of his reputation as a "Communist" was that when Douglas Hyde was quitting the Communist Party in England, Gerry was his Catholic newspaper contact.)

Three of the younger men hired by Gerry went on to notable careers: Mike Long is now a senior editor of *The National Geographic*; Steve Gavin became a major writer with the Hearst paper locally and elsewhere; Frank DiFilippo became press secretary for Governor Marvin Mandel.

Bob Ostermann succeeded Gerry in August 1960 and relied heavily on Steve and Frank. Gerry had told Bob that as the consulting editor I was "everything and nothing." Steve and Frank led Bob to emphasize the second part of my curious identity and to resist my already ill-defined authority. "Political" editorials soon began to appear attacking J. Edgar Hoover and Richard Nixon; articles and headlines began to appear that I regarded as in bad taste. Each Friday morning I had to brace myself for outraged phone calls from Monsignor White, the archbishop's secretary. I got the blame, although my role was still vague and nobody would clarify it.

Finally, Ostermann, Gavin, and DiFilippo all resigned suddenly and around the same time in early 1961.

Dave Maguire was the third editor I worked with. He came from the local Hearst paper in April 1961 and eventually resigned in mid-1965 when he felt he had lost Cardinal Shehan's confidence. At times he also surely found it hard to deal with me. Several local priests complained that he neglected to highlight their activities. The cardinal himself took offense when Dave did not immediately reprint an article he had written for *America* magazine and hadn't even mentioned to us at the paper. He also took offense at some features Dave ran about racism in Baltimore parishes. (The Jesuit-run *America* specifically praised one of these.) During Dave's tenure I was made executive editor and gained more authority.

Finally, at the recommendation of *America*'s editor in chief, Thurston Davis, I interviewed Ed Wall, a convert who then edited the leading newspaper in Hawaii. The cardinal hired him in the summer of 1965 and in the following year I, myself, resigned. My last issue was the last issue of 1966. Since then, there hasn't been a priest on the *Review* staff. My great contribution was to declericalize the paper. When Ed Wall spoke of resigning shortly after I did, the cardinal threatened to close the paper down.

So, it turned out that I worked with four editors during my seven and one half years with the *Review*. I started six months after Pope John XXIII made his call for a Council. I resigned in great disillusionment a year after the Council ended. But the nearly four hundred issues of the *Review* with which I was associated appeared during a dramatic time in the church, in the world, and in American national life. The experiences I underwent made a profound impact on my life and thoroughly altered my attitude toward church authority and the priesthood itself. But more of this later.

⚘

Correction: In yesterday's edition we said that Mr. Jones was a
defective on the police force. We meant to say, of
course, that he was a detective on the police farce.

Midnight, June 18–19

I am seated at the desk of my study, in the second-floor back of the only home I ever owned. I am puffing on the gift pipe and the gift tobacco sent to me by an eighty-one-year-old widow friend in Miami. On my radio, Beethoven's *Second Symphony* is being played by the Vienna Philharmonic. The announcer said that the Vienna-based genius composed it at a time when he had grown aware of his doom of deafness. I've read that this restless genius had seventy-one different addresses during his thirty-one-year stay in Vienna.

I have just returned home from a gently festive evening with my oldest nephew, Frank, and his friend Clinton MacSherry. (Clinton calls me "U.J." for Uncle Joe.) They treated me to dinner at Connolly's Seafood Restaurant at harbor's edge. But first they went with me to College Park as I once again gave the eighty-nine-year-old Katherine Anne Porter absolution and Holy Communion. Frank had met her once before, but this was a prized first for Clinton, who attends Trinity College in Hartford and specializes in literature.

On this, my twenty-third visit to Katherine Anne, she seemed unusually serene. When Clinton told her that her short story *The Grave* was his favorite, she said she loved it. She had a book by Cleanth Brooks on her bed, and said that *The Grave* was also his favorite. When we were leaving, the nurse showed Clinton the colorfully decorated wooden coffin that Katherine Anne keeps in her closet.

After our leisurely dinner, we all strolled around the charming inner harbor for about an hour—the breeze was delight in motion. On pier four we stopped in at the new Chart House Restaurant for a liqueur, which we sipped while looking out a large upstairs window opening onto the harbor and the illuminated downtown buildings.

It is now midnight and my digital watch flashes freshly the magical numbers 6:19. I have made it past the first half century—the first male in my family to do so. *Deo Gratias, Alleluia!*

Tonight Frank asked me whether I dreaded this milestone. Not at all! I regard it as quite an achievement. Words from that tenderly triumphant hymn "Amazing Grace" express a key sentiment now pervading me:

"Through many dangers, toils and snares I have already come!"

The day which led to this midnight hour found me housekeeping in preparation for tomorrow's guests. I also picked up the April section of this book from my typist and drove around awhile in search of gas.

Presidents Carter and Brezhnev signed the Salt II Treaty today (yesterday) in Vienna—the anniversary of Napoleon's defeat at Waterloo—and while I was eating my seafood dinner our President was already back in Washington addressing a televised joint session of Congress. Not even for very special private milestones does history pause.

A rare letter came from my only living brother: "Hope you had a good birthday. I have lost fifty pounds and have a hard time getting my breath. . . . Love always, Tommy."

Being fifty means I have lived through 18,250 days, more than twenty-six million minutes, and two billion heartbeats: a fatiguing consideration.

I share this birthdate with Blaise Pascal and a fellow Baltimorean, the Duchess of Windsor, widow of the former King Edward VIII. My actual day of birth overshot by three days the silver anniversary of James Joyce's "Bloomsday" in *Ulysses* (June 16, 1904).

It was a doleful deathdate in 1756 for 146 British soldiers in the Black Hole of Calcutta; in 1867 for the Mexican Emperor Maximilian, and in 1953 for convicted spies Ethel and Julius Rosenberg. More cheeringly, the Magna Carta was signed and the First Ecumenical Council (Nicaea, A.D. 325) opened on this day.

I was born by facial presentation at Baltimore's Mercy Hospital, which is about a mile southeast from where I write and which has been almost completely replaced by a modern building. I was born in mid-week, on a Wednesday, and about midway between President Hoover's inauguration and the Wall Street Crash. That made me a pre-Depression partus; I was also pre-Plutonian, since the ninth planet had not yet been discovered. According to the anonymous nursery rhyme, I was due to be "full of woe" as a Wednesday child, or "loving and giving" according to an alternate version.

I am about to go to bed and the radio is playing selections from Scott Joplin, who wrote "The Wall Street Rag."

※

I slept and dreamt that life was joy.
I woke and found that life was duty.
I worked and found that duty was joy.
Rabindranath Tagore

I awoke to a day of perfect weather. I picked up nephew Jimmy (the youngest Gallagher by twelve minutes) and took him to his eye doctor. While he was there I paid a visit to the graves of my parents and my older brother. After taking Jimmy home, I returned downtown for the noon Mass in the chapel at Mercy Hospital.

Realizing that I had never seen my birth certificate, I stopped at the State Office Building and for $2.00 learned that I was born at 5:20 A.M. and that my doctor was Thomas K. Galvin. My younger brother, from whom I heard yesterday, is Thomas Galvin Gallagher. The document declared me legitimate, a status which would come as a surprise to some.

It turns out that all these years I have just been "Baby Boy" Gallagher—apparently I was born without a decided-on name. So, for another dollar and with the service of a notary I became John Joseph today in the eyes of the state, though in the affidavit the notary mistakenly changed my mother's last name from Doyle to Douglas. (You win a few and lose a few.)

Both my father and my mother had brothers named John and Joseph, and my father's father was John Joseph. So, I was named after five people, all now dead. I have no recollection, though, of ever being called John. Taken together, my two Hebrew forenames and Gaelic surname yield this piquant translation: "The Lord is gracious. . . . He will increase . . . foreign aid."

A number of birthday phone calls and greeting cards came today, though my party won't be until Saturday. This calendar date coincided with some special memories in my life: in 1939 I served my first Mass as an altar boy; in 1955 I performed my first baptism—it was also Father's Day, the parents' first wedding anniversary, and Tavia McRae Covington was their first child. The first issue of the *Catholic Review* to carry my name on its masthead bore this date in 1959; in 1961 on my thirty-second birthday I spent my first day in Europe, France, and Paris, gazed at the Notre Dame Cathedral, and ascended the Eiffel Tower.

At the Montreal World's Fair I bought a copy of page one of the New York *Times* for June 19, 1929. Five stories dealt with a new Anglo-American Call for Peace and Naval Disarmament; four stories dealt with Prohibition; one noted that Congress was recessing today; another that "Mexicans Find Basis for Church Peace"; and one spoke of a nationwide hot spell and a record temperature in New York City. (I recall my mother saying that I was born on a very hot day.)

The Baltimore *Sun* for this day in 1929 promised "continued warm" weather; it highlighted the call for world peace and carried stories about bootleg liquor and border killings; the only photo showed a Mexican archbishop involved in peacemaking negotiations there; an alleged opium yacht fled Cuba in a hail of bullets; the Lindberghs ended their honeymoon cruise, and the colonel headed for Mitchell Field, Long Island, to be part of a search for a safe and "foolproof" airplane. In Annapolis a Negro failed the physical for entrance into the all-white Naval Academy.

Today's front-page concerns—the Salt II Treaty, a DC-10 crash, racial justice, and drug busts—seem almost a continuation of the headlines of a half century ago.

About 9 P.M., Pete Garthe arrived from Michigan with wife, Fran, and children Susan and Chrissie. They plan to stay till the weekend. Pete was a student of mine at Paca Street; he toured Ireland with me in 1967, and I baptized his second daughter a year ago in Grand Rapids, where he is a "referee" in the juvenile court.

Just before midnight we had crab cakes and beer together—a worthy Maryland substitute for ice cream and cake on my special day.

❦

. . . the closer I move to death
. . . the louder the sun blooms
And the tusked, ramshackling sea exults.

❦

O may my heart's truth
Still be sung
On this high hill in a year's turning.
From birthday poems of Dylan Thomas

June 20

This world is a wonderful place for a battle, but a terrible place for a truce.

G. K. *Chesterton*

June 21

Summer arrived sometime today: my mandala calendar said it was this morning; the TV weatherman said it was this evening. In any case I spent most of the day driving to Ocean City, Maryland, and back with the four Garthes. The drive was about three hundred miles round-trip.

On our way to the beach we detoured to take a look at the Maryland State Tree—the Wye Oak, which is over 450 years old and is "the largest white oak in the U.S." Ten years or so ago former Governor McKeldin gave me one of the small crosses made by prisoners from a large branch that had fallen from the tree . . .

Stasia Doyle, my oldest living aunt, turned seventy-six today. It was on her sixtieth birthday that Cardinal Montini was elected to succeed John XXIII as Paul VI. I recall very clearly watching him appear on St. Peter's balcony in an early morning TV special that day. This, I knew, was the man who would have to deal with the birth control issue and I pitied him.

I phoned the Jesuit Gus Weigle that day to tell him the papal news. He was giving a retreat at the Roland Park Seminary to the second half of our diocesan priests. I had been there to enjoy his talks the previous week. He cited the word St. Ignatius used for the spiritual quality of detachment—it was "unstuckedness," a word with much more humane and realistic overtones than the ideal of some kind of bloodless aloofness. The latter ideal was at times quite successful in producing "immaculate misconceptions," as the Dominican Gerald Vann once phrased the danger.

Gus was a hearty ecumenist and belonged to the original ecumenical commission established in 1962 by Archbishop Shehan. He told us that in Austrian Catholicism all is approved unless forbidden; in German, all is forbidden unless approved; in Italian, all is approved even when forbidden. He urged us to go ahead and do brave new ecumenical things and find out later whether higher authorities approved of them.

While I took his retreat, Gus told me stories about an especially pious former editor of the *Catholic Review*. He was fond of captions like "Note the prayerful way the bishop folds his hands" or "Observe the gleam of sincerity in the bishop's eye."

This editor's supreme delight was a story which combined religion with patriotism. During World War II he heard of a Baltimore soldier who had been taught by the Madams of the Sacred Heart, and who now encountered some sisters from that very order in the South Pacific war zone. His headline for that story was memorable: "Lonely Soldier Comforted by Madams."

I took many pictures at the second session of Vatican II. Mutual friends invited me to show these after a Saturday dinner which Gus attended. He had a bad cough, and his doctor host insisted that Gus pay him a visit on the following Monday. The doctor took tests and told Gus his heart condition had notably worsened. He could either take good care of himself and live maybe five more years, or be his natural self-forgetting self and blaze out in the midst of activity. Gus, who knew what he wanted, died that Friday as he prepared to return to the afternoon half of an all-day ecumenical conference in New York.

In honor of Gus Weigle and all ecumenical theologians: "The opposite of a true statement is a false statement. But the opposite of a profound truth may be another profound truth."

Niels Bohr

June 22

W. H. Auden said something that makes a keen introduction to what I'm going to say next:

> The image of myself which I try to create
> in my own mind in order that I may love
> myself is very different from the image
> which I try to create in the minds of others
> in order that they may love me.

Because we human beings find it very hard to know ourselves or to show ourselves with any completeness, we also find it hard to discover how much we are like others and how much unlike. Nevertheless, I'm going to be reckless enough to permit a glimpse at the distinctive inner man who has been doing all this remembering.

First, take an unmoneyed Irish Catholic male from Philadelphia who is big and strong and bright and mechanical and musical and witty and worldly and gregarious and twenty-nine and a budding alcoholic and marry him to

an unmoneyed Irish Catholic female from Baltimore who is lovely and tender and cheerful and devout and rather simple and twenty-five

and give them three sons in four and a half years, and take away their home and several good jobs during the Depression,

and you have the setting of my formative years as my father's drinking and my parents' quarreling grew terrifyingly worse.

It seems my father isn't around very much, and when he is, I know there will be arguments and drunken stumbling and maybe physical violence, and once a knife is used threateningly so I hide the cutlery during subsequent clashes and on another occasion my father tries to choke my mother while she's sleeping because he thinks she has taken his money so she screams and a policeman comes and arrests my father after chasing him through the backyard and down the alley and I go to the trial and the judge asks the lady upstairs whether she ever saw Mr. Gallagher drunk and she says Judge I never saw him sober and everybody howls and they send my father to jail awhile and I tell my mother I'll leave home if she ever takes him back again which she does anyway and meantime I sit with her on wooden benches while she waits to get some powdered potatoes from the welfare and when my old man comes back from the cut sure enough he gets dead drunk again and after my mother nurses him back he makes some crack about her nitwit family so she picks up the nearest available projectile in the form of a mustard jar and wings it across the room where it cracks him in the skull and leaves him bleeding and I don't blame her and anyway it's better than a knife so in summary you might say I was in the middle of conflictual parents.

Put me, too, in the middle of my two brothers; the elder one, who is very intelligent and studious and nervous and driven and dutiful and affable in the midst of his migraine headaches, and the younger one, who is rebellious and sullen and wayward and openly craving our father's affection. Tommy tries to sit on our father's lap and that giant says, "Get down—you're too old for that."

And once the Good Humor truck comes by and our father buys himself some ice cream but none for us because "you've already had your fun." And he lets little Francis burn his hand on a hot bulb because it will teach him a lesson; and at the beach he won't pick us up when our tender feet are walking across the scorching sand because the experience will toughen us up. How could we realize that somehow we dwarfs were in competition with that Goliath?

In the midst of all this bitterness comes a curiously tender moment: my reeling father abuses my mother and I warn him, "If you do that again I'll hit you." "What did you say?" my hulking parent demands. I repeat my suicidal threat. "Little boy," my mixed-up father says as he pats me on the head, "I'm proud of you." I don't remember this episode; my mother told me of it when I was much older, though one time she said it was Francis who bearded the lion. I do remember Francis and myself once making noises upstairs and throwing apples down the steps to distract our shouting parents.

Out of all this chaos some basic dilemmas emerge: my father is strong and bright, but he doesn't love me and hence can be cruel. So "head" is heartless but powerful. My mother is loving but overwhelmed and overprotective and sickly and full of apprehension and sighs a lot and belongs to a gloomy and emotionally unstable family. So "heart" is mindless and vulnerable. If my father rejects me it's because I'm not lovable. If my mother accepts me it's because I'm not strong. So where do I gravitate? On whom shall I model myself? Uncles are practically nonexistent. As for my brothers, shall I be uncomplaining like Francis, who gets scary sick spells, or shall I vent my rage like Tommy, who gets in trouble and makes more trouble for mom?

Unwittingly, I'm fashioning models for the future: God the Father as powerful creator but cruel lord of cruel history; Mother Church as bewildered and irrational and not very smart; and Jesus as the brave and the dutiful brother who dies young and everybody praises him for his success and efficacy while you feel like a failure.

Behold the trap I'm in: my home situation—my childhood world —afflicts me with the pain of fear and the fear of pain; the fear makes me angry, but I dare not add my anger to an already intolerably explosive situation. If I did I would hurt my hurting mother and make myself feel even guiltier, or else I might get hurt even more in return. So I repress the anger and it feeds depression. All of which merely increases the pain, the fear, the anger. Dr. Whedbee will tell me when I'm almost forty that I have enough rage inside me to blow up Baltimore city.

Now all these searing experiences happen to a boy who inherits his father's unusual brightness and his mother's unusual tenderness and devoutness. So I have his head and her heart. But no matter how much I see—and my IQ is later scored as exceeding 140—it never seems enough to make me understand what I am feeling and what to do about assuaging my chronic existential aches. No matter how much I know, it's never enough to protect me from the dangers of not knowing in an inscrutable cosmos brimming with perilous surprises.

But to protect myself, to overcome the feelings of emptiness within, I must know everything. To endear myself I must help everybody be at peace within and without. Thus my Quixotic mission is to delete conflict from a universe which is, alas, inherently dialectical. (Hear Robert Frost: "Nature within her inmost self divides / To trouble men with having to take sides.")

Feeling rejected by my God-figure and knowing the pain of it, I must not reject or even appear to reject anyone. (Before I ever heard of Shelley I, too, wished "no living thing to suffer pain.") I couldn't stand the guilt of it, and I would dread the rage of the rejected. And I am afraid to be afraid lest I unleash within myself an anger which might prove murderous. (Like many oversensitive people, I exaggerate how much other people need me, how much pain they are feeling, and how destructive anger is likely to be— either theirs or mine.)

So here is the cluster of resulting characteristics which polychrome my psyche:

Perplexity . . . the need to know . . . curiosity . . . delight in knowing . . . astonishment at existence . . . the sense of mystery . . . information remembered and marshaled like weapons of self-defense . . . a sense of mental inadequacy.

Fear of insanity, of conflict . . . nameless panic . . . emotional vulnerability . . . turbulence . . . self-doubt in most cases, stubbornness in a few . . . guiltiness . . . mild hypochondriasis . . . melancholy envy of my ubiquitous betters . . . a sense of emotional inadequacy.

Sociability . . . congeniality . . . lonesomeness . . . longing to belong . . . fear of rejection . . . distrust of group thinking or mob action . . . verbal playfulness . . . defensive and defusing humor . . . *faim* for fame and some shame at same . . . if I can do it it's trivial; if I can't it's crucial . . . a sense of social inadequacy.

Tenderness . . . tearfulness . . . sympathy . . . empathy . . . religiousness (much battered and currently in the shop for an overhaul) . . . keen capacity for delight . . . love of music . . . clamorous sensuality . . . unathleticism . . . some bodily laziness . . . heavy sleeper . . . a sense of physical inadequacy.

Serenity has come to the degree that I have learned and accepted and remembered these arduous simplicities:
  (1) I'm lovable enough and strong enough and don't need whatever bonuses being more lovable might bring;
  (2) It's all right to be inadequate;
  (3) I'm probably no more inadequate than the average person and may be more adequate than many of the successful people whom I envy or whose admiration I seek;
  (4) Inadequacy has its compensations;
  (5) Adequacy has its drawbacks (cf. the saber-tooth tiger, now gloriously extinct).

※

> And then, crying his sorrow, he crawls
> To his bed: the world, and his home, hurt him
> With their emptiness.
> *Beowulf*

June 23

Because my birthday occurs in the latter part of June, my schoolmates have always been scattered by that time. That was even more true during my seminary years, when my school friends would have returned to their homes all across the States. The result has been that I've never had a birthday party attended by any substantial number of my friends.

This year deserved to be different and the occasion was postponed until this weekend day. My brother's widow and children had been wondering how to solemnize my semicentennial when I approached them about the idea of a party for friends at their commodious house. They readily agreed.

The weather turned out to be mannerly and the bar was safely placed in the spacious Gallagher backyard. The dining room was graced with a colorful bouquet of flowers and abundant sandwich material and pastries. A cluster of fifty balloons decorated the sidewalk stairs.

Fifty-three guests and five children attended, plus fifteen family members.

Seven priests were on hand, including the priest who "sent" me to the seminary in 1943, Dan McGrath, and my most faithful adviser, Gene Walsh.

Of the three nuns present, Sister Bernarde had taught me to be an altar boy in 1939.

Thirteen of the guests were former seminarians, fondly known as D.R.Q.s (Dirty Rotten Quitters). Most were accompanied by their wives (one apiece); I had a role in the weddings of almost all.

A key part of the fun and felicity was having friends meet one another for the first time, or having separated friends renew acquaintances.

Latter-day friend Mary Meyer made the prize comment: "This was the most congenial collection of people I've ever met."

It was a unique and supremely satisfying day, as full as the dreams which overtook my grateful yielding to sleep.

> Think where man's glory most begins and ends,
> And say my glory was I had such friends.
>
> W. B. Yeats

June 24

After 10:30 A.M. Mass for my Loyola group, I had breakfast with Nanci and John Corcoran, who came from Pittsburgh for my special day. We three then drove to Texas, Maryland, for the 12:45 P.M. Mass. Today was the feast of the birth of John the Baptist, and I congratulated all Johns, Jacks, Ivans, Iains, Ians, Jans, Juans, Evanses, Shanes, Shauns, Jeans, Hanses, Giovannis, Joans, Joannas, Johanns, Jacksons, Joneses, Jenkins, and Jennings.

The Gospel spoke of John as growing into maturity; I cited by way of contrast someone's observation that we grow hard in certain places, soft in others, but we too seldom ripen. I also recalled Jacques Maritain's kindred comment that as we grow older our heads tend to get soft and our hearts hard, whereas it ought to be the reverse.

Since the Corcorans are heading for Williamsburg tomorrow, I phoned some Williamsburg friends, Ann and Cy Brunner, and learned that they narrowly escaped death by electrocution a few weeks ago. They were trying to lower the extension of a metal ladder when it hit a 22,000-voltage wire, knocking out electricity in the neighborhood for several hours. Though both sustained third-degree burns on their feet, Ann and Cy saved each other by sharing the voltage. Now there's a parable of the ideal marriage.

✿

If you want a perfect church, just get rid of the people.

June 25

All of the Gallaghers who hosted my party (except nephew Frank) headed northeast today for the New Jersey shore and a three-week vacation in Avalon.

On this day in 1961 I arrived in a French city that is a rhyme-sister of Avalon, the Avignon of the medieval papacy. I saw the now-collapsed bridge which supposedly inspired the French nursery rhyme *Sur le Pont d'Avignon*. We saw in that castled town many gypsies with desperate-looking children. Rumor held that the mothers abused the children by way of eliciting sympathy and money from the tourists.

In Avignon I also discovered the lure of intoxication. A "pledge" I took in the seminary had kept me away from alcohol, but Archbishop Keough dispensed me from it for my trip to Europe. He had studied there before the Great War, and still deemed the drinking water unsafe. At Avignon I had drunk wine during supper, which consisted of the almost inevitable *poulet* (chicken) with which our hotel chefs tried to make us feel at home.

Afterward I found a little cafe outside the city walls, where I could watch the Rhone River darkening with twilight. I sipped some cold beers and gradually slipped into my first alcoholic high. I felt like a helium-filled dirigible cut loose from my earth-bound moorings. "At last," I sighed to the ghost of my pixilated progenitor, "I understand!"

※

I think I'll have another drink; it makes you so witty.

June 26

On this day in 1975 I agreed to take over as general editor for the bicentennial edition of *The American Catholic Who's Who*. This assignment put me in touch with such unhackneyed names as Outerbridge Horsey, a social worker named Toogood, and "Pascal Pompey Pirone, plant pathologist." Among the curiosities which escaped my rushed and blood-shot eyes: Jean Kerr and Walter Kerr were married to each other on separate dates and had an unequal number of children.

Thirteen years ago today I experienced a rarity: the last Mass celebrated in a church. In this case the church was that of St. John the Evangelist in Baltimore's once famous and heavily Irish "tenth ward." This was the church in which my parents had been married just forty years earlier. Now the neighborhood was mostly black and non-Catholic.

The closing of St. John's occurred on a Sunday morning. The usually empty church was now bulging at the seams with former parishioners who had heard of the imminent finale. The aisles were packed. Hymns were sung lustily from darkened and dog-eared hymn cards—old favorites such as "O Lord I Am Not Worthy" and "All Hail to St. Patrick." With tears streaming from their eyes, and children in their arms, men and women worked their way to this communion rail for one last time.

Since there were so many communicants I was drafted to help distribute Communion. By chance my mother was one of those to whom I gave the Eucharist. This being a Sunday, not many visiting priests were in the sanctuary. One of them, though, was Monsignor Harry Graebenstein, then of the Washington diocese, who had presided at my parents' wedding that day in June 1926. I can't recall that I had ever met him before, and he died shortly afterward.

It was a unique and wistful occasion, and a branding-iron lesson in mortality, the poetry of coincidence, and the power of childhood religious memories.

The most important thing about me is that I am a Catholic. It's a superstructure within which you can work, like a sonnet.

Jean Kerr

June 27

Four years ago tonight I shook hands with President Gerald Ford, who became thereby, as George Allen would say, the only President ever to meet me. (I had met J. F. Kennedy only as a senator.) Earlier that day I had conducted in Georgetown a wedding rehearsal for the daughter of my friend Dr. John Harvey.

President Ford was a friend of Harvey relatives and used to stay at their Michigan house in his football days. So, he was invited to attend the rehearsal dinner in the Army-Navy Club, which isn't far from the White House. The Secret Service wanted a list of all of us guests ahead of time. When we arrived at the club, a swarm of very serious-looking men checked us out one by one, and checked with each other by walkie-talkies.

Finally the Chief Executive arrived looking quite tan and relaxed, and dressed in a seersucker suit. When I was introduced to him he mentioned that he had recently visited Pope Paul and found him not so infirm as rumors had implied. He said he thought the pope's English was good, but he relied heavily on a translator. We were interrupted at this point, so that was the end of our conversation.

Dr. Zassenhaus told me she was once talking with President Johnson at an embassy reception when she reached into her purse to get a Kleenex for her sniffles. About three Secret Service men practically jumped her, and the President apologized for their wariness.

In the August before his assassination, President Kennedy visited the home of Senator Joe Tydings near Havre de Grace, Maryland. My older brother and his wife were invited to be part of a small group discussion of the upcoming elections. Frank said he saw the military man sitting nearby with the famous red box that could set off a U.S. nuclear attack or counterattack. Bringing a fresh drink to the President, my brother asked him, "How do you know this isn't poisoned?" JFK just smiled and said, "It probably wouldn't happen that way."

꙲

It's not that I'm afraid to die. I just don't want to be there when it happens.

Woody Allen

June 28

You wouldn't care so much what others think of you if you realized how seldom they do.

June 29

Fame is the advantage of being known by people who don't know you, of being known for being known.

June 30

At the 5 and 7 P.M. Masses at St. Joseph's, Texas, I preached on some of the secrets life had taught me about itself. After the first Mass, a young girl about twenty years of age said that she would have preferred quotes from the Bible to the quotes I used in my sermon. "Did Shakespeare know the Lord?" she inquired.

I suddenly realized I was facing a person whose narrow kind of religion I loathe. I told her that Catholic tradition regards God as the author of a second book, too—creation and the gifted human beings who see life in their own special way and talk about it with special beauty and power. I cited St. Ambrose's belief that whenever truth is spoken it is spoken by the Holy Spirit. I doubt that I converted her. . . .

As Independence Day 1966 approached I pondered over what I could write as a timely editorial in the *Catholic Review*. The U.S. had been suffering and inflicting casualties in the Vietnam War for over five years; our military involvement was growing month by month and the violence escalating. Having recently worked on the translation of the documents of the Second Vatican Council, I was well aware of the church's most current teachings on the subjects of patriotism, conscientious objection, and the dangers and moral limits of modern warfare.

As I began to summarize these teachings for an editorial, it suddenly occurred to me that such a summary would gain much wider attention and have much deeper impact if it appeared as a pastoral from Cardinal Shehan. He had just returned from Rome, where Pope Paul VI had again lamented the tragedy of the war in Vietnam. So, I gave the cardinal a draft of what I had written.

To my considerable amazement he speedily acquiesced in the proposal and accepted the draft *in toto*. He added at the end two sentences which I thought debatable, but I felt he was entitled to make such additions to what would appear under his own mantle: "That our President has earnestly sought such negotiations in the past, we cannot doubt. That he and our other national leaders would gladly enter into such negotiations now we firmly believe." (I did persuade him to change "we cannot doubt" to "we do not doubt.")

We were due to go to press on Thursday, June 30; on the previous day for the first time the U.S. had bombed oil depots in the Hanoi-Haiphong area. The cardinal suddenly worried that his pastoral might seem to be a response to that bombing, whereas the pastoral studiously avoided dealing with specifics and proposed only general principles. He was considering withdrawing the pastoral at the last minute, but my lawyer brother dissuaded him from doing so. To avoid misinterpretation, the pastoral was clearly dated June 28.

It was a sign of how little moral guidance the U.S. hierarchy had given their people on the Vietnam War that the pastoral created a sensation. As "moderate," "balanced," and "nonspecific" as it was, it was the first of its kind by a U.S. Catholic bishop. It was reported by the major Baltimore newspapers, and was a front-page story in that Sunday's New York *Times* ("Cardinal Urges Restraint in War"). It was completely reprinted in *The Catholic Mind*, *The Catholic World*, and *Ave Maria* magazines.

In editorials, *Extension* magazine called the pastoral "magnificent"; the *St. Anthony Messenger* read it "with pleasure and gratitude"; *The Sign* called it "an important document"; *Ave Maria* greeted it as "wise and welcome"; *America* spoke of its "added significance" in view of the Hanoi-Haiphong bombings; *Commonweal* found it a manifestation of what had hitherto been hidden: that the American church was concerned about the methods and peculiar madness of modern war.

The London Tablet carried two stories about it. In his syndicated column, Paulist John B. Sheerin called it "superb"; Lou Cassels, religion editor of United Press International, spoke of this "wise Cardinal" in a column syndicated in 214 newspapers; he said the pastoral deserved to be read far beyond the boundaries of the Baltimore Archdiocese.

A group of Baltimore priests, ministers, and rabbis immediately announced their support for the cardinal's words. The American Pax Association, a predominantly Catholic group, sent the cardinal a message of gratitude, for "by taking the lead in reminding the faithful that Vatican II gave a peace message to all humanity . . . you have accomplished a breakthrough." Three months later, Atlanta's exemplary archbishop, Paul Hallinan, and his auxiliary, Joseph L. Bernardin, issued a pastoral on "War and Peace" in which they refer to the cardinal's "splendid" pastoral. In a letter to me, the archbishop stated, "You know that your own Cardinal's pastoral was the inspiration for that of JLB and me."

This story has a less edifying sequel. A month or so later the cardinal told me with astonishing agitation that some letter writer in an Ohio Catholic paper had reacted to his pastoral by calling him a "communist." In late August the cardinal wrote an open letter to the National Commander of the Catholic War Veterans, who had conferred some honor upon him. He took the occasion of expressing his thanks to cite "distortions" of his pastoral. "Insofar as attempts have been made to interpret my pastoral as a condemnation of American presence in Vietnam, I would point to the fact that I made no such condemnation. . . . Our presence in Vietnam and the reasons which have prompted us to involve ourselves there are honorable. I approve of them." [When the pastoral and this letter were officially published as a leaflet, the last four words were significantly omitted. Also, when the cardinal's Memoirs appeared in 1982, they contained no reference whatsoever to this pastoral letter nor, in any context, to its ghostwriter.]

Published in the Catholic Review on August 26, 1966, this qualifying letter produced justifiable but (to me) tragic headlines: "Cardinal Supports War," said the National Catholic News Service. The National Catholic Reporter announced, "Shehan Backs Viet War." My judgment was that the cardinal had undone much of the good effect of his personally noncommittal pastoral.

Nevertheless, on November 18, 1966, the National Conference of Catholic Bishops issued a brief statement on peace which followed and paraphrased the earlier Shehan statement. And on April 5, 1968—by coincidence, the day after Martin Luther King's assassination—the cardinal issued another statement affirming that "ultimately a withdrawal of American troops must be brought about."

In the meantime, in August of 1967, an article appeared in the *New Blackfriars*, an influential magazine published by the Dominican Fathers in Oxford, England. The author, Ian Linden, wrote of the original pastoral, "The value of the pastoral is becoming ever more evident as the war continues; at the time it was a brave and forthright act of leadership when moral leadership was at a premium."

That damnable war would continue for nearly eight more years, though the U.S. withdrew in early 1973. My own battle with the cardinal quickly escalated so that I submitted my resignation as editor about two months after his pastoral. The occasion was an editorial about napalm bombs which he vetoed. But more about that in a later entry.

Meanwhile: this impression. What did the generality of U.S. bishops think about the Vietnam War? They didn't *think* about it at all. Like so many Americans at the time, they were naïve, anti-Communist patriots who believed that "the President and his advisers know best." (Remember Cardinal Spellman's "My country, right or wrong" remark in Vietnam?) That's why I was never much interested in their opinion on specifics. But I did expect them to promote the views on war which they had voted on at Vatican II. Amazing, that such consistency should be considered remarkable! (For the original text of the "Pastoral Letter on Peace and Patriotism," see Appendix B.)

The first casualty when war comes is the truth.
                        Senator Hiram Johnson

July 1, 1979

Success nourishes them. They can because they think they can.

Vergil, The Aeneid

July 2

Five years ago today I ended my drug research program at Spring Grove Hospital. Ten sessions were the legal limit. I stopped after six because I was going through a considerable amount of inner turbulence at the time, and I grew afraid of plunging into the depths any more than I already had.

Here are some memories of the final four sessions, some of which lasted longer than six hours. My director was always Bill Richards, who was once interviewed by Mike Wallace on *Sixty Minutes*. There he talked about his drug work with alcoholics and the terminally ill. I belonged to a third class—the emotionally turbulent who want to deal with pain from the past. In theory the drug breaks down your old defenses and allows you to relive pains from the past, but this time to accept and absorb them, so that they are no longer like giant-seeing pebbles in your psychic shoes. As Marcel Proust observed, "We are healed of a suffering only by experiencing it to the full."

Third Session: 12/7/73

Janet injects two needles into me (105 mgs.): she recalls the remark I made at the previous, second, session—about feeling as though I were hit by a Mack truck. Bill says, "Remember, it's your Mack truck, your very own; it's not a hostile outside force."

I sink down more quickly this time . . . deeper flashes of color, velvety blue. I feel that I am coming home again; this is the real me, my real world. . . .

Grotesque, distorted faces: am I in a hospital room? are these faces looking down at me? do I see blood? is this my birth scene?

The secret . . . the secret . . . beneath the pain and the energy at the center—break it open—it's a madman, a not too fearsome maniac. . . . (Is it the Wizard of Oz?)

Am I God visiting the earth? I didn't mean to stay, but I find its ridiculousness charming. I'll come back and marry the earth.

Sexual communion: two bodies linked and acting like a nutcracker trying to break open a nut because there is a secret inside— THE secret.

I realize it doesn't make any difference if I die, if anyone dies; joy, pain, past, and future are all mixed together, so it doesn't make any difference. But if this is so, will I die right now? I wouldn't want my mother and my nephews and nieces to suffer the shock of my dying— but didn't I just see that it doesn't make any difference? I'd better think about something else, quick.

My awareness is standing on weak, spindly legs which can only just bear the weight of the awareness. If I add the weight of being aware of the awareness, of making the object subjective, the whole reality crumbles and collapses. Yes—that's why I can't remember these secrets. They are too big for one mind—even to remember *that* fact is probably too big for just one mind.

I am busy appropriating a lot of unclaimed pain.

When I sink into these depths I have the feeling that "life" has been the dream and that now I am waking up, and the waking up puts everything into a resolving perspective, explains everything, justifies everything.

Will I discover the secret of life just as life is ending for me? Would that be too late—or is that life's purpose? Is the play the learning of the lines rather than the delivering of them to a compact, attentive audience? Is the real audience the people you meet as you are trying to learn the lines by heart—the bus driver? the waitress?

This is the truly dreadful: not what you run from, but the running from.

There are so many little dyings that it doesn't matter which of them is death.

Kenneth Patchen

Fourth Session: 1/22/74

For this session 120 mgs. of DPT were used. I remember seeing a vertical collection of silent, unsmiling kings from past ages, watching over the descent of their people from lookout points, one below the other, down the mountainside of history. . . . I, too, am watching over my family and my students along with the kings, who wear fur hats and have their fur collars turned up . . . someone should go up and kiss these shivering, unsmiling kings, bring them delight—like Scheherazade dancing in a hall of mirrors with an amulet bouncing against her belly . . . they have been so busy watching and protecting, they have forgotten how it is to be loved . . . tears stream from me as I think of loving and kissing them . . .

People love me because they have poor eyesight . . . in heaven you wouldn't have to worry about people's eyesight getting better, because their love for you will make you beautiful. . . . I was such a lovable, attractive, kingly child, sitting serenely in my rocking chair with my curly hair and my direct, confident eyes—how could anyone (like my father) look at me and then not want to come back and look at me again?

❦

He brought so little to what he saw that he saw what was there.

Fifth Session: 2/21/74

I was given 150 mgs. of DPT—five times the strength of my first dose. . . . On my four previous trips I had seemed to spiral down. . . . This time I just caved in at once and attained a very deep and seemingly tranquil level. I'm a diver repairing a submarine on the ocean bottom. When I surface I forget what I did but am confident I did something needful.

The main image that I can remember dealt with simple, peasantlike people, such as Grandma Moses might draw—wooden, stiff, unsophisticated folk in plain clothes and baggy pants such as Dutchmen might wear. It seems these people are having their first experience of the overwhelming quality, the excessive terror and beauty of existence.

Perhaps to distract himself from too bright a vision of reality, someone—was it myself?—writes down his own immediate, spontaneous reaction to it. Then he reads what he wrote and discovers he has written a hymn, a hymn being somewhere between a curse of rejection and a totally serene cry of affirmation, between an execration and an exaltation.

It seems that these primeval, primitive people did not realize how they felt about existence until they read what had been written. It is vital that by my writing I keep on preserving these pristine responses, keep them from being vulgarized, commercialized, trivialized, prettified. It was good to discover that the hymn was something that people could sing together. . . .

My sense of childhood loneliness seemed like being born in the room next to my mother, and having a father who would never have any children.

❦

It is always daybreak.

Norman O. Brown

Sixth Session: 3/28/74

For the first time the quantity was not more than the previous session—150 mgs.: flashes of white light, some awareness of increased heartbeat, swirling colors . . . down, down I sink, trying to let go completely. The music invades me. I'm so impressionable a false note could pulverize me. The beauty of it and of the light I see seems almost murderously painful. . . .

Little men climb back over the edge of my awareness and drop inside me. They act dim-witted, inebriated. They seem to know each other and to know the deepest part of me. It is as though we belong to a secret club, that we are really the ultimate people, but that we cannot normally let on that we know one another or even that we exist. We all seem to be grandfatherly types: like elders of the clan. . . .

There is a clear picture of the whole country (world? cosmos?) as a gigantic machine which has run down. It needs only a nickel to get going, but all the nickels have melted in an oppressive heat, and anyway, everybody, myself included, is too tired to insert a nickel. . . .

A poem: after all the wind and rains I am surprised to find that I am still a candle of astonishment burning before the shrine of existence. I am afraid I might blow out before I burn out—by coming to hate life, in response to pain or disappointment.

As I am surfacing I become aware of the music: I hear Pachelbel's *Canon in D* for the first time. I see a rose unfolding, and at its heart is a rose unfolding, and at its heart is a rose unfolding . . .

Also, as I surface, I realize that as in the past few sessions I went so deeply that I can't remember much.

Bill Richards had talked about a drug experience which I don't think happened to me, but which he seemed to regard as the supreme possibility. It is a kind of ego-death, in which the self lets go totally and thereby undergoes a dying of sorts—only to discover that a better self is born, one which is anchored confidently in the Universal Self. I doubt if this is the kind of experience you could forget or mistake. If I have no memory of such it is probably because I wasn't ready for that kind of surrendering.

The whole experience seems to have weakened my practical memory. That could be a promising sign. When you stand on a hillside you gain a tidy overview of the town below. When you descend and enter the town and partake of its hurly-burly life, you may feel that you have lost your clear vision, but you are actually coming to know the town better in its messiness than you did in its simplicity. Now if you return to the hillside, your clarity of view will have more depth to it. Such, at least, is how I console my growingly forgetful self.

☘

> Drawing near to its desire,
> our intellect is lost in such depths
> that memory cannot follow it.
> *Dante,* Paradiso *I*

July 3

Let a man marry or not, as he chooses. In either case he will repent of it.

July 4

The Fourth of July: a customary day for Americans to go a-picknicking. On this day in 1963, I went a-picketing—for the first time.

Though Gwynn Oak Park in west Baltimore was in a growingly Negro area, it still remained a segregated amusement park. If memory serves, there was no Maryland amusement park open to blacks. Dr. Eugene Carson Blake, chief executive officer of the United Presbyterian Church, U.S.A., and a president-to-be of the World Council of Churches, decided to join the Baltimore chapter of the Congress on Racial Equality (CORE) in a protest at the park on the July Fourth before the famous August March on Washington.

Informed of these plans, Father Joe Connolly and other members of Baltimore's Clergymen's Interfaith Committee for Human Rights decided on short notice to join Dr. Blake and Bishop Daniel Corrigan of the National Council of Protestant Episcopal Churches. Looking for other priests to join him, Father Connolly phoned me on July 3. So the next day I went directly to the park and began picketing before the main contingent arrived. Four chartered buses from New York and one from Philadelphia drove down to swell the number of protesters.

Father Connolly invited some Franciscan nuns to join us, but they said they would need the permission of their out-of-town superior. So, Joe phoned that superior and was told that it would be unseemly for the nuns to be involved in such a public protest.

"But," argued Father Connolly, "your holy founder, St. Francis of Assisi, once publicly stripped himself before his bishop and family."

"Yes," parried the superior, "but he was an extremist."

At the park I tried to distribute copies of Archbishop Shehan's recent "Pastoral Letter on Racial Justice." Some bystanders refused them; others took them, tore them up, and tread on them.

I heard one bystander say she was ashamed to be a Catholic. Another said he would never go to church again. Hearing these remarks and the taunts of some red-necks, I soon learned what an unpleasant experience it is to be a picketer. I marveled that black picketers elsewhere had been so patient.

Joe Connolly and Monsignor Austin Healy of Baltimore arrived around 3 P.M. and accompanied several Negro ministers who tried to gain entrance. They were all refused, and when they persisted, they were arrested. I envied Joe and the others who came and went so swiftly while I and others paraded about absorbing the heat of the sun and of the bystanders. Joe said that he and Monsignor Healy had the quasi-permission of the archbishop to get arrested. I think that the archbishop's precise statement was that these two priests could stay by the side of Dr. Blake.

Altogether 283 persons were arrested, including thirty-six Protestant, Catholic, and Jewish clergymen. A second protest was held the following Sunday when 101 persons were arrested, including twenty clergymen (but no priests). The archbishop had in the meantime directed that no priests partake in such demonstrations without his permission. This directive produced varying headlines in the Catholic press: "Prelate Forbids Priests . . ."; "Baltimore Clergy Are Told to Eschew . . ."; "Prelate Limits Clergy Participation . . ."; "Baltimore Archbishop Lauds Clergy Stand. . . ."

By the time of the second demonstration, banners had been made for protesters to carry. One rabbi picked up a banner at random and later discovered that his bore the words "We Are All One in Christ."

The park was eventually integrated, but it suffered financial losses and finally closed at the start of this decade.

The experience taught me one thing: if you want to make a splash (for whatever reason) do it on the Fourth of July. Practically no other news happened on that day. By early the next day the *Evening Sun* had even found time to publish an editorial entitled "Example of Decorum" and citing the dignity and effectiveness with which the protest at Gwynn Oak had been staged. That same day, page one of the New York *Times* carried a photo of Dr. Blake in collar and straw hat, ducking to enter a paddy wagon.

This ecumenical event was, I believe, the first of its kind in U.S. history. Thereafter there would be less ducking on the part of clergymen when there was a need for direct involvement in movements of social protest.

❧

> No man, white or black, shall ever drag me down so low as to make me hate him.
>
>   *George Washington Carver*

July 5

Bishop Frank Stafford and I went to a downtown lunchroom and chatted about old times. Somewhat younger than I, Frank, too, had direct experience of Cardinal Shehan's ambivalence about speaking out on the Vietnam War. "Your relationship with the cardinal was destructive, wasn't it?" he asked with a kind of detached sympathy.

Frank put me in mind of various warnings I had heard through the years about dealing with bishops: "Don't monkey with the buzz saw"; "Stay out of the engine room if you want to sail smoothly on the Barque of Peter"; "From a distance a bishop gives light; up close he burns." There is even an old Latin saying: "*Cave a prelato sicut a peccato* (Flee from a bishop as you would from sin)." Broadening the motto, the philosopher Kierkegaard reportedly told his nephew to stay away from the clergy and avoid one more sin.

Such bishop-fear apparently strikes even bishops. The rightly admired Monsignor George Higgins of the National Bishops Conference once told me that his long years of association with bishops had proven one thing: bishops are more afraid of other bishops than any priest is of any bishop. What they fear, I suppose, is appearing to be wrong or ill-informed or stepping out of line or failing in orthodoxy or in loyalty to the Holy See. Often, then, the sensible procedure is to do nothing, take no risks, launch out into no deeps.

If you are very, very careful nothing very bad or good will even happen to you.

July 6

Parents grow down so that their children can grow up.
                                                    Judy McGinn

July 7

I rose early to drive forty miles or so to the Georgetown area of Washington, where I assisted at the funeral Mass of the father of one of my most gifted students. Mr. Karl Kunz, Sr., who had worked as a lawyer at the Justice Department for several decades, died this week after a serious operation.

His son Karl had studied for the priesthood at old St. Mary's on Paca Street, eventually went into the Peace Corps, worked in Thailand, and later returned there to marry a Thai girl.

In the church of Our Lady of Victory was the gentle, artistic wife and her five other children, all talented in various ways. It was an affecting, familiar scene for me—the parent fading away, the spouse lingering on in aloneness, and the children moving forward to be the elders in a world from which they too will fade away sooner than they think.

I was driven to the Mount Olivet Cemetery with the kindly pastor. The driver told us that Mary Surratt, the first woman in U.S. history to be hanged by the government, is buried here. She was condemned for her supposed role in Lincoln's assassination.

Her son had been a seminarian at the old St. Charles Seminary whose successor I attended. He pulled out of the conspiracy when he realized that Booth meant to kill the President and not just kidnap him. A receipt for a pair of shoes he bought in Elmira, New York, on the day of the assassination helped establish his alibi when he stood trial two years later. Some mysterious person still places flowers regularly on his mother's grave, who died on this day in 1865. She had attended Mass every day during the previous Lent.

The pastor invited me to offer the prayers at the grave. As the family walked back to their cars, most of the children and their spouses formed a single line with their mother and locked their hands around each other's waists. I never saw the like before, and it was as powerfully touching as it was spontaneous.

> Each alone on the heart of the earth,
> Impaled upon a ray of sun:
> And suddenly it's evening.
> *Salvatore Quasimodo*

July 8

Two years ago today, I arrived with poet-friend Elliott Coleman in the fabulous city of Oxford. Our mutual friend, Michael Lynch, was in charge there of an Antioch Abroad summer school of creative writing. Michael, who had taught me at Johns Hopkins, had invited me to teach a class in "poetry writing." The program was centered in Plater College, a set of modern buildings in the suburbs of the city. The area was known as Headington; C. S. Lewis and J. R. R. Tolkien, of *Hobbit* fame, had lived nearby.

Visiting downtown Oxford that day with Michael, I couldn't believe that just anyone could stroll at will down these legendary streets and walk through the neatly groomed grounds of fabled colleges like Trinity, Balliol, and "Maudlin." Surely you needed special written permission from God or the Queen.

I know we Americans have a reputation for naïveté as tourists and as furious place-collectors. A priest-friend of mine said he was once standing outside the drab cathedral of Bologna when a car pulled up. "Is that the cathedral?" a Yankee voice inquired. "Yes," answered my friend. "Check it off," he said to his partner as he zoomed away.

And then there was the cartoon of an American couple bearing down grimly on Chartres Cathedral. "You do the outside," said the man, "and I'll do the inside."

Lucky for me, I was going to be able to spend six weeks and more doing Oxford. How could a trip be unlucky which had begun aboard a 747 on 7/7/77?

🌳

At Oxford in July, countless gardens vie to make their artistry most splendid. Here the War of the Roses never ended.

J.G.

July 9

Gratitude is the least of the virtues; the lack of it, the worst of the vices.

July 10

Desire has a long memory; gratitude, a short one.

July 11

The news has been full of Skylab and its predicted fall to the earth. Someone has been selling anti-Skylab spray. If it fails to work, you can get your money back. A recent *Sun* editorial noted that 300,000 pounds of meteors hit the earth each year. About once every thirty years someone is injured, but no known death has ever resulted.

Well, after six years in orbit and 875 million miles of travel, Skylab finally fell to earth early this afternoon. Most of its parts fell into the Indian Ocean, though some hit a sparsely populated part of southwest Australia. Happily, there are no reports of deaths or injuries.

Jim Bready of the *Evening Sun* is a stringer for *Time* magazine. This morning he phoned to tell me *Time* plans an article on preaching in America. Did I have a tape of myself giving any sermon? (No.) Could I provide him with one by Monday? (Yes.)

Sermonettes produce Christianettes.

July 12

I had a visit today from a young Illinois priest who has burned himself out in a large suburban parish. He was visiting friends on his way to a year's recuperative stay in a monastery. At his farewell Mass a liturgical dance was performed. One parishioner said she had heard many a prayer, but had never seen one before.

Rusty, who was a student of mine, is keenly interested in prayer. While meditating some time ago, he began to visualize himself as a fetus. He gradually became aware of a friendly presence, then of some distress, and finally of grief at the loss of that presence. The experience was so profound that he contacted his father and asked whether he was a twin. "Yes," replied the astonished father, "you, too, nearly died at birth. We decided not to tell you."

While in Berlin recently, where a documentary was being made on her life, Dr. Zassenhaus was disheartened to discover that two childhood friends whom she and her family had bravely defended during the Nazi period were quite worried about appearing in her film. In fact, one refused to do so, while the other had to apologize that her husband and children did not want to meet her. Germans, said Hiltgunt tonight, are still afraid of one another, and inclined to duck from getting involved. "It's as though nothing has changed."

On this day in 1968 the seminary rector at Paca Street told me that my own Cardinal Shehan was considering not sending Baltimore students to that seminary if I continued to teach there. That was a few months after the publication of my "Open Letter to the U.S. Catholic Bishops," and after I had let Father Phil Berrigan use my return address in a letter he was sending from jail to those same bishops. (Two auxiliary bishops replied and sent money: Thomas Gumbleton of Detroit and Bernard Kelly of Providence. The latter later resigned from the episcopate. The present archbishop of St. Louis, John May, sent a friendly but disagreeing letter.)

The rector, Bill Lee, admirably said he would back me up. I decided not to make the seminary suffer, so I was planning to pull out after my return from a summer trip to the Holy Land.

⚜

This wine is not the best. The grapes did not suffer enough.

July 13

Some men show the way by carrying torches, others by making torches of themselves.

July 14

A decade from today the French will be celebrating the bicentennial of the storming of the Bastille prison in Paris, and the birth of their national holiday. On this day in 1961, I sailed up the Rhine River and passed the rocky spot where the legendary Lorelei lures sailors to death with her singing. A few in our group were trying to sing the "Marseillaise"—probably with similarly deadly effect—when some Frenchmen aboard picked it up and sang their national anthem with great gusto, not to mention *élan* and *esprit*.

"Nothing happened today."
Marie Antoinette's diary comment on the original Bastille Day

July 15

> Your lot is mortal, but not what you long for.
> *Burial inscription near Dylan Thomas' grave in Wales*

July 16

Katherine Anne Porter phoned last Friday, convinced that this time "I am really dying." When I phoned yesterday I asked whether she would mind if I brought two of my Hopkins' classmates with me when I came today. "No, indeed," she replied, "I like to see people like that."

In her hour-long talk with Carolyn and Jim Bennett and myself, she mentioned how she had relished watching a recent thunder and lightning storm from her fifteenth-floor bedroom window. "When I was a child I used to lie outside on the ground when a storm came. My father said, 'That's dangerous.' I told him, 'I know.' And so he dropped the matter."

The retired archbishop of Los Angeles, James Cardinal McIntyre, died today. A conservative churchman, he tried to restrain some of the more change-minded nuns under his jurisdiction. One such nun was asked how she felt about his repressive efforts. "Well, as you know, we are spouses of the Lord, Whom we still love and wish to serve. Let's just say we are having some in-law problems with His clerical brethren."

Many communities of sisters now allow their members to choose between the old habit and more modern dress. Four nuns went dining once in a restaurant. Two wore the old habit and two dressed modern. When they asked for the bill, the waitress told them that some kind gentleman had already paid for the dinners of the two "nuns."

One moribund older nun who had tried out the new habit was discussing her funeral with her superior. She asked that she might be buried in the old habit. "Of course," said the superior, "whichever way you'll feel more comfortable."

In these polarized times religious groups are not always comfortable with their superiors. I heard of one such group which had just elected a new superior. A minority group was quite unhappy about the results and arranged to have the following telegram delivered at once to the community residence: "Sorry couldn't be with you today. [Signed] Holy Spirit."

The trouble, of course, is that the Holy Spirit is sometimes hard to recognize. I understand that there is a painting somewhere which shows a group of Franciscan superiors bowing their heads as they pray for heavenly guidance in the selection of their new father general. Meanwhile, over in the corner, another Franciscan is using a broom to keep out a dove which is trying to fly through the window.

In the last two decades much of the traffic has been in the opposite direction as monks and other religious have flown their communities. Some years ago a story was circulating about one particular monastery which had lost a very high percentage of its members. Finally this sign appeared one day on the community bulletin board: "Will the last one out please extinguish the sanctuary lamp and turn off the lights?"

For their part, the laity, too, have felt the seismic shocks of all these changes in the church. I recall giving a tour of Baltimore's new cathedral in the early sixties. I had just pointed out a window depicting the Last Supper and giving the names of all the participants.

"Is that Judas up there?" a woman asked me.

"Why, yes," I replied.

"Judas, in a stained-glass window?" She sounded disbelieving.

"Oh," I clarified, "that's not to honor him, but just because he was there."

"Oh," she sighed with relief, "I was afraid there might have been some recent developments!"

❧

What they were saying to each other was only, *Love me, love me in spite of all! Whether or not I love you, whether I am fit to love, whether you are able to love, even if there is no such thing as love, love me!*
Katherine Anne Porter, in the only lines in Ship of Fools *which are italicized for their own sake*

July 17

On this day in 1973, I was resigning myself to the fact that lack of funds would make this my last day in psychoanalysis. Almost two years earlier I had begun seeing Dr. Riva Novey several times a week. She had been part of a program on counseling given to the faculty members of the seminary where I was teaching at the time. (In fact, her office was about five minutes from the seminary.)

I liked her style and her approach. She was a distinguished-looking woman, perhaps in her late fifties at the time. She struck me as calm and perceptive, gently disciplined. I began seeing her in September 1971 and concluded on this day in 1973—285 sessions and $8,550 later. The archdiocese helped me with the payments, but the bulk came from my diminishing savings.

When I terminated treatment, Dr. Novey pointed out that in psychoanalysis the first two years are considered as just introductory. I knew that more work needed to be done on my unconscious; that's why I first made contact with the research program at Spring Grove Hospital during this same month in 1973. That program was free, would last less than a year, and concluded the following July.

As I talk about all of this I keep thinking of a cartoon I once saw: a man and woman are walking along a beach, and the woman is saying, "Yes, dear, I know your childhood was traumatic, but it is *so* boring." Let me just say, as swiftly as I can, that I'm not sure just what good effects resulted from the psychoanalysis. It happened to occur during the time when my older brother died suddenly, my mother was acutely distraught, and my eldest nephew nearly died during a 120-day stay in the hospital.

It was certainly helpful for me to be able to ventilate feelings freely during that period of time. (Sometimes, though, I was so preoccupied with immediate urgencies that I could not focus on my own interior world, so I just canceled some sessions.) I should point out that psychoanalysis is hard work for the patient; it is no facile task to speak out your most random, unguarded thoughts and mental associations in the presence of another person (and in this case, to a woman who could almost have been my mother).

I had lots of dreams, of course, and came to see them as coded messages for Dr. Novey herself. Part of me was jealous of her beautiful Irish setter; another part resented that she was taking all that money from me; still another part viewed her professional "coolness" as a kind of hostility or rejection. Once, when hearing me recount a dream, she abandoned her "cool" and exulted, "There are times when I am so glad I became a psychoanalyst!"

I suppose the most dramatic moment came when I was casually recalling that childhood day which I have already mentioned—when my mother broke her leg and had to crawl home from church during a snowstorm. I can still see my father in pajamas dashing down the inside stairs after he heard my mother's cries. As I recounted these memories I began to shiver so thoroughly that Dr. Novey put a quilt over me. (She was careful not to appear too motherly.) I came to realize that in my memory my father stays frozen on the stairway, and hence my mother stays frozen in the snow. I realized, too, that as fearful as this moment was, it had its beauty: my father was showing concern for my mother.

My most difficult moment occurred when, in trying to be totally honest, I mentioned my impression that the doctor would occasionally be reading her mail instead of paying attention to me. (She sat behind me as I lay on the couch—which I did most of the time.) Perhaps trying to soften that remark, I suggested that this might have been her way of testing to see whether I could really say what I was thinking. She said that there was no need to play games.

Speaking of the couch, I understand that the prone, dream position makes it easier for the patient to concentrate on what is going on inside himself. By sitting out of view, Freud hoped to keep the patient from reacting to any real or supposed facial expressions he might be making as he listened.

Among the emotional dynamics which Dr. Novey pointed out and I found most intriguing were these: a person tends to recreate a failed kind of relationship, as though in the stubborn hope of being successful at it this time. (Attention, all you folks who keep falling in love with the same kind of disappointing person.) She said that a person who had a deprived youth can actually grow resentful of the young people he later helps, because (thanks to him!) they have what he never had. Finally, there is a reaction called "closing-door panic," in which all the patient's emotional symptoms return at the imminent prospect of losing the doctor's support. (She also said that the amount of human distress in the world is infinite, and no one can change that.)

This business of psychotherapy is so paradoxical: the doctor has to get you to depend on him so that you can take the risk of trying out your flawed reactions on him; he in turn must avoid the temptation to counterattack in a flawed way; then he has to get you to un-depend on him as you grow in your ability to use your new and im-proved reactions on the everyday people in your life. Still, as one therapist told me, some patients get better without insight; others gain insight but don't get better.

A therapist, who is no less human than any of his patients, can never take away life's basic problems. (Even Freud said he could only replace hysterical misery with everyday unhappiness.) But he can help free the patient from artificial problems so that he or she can more creatively wrestle with life's genuine dilemmas with the help of genuine strengths and out of genuine needs. Moreover, the doctor can't tell you whom to phone, only how to use your emo-tional switchboard rationally.

I'm not sure how Dr. Novey took it when I mentioned that "ther-apist" can be spelled "the rapist," and "analyst" as "anal-yst." In any case I was quite touched when, on learning of my mother's death, she phoned me eighteen months after our sessions had ended. She invited me to pay her a visit without charge.

I had frequently complained about my mother's frequent com-plaints—which were understandable but which depressed me and emasculated me by making me feel unable to solve her problems and thereby make her happy; moreover, as a priest, I was angered that she made me feel angry and guilty and thereby scarred my self-image. Dr. Novey had originally told me, "You can't change your mother; you can only change your attitude toward her." On this oc-casion I asked, "How is it that no one ever told me how much I loved my mother?" She just quietly replied, "If you hadn't loved your mother, you couldn't have loved anybody."

Dr. Novey had told me late in our original sessions that she would not normally have said it, and she had never said it to any other cler-gyman, but she felt that the ministry was so destructive for me that I should leave it. I certainly gave her enough reasons for coming to that conclusion.

❦

It is sometimes just at the moment when we think everything is lost that the intimation arrives which may save us; one has knocked on all the doors which lead nowhere, and then one stumbles without knowing it on the only door through which one can enter—which one might have sought in vain for a hundred years—and it opens of its own accord.

Marcel Proust in Remembrance of Things Past, *Vol. 8,*
Andreas Mayor, translator

July 18

Invited or not, God is present.

Inscription over Carl Jung's doorway

July 19

When the finger points to the moon, the foolish man looks at the finger.

July 20

It isn't every day that one of your life's most memorable moments is also one of the supremely unforgettable days in the history of humanity. Such a coinciding took place a decade ago today, when the first human foot was planted on the moon. I was in Richmond, Virginia, that Sunday, visiting my friend Mike Schmied. Like millions of other earthlings, I sat transfixed before a TV set for more than eight continuous hours. I still have the front-page headlines of the *Evening Sun* for the following day. It was dated "Moonday, July 21, 1969" until some prosaic editor "corrected" the dateline in later editions.

All that exhilarated "looking up" found a tragic contrast that weekend in an accident which long had the nation "looking down" at the moon-responsive waters of Chappaquiddick, where Mary Jo Kopeckne drowned in a car driven by Senator Edward Kennedy.

Unlike the cow in the nursery tune,
or spacemen aloft in their metal balloon,
I don't think I'll ever get over the moon.

J.G.

July 21

Last week, as I was preparing to inscribe a book about the German poet Rilke for Dr. Zassenhaus's birthday, my eye caught a statement in the book to the effect that a certain line (in German) was the most celebrated one the poet ever wrote. Though I wasn't quite sure what the line meant, I included it in my inscription: "*Wer spricht von Siegen? Überstehn ist alles.*"

At the time Hiltgunt told me it means "Who speaks of victories? Endurance is everything." Today on the phone she told me that she was quite overwhelmed by the inscription because it was the very line she kept repeating to herself while she was doing her dangerous anti-Nazi work during World War II.

Her mind seems full of such memories. After we saw the movie *The Magic Flute,* she told me a story about the famous aria sung at the start of the final act by the basso profundo high priest, Sarastro. This haunting solo is a prayer for wisdom and safety in danger, and fruitful triumph over trials. As a brave girl in her twenties, Hiltgunt would get the Scandinavian prisoners whom she befriended to sing this song with her when her visits with them were ending.

When she finally visited Scandinavia many years after the war, one of those prisoners sought her out to present a monogrammed wooden spoon which, with the help of a nail, he had been carving for her in prison but never had a chance to give to her. He said his heart was still consumed with hatred for the Nazis. "Then," she admonished him gently, "they still have you in prison."

You feel you are hedged in; you dream of escape; but beware of mirages. . . . If you run away from yourself, your prison will run with you and will close in because of the wind of your flight. If you go deep down into yourself, the prison will disappear.

Gustave Thibon

July 22

"Snuffy" Nevins died today at ninety-five. He was the oldest of the priests living at the archdiocesan old folks' home. Snuffy taught

me moral theology for two years at St. Mary's, where he was famous
for his one-liners. Quite short himself, he used to say that anything
over five feet four was "an excess of vulgar matter."

I'm sure that many hundreds of priests across the nation still recall his practical and pointed observations about Christian morality.
In the treatise on self-defense, for instance, our Latin textbook said
that the self-defender is obliged to observe due proportion. Said
Snuffy, "That means, don't kill him any more than you have to."

I had a timely occasion today to recall his comment about suicide:
"A man must be pretty hard-pressed to take his own life." My niece
Mary Ellen told me tonight that a young acquaintance had hanged
himself. He was a fine athlete, had recently married, and "had everything to live for." He didn't drink heavily or smoke pot, and seemed
to have it all together.

Looking back over my fifty years, I find it remarkable that apart
from the seminary doctor I have known no relative or acquaintance
who took his or her own life.

❧

We must come to recognize the sacredness of being alive in our
own time.

Walter Lowenfels

July 23

On this day in 1968 I arrived for the first time in Athens and
gazed up at that astonishment known as the Acropolis, three hundred
feet above the city. I learned that quite a few ancient Greek cities
had an acropolis, a "city highpoint" to which the inhabitants could
withdraw in time of attack and better defend themselves. Later in
that 1968 trip I saw the acropolis of Corinth, the highest of them
all, which rises some two thousand feet above sea level. For its
heights of beauty, though, Athens topped them all. Gracing it still is
that marvelous temple dedicated to the virgin goddess Athena—the
Parthenon, from the Greek word for virgin. This zenith of classical
architecture hasn't a straight line in it. Straight lines looked curved
from a distance, so the lines of this building were curved to make
them look straight.

When the Nazis conquered Greece they ordered a Greek soldier to lower his country's flag over the Acropolis. With great dignity he obliged, but then furled the flag around his body and threw himself off the edge of that historic site.

I had a letter recently from one of my few correspondents who is likely to quote Greek at me. Bill Sharpe is a scholarly medical pathologist who studied at Johns Hopkins when I was assigned to the nearby old cathedral. In those days he, as a born Catholic, was wrestling with the basic question of belief in God.

He has since settled reasonably peaceably into the Episcopal tradition, and the tables have been turned somewhat. In several critical times in my life, he has argued for my staying in the Catholic priesthood. In his latest letter he wrote, "Are you still wrestling with the angel? You know my views well enough . . . that however you earn your living or spend most of your time, your Orders are essential."

I talked by phone today with niece Mary Ellen and nephew Frank. They are still dumb-struck by the suicide of their young acquaintance. Someone arranged for a psychiatrist to talk with the young man's closely knit family. This particular suicide seems so incomprehensible, from what I hear. I was told that in his suicide note the recently married man said something about his failing to live up to expectations, and feeling his mind was slipping.

I've heard some suicides blamed on happiness or achievement—the victims were too afraid of relinquishing the sadness which had become the most secure part of their selves, and was their last link with their parents!

I think many of us would prefer to feel guilty about the suicide of someone close rather than accept the more terrifying fact that in some cases at least the suicide is nobody's "fault." Any human act that seems so irrational reminds us comfortably that such irrationality can erupt in our own lives too, no matter how sensible they seem.

You must live out your whole life to realize that it doesn't belong to you.

Osip Mandelstam

July 24

He who is not busy being born is busy dying.

July 25

God sent food, then the devil sent cooks.

July 26

Hunger is the best sauce.

July 27

The Indian guide said that he had never actually gotten lost, but he did admit that once he was confused for several weeks.

July 28

You see a thing for the first time only once.
                                             Theodore White

July 29

If it is nothingness that awaits us, let us not live in such a way that it would be an appropriate fate.
                                             Étienne de Sénancour

July 30

On this historic day in 1968 I was in the midst of my first visit to the Holy Land and left the Mount of Olives for a trip to Bethlehem, the birthplace of Christ, and to Hebron, the burial place of the Jewish patriarchs. Both places are but a relatively short distance south of Jerusalem. I was surprised to learn that Bethlehem lies at an altitude somewhat higher than Jerusalem. I said Mass in the Church of the Nativity, at the downstairs altar in the grotto where tradition says Christ was born. My group sang carols and created its own version of "Christmas in July."

There is a metal marker on the floor indicating "the very spot." The walls around that marker were scorched by a fire some years ago. I was told that none of the religious groups who administer the shrine will admit that any of the other groups has the right to repair that spot. So it remains ugly, and an ugly witness to the division among Christians.

For our evening entertainment, our guide took us to an outdoor restaurant called the Jerusalem Gardens located behind the Christmas Hotel—a neat touch for us out-of-season carol singers. There we sipped arak (a kind of anisette), ate salads with pita bread, and smoked a hubbly-bubbly (alias a houka pipe).

I for one needed all the entertainment I could get. I'll quote the journal entry I made this day in that turbulent year of 1968: "Going into breakfast, I bought a Jerusalem *Post* from a newsboy and read the disastrous front-page news about Pope Paul's encyclical condemning birth control in traditional terms. More than ever I do not see how I can function as a priest . . . since my whole being (intellect and emotions) revolts against the harshness and inhumanity of this position.

"I can foresee only increased tension and agony and bitterness in the church, a collapse of discipline, and perhaps an eventual oath-taking loyalty purge. Many theologians and other priests, perhaps even some bishops, will repudiate the pope's decision and may leave the church. Surely this is one of the gravest crises in the history of Roman Catholicism."

I still have the clipping from the Jerusalem *Post*. Under a photo of a Vatican attendant delivering copies of the encyclical to newsmen the headline reads, "Pope Condemns Birth Control." Another story cited various Catholic reactions. A spokesman for New York's Archbishop Cooke said the pope's decision would require the assent of all Catholics "even under the pain of serious sin." But in Holland spokesmen for two dioceses said that "as long as the church was divided on the issue, decisions rest with the consciences of the married couples themselves."

In this unpredictable world you could still always depend on the U.S. Catholic hierarchy in its readiness to lower the boom on sexual matters! For myself, in my depression, the fact was not lost upon me that this devastating document from the Holy See was issued while I was at the Dead Sea—the lowest spot on earth, whose waters can buoy you up, but can also blind and kill you.

✤

Pain makes man think. Thought makes man wise. Wisdom makes life endurable.

Sakini in The Teahouse of the August Moon *by John Patrick*

July 31

When God erases, He is beginning to write.

Jacques Bénigne Bossuet

August 1, 1979

After my seminarian companion Mike Schmied and I got settled in the Nazareth Hotel on the edge of Nazareth eleven years ago today, I made the following notes in my travel journal:

"In the pleasant afternoon air I sit on my balcony, looking out and up to this sacred city. . . . Israeli soldiers with machine guns are in good supply, jets and helicopters have been flying overhead. There are about twenty Israeli flags at this intersection. A sign just in front of me says in Hebrew, Arabic, and English "Welcome to Nazareth." A road sign says 36 kilometers to Haifa, i.e., 22 miles to the Mediterranean; 34 kilometers (21 miles) oppositely to Tiberias on the Sea of Galilee.

"Yesterday's International Edition of the *Herald Tribune* . . . tells of eighty-seven U.S. Catholic theologians, speaking through Charles Curran, who assail Pope Paul's encyclical on birth control, say it is not infallible or binding under pain of sin on those who conscientiously feel otherwise.

"For the first time in ten days I am out of a big city. . . . It is much smaller and quieter here. I see the hills and the valleys, the tall cypress trees, slopes dotted with white stucco houses, some covered with light red (almost orange) roofs, some slopes parched and barren-looking, or quarried into. . . .

"I have often 'resisted' these shrines and holy places in Palestine —by nature I seem now so suspicious of piety and legends and so incredulous . . . still, I find myself . . . feeling attracted by this simple out-of-the-way village—I want to consider that for many years Jesus knew the shape of this setting, these hills, saw the sunrises and sunsets here, saw the moon silver the slopes. . . .

"Who can deny the impact which Christ's words and life and belief in Him have had on the past nineteen centuries. . . . Has Christ been spoiled for me by so many doctrinal squabbles and distinctions and side-takings? . . . Still I know how much of value I have gained through the institution of the Church, how Christ originally came to me through it, was made real to me by it, in its members I saw, from time to time, what Christ must have been like; so many of my friends, so happy memories are entwined with the Church . . . a considerable amount of pure water makes its vivifying way through those rusty, leaky pipes."

This man has insulted Christ in my presence. . . . But in insulting Him he has never asked himself: "Whom are we to put in His place?" . . . I believe that there is nothing finer, deeper, more lovable, more reasonable, braver and more perfect than Christ.

Feodor Dostoevski

August 2

Rationality is unmusical religion.

Max Weber

August 3

A madman is someone who has lost everything but his reason.

G. K. Chesterton

August 4

Traditionalism is the dead hand of the living. Tradition is the living hand of the dead.

Jaroslav Pelikan

August 5

We do not possess the truth. At best the truth possesses us.

August 6

The truth belongs to God alone. But there is a human truth, namely, to be devoted to the truth.

Martin Buber

August 7

This time last year I was visiting former student Pat Corcoran in upstate Pennsylvania when I heard the news of Pope Paul's death. Around midnight I began writing an article about him for the *Evening Sun*. Then I rose early to retype it and mail it off. I thought I had better call editor Brad Jacobs to tell him it was on its way. "I've been trying to get ahold of you," he said. "Hang up, phone back collect, and dictate the article to my secretary."

Exactly a decade earlier, in the new Rome of Constantinople (Istanbul), also built on seven hills, I had my audience with the Pope of the East, the Ecumenical Patriarch Athenagoras. Mike Schmied and I had arrived at his headquarters by 9:20 A.M. By then there were about fifteen people waiting in the plain room. His secretary included us two in a group of six or so, who seemed to be Greeks accompanied by some visiting French relatives. As we entered the office of the tall, bearded, black-robed, and octogenarian prelate, he gave each of us a kiss and an embrace.

He sat us around his desk—a plain affair, crowded with letters, some books, and a picture of himself meeting with Pope Paul in Jerusalem. On the wall was a second photograph of Paul and himself, and one of the first Turkish President, Attaturk. On a nearby table was a picture of President Lyndon Johnson—the patriarch had once served in the U.S.

Eventually he addressed Michael and me. When I told him we were from the States, his eyes brightened and he sang a line or two from "God Bless America." When I further stated that Cardinal Shehan was my bishop, his eyes lit up even more. At the end of the Second Vatican Council, both Rome and Constantinople repealed ancient and mutual excommunications, and for the occasion Cardinal Shehan was sent to represent Pope Paul in Constantinople. "I love your bee-shop," he told me in heartfelt tones.

Before long an aide came into the room with cool and welcome glasses of water. Each of us also had a turn at scooping out a spoonful of some white, gelid, and tasty concoction resembling ice cream.

By now the patriarch had seen my camera and without further ado he instructed his aide to take my camera and snap a picture of all of us standing with him. With another embrace and kiss the audience was over, but the rest of the group gave me addresses so that I could mail copies of the pictures to them.

I eventually sent the copies. Some months later I received from France a box of candy filled with various liqueurs. It took me some time to figure out who sent the box. The transatlantic gift was an apt symbol of the truly ecumenical patriarch's sweet and spirited personality. His death four years later meant something quite personal to me.

❦

The song I came to sing remains unsung. I have spent my days stringing and unstringing my instrument.

Rabindranath Tagore

August 8

The city of my birth celebrated its quarter of a millennium today —which means it is five times older than I am. The *Evening Sun* published my essay on how the world looked fifty years ago, when the city observed its bicentennial and I my fiftieth day of life.

I drove in the 98-degree temperature to Katherine Anne Porter's, where I said prayers for her, gave her Holy Communion, and fixed her rosary with the aid of a paper clip. She said the cross was missing; I told her she was carrying it.

She confided again, "I am going to die, and I'm glad of it." Later she wondered, "What will it take to kill me?" She spoke of having had some guests earlier this week. "They just sat around and chatted with one another while I just listened. Imagine! For once in my life I let somebody else dominate the conversation."

I returned to town about 8 P.M. and decided to have a light supper at Chiapparelli's, where President Carter lunched yesterday. Before sleep I went over the speech which Bishop Frank Murphy dropped by this morning for my comments. It's about the ordination of women. (You know of course that at Vatican III bishops will bring their wives, and at Vatican IV bishops will bring their husbands.)

A city ten times older than Baltimore preoccupied me on this day in 1968. I left the new Rome of Istanbul and flew to the old Rome on the Tiber. I was saying good-bye to Turkey, where over the taxi radio I had heard that day some woman singing "Hello Dolly" in Turkish.

When I arrived in Rome after the two-hour flight I learned that Richard Nixon had been nominated for the presidency. Six years later I would listen on this night to his resignation speech. During the Watergate hearings I had tried to follow the advice of a priest-friend of mine: "Let's not prejudge the s.o.b."

A final word for today about my birthday city. The Irish seaport town of Baltimore is said to mean in Gaelic "The place of the house big: baile-tig-mor." The big house in question was probably the castle of the once-ruling and piratical O'Driscoll family. The ruins are still visible and achieved their status of ruins in what some would call a very Irish manner.

It seems that some Portuguese ships were heading for Waterford with cargoes of wine. A storm threatened the ships, and O'Driscoll and his men dashed to the rescue. The grateful Portuguese broke out some wine to toast and host their rescuers. When the Baltimoreans realized how superb the wine was, they decided to imprison the foreigners and seize their cargoes.

Word got to the men of Waterford, who were so outraged that they marched on Baltimore, pillaged the town, and demolished its castle.

Nobody has yet been able to establish any link between this Baltimore or any other Irish Baltimore and the English Catholic family of the Calverts, who were given an estate in central Ireland by King Charles I and whose heads called themselves Lord Baltimore.

The Irish are a very fair race—they never speak well of each other.

Samuel Johnson

August 9

On this day in 1968 I was winding up my last visit to Rome. Ever since Pope Paul had issued his anti-birth control encyclical at the end of July, I had been reading in English-language newspapers various statements of reaction. Some of these seemed unjustly harsh toward the pope as a person. Gradually the idea came to me of making a statement of my own.

For more than seven years, as an editor of Baltimore's *Catholic Review*, I had been used to making public comments on church matters. I had studied and promoted the role of public opinion within the church. Church leaders need to know the honest thoughts of various members of the church; the respectful expression of such thoughts is a duty.

Until I arrived in Rome I had not had the time to prepare much of a statement; nor had I been able to read the complete text of the encyclical. Now I had the time and the text; also I finally had a newspaper contact, since the Baltimore *Sun* had a Rome bureau to which I could release any statement.

I had mixed feelings about making any statement, but I felt it would be easier for me to do so on this last stop before my return to the States. Since the statement was not going to be published in Rome but in the U.S., I did not weigh the indelicacy of making the statement in the pope's own diocese. But some, including my own cardinal, would take special offense at this aspect of my statement. For his part, Mr. George Mahoney would later accuse me of flying to Rome expressly to make my statement. (Incidentally, I learned on this day in Rome that Spiro Agnew, who had defeated Mahoney for governor of Maryland, had been chosen as Richard Nixon's running mate.)

When I made contact with the *Sun* bureau on this day I was heartened to learn that seventy-two Baltimore priests, including a monsignor and some seminary faculty members, had already issued a statement upholding the right of conscience for married people in this whole matter of birth limitation.

If venereal delight . . . were permitted only to the virtuous, it
would make the world very good.

James Boswell

August 10

This was the day in Rome of 1968 on which I gave my statement
on Pope Paul's encyclical to Bill Schmick at the *Sun*'s bureau.
Young Bill was the son of the *Sunpaper*'s president, and he showed
a touching concern for my personal situation at the time.

The same was true of Patrick Gavan-Duffy Riley, a kindly correspondent at the Rome bureau of the U.S. Catholic News Service. I
had known Pat, distinguished by his eye patch, from my Vatican
Council days. He is a very well-read and intelligent conservative,
and has since become the publisher of the *National Catholic Register* in the U.S. I still cherish the name card he dropped off at the
Grand Hotel that day, "with prayers for the best option."

The main motive for my statement was a simple pastoral one. I
was not supporting contraception as such, nor was I denying the
selfish, anti-life dangers of a contraceptive mentality. I was taking
God quite seriously. I was also taking quite seriously the concept of
mortal sin as involving the risk of everlasting separation from Him.
My own life experiences had made the abstract notions of utter
dread and absolute rejection painfully real to me.

As a confessor, I had known the agony of married penitents who
felt trapped between their insistent sexual needs (or that of their
partners) and the extreme advisability of having no more children.
From my own immediate family life I knew the reality of nervous
breakdowns and mental collapses, and the horrors of them.

As I read the encyclical I understood the pope to be solemnly
teaching that every act of contraception is objectively a mortal sin.
Of course, this was the teaching of the church when I was ordained.
But as a confessor I had growingly found this teaching a hard, too
hard saying. At times I felt I was pushing husbands and wives toward nervous breakdowns—or into abortions, which have always
profoundly revolted me. It was also unsettling for me to imagine the
amount of rage that I must be stirring up toward myself—though I
always tried as a confessor to be as kind and considerate as possible.

But as my internal questioning was reinforced by the vocal questioning and dissent aroused on all sides by the Council, I found the traditional teaching ever more repugnant. By the time that I learned that the majority on the birth control commission (including my own cardinal) had voted for a new approach to the problem, I had already reached a point of no return intellectually and emotionally. There was a seemingly simple all-or-nothing rationale to Catholic teaching on sexuality. At that time there was also such a rationale to my allegiance to the church. Or so it seemed in those frightening, sanity-threatening times in the late sixties, when the logical implications of my independent thinking forced me to confront my own sexuality in disruptive ways.

A less immediate concern behind my statement was the reality of world hunger and starvation. At times I found this reality profoundly depressing, and the source of severe temptations against belief in a personal God. How could a just and loving God allow such mass misery? The old question and the old attempts to answer it had not changed; but now the church herself seemed to be exacerbating the question.

In view of my fiercely negative feelings toward the church at the time, I did not find it surprising that my faith in Christ, "the founder of the church," was equally under attack in my emotions and thinkings. How could Christ be divinely present in a church which was in such a colossal mess? I guess we all set up limits to divine respectability.

Nor was it surprising that I had to wonder about the ability of my own sanity to handle the schizoid thoughts and feelings that resulted from that encyclical of July 1968. Talk about cognitive dissonance! Spiritually and psychologically I was pulling from my face an oxygen mask I had been born with. Could I survive without it? The very question caused palpitations that sounded as though the answer was no.

As I walked around Rome on this day in 1968, I came across a statue of Giordano Bruno, the Dominican priest whom the loathsome Inquisition burned at the stake on that spot in 1600. (The anticlerical post-1870 Italian government put the statue there.) Of course, I had no fear of physical reprisal from the church. But I had already learned that there is more than one way to be put to the stake; and when you love conflicting values, you put yourself there.

In some terrifying way the church as mother, God as father, and even Jesus as brother seemed to be dying in Rome that day. My public statement was a death warrant, a death certificate, a birth certificate, and a declaration of independence—all wrapped wrenchingly but inescapably into one.

That same day I had a letter from my older brother. He said that even the cardinal now wanted me to return to teaching in the seminary! I phoned Francis to alert him about my forthcoming statement. He was supportive, but advised, "Don't turn any sharp corners too fast." Others would turn corners too. On this day in 1969 I learned that Bishop James Shannon, friend and hero of mine, had left the episcopate and married.

> The frown of his face
> Before me, the hurtle of hell
> Behind, where, where was a, where was a place?
> *Gerard Manley Hopkins*

August 11

Eleven years have passed since I stood in the heat of the papal courtyard at Castel Gandolfo and heard Pope Paul VI give his Sunday noon blessing "to those who accept Our encyclical and to those who do not." This was to be my last day in Rome: and as disturbed as I was by *Humanae Vitae*, I could not miss what proved to be my last opportunity to see the pope. He would die there on an early August Sunday one decade later.

It was a stiflingly hot day, and the visitors in the courtyard were packed wall to wall. If you fainted you would have had nowhere to fall. Finally the thin Holy Father came out on the little balcony. From the enthusiasm of the crowd you could never have guessed that the church was in an uproar over the lonely decision of this single human being—single in both senses.

I realized that no matter how he had decided he would have been savagely criticized. I had to sympathize with him for that dilemma. I could feel the tug of a simple faith in his guidance. And why not say, sure, the pope may be right in theory, but sin is inevitable and God is all-merciful? No, I felt strongly that I had to resist that easy way out. And by so doing, was I not being loyal to the Catholic teaching on the primacy of conscience? But being a self-doubter—who are *you* to disagree with the pope?—I had to wonder whether I was hurting the church and general morality in a way which was truly against the will of God. "Remain in me," Christ had said in that morning's Gospel.

As I stood gazing up at this fragile-looking man dressed in white and pinioned at the aching center of the post-conciliar church, I had a sense of the dizzying developments of history and how wildly they buffet us. I knew that my own statement rejecting *Humanae Vitae* was appearing in the Baltimore *Sunday Sun* that same morning. Later I would learn that a front-page article including my picture stated, "Monsignor Gallagher Opposes Birth Stand." A smaller headline continued, "Baltimore Priest Calls Encyclical 'Tragic, Disastrous'; To Resign Title."

Apparently someone from the *Sun* had contacted Cardinal Shehan. Underneath my article was a second one: "Comment by Cardinal." "I have no direct word . . . on the basis of the news report, I regret Father Gallagher's action." Then, recalling my role in translating the documents of Vatican II, the cardinal quoted a section to the effect that a "religious submission of will and mind must be shown in a special way to the authentic teaching of the Roman Pontiff, even when he is not speaking *ex cathedra*."

It was Cardinal Shehan who had obtained for me the title of monsignor in the spring of 1965. The honorary title indicated that the holder was in some sense a member of the pope's personal household. At the end of my statement I noted that since the title implied a special allegiance which I felt I could not conscientiously give, I was planning to resign it. (I wasn't sure, though, how a person would go about doing such a thing.)

As it turned out I simply ceased using the title myself. In the cardinal's comment just quoted, I noticed that he did not call me monsignor. Later he expressly told me that I should not use the title, and official letters from the archdiocesan office still do not use it. Nonetheless, the latest edition of the official Vatican directory still has me listed with my old title. In any case, I was surprised at the amount of attention given to this symbolic afterthought of mine. It was mentioned in *Newsweek* and *The Reader's Digest* and figured in two novels: Ralph McInerny's *The Priest* and Clay Blair's *The Archbishop*.

This is the statement I wrote in the Eternal City:

I have keen sympathy for the harrowing decision which faced Pope Paul, who is so admirable a human being. But I feel an even more compelling sympathy for the mounting problems of starvation and overpopulation which afflict humanity, and for the lacerating distress of countless wives, husbands, and children.

That is why I find the recent encyclical so tragic and disastrous. As was his unique duty, the pope has preserved the inner logic of papal authority, but has gravely wounded its rational acceptability. I fear he has also damaged his magnificent efforts of leadership against the global scourges of war and social injustice.

Such is the mystery of God's will, and such the plight of human nature, that His Holiness may indeed be right, despite the contrary convictions of many wise and saintly human beings inside the church and out.

But is there never an objective circumstance in which contraception is not so grave an offense against God that a man's eternal salvation is jeopardized by the practice of it? Increasingly I have found this view so intellectually, emotionally, and spiritually repugnant that I would be false to my deepest self if I pretended agreement.

There was a time when Catholic loyalty probably meant approving the torture of heretics. I hope I would have drawn the line at that point. In any case, I cannot and will not have a part in torturing Catholic consciences on the rack of this shattering decision.

Pope Paul has undoubtedly followed his conscience at great cost. Individual Catholics must feel free to do the same. Like many other priests, I must now ponder what honest options lie open to one who was ordained to represent the church, but who regrettably finds himself in such radical disagreement with its official position on such a serious issue as birth control.

This is a time of exquisite agony for Catholicism, hence a time for extraordinary honesty, compassion, and forbearance. An excruciating burden has fallen on the shoulders of bishops, confessors, seminary teachers, theologians, and all who represent the church in official ways. In the tumultuous times ahead, great pain and confusion will afflict conscientious Catholics, especially "the little ones" without theological sophistication.

I only hope that such Catholics will turn afresh to the

simplicity of the Gospels and to Christ's message of concern, love, and forgiveness. Humanity at large is in its own agony, and disciples of Christ must not permit their own family problems to deflect them from their duty to embody the divine pity in every aspect of their lives.

A minor personal point perhaps needs saying. Since the title of monsignor should imply some special allegiance to the Holy Father and since I can no longer extend such fealty, except in affection, I intend to resign the title, not in anger but in simple honesty.

I hope that kindly men everywhere will, if they can, pray for Pope Paul and the Christian family which wants to look to him for guidance and solidarity as they struggle to bring God's mercy into a torn and sorrowing world.

Faith is what's left after you thought it was all gone.

                                    J.G.

August 12

I paid a visit tonight to my cousin with cystic fibrosis at Hopkins. He had a coughing spell which hurt just to watch. He's a brave youngster, persisting in his dance of wit and courage as the walls close in. When he heard another sick youngster making a scene the other day, he said, "Why doesn't he just yell 'ouch' and let it go at that?" Tonight he mentioned that he had had no vacation this summer. "But I might have had to spend the whole summer in the hospital—there's always a bright side."

Some years ago, Mike was the Maryland poster child for cystic fibrosis. Then he was the national choice and was flown to Hollywood to make a promotional film with a star. Earlier this year I suggested that he write a book about having been sick his whole life; he actually started it enthusiastically, but lacked the pep to continue. About the same time I gave him a prayer card which contained these words: "I asked for health that I might do greater things; I was given infirmity that I might do better things." Can such words mean much to a thirteen-year-old?

I have been meaning to touch on the topic of death with Mike.

Tonight I referred to his tennis bag, and asked him what he would do if I said I was going to stuff it full of jewels. "I'd empty it out," he answered, right on target. "Well," I continued, "lots of wise and holy people say that the purpose of life is to empty ourselves out so that God can fill us up with Himself. Sickness helps us to empty ourselves out. People who live a long time can get so attached to things that pulling away from them is like having adhesive tape stripped off a hairy arm."

Mike looked as though he was trying to drink these thoughts in. He brightened and said, "I should have said I'd get a bigger bag." Yours is plenty big, Mike.

> I learned that grief has a great purgative value. Since God cannot fill the soul until it is emptied of all trivial concerns, a great grief is a tremendous bonfire in which all the trash of life is consumed.
>
> *Claire Boothe Luce*

August 13

Pope Paul VI was still evoking statements from me a year ago today. Only this time I was lamenting some aspects of his funeral, which I had witnessed on TV the previous day. An estimated one billion persons watched the funeral. What a chance for the church to show its catholicity, its universality! Yet there wasn't one woman, one layman, one young person, or one nonwhite churchman immediately connected with the funeral liturgy. (Even women and laymen can participate in readings at an ordinary Catholic funeral.)

I couldn't believe that such a bad "sign" had been perpetrated by the Vatican planners. I said so in my article, which triggered some angry letters-to-the-editor. I mentioned my reaction to Bishop Frank Murphy, who mentioned it to our archbishop, who was going to contact the apostolic delegate in D.C. But the same basic bad image was repeated three more times in the next two months, with the installation and funeral of John Paul I, and the installation of John Paul II. In the last case, though, I think there was at least a procession of youngsters at the Offertory, and there were some shots of a choir of nuns.

More than one observer of Catholic affairs has stated that the greatest argument for the divine guarantee behind the church is that during all these centuries it has survived the colossal contributions of the clergy toward its utter destruction.

✣

Now I am a priest, with a boundless capacity for thwarting good, and for turning wine into water.

August 14

It wasn't until Pope Paul died last year that I realized that my own father, born on this day in 1897, was one month older than the pope, and about seven months older than Cardinal Shehan. Talk about father figures! I've already mentioned that my father was drafted on the last day of World War I; World War II ended on his forty-eighth birthday, but his life had already ended.

I was visiting the Wildwood, New Jersey, home of his stepmother and half brother when V-J Day arrived. After President Truman made his announcement of Japan's surrender on 7 P.M. radio, whistles blew, horns honked, and it seemed that everybody in the seaside town spontaneously went to church. No sooner would the sacristan bring out a new supply of votive lights than they would be all lit by worshipers.

It was off this New Jersey coast that German spies had slipped ashore, were caught, and later executed. On these same shores oil slicks used to appear from sunken U-boats and cargo ships. (Of the 40,000 German U-boat men in that war, 28,000 were killed.) Quite a few Americans were sure that we were going to beat those "Japs" in no time after Pearl Harbor, but it had taken nearly four years and two atom bombs to do so. According to one joke, we had won by giving the Mikado "atomic ache."

On this day in 1968 I had returned to Baltimore after twenty-one days abroad, and faced my own private battles resulting from my statement against the birth control encyclical. I phoned my mother and asked her whether the *Sunday Sun* article had brought any repercussions on her. She said one fellow tenant, a woman, had given her an unfriendly shove and exclaimed, "Your son!"

"I tell people that you are a man and have a mind of your own and know more about the subject than I do. Besides, to tell the truth, I'm confused myself." This was a rather upbeat reaction from a mother who was generally inclined to be overprotective of me. I was proud of her. My older brother told me that people treated him as though there had been a death in the family. He was probably referring to loyal Catholics who were embarrassed by all the public hassle.

The *Sunday Sun,* noting my statement, ran a rather curious editorial reminding its readers that the church is not a democracy. Several letters in the *Catholic Review* were soon to speak sarcastically about my resignation of the monsignorate. One lady suggested that I go into the press agent business "at which he has proven himself so astute." In reaction, a later letter expressed absolute shock that the *Review* would publish such a poison-pen letter. "I was his friend, I am his friend, and I will be his friend." The truth was that I loathed all this public to-do.

Altogether private was the visit I paid to Cardinal Shehan eight days after my statement appeared in the *Sunday Sun.* I talked to him for about twenty minutes in his seventh-floor office in the Catholic Center. (He was heading for Bogotá, South America, later that day in conjunction with the pope's visit there.)

> We greeted each other with genuine warmth. . . . I immediately mentioned that I had largely made up my mind to leave the seminary . . . I wanted to know his mind. At first he said my seminary acceptability would be up to the Sulpicians. I asked whether he had any minimum conditions, such as some public retraction from me. (His secretary, Frank Murphy, had mentioned this possibility earlier.) The cardinal said he could scarcely do otherwise . . . since I had "insulted" the pope, particularly by making my statement in Rome, also (though seemingly less importantly) by renouncing my monsignorhood.
>
> I told the cardinal I couldn't retract my essential statement and had made it in Rome as the first place I could find a news bureau I was acquainted with.
>
> When I said priests would be required by the encyclical to say it would be a serious sin to practice contraception under even the direst conditions, he replied "Did the pope say that?" I said it seemed presumed ("intrinsic evil". . . "go to confession").

I said I would probably find a place to live and do some writing or schooling. I said I didn't envisage asking for laicization at the moment.

He asked me again about writing the history of the archdiocese. I thanked him for making the offer under the circumstances, but said I didn't have the emotional energy to abstract myself from the twentieth century—though the prospect seemed at times an enticing idea. We both laughed. He asked me to let him know if he could be of any help.

Later that day I talked for an hour with Bill Lee, the seminary rector. He was personal and sympathetic, but said he didn't think I could very well stay on in the seminary without the sort of statement mentioned by the cardinal, especially since most bishops would know of my original statement through the Catholic press. The rector seemed disturbed himself about the encyclical but didn't see himself as about to leave the church.

⚜

Polemos panton pater: Strife is the father of all things.

Heraclitus

August 15

On this feast of the Assumption of the Virgin, I offered an afternoon Mass at the nearby church of Corpus Christi. (I read somewhere that the Jewish philosopher Henri Bergson had two paintings of the Assumption in his bedroom.)

Outside the church I met Paul Purta, the former head of the Sulpicians, who resigned recently from the priesthood. He thanked me for my letter of best wishes, and said he had received only two other such. He commented on the pains of adjustment and the temptation to fall back into a safe haven.

But he feels that for him there is something invalid in ministry as it is presently constituted. He spoke also of the institutional dishonesty of bishops on the subject of celibacy, and their general inability to admit the reality of sin and error in the institution. Paul is a gutsy man.

✢

The first step in greatness is to be honest.

Samuel Johnson

August 16

True democracy begins with the free discussion of our sins.

W. H. Auden

August 17

A dozen years ago I spent this night under the Roman stars, listening to an elaborate production of Verdi's *Aida* in the ruins of the Baths of Caracalla. The experience seemed like the ultimate variation on the practice of singing in the bathtub.

Water was much on my mind two years ago when a six-inch downpour of rain flooded the London subways and frustrated my plans to use a special all-day pass I had purchased. The newspapers were filled with the news of Elvis Presley's death and the BBC made a rare interruption of its programming to announce the event. The singer made front-page headlines for about four days in a row. Members of a British fan club were urged not to commit suicide.

Thirteen years ago today, while I was still an editor of the *Catholic Review*, I paid an ominous visit to Cardinal Shehan. But first, a bit of background. Two weeks earlier I had received a special delivery letter which the cardinal had sent from New York:

> For some time now I have wanted to establish the "parish coverage" plan for the support of the *Review*. This, however, can be done only with the good will and cooperation of both our priests and people generally. . . . To cultivate the necessary good will, I believe it is necessary to exercise great care in three particular fields: a) the question of race relations; b) the war in Viet Nam; c) Red China and the U.N.
>
> Before any editorials or special articles on these three

subjects are published in the *Review*, I believe that there
should be a conference between you, Ed Wall, the Bishop
and myself. . . . After my return I should like to have a
conference with you, Ed Wall, Bishop Austin Murphy and
myself.

Ed, a convert who had never worked for a Catholic paper until he
was hired at my recommendation a year previously, told me that the
cardinal had had an agitated conversation with him in July, suggesting that Ed the layman should censor me the monsignor when I
tried to editorialize about controversial issues. He told Ed "I have
written my pastorals on racial justice and the Vietnam War. Why
must the *Review* keep on dealing with these subjects?" (This, of
course, despite statements in his pastorals and elsewhere that these
ongoing problems required persistent attention.)

At the time of this August 17 meeting, I still hadn't caught on to
the cardinal's strategy of undermining me through Ed Wall, who as
a layman would presumably find it harder to argue with the cardinal
than I would. On this occasion I pointed out to the cardinal how
difficult it would be in practice to try to arrange a hurried conference with three busy people every time I wanted to deal with these
controversial subjects.

I also raised the question as to who was saying that my editorials
were all that controversial. I have reason to believe that his adviser,
Monsignor Joseph Nelligan, a kind of *eminence gris*, was my enemy
behind the scenes. When the Vatican once contacted me secretly
about this man's qualifications to be a bishop I had given him a generous recommendation. (Did that hurt his chances? He was never
named a bishop.)

Apparently swayed by my arguments that day, the cardinal backed
down and said that I need not submit any editorial to him unless
Mr. Wall judged that it was so controversial or problematic that the
cardinal should pass judgment on it. With that understanding I
thought I had been given a workable arrangement. Within two
weeks I would discover otherwise.

⚜

Don't wait for the Last Judgment. It takes place every day.
Albert Camus

August 18

Creativity is the acceptance, ultimately, of oneself as present, mysteriously, impermanently, on this limitless occasion.

John Cage

August 19

We're made in no fit proportion to the universal occasion.

Christopher Fry

August 20

A bore is someone who insists on talking about himself when you want to talk about yourself.

August 21

Shortly after I arrived in Oxford in the summer of 1977, I met Father Fred Copleston, a Jesuit philosopher whose books I had used as a student and later as a teacher. Precisely because he is not flashy, I used to call his paperback on St. Thomas Aquinas "Flashy Fred and His Favorite Friar." He laughed when I told him this.

He once had a BBC debate on God with Bertrand Russell, who later spoke of the Jesuit as the most gentlemanly adversary he had ever encountered. I could see this quality for myself as I asked him whether he was working on a new book. He said he was writing his philosophical memoirs. I told him I looked forward to reading them. "You shouldn't really bother. Most of the time I come down on the side of common sense, and you know how dull *that* is."

He told me that regrettably there aren't many famous philosophers buried at Oxford, though many taught there. He did mention the graves of Karl Marx and Herbert Spencer in London. "They're buried just across from each other." After I left Father Copleston at the Jesuit House in Oxford—Campion Hall—I had to smile at seeing nearby a department store called Marks and Spencer, which is like an English Woolworth's.

Some weeks later, on this day in 1977, I took the tube from London to the Highgate Station, and walked up the daunting hill to Highgate Cemetery. It is immense, and I had no idea where to begin looking for the grave of Marx. After a few minutes I saw a man in overalls coming down a path. I approached him and began, "Pardon me sir, could you tell me . . ."

" 'e's down there," came the reply before I finished the question. "Well, thank you," I said. "And what of Christina Rossetti?" (I knew that that delicate poet was also buried here.)

"Well, I don't know about 'im—but the 'ead one—'e's gone."

The section containing Christina Rossetti's grave was closed off, so I never did discover whether the grass was green above her, as she asked for in her haunting poem *When I Am Dead, My Dearest, Sing No Sad Songs for Me.*

I found the Marx grave where my adviser had indicated. A gardener was tending the plot around it, which was neat and flowered. ("It's a Communist plot," I've heard it said.) There is a great black bust of the bearded Marx above the tombstone, looking like Jehovah. It was Sunday, and I could hear church hymns floating down on the grave from the hillside. Many people do not realize that Marx's words about religion as the opiate of the people were originally spoken in a compassionate way. "Religion," he said, "is the sigh of the oppressed creature, the heart of a heartless world."

His grave contains two quotes from the master himself: "Workers of All Lands, Unite." And: "The philosophers have only interpreted the world in various ways; the point, however, is to change it." A young man from Switzerland stood by as I read these words. Other visitors, too, came while I was there.

About twenty paces away, on the other side of the path, was the grave of one of those philosophers Marx may have had in mind, Herbert Spencer.

In capitalism, one class oppresses the other; in communism, it's the other way around.

                                                    U Thant

August 22

I have no religion. That's why I think about God all the time.

August 23

If you have two cloaks and your neighbor has none, you are a thief.

St. John Chrysostom

August 24

We must help the poor in such a way that they will forgive us for helping them.

St. Vincent de Paul

August 25

Charity means seeing Jesus in others without requiring them to act like Jesus.

Carlo Coccioli in The White Stone

August 26

While love is very penetrating, it penetrates to possibilities rather than to facts.

George Santayana

August 27

If you treat men as they are they will never improve. If you treat them as you would wish them to be, they will begin to improve.

Goethe

August 28

While writing editorials for the *Catholic Review* I began toughening my hide against hostile reactions. In response to my Vietnam doubts one reader wrote: "If you aren't a dedicated Red, or a sympathizer (one and the same), then you are an incompetent fool who should be defrocked for the salavation of the Church. There must be a special place in Hell for men of your caliber, regardless of the reasons why you preach treason."

Treason wasn't my only sin. Once the *Evening Sun* carried a story about a panel that included Dr. Zassenhaus, an Episcopal priest, and myself. Pictures accompanied the story; my partners wore formal attire; I sported a sport shirt. Presumably these were old photos from the files. Someone sent me a clipping of the story. My partners had "Lady" and "Gentleman" written across their photos. Mine said "Bum." In case I missed the point, a sentence was added: "If you want to be a priest, put your coller [sic] on!"

By this time last year my article on Pope Paul's funeral and its exclusively white, elderly, clerical, and male flavor was being irately counterattacked in letters-to-the-editor in the *Evening Sun*. One lady thought it odd that "if Father Joseph Gallagher is so discontent with the Catholic Church he continues to remain in it . . . with his typewriter he continues to chip away at the rock of the church . . . why do theorists like Father Gallagher feel that they walk on water with their typewriters? The Roman Catholic Church has survived Luther and Calvin. I am sure it can survive Gallagher and his kind. These malcontents could form their own church. I even have a name for them: New Ultimate Thought Society: NUTS."

Earlier that summer, commenting on civil rights for homosexuals, I had tried to argue for a compassionate understanding of the emotional plight of many members of this "last minority." That had started its own round of letters-to-the-editor. One saintly priest wanted to know whether I would also urge sympathy for people who practiced bestiality and necrophilia.

A Catholic layman, referring to me as "Good old Father Joe," invoked Cardinal Shehan's belief that the church's main terrorists and snipers operate from within. This correspondent proceeded to expand on my liberal, corrosive, and destructive activities. After admitting that the amazing thing about me was that I was still around when most of my destructive confreres had left the church, he suggested that I put my inconsistent and self-centered moral philosophy to good use by applying for the then vacant position of technical adviser to *Playboy* magazine. (How, I wondered, did he know it was vacant?)

One good result of such letters is that kindly people often come to your defense. So it was that a lady who described herself as impartial, i.e., nonreligious and heterosexual, wrote that there was nothing in my "rational and dignified statement on homosexuality to warrant the venomous attack" mentioned above, but that the attack was a sad commentary indeed on the "ennobling influences which the two thousand-year-old tradition of the Church has had on that particular gentleman." Thank you, Lisa Crone, whoever you are. . . .

Today's feast of St. Augustine of Hippo coincided with three memorable moments in my life. I've already mentioned the 1963 March on Washington for civil rights, when Martin Luther King gave his "I have a dream" speech. I was among the estimated quarter of a million people who paraded that day in the capital. There was a joyfulness to that event which reminded me of a church picnic. I can still see the smiles and waves that Washington blacks gave to our bus as we headed home in the evening—after some of us had bathed our tired and torrid feet in the reflecting pool in the Mall.

I was spending two weeks as substitute pastor in the Caribbean island of St. Croix at this time in 1971. Having been told that this island is the easternmost point of land that belongs to the U.S., I drove before sunrise on this feast to the easternmost accessible point of land on the island, and celebrated Mass to the rising of the sun and the splashing of Atlantic waves. George Riddick, a then seminarian who is now a military chaplain, was my sole congregation.

On this feast in the previous year I was "south of the border," winding up my maiden voyage to Mexico. My two seminarian friends and I had heard of the restaurant Seps de Paris in Mexico City as a place where you could get good steaks cheap. We decided to treat ourselves, and were given a table right by a window facing the street. When the steaks arrived, two of us found ours to be tough, and we were grumbling appropriately. Suddenly we noticed a peasant woman with two children gazing through the window, wide-eyed at our "feast." I have never switched points of view so abruptly.

We beckoned her older child into the restaurant and gave him some of our food. . . .

On one of the feasts of Augustine which I spent in my native Baltimore, I was visiting my mother at Mercy Hospital. She had undergone surgery that morning and was doing well. As I was leaving her the night before, I had mentioned that the next day was the feast of St. Augustine, and that I would pray to the saint for her at Mass. As I was leaving her on this night, she asked me to tell her roommate whose feast day it was tomorrow, when *she* was to undergo surgery. I regretted to announce that it was the feast of the Beheading of John the Baptist.

☘

Feed the man who is dying of hunger, because if you have not fed him you have killed him.
        Statement of the early Church Fathers, quoted by Vatican II

August 29

Two years ago I said good-bye to Oxford. Before leaving I summarized for the *Evening Sun* some Britannic impressions, including these:

> Eight chilly summer weeks in England during Queen Elizabeth's silver anniversary. Amid an avalanche of impressions, what stands out?
>
> The fact that the Thames, "liquid history," was once a tributary of the Rhine; that greater London measures more than six hundred square miles; that its metropolitan population of twelve million comprises about one fourth of the population of Great Britain.
>
> This capital city features statues of Washington, Lincoln, and FDR, and has a Carter Lane.
>
> For lovers of quaint place-names London provides Rotten Row, Spital Square, Houndsditch, Threadneedle Street, Turn Again Lane, and the churches of All-Hallows-by-the-Tower and St. Vedast-Alias-Foster. (Oxford has its Quak-

ing Bridge; Cambridge its St. Bene't Street, and there's the
town of Bury St. Edmunds.)

People who have been shot or are otherwise externally
injured are said to be "ill" . . . never bring red and white
flowers to a sick person—they are a bad omen (blood on
sheets? the War of the Roses?) . . . if you give anyone a
knife as a gift, give then some money too, to emphasize
your friendly intentions.

England, the size of New York State, is full of plaques.
An English boy is said to have asked his father about the
names on a plaque in the back of a church. "They are the
parishioners who died in the service." "Which one, the
10:30 or the 12:15?"

Oxford's river has a section known as Parson's Pleasure
where even non-parsons traditionally swim or sunbathe
without benefit of swimwear . . . keep your eye on the location of the apostrophe and you'll not confuse Queen's
College of Oxford with Queens' College of Cambridge . . .
every year on his birthday a new quill pen is placed in the
hand of Shakespeare's bust over his grave . . . each year on
King Arthur's birthday his birthplace statue is adorned
with a floral wreath sent by an anonymous Yankee . . . another anonymous donor sent 174 rose bushes to honor
Winston Churchill's churchyard grave.

A young American girl asked an Oxford taxi driver what
the temperature was. He said he knew only hot and cold.
Her mother said, "Well, it wouldn't help us anyway; over
here they give the temperature in centipedes."

There's a church across the street from the site of Shakespeare's death. I wondered whether the immortal bard
might have attended that church, so I asked a teen-ager
who seemed connected with the place, "Could you tell me
how far back this church goes?"

"Only to that wall, sir."

❧

Time is God's way/of keeping everything from happening at
once.

Jack Marshall

August 30

The world will never know peace until the brave pacifist is as much of a hero as the brave soldier.

August 31

The chain of evil can be broken only by one who is willing to sacrifice himself in Christlike fashion, to absorb evil and suffering into himself, without yielding to the temptation of causing others to suffer.

Simone Weil

September 1, 1979

Forty years ago this morning my mother came into my bedroom at 403 East Twentieth Street (a mile east of here) and told me that "the war" had broken out; a war that would put 70 million in uniform and 35 million in the grave. It would leave hanging over humanity a mushroom cloud which would change everything except, as Einstein lamented, our way of thinking. After Germany invaded Poland, Britain and France declared war on Hitler's Nazi government. I thought of Hitler and his horrors yesterday when I attended the Munich Festhalle in the German part of the Busch Gardens near Williamsburg, Virginia. It was hard to relate the singing, drinking, dancing, and pastries to the Bavaria which produced Hitler, and to the Munich beer hall where he staged his *Putsch*.

Another war was decisively on my mind thirteen years ago today. Earlier that week I had written an editorial about the accidental dropping of napalm on U.S. troops in Vietnam. The newspaper accounts made clear the barbarity of this bomb, which we had been using on the Vietnamese. I seized the occasion to stress the dreadful nature of our involvement in Vietnam, and the urgency of concluding the war.

My fellow editor at the *Catholic Review*, Ed Wall, suggested that the editorial be sent to the cardinal so that he could see ahead of time that nothing was objectionable about it. I reminded Ed of the agreement: I need send the cardinal only items about which he himself had questions.

But Ed said that the cardinal had been much more upset in their discussions of my Vietnam pieces than he had apparently been with me. If the cardinal saw the editorial ahead of time he would know that there was no need to worry about it. I reluctantly agreed, suspecting that a bad precedent was being set.

That was on a Tuesday. On the next day I was stunned to learn that the cardinal was opposed to the publication of the editorial. About 4:45 P.M. I went to the cardinal's office on the seventh floor of the Catholic Center. (Our newspaper offices were on the second.)

The cardinal said I was sniping at the President. I said the editorial actually praised his peace-seeking efforts. But, in any case, is a paper based on Gospel values the only one which is not free to question the conduct of a war?

I asked whether my words were against faith or morals. He said they were imprudent.

I pointed out that by the agreement of August 17 the editorial didn't have to be shown to him ahead of time. He said Mr. Wall must have had some objection if he sent it up.

When I told him Mr. Wall's reason, he banged the desk and asked if I was saying that he said one thing to Mr. Wall and another thing to me. I forget what I answered.

Then I told this man who was chosen by the Vicar of Christ to be a prince of the church that I could no longer guess his mind even if I wanted to sacrifice my convictions to his fears. I asked him who said my editorials were hurting the paper and archdiocesan projects. "We have had very few cancellations, and even five hundred would be only one percent of our subscriptions."

"No one said five hundred had canceled."

"You act as though the President is going to alter his war policy as a result of my editorials. I don't take them *that* seriously."

"You contradict yourself. You say editorials are important and now you say you don't take them seriously."

"*I* take them seriously, but I don't think the President will."

"You say I contradict myself, but you won't allow that you contradict yourself."

The cardinal looked quite angry and ashen. He gazed down silently at his desk awhile and appeared very pale and weary and burdened. The windows behind him showed a darkening city.

"I'm going to have a meeting with some lay advisers tonight and I'll see what they say about the editorial." (I later discovered that this group included one of my wealthy cousins.) As I left, after about forty-five explosive moments—the worst I have ever had with a superior—the cardinal made some attempt to apologize for his anger.

Very little in my docile background had prepared me to look my religious superior straight in the eye and tell him, in effect, that in this matter I was following the inspiration of the Gospels and Vatican II, and he was not. I am still glad that when this watershed moment arrived in my life, the cause was something as brutal and loathesome as the savageries of modern warfare. And to think that a medieval Ecumenical Council condemned the crossbow as inhumane!

The next day was September 2, press day for the *Catholic Review*. I pulled into my parking slot in the Catholic Center garage just as the cardinal was pulling into his. It was about 9:10. He walked over to me and, looking somewhat uneasy, said to me, "Joe, we can't let that editorial go in." I merely answered, "All right," but I knew that a moment had come which would change my whole life and my basic attitude toward church authorities.

Just a week earlier the *Review* had published the cardinal's letter about the war to the Catholic War Veterans. In it he said, "The necessity of continuing discussion concerning our position and the means we adopt to reach our objectives is one which we can ill afford to forgo in a democratic society."

This is what I wanted to say in the suppressed editorial, entitled "The Horror of Napalm."

The tragic mistake by which American airplanes recently dropped napalm bombs on American soldiers in Vietnam has undoubtedly made Americans more than ever aware of the terrible nature of the war in Southeast Asia.

Napalm is a bomb composed of jellied gasoline. As recently described by newsman Jack Kofoed of the Miami *Herald*, napalm "burns people to death in the most excruciating way. . . . Napalm falls on a body, burns through the skin, eats away the tissue, muscle and bone, burning people into blackened, screaming shards."

Most of us had probably heard about the workings of this new type of bomb before we saw the recent pictures of our own men wounded by it. A member of a CBS television team happened to be near the site of the tragedy, and added these words to the pictures:

"We hit the dirt. I put my head up and the jungle in front of us was on fire. Running out of it were dozens of men, their clothes ablaze, some of them screaming, some rolling in the mud. . . . We reached them just as the medics were cutting away bits of skin and blackened uniforms. Another trooper, his face a mass of blisters, his hair burned away, spoke softly through blackened lips."

The enemy in Vietnam has undoubtedly resorted to merciless, barbarian cruelty—not only against combatants, but against helpless and innocent civilians as well. Still, as these savageries beget one another, and seemingly justify one another, a Christian is surely entitled to be revolted and sickened by the refinements in agony which modern man is able to inflict on his fellow human beings, his brothers under God.

Accidentally bringing home to America in a most vivid way the terrible cost of this war, these latest photos should spur the Christian to pray and work harder than ever to bring an end to this war as speedily as possible, as humanely as possible. Every effort of President Johnson to do so deserves the most cordial support.

Meantime, General Westmoreland's determination to see that civilian casualties are minimized merits high praise. As he rightly stated, one such casuality is too many. May the day soon dawn when such accidents won't have to happen, because all mankind will have learned to say with Pope Paul, "No more war. War never again."

🌳

Nationalism is an infantile disease. It is the measles of mankind.

Albert Einstein

September 2

The trouble about man is twofold. He cannot learn truths which are too complicated; he forgets truths which are too simple.

Rebecca West

September 3

It is well that God has made war so terrible, else men would fall in love with it.

Robert E. Lee

September 4

Faith begins as experiment and ends as experience.

September 5

The fact of the religious vision, and its history of persistent expansion, is our one ground for optimism.

A. N. *Whitehead*

September 6

On this day in 1966 I put on Cardinal Shehan's desk a brief letter of resignation as executive editor of the *Catholic Review*. Over the previous Labor Day weekend I had composed a four-page letter of resignation spelling out what his rejection of my napalm editorial had made "blindingly clear: that you and I have radically different convictions about the nature and duties of a Catholic editor."

I also drew up a fifteen-page résumé of past actions and criticisms by the cardinal which had left myself and the editorial staff in considerable confusion about his true attitude toward the paper and its function, or even about how to follow his directives. I cited the advice he wrote to me from Rome during the Second Vatican Council: "In dealing with the Council I think a good policy would be: not to editorialize on the account of someone who was not actually at the Council, or, if he was present, did not understand what was actually happening [November 16, 1964]." Apparently I was suppose to be able to make these distinctions from several thousand miles away.

Anyway, priest-friend John Gray (who has meantime left the ministry) advised me against sending these two lengthy documents. Accepting his suggestion, I merely wrote, "I regret that it has become compellingly clear to me that I can no longer continue working with the *Catholic Review* and preserve a good conscience, self-respect, and basic loyalty to my convictions about the function and duties of a Catholic editor. For this reason I am hereby submitting my resignation . . . also . . . I wish to take a leave of absence from the Archdiocese."

About noon the cardinal called me to his office and said he wouldn't accept my resignation or grant a leave of absence. I said that I could continue only with the understanding that I would write no more editorials, but only signed columns. (The cardinal seemed always to be worrying that readers would think he wrote the editorials.) Later the cardinal would say that he never gave final approval to this arrangement—though I published my signed columns for the next three months.

Showing himself a little more personal than usual, he said, "I guess I hate to have the paper criticize some prelate with whom I may have supper the next night." (I wasn't aware that we did that much criticizing of specific prelates. On another occasion he said to me, "I suppose you think I'm being venal"—apparently in reference to the implication that the paper should avoid controversy lest archdiocesan financial projects be hurt.)

Trying to justify my state of dilemma, I mentioned that I had drawn up a list of restrictive episodes, and stated my view that they would give scandal if they were publicly known. Later I learned from my brother that during the rocky months ahead the cardinal feared that I might call a press conference and publish that list . . . something I never considered doing.

My brother also told me that my reference to "good conscience" in my letter of resignation particularly nettled the cardinal. I was on record as saying that I was being asked to act against my conscience —though my letter carefully avoided saying explicitly who was causing me the problem. My brother implied that the cardinal wanted me to take back that remark, and in writing. I never did.

In order not to put him on the spot, I had tried to keep my brother out of this conflict between myself and the man whose attorney my brother was. Though we had offices in the same building, the cardinal and I, during these stormy weeks, did not talk directly to each other, but communicated by occasional letter. (It's too bad we didn't sit down quietly and have a heart-to-heart talk.)

Thus on September 26 the cardinal wrote, "One who I have every reason to believe is very close to you informed me that you regretted the submission of the resignation. . . . At that time I stated to the above-mentioned person that it seemed to me that since the resignation was submitted in writing, it ought to be withdrawn in writing. This he seemed to think reasonable."

In what was becoming a kind of cat-and-mouse game, I answered by letter on September 28, "I am sorry that some failure in communication seems to have intervened. . . . Although I indeed regretted the necessity of having to submit my resignation under the circumstances which existed at the time, I could not regret having acted according to my conscience. Hence, I am at a loss in guessing how some third party could have gained the opposite impression."

In his letter the cardinal also told me that he was establishing an executive committee which would take over complete responsibility for the *Review*. The members were to be his auxiliary bishop, Austin Murphy; his chief fund raiser, Monsignor Thomas Mardaga (future bishop of Wilmington); and the pastor who was widely deemed his closest confidant, Monsignor Joseph Nelligan—all men unencumbered by any journalistic experience. I was to learn later that the cardinal also turned over to them the matter of my resignation.

Lord, make me right, for You know how hard I am to change.

September 7

No faith-healing today, due to the illness of the pastor.

September 8

A man's character is dyed the color of his leisure thoughts.

September 9

The only secular thing on earth is the secular heart of man.

A. C. Bradley

September 10

Not how the world is, is the mystical, but that it is.

Ludwig Wittgenstein

September 11

The greatest philosophical question is why there should be something rather than nothing.

Gottfried Wilhelm von Leibniz

September 12

The most incomprehensible thing about the world is that it should be comprehensible.

Albert Einstein

September 13

I put my talent into my work, but my genius into my living.

Oscar Wilde

September 14

On this day in 1966, while my editorial disagreement with Cardinal Shehan remained unsettled, I picked up the September 16 issue of *Commonweal* (the national Catholic lay-edited weekly) and was appalled to read in John Leo's "News and Views" column that after Shehan "allowed his name to be signed" to the pastoral on Vietnam, he had "ordered his diocesan paper not to print anything more about Vietnam dissent" because of "heavy negative reaction from pro-war Baltimoreans."

On these matters I had had no contact with John Leo, who now works for *Time* magazine. I am not sure how he came by this information, even in its garbled form, but I suspect that it derived from a Baltimore layman to whom I had confided some of my troubles. Perhaps both he and Leo thought they were helping me by putting public pressure on the cardinal, but I feared that the cardinal would think I had leaked this information to embarrass him.

I immediately dropped a memo to the cardinal and included a letter that I planned to send to *Commonweal*. As I now remember it, he sent me word that he didn't much care what Leo or *Commonweal* had to say. Framing my letter to the magazine was a delicate affair, since Leo's implications were not altogether inaccurate even if his facts were partly inaccurate.

Leo argued with me over the phone. When the letter finally appeared in the magazine, it was a shortened and somewhat softened version of the original. But I still felt betrayed by my Baltimore friend, and I still feared that the cardinal thought I had betrayed and demeaned him. This wasn't the only time during the whole episode that I had to deal with patricidal guilt feelings, at a time when the cardinal was undergoing radium-seeding treatment for a gum cancer.

🌳

Journalism: history in a hurry; criticism of the minute at the minute.

September 15

Everybody wants to be somebody, but nobody wants to grow.
                                                            Goethe

September 16

Most men are not wicked. They are sleepwalkers, not malefactors.
                                                        Franz Kafka

September 17

My priest-friend at Georgetown told me some months ago that the magazine *Christopher Street* was due to have an article soon on him and his declared homosexuality. When I saw the latest issue on the newsstands today I had no doubt that this would be it: the cover showed a priest trying to separate two men; the central words were "A Cruel God: The Gay Challenge to the Catholic Church." Two other items on the cover announced an article on "The Comedian as Nun" and "A Gay Novel by a Catholic Priest."

The section that dealt with Bob was part of a long article by a former candidate for the Christian Brothers, Tom Dlugos. He also interviewed several priests and a nun who have worked with gay Catholics, and several anonymous Catholic priests who are gay.

The article struck me as quite accurate and fair-minded. One actively gay priest (presumably from the Washington Archdiocese) even took Bishop Sullivan's part against Bob. The priest estimated that about 10 percent of the priests of his diocese are gay, though not all are "practicing." Another non-gay priest who has been working closely with gay Catholics in and around Boston said he was told that 80 percent of current seminary applicants are gay.

"But why not?" he asked. "If a young Catholic discovers he is gay and wants to live a gay life, God and society and the Church and even his own mother will hate him—he is even supposed to hate himself. But if he becomes a priest, everybody will love him."

I'd be willing to bet that in my seminary days the percentage was nowhere near that high. (Consider all the priests who have left the ministry in order to marry!) But I did deal with a group of seminarians a few weeks ago and was struck by the seeming preponderance of young men who gave an impression of femininity and delicacy—though I realize how misleading such impressions can be. One of the huskiest athletes I ever taught was a seminarian who dropped out and is now living a gay life-style while doing dedicated social work.

When my friend Father Richard Ginder was discussing his memoirs with a prospective publisher, the latter asked him to add something about sexual activity in the seminary where he taught and I was a student. "There wasn't any!" said Dick, who is by no means a prude.

For whatever it proves, I would have to agree with the teacher of my adolescence. I spent twelve years in all-male boarding schools. In all that time I never once encountered or even heard of any resident homosexuality. After I left the seminary I did hear of one case dating to my time. On the eve of assuming the obligation of celibacy, a seminarian was approached by a younger student who devoutly pointed out that the deadline of possibilities was at hand, and who volunteered to be a gathered rosebud while the older student mayed!

It was probably always too simplistic to say that there are three sexes: male, female, and clergy. When Baltimore's auxiliary bishop, Jerome Sebastian, was once caught observing the charms of a passing woman, he explained: "Just because I'm on a diet doesn't mean I can't look at the menu." In Rome, during the Second Vatican Council, I heard a group of older and knowledgeable U.S. priests discussing the vow of celibacy. No one contradicted the priest who estimated that 75 percent of U.S. Catholic priests had kept their diet of celibacy perfectly. ("It's as tough to keep," opined one practitioner, "as you think it is.")

That of course was before the monumental exodus of twelve thousand U.S. priests from the ministry in the post-conciliar years. It was also before so many questions arose about the wisdom and the justice of the celibacy requirement, and before the sexual revolution of the sixties caused so many waves in a U.S. Catholicism which had inclined to be puritanical.

Even before all this, there was the relatively rare but usually hushed-up clerical scandal. (Canon Law itself felt obliged to deal with priests who used the confessional for sexual solicitation or who attempted to absolve a sexual accomplice.) One of the most admirable of my fellow Baltimore priests is Joe Connolly, an ex-Marine and a sterling, battle-scarred hero of civil rights, liturgical renewal, and ecumenism. During a public discussion he was once questioned by a professional priest-baiter in the audience.

"What would you say if I told you I was propositioned by a priest?"

Joe looked at the man for a few seconds and then replied: "Well, I don't know about his morals, but I can't say much for his taste."

❦

> Sexual life was given to man perhaps to divert him from his true road. It's his opium. . . . Without it, things come back to life. It is not immoral, but it isn't productive.
>
> *Albert Camus in his* Journal

September 18

> A wicked man is but a child grown strong.
>
> *Thomas Hobbes*

September 19

> Most of us would rather be wrong than appear ridiculous.

September 20

When I was in junior college, I had Father Porter White as a Greek and speech teacher. Aware of my interest in poetry, he was the first person to urge me to read T. S. Eliot's *The Waste Land*. In the copy he lent me, I read in the "Fire Sermon" section: "O the moon shone bright on Mrs. Porter / And on her daughter / They wash their feet in soda water." (Those words, preceding the section entitled "Death by Water," may have been among the few lines I understood at first reading.)

When I arrived at the cathedral rectory in June of 1955 for my first priestly assignment, I discovered that I would be sharing a bathroom on the third floor with my erstwhile poetry-pusher. He was assistant chancellor at that time, and Archbishop Keough's secretary.

Now Porter, a busy man with a sinus condition, was no addict to noiseless behavior, so I soon became accustomed to various slammings of doors and congestive harumpings emanating from the room next to my bedroom-study.

Twenty years ago today, however, as I sat writing a morning letter and half listening to a radio sermon, I heard rather strange noises in the bathroom. I didn't want to appear nosy, so I tried to dismiss the sounds from my mind. But they persisted and grew increasingly unusual. I waited until I finished my letter and then knocked on the door.

When I opened it to a presumed "Come in," a macabre sight awaited me. There was Porter White, fully clothed in his monsignorial robes, thrashing about in a bathtub containing several inches of scalding water. (Was the water dyed red by then, or has my imagination invented that detail?) I turned off the hot water instantly and tried to pull Porter from the tub. His clothes were piping hot and burned my hands. I led him to his nearby bed and proceeded to pull his clothes off of him. Steam was still rising from them.

I never did learn precisely what had happened. My guess is that he leaned over the bathtub and turned on the water as he tried to get rid of some phlegm. He may have been taking some stupefying medicine for a bad cold. Then, I think, he lost his balance, fell into the tub, and struck his head. (The old bathtub had a metal contraption that could easily slide down and plug up the water.)

I ran over to the church for advice from the rector, Monsignor Hopkins, who was master-of-ceremonying a Mass with Archbishop Keough. "Call an ambulance and take him to Bon Secours Hospital." I waited at the hospital until the archbishop and rector arrived. Porter White remained there for several weeks, then insisted that he was well enough to accompany the archbishop to Rome. There he had a relapse, was anointed, and nearly died. But he's the only man whose life I can reasonably claim to have saved directly.

As I was leaving the hospital that day, I was waiting at an elevator with the archbishop and the rector. A bouncy teen-age girl who was being discharged came up beside us, scrutinized us, and then shouted, "Why, it's FATHER GALLAGHER!" Perhaps she knew me from some high school talk I had given, but I was mightily embarrassed in the presence of these better-qualified celebrities.

Once, as a member of the Paca Street Seminary faculty, I was shepherding a visiting prelate of the Eastern Rite. He had asked to use my shower across the hall but was in there so long that I began to worry. (Did he know how to use the faucets; had he scalded himself?) I knocked at the door but could hear no answer above the splashing of water. Now really worried, I used a chair to look through the steamy glass window over the door. (Imagine my chagrin if someone had come down the hallway and seen me!) The dignitary was washing his clothes in the shower. . . .

Tonight I began giving a ten-week course in *The Divine Comedy* at Columbia, Maryland. My young friends the Rosiers have just moved there, so I had supper with them and their three children. Ron has a bridge partner who grew up in a neighborhood blessed with only one Catholic youngster. This papist was, alas, fat and sissified and much picked upon. Perhaps he was even called a "Cat-Licker," as I was in my tender youth. In any case one marvelous day he was taught that non-Catholics can be saved only if they don't realize that you have to be Catholic. So he sought out his tormentors at once and announced, "You can't be saved if you know you shoulda been Catholic. Well, now you know, so you'll all be damned."

❧

Calvinist Examiners: "For the glory of God, would you be willing to be damned?"
Seminarian: "Yes. And for the glory of God I'd be willing for all of you to be damned too."

September 21

Give your child a spanking every night at bedtime. If you don't know why, he does.

September 22

Justice is what happens when two thieves get together.

September 23

The law in its majestic impartiality forbids both the rich and the poor to sleep under the bridge.

Victor Hugo

September 24

I delivered to the *Evening Sun* an article about the pope's upcoming visit to the U.S. We've come a long way since 1854, when the visit of a papal representative caused near riots in several American cities and the churchman in question had to sail secretly from New York harbor. That was also the year when the stone sent by Pope Pius IX for the Washington Monument was stolen and reportedly chucked into the Potomac.

Many young Americans would be surprised to learn of the judgment of Arthur Schlesinger, Sr., that anti-Catholicism is the deepest bias in U.S. history. Also surprising would be poet-historian Peter Viereck's description of U.S. anti-Catholicism as the anti-Semitism of the intellectuals.

In any case, on this day in 1963 this American arrived in Rome for a month's working vacation during the second session of the Second Vatican Council, where U.S. bishops would be an outstanding force behind the Council's long overdue declaration on behalf of religious freedom. As a journalist I was able to obtain a Vatican press pass. ("Forgive us our presspasses" was the joke.)

This pass, however, didn't gain me access to an actual Council session, so I borrowed the pass of a Council *peritus* (expert), pasted my photograph over his, and won a seat at the sidelines of history-in-the-making. Immediately after the opening Mass that morning of October 7, the Council secretary, Archbishop Pericles Felici, honored my presence by solemnly announcing, "*Lamentandum est quod aliqui adsunt in hac aula sine auctoritate* (It is to be regretted that

some people are present in this hall without authority.)" Two Baltimore priests who knew of my daring and who were lawfully seated
in a balcony across from me in the nave of St. Peter's instantly
pointed accusatory fingers in my direction.

That was also the day when Maximos Saigh, the crusty patriarch
of the Melkite Rite, refused to give his speech in Latin ("It is not
my language"), but used his customary French. Then his priest secretary had to get up and give the speech all over again in the official
lingua Latina.

But getting back to this day in 1963: I had lunch at Ernesto's
with novelist Paul Horgan. He was in Rome working on his biography of Sante Fe's great archbishop, Jean Baptise Lamy, who had attended Vatican I. The novelist wanted to get the feel of a Council,
and wanted to meet me because as archivist of the Baltimore Archdiocese I had letters from Lamy under my care.

The author proved to be a genial gentleman, with a cultivated
manner of speaking. Morris West's *The Shoes of the Fisherman* was
quite the timely rage then, and Mr. Horgan did not try to disguise
his lack of admiration for that novel. Months later he visited the
Baltimore archives, and I was able to send him copies of letters he
deemed important. Lamy, by the way, was the hero of Willa
Cather's *Death Comes for the Archbishop.*

That Roman fall of 1963 brought me two less enchanting encounters with U.S. Catholic laymen whom I had held in admiration. One
afternoon I found myself standing on a street corner near St. Peter's
with one of those laymen and Mr. Paul Blanshard, author of the
anti-Catholic *Catholic Power and American Freedom.* Though unknown to them, I knew of them and they undoubtedly knew of each
other.

Looking dapper and benign, Mr. Blanshard asked whether the
Council might indeed issue some statement on behalf of religious
freedom. Mr. N. answered at once that not only might the Council
do so, it must do so. Noting my collar, Mr. Blanshard looked to me
for confirmation. "Is that right, Father?"

I was about to say that Mr. N. was quite possibly correct as far as
I knew, when the young layman in question fairly screamed out, "I
know as much theology as *that man.*" Indeed, he probably knew
more, but what he didn't know was who I was and whether I
merited that withering discourtesy. Alas, I concluded, not all of
Pope John's devotees share his sunny disposition.

That fact was reinforced soon afterward when I attended a press conference given by U.S. Catholic experts at the far end of the street leading to St. Peter's. Rumors were afoot that Vatican bookstores had banned certain "liberal" books on the Council. This issue came up at the conference, and a member of the audience raised his hand to say that he had recently interviewed the conservative Cardinal Ottaviani, who denied that there was any such banning. The interviewer was Dale Francis, a gentle-mannered convert and newspaperman.

After the conference one of the authors who was said to have been banned made his way over to Mr. Francis and challenged his statement about Ottaviani. Trying to answer the angry Mr. K., Dale Francis stumbled somewhat in his reply: "The cardinal told me to say . . . I mean, the cardinal said . . ." Mr. K. interrupted, "You mean you slipped!" Nothing like calling a man a conspiring, incompetent liar to his face. I began to think that the most important thing about one's heroes is not meeting them.

I don't know that anyone has written a book which tries to capture the human drama of Rome during Vatican II. Weldon Wallace of the Baltimore *Sun* was writing a novel about a Baltimore seminarian who was studying in Rome during the Council, but I understand he has set it aside at least for a time.

I did hear that a nationally prominent U.S. journalist was going to write a novel about conciliar Rome with characters based on actual personages, but I have heard nothing further. Will he tell the story of a religion editor who thought an eminent Jesuit was paying too much attention to his wife at their cocktail parties, so with butcher knife in hand he was found chasing the priest down a midnight Roman street? A pope once said that every Council has three parts: the human part, the diabolical part, and the divine part.

Whatever the prose situation, Vatican II did find its way into a memorable limerick. About a year after the end of the Council, British theologian Charles Davis left the priesthood and the church, and married a woman named Florence Henderson. For many of Father Davis's admirers this was a painful development. But someone tried to lighten the situation by thus recalling in rhyme a meeting of bishops held in Florence, Italy, during the late Middle Ages:

> "Charles Davis said with abhorrence:
> 'The Church has no biblical warrants.
> 'Vatican Two may be okay for you,
> 'But I'll take the counsel of Florence.' "

When the Earl of Kildare was criticized for burning down the great Cathedral of Cashel, he said he was truly sorry, but that he had been falsely informed that the archbishop was inside.

September 25

Today is the first anniversary of one of my most humbling and instructive experiences ever. Last year at this time my young friend from the Children's Village, John Standafer, was living with me, while a sultry girl roomed on the top floor. I knew well that John, who was about to leave for a legal job in South Dakota, was starved for, uh, feminine companionship.

I had told John that I would spend the night with friends in Washington, but there was a change of plans, so I returned home about 1:30 A.M. As I approached my house I noticed that the lights on the top floor were still on. When I entered the house, I presumed that John would be asleep on the first floor. Instead, his light was on and his bed empty.

I waited for about an hour for him to come downstairs, and then finally went to bed myself. After awhile I heard soft footsteps and a flicking out of lights. I boiled as I thought of what the upstairs girl would be telling her friends about the amenities provided by her clergyman landlord.

John slept so late that I finally woke him and instantly berated him for what I regarded as a betrayal of friendship. He sleepily denied my charges. He said he had been out with one of his girl friends from Washington, and that they had decided to get married. What a corny excuse, I thought! I phoned the girl friend and discovered that John was telling the truth. It was the worst act of rash judgment I ever committed, and it taught me a lesson about circumstantial evidence. . . .

A few years ago I could have been the blushing victim of such evidence. Visiting a former seminarian in Atlanta, I was invited to do my own laundry since his wife was away on a trip. When the dryer stopped I immediately transferred the clump of clothes to my suitcase. After I returned home I discovered among my belongings a piece of my friend's wife's unmentionables. I returned it in a plain brown wrapper.

On its network news this week, ABC has been running a series on "Catholics in America: A Church in Turmoil." The occasion is the pope's arrival here next week. A ghost out of what seems my distant past appeared in a network interview with Father Gommar De Pauw. I first met the Belgian-born priest during a summer visit in the late 1950s to Maryland's Mount St. Mary's Seminary, where he taught moral theology.

A stocky, heavily accented man, he was most hospitable to me and my companions. I've always remembered a Latin saying he told us about drinking wine and milk in sequence: "*Lac post vinum est divinum; vinum post lac, testamentum fac.* (Milk after wine is divine; wine after milk, make out your last will.)"

When on my recommendation Archbishop Shehan established the nation's first Catholic ecumenical commission in January 1962, Father De Pauw (who was incardinated into the Baltimore Archdiocese) was appointed a member, possibly at my suggestion when I drafted the pastoral announcing the commission. Only later did I learn that the priest considered that the writings of C. S. Lewis belonged on the Roman Index—a most extreme position. I was further told that he used to put notes inside some books in the school library, declaring that these works properly belonged on the Index and should not be read without special permission.

As Vatican II progressed and liturgical changes began to be introduced, Father De Pauw set about establishing the Catholic Traditionalist Movement. He was upset about the removal of Latin from the Mass and other "heretical, Protestantizing" changes in Catholic tradition. When Archbishop Shehan tried to resist his anti-conciliar activities, the priest began to insist that he had the pope's blessings and the support of high church figures. He was a close friend of a German archbishop who had been exiled from China; Cardinals Spellman and Ottaviani were rumored to be backing him privately against the liberal currents in the church.

At one point Archbishop Shehan was on the verge of releasing Father De Pauw to the diocese of Tivoli near Rome but changed his mind at the last moment. Although as editor of the *Catholic Review* I was somewhat closely involved in the struggle against the claims this priest was making, I never really knew what was causing the archbishop's extreme agitation on the subject. Once, when the priest was due to see the archbishop and accept or reject an ultimatum of obedience, I saw the newly created cardinal pace the rug of his study like a caged animal. I knew that he was not telling me the whole story.

Later, as the priest grew more defiant and went back on his agreement with the cardinal, my brother, as the archdiocesan lawyer, tried to serve on him a showdown letter from the cardinal. The priest was being interviewed by David Susskind on a TV station (in New Jersey, I believe), and his confrontation with my brother and his refusal to accept the letter produced a photograph widely used in United States papers. It also produced from the priest a reference to my brother as the cardinal's "portly henchman."

Still later, Father De Pauw returned to Baltimore for a rally at the Civic Center and an appearance on a radio phone-in show. The producer of the show feared that supporters of the priest would clog the phone lines, so he gave me a private number to call. The priest did not recognize my voice at first when I asked him about his insistence that he had never gone back on any agreement with the cardinal. After he repeated that claim, I asked him about a letter of his which I had seen and which disproved his claim. He sputtered a bit, deduced who I was, and told me to get off the line.

It is ironic that I began the year 1966 defending the cardinal against an anti-Council priest, and ended it with my own struggles against the cardinal and what I considered his failure to back up the Council's attitude toward modern warfare. I have pretty much disappeared from the official church scene, but Father De Pauw carries on thirteen years later as the head of his Traditionalist Movement.

Certitude is being wrong at the top of your voice.

September 26

Today was the seventy-third birthday of the most poetic poet I've ever known. He is Elliott Coleman, a tall, gaunt man with silky white hair, a Van Dyke beard, an elegant voice, and achingly blue eyes. I met him through his friends and mine, the Jacobsens. At the last minute in 1971 he admitted me into what was supposed to be his last year of teaching poetry writing at Johns Hopkins.

As fellow bachelors we became close friends—almost father and son. I helped to get him admitted a few years ago into Stella Maris, the archdiocesan retirement home. He went to England for a year, then in weakened condition returned last May to Stella Maris. His friends are glad to help him, a man who spent himself generously for his students over long years. As a result, he so neglected pushing his own career as a poet that poet David Ray in *Contemporary Poets of the English Language* calls him "one of the most neglected poets in America."

It was an experience to see some story or *bon mot* delight Elliott. He would raise his right hand to full height, swoop down on his thigh, slap it spankingly and pronounce the word "mar-velous" as though he had just invented it. But at heart he was a lonely, melancholy man, appalled at the world's perfidies and sorrows. He served for a while in his younger days as an Episcopal deacon. When he wasn't a troubled believer he was a troubled unbeliever. ("Never look," he warned in a poem, "unless you are ready / for everything / or nothing.") In either case, there was something saintly about him, something endlessly refreshing and endearing.

Once I offered him a pair of dark glasses as we drove about in the glaring sun. "No thanks," he said, "I feel that I have so little time left to look at the light that I can't bear to put any darkness over my eyes."

On another occasion I asked him whether he had heard any good concerts lately on his TV. He mused for a few seconds and then answered, "When you have to stop and think, the answer is no."

Once I was involved in a baptism and dinner party for a couple with three young children. The parents were going to break up later that week, yet everything seemed cheerful and civilized. Said I to Elliott, "I felt as though someone should get up and scream." Said Elliott to me, "Someone should always be getting up and screaming!"

Today I took Elliott out for a birthday lunch at a favorite Chinese restaurant. At Stella Maris the fellow residents in his dining hall usually sing "Happy Birthday" at breakfast to any celebrant. Elliott had let it be known that he detests that song. So instead the elderly ladies and gentlemen all came to his table after breakfast and shook his bony, fine-veined hand. "I was rather touched by their kindness," he admitted to me. "I should have let them sing the damned song!"

Quite a few years ago, when Ezra Pound was confined in a Washington mental hospital, Elliott visited him and later sent him a birthday gift. Pound responded with a post card containing only three words: "Presence, not presents." Those who know and love Elliott and accept his radical sadness and battle-frayed nervous system know that his presence is the best of presents.

.... only the brave are any good;
They're dead: and I am dazzled by their blood.
Elliott Coleman

September 27

Old age is not for sissies.

September 28

As for old age, well, all the sugar is in the bottom of the cup— and when you get there you'll have diabetes.

September 29

Last year on this day, at 7:10 A.M., my phone rang. It was my eleven-year-old nephew Pat Gallagher asking me if I had heard the news. No, I hadn't. "The pope died last night." It was a shocker all right. I knew the *Evening Sun* would want an article. I checked my source books and found that no pope since Leo XI in 1605 had served for a shorter time than John Paul's thirty-three days. I also learned that between 1590 and 1591 three popes had died.

By 7:30 A.M., I had the outline of an article in my mind and phoned my contact editor at the *Sun*. Brad said that the editorial page was pretty well closed out for the day and included an editorial on the dead pope. But he would certainly use my article the next day.

I went ahead right away anyway and delivered a typed article to the *Sun* by 9:15 A.M. Brad decided to rearrange the editorial page and insert my article immediately. In the process he shortened my piece a bit and left out some connecting sentences. So my quote from Pope John Paul's favorite, Mark Twain, came on somewhat abruptly: "Try to live in such a way that when you die even the undertaker will be sad."

In all my writing career this article was the speediest from conception to publication. In its own way it was an apt tribute to the swiftness of this winning pope's papacy. Attracted to journalism himself, John Paul I would have understood the satisfaction a free lance gains from such a performance. . . .

Fifteen years earlier, aching from my walk around the Roman wall, I had my first up-front experience of a papal ceremony. On this day in 1963, Paul VI opened the second session of Vatican II—his first as pope. My journal sketches some impressions: "We left the Villa Nova house by special bus about 7:50 A.M. for St. Peter's and walked into the Basilica by way of the Vatican Museum. I had a fairly good seat in the right transept, about twenty seats back in the journalists' area. (Vatican I was actually held in this transept, when there were fewer bishops attending.)

"A Protestant clergyman-journalist who had been devoutly reading his New Testament walked out in disgust during the Mass because of noisy and rude tourists who crowded illegally into the press area. Some of these were Italian nuns, who (it is said) use pencil sharpeners on their elbows before they attend papal audiences. Pope Paul spoke for sixty-three minutes in Latin and made an historic apology for the Catholic faults which precipitated the Reformation. While he talked, newsboys were passing out tear sheets of the speech from *L'Osservatore Romano*. They weren't much help if you couldn't read Latin."

Journalism is the first rough draft of history.
Philip Graham

September 30

Pope John Paul II arrived in Ireland yesterday for a three-day visit, and massive crowds—perhaps half of the nation—turned out to greet him in Dublin and Drogheda. Addressing himself to all men and women engaged in violence, he pleaded, "On my knees I beg you to turn away from the paths of violence and to return to the ways of peace."

After my three morning Masses I returned home to pick up my visiting priest-friend, Paul Philibert, O.P. We headed for St. Mary's Seminary in Roland Park, where we have both been faculty members, and which is celebrating its golden jubilee today and to-morrow.

At 4:00 P.M. began a festive Mass with Cardinal Shehan as main celebrant and Richmond's Bishop Walter Sullivan as preacher. Among other dignitaries in the sanctuary were Bishop Gossman of Raleigh and Father William Lee, president of the seminary.

My memory was easily transported back to this day in 1968 when I was at the center of a meeting that involved the cardinal, Bishop Gossman, and Father Lee.

The time was two months after Pope Paul's encyclical *Humanae Vitae* and my public statement lamenting it. Cardinal Shehan had said he did not see how I could be allowed to return to teaching at the seminary if I did not publicly withdraw my statement. But in the meantime Washington's Cardinal O'Boyle had suspended some forty of his priests who had also issued a statement against the en-cyclical. Reports were circulating that Cardinal Shehan might be asked to serve as a mediator. Dr. Whedbee, the psychiatrist whom I was seeing at the time, suggested that my own cardinal might now be willing to be more compromising about my return to the semi-nary. That led me to seek the meeting which occurred on this day eleven years ago.

I was not asked to make a public retraction of my opinions about the anti-birth control encyclical. But I was asked to write a letter to the cardinal expressing "to the Pope your apology for what some may interpret as an affront, expressed or implied, in the statement you issued in Rome."

I also agreed not to use the title of Very Reverend Monsignor, nor to speak against the encyclical and its doctrine. If I spoke about con-traception or heard confessions I was to present the teaching of the encyclical as the authentic and official doctrine of the church.

It was not hard for me, who had already said my piece, to make these agreements. In the meantime various conferences of bishops around the world had issued statements which allowed for the role of individual conscience in the practical solution of contraceptive di-lemmas, and which conceded that a conscientious use of contra-ception could occur without subjective serious sin. Had the original papal document made these statements I would have had much less difficulty with it.

In the weeks prior to this agreement I had felt acutely lonely and alienated. This is why I was attracted to the chance of returning to the seminary community. Why did the cardinal and the seminary officials accept this compromise? I believe they felt a genuine concern for my well-being and also thought it would be good for the ecclesiastical morale of many of the seminarians who knew me to find me once again in their midst.

> If any man can convince me and bring home to me that I do not think or act rightly, gladly will I change, for I search after truth, by which no man has ever yet been harmed.
>
> *Marcus Aurelius*

October 1, 1979

Quite a bulging day today: the pope arrives in the U.S., President Carter addresses the nation about Russian combat troops in Cuba, the U.S. ends seventy-five years of control over the Panama Canal, the Jews are celebrating Yom Kippur, the odd-even gas-rationing plan ends in Maryland, and my seminary class holds a reunion luncheon.

Thirty-eight had said they would show up at the luncheon; I had to guarantee thirty-five at $7.00 a person. Eleven classmates did not show up, including a doctor of psychology who phoned me some weeks ago and wanted me to make special arrangements for him to address all the alumni at the seminary banquet. Four people showed up without reservations. In the end, the banquet manager, himself a former seminarian, decided to charge me only for the number of lunches actually served.

Some of these classmates had not seen each other for thirty years; four of them brought wives along whom many of us had never met before. Some had children as old as we were when we last met. One classmate had licked a fight with cancer some years ago; another was undergoing chemotherapy; a third was gracefully losing his battle with a rare muscular malady called Charcot-Marie-Tooth's disease. It is hereditary, and now his twenty-five-year-old daughter is suffering from it. When Tom apologized to her, she said, "If you can bear it, so can I."

After our private luncheon, we headed for St. Mary's Seminary and a 4 P.M. Mass. Scripture scholar Raymond Brown preached. In the presence of a number of bishops, this contemporary and fellow alumnus of mine said that no church authority can forbid us to use our minds or countermand our loyalty to Christ. "People know their priest can be wrong; priests know their bishop can be wrong; bishops know Rome can be wrong." (I noticed he didn't say the pope.)

Seated next to me was a young man I first knew when he was a Catholic seminarian. Not long after ordination he left the priesthood, married, and is now the pastor of a Lutheran church. He was warmly "Amening" the sermon. I know several other priests who have been able to embrace a spouse by embracing other Christian traditions.

Also in my pew was a priest-classmate who resigned from the ministry because of all the changes. He has remained unmarried, but feels alienated from the church. He told me he is just waiting to die. He didn't receive Holy Communion, but accepted a handshake from me when I returned from the altar. We had a communion of the hands. At the "kiss of peace" some alumni found themselves shaking hands with a gay-rights ex-seminarian wearing a ring in his left ear.

These alumni occasions often have poignant aspects. Once I was in a pew with a former seminarian who still desperately wanted to be ordained, but who had been rejected by the faculty. Near us was the faculty member who had led the fight against him. The priest had in the meantime left the faculty and the priesthood, and was present that day with his wife.

It is amazing how much life resembles a bad novel.
Guy de Maupassant

October 2

Fear not your enemies, for they can only kill you. Fear not your friends, for they can only betray you. Fear only the indifferent, who permit the killers and betrayers to walk safely on the earth.

October 3

The hero is he who is immovably centered.
R. W. Emerson

October 4

I begin to suspect that a man's bewilderment is the measure of his wisdom.

Nathaniel Hawthorne

October 5

I am often wrong, but never in doubt.

October 6

I drove to the new cathedral parking lot and boarded one of the six buses taking about 250 Baltimore priests and deacons to St. Matthew's Cathedral in Washington, where the pope offered Mass for about a thousand priests from the general D.C. area. The buses left at 9 A.M. By 10:45 I was filing into the cathedral between large crowds, some of whom carried picket signs in favor of women's rights in the church: e.g., "The Vatican is not an equal opportunity employer"; "Sexism is a sin. Repent." My purple ticket gained me entrance.

Inside the cathedral, we Baltimoreans were given the remaining seats, which were not the best. I managed to slip into a side aisle, and met Bernie Gerhardt, a priest-friend from of old who is on the cathedral staff. Eventually he gave me an ideal seat in the fourth row off the center aisle.

Just in front of me today were admired priest acquaintances from former days—Monsignors George Higgins, of social-action fame, and Frank Lally, erstwhile editor of the Boston *Pilot*. George told me that his former confrere, Father John Cronin, was unexpectedly recovering from a serious heart attack. John has always been an avid newspaper reader. When his family was leaving on the night he was expected to die, John reminded them to leave money for the next day's Washington *Post* and New York *Times*.

Among the friendly crowd of priests was Wilmington's Father Pagano, the exonerated "gentleman robber" suspect. I congratulated him on his good luck. (The real robber gave himself up in the midst of the priest's trial.) Behind me in the pew was Father Jim Montgomery, who conditionally baptized President Johnson's daughter Luci when she became a convert during his presidency. (When she was later married at the National Shrine, it was said that the President wanted a small wedding so he had invited only the immediate country.)

Twenty minutes behind schedule, the pope arrived at 11:50, and was uproariously greeted by the crowd. Mass began about noon; he gave an eight-minute sermon on the Virgin Mary, and finished the liturgy about 1:10. I had a close, direct view of him and took about fifteen photographs. He seemed physically weary. He said the Mass prayers quite deliberately, despite the fact that he was due at the White House at 1:30. Curiously, he said nothing special to us as a group of priests. Bishop Frank Murphy was in the sanctuary and noted that, although the deacon extended his hand to receive the Host, the pope put the Host in his mouth, old-fashioned style.

About twenty minutes after the Mass ended, the pope appeared on the balcony of the next-door rectory. The crowd had been chanting, "Pope John Two, We want you." When he came out he replied, "Pope John Two, He wants you." Finally, he warned the enthusiastic crowd, "I will tell the President of the United States that I am late because of you."

I waited on the corner of Connecticut and Seventeenth Street until the papal motorcade passed by not long afterward. A thin young black man was selling fruit near the corner. "Buy this historical fruit which the pope passed by," he shouted good-naturedly. "Let your stomach go down in history," he continued. An NBC cameraman filmed him and his fruit.

My bus finally arrived, and returned me to my car about 3:30 P.M. I wolfed down a hamburger and headed for St. Jerome's church in south Baltimore. There a deacon friend of mine, a former counselee, was taking vows in an order known as the Sons of Charity. They take a special interest in poor working people, and often work at regular jobs in their midst. Seven members of the order—from France, Spain, Mexico, and Canada—were on hand as Bob Newman took his three-year vows of poverty, chastity, and obedience.

Bob, who sat up front with three young black boys, gave a very simple, honest, and moving talk before pronouncing his vows. It was quite a dramatic contrast, going from the pope, the crowded cathedral and TV cameras, to a poverty-area church with about fifty people in it and a young man who wants to love the poor as Jesus did. The cheers were for Washington but the tears were for Baltimore.

🌾

There is always more misery in the lower classes than there is humanity in the upper.

Victor Hugo

October 7

It is strange that we should see sublime inspiration in the ruins of an old church but see none in the ruins of a human being.

G. K. Chesterton

October 8

The pope is back in Rome and life in America is back to normal. A friend of mine, Sally Jenkins, who is a mother and a grandmother, told me the pope had won her heart but not her head.

🌾

Man is born broken. God's grace is glue.

Eugene O'Neill

October 9

I always expected the worst, but it was always worse than I expected.

Henry Adams

October 10

A totally unexpected snowfall hit Maryland this morning, dropping six inches in some places. The paper said it was the earliest measurable snowfall in Maryland history.

In the early afternoon I went to a public service hospital near Johns Hopkins University. A cardiologist there is a friend of a friend of mine, and he has agreed to give me a heart stress test in view of my intention to begin regular jogging. I did the first jogging of my life on the twentieth of last month. I ran around the reservoir in Druid Hill Park—a distance of about a mile and a half. While I was resting once, a black jogger who at first looked rather fierce asked me as he passed by, "You all right?" This was my first indication that the fraternity of joggers surmounts even racial barriers.

Today Dr. Lange had me take an EKG before the stress test. For the latter I was dressed in shorts and tennis shoes, with five electrodes pasted to my chest area, and blood pressure apparatus around my right arm. I signed a paper saying I realized that I might get a heart attack while performing the test. Then I walked briskly for nine solid minutes on the treadmill, which increased its speed twice. About every two minutes the doctor checked my pressure while I kept pacing.

When the treadmill stopped I was just about at my limit of persistence, and I began to feel the pressure around my neck which I first noticed the second time I jogged. The doctor said the EKG taken while I was pacing indicated that toward the end I was beginning to have trouble getting the blood supply I needed for my heart muscle. Otherwise the indications were good. He prescribed some nitroglycerine for me to take if the neck-area pains returned while I'm jogging. He said he had to reassure some patients that the medicine wouldn't explode if it gets jogged by a jogger.

❦

The optimist believes that this is the best of all possible worlds; the pessimist fears that the optimist might just be right.

October 11

On this day in 1962, in the presence of some 2,400 bishops, Pope John XXIII opened the Second Vatican Council with his call for the medicine of mercy. Like today, that date was a Thursday, and I was at the print shop putting the *Catholic Review* "to bed" while watching the Vatican ceremonies via Telstar.

We had made arrangements with Reuters news agency to get a

quick copy of the pope's opening talk. Even so we had to delay going to press until about 7 P.M. I recall finding twenty-seven typographical errors in the first galleys of the talk. We used linotype machines, so a whole line had to be reset if it contained one mistake. When the corrected galleys appeared, I found that the typesetters had made nineteen new mistakes in the process of hurriedly correcting the old ones. Maybe that's a parable about any human efforts to reform things. (One of Pope John's mottoes was something like "See everything; overlook a lot; correct a little.")

I was on a month-long visit to Rome when the first anniversary of the Council opening occurred. On that day I made a special point of visiting Pope John's tomb and blessing in its presence the Council medals I had purchased.

Today I paid my twenty-seventh visit to Katherine Anne Porter. Once again I read the handwritten note which was Scotch-taped to her door: "Please do not knock at any hour without an appointment. Please do not call me by telephone unless I ask you. I am not well and need quiet." Her signature had been cut away—you could still see the top edges of it.

When I asked her how she was, she said, "I'm dying, thank God."

She spoke of a current irritant. "Does it keep you from being peaceful?" I asked. With great vigor she responded, "I'm as peaceful as hell!" Then she made an impish grimace, looked heavenward, and blew a kiss in that direction. "That's a joke," she said of her earlier comment.

When I prepared to leave she pulled me to herself forcefully: "I'd be a fool not to realize that a terrifying thing is going on. I am going to a place where I've never been. This is a great moment in my life."

※

God knew I was going to be pope. You'd think He would have made me more handsome.

Pope John XXIII

October 12

A baby is God's opinion that history should continue.

October 13

Our ideals are like stars: we never reach them, but we guide our courses by them.

October 14

The chief flashback for this day takes me a quarter of a century into the past as I knelt in the chapel of St. Mary's Seminary, Roland Park. The new chapel had just been dedicated earlier that week, and I was in my last year of seminary. The whole community regularly went to the chapel after the noonday meal for a few moments of prayer. One of our classmates, a close friend of mine, was missing. This Joe Nunes had returned to Providence, Rhode Island, to pursue his last year of studies while acting as a prefect in the minor seminary there.

Our rector, Father Laubacher, now broke the silence from the back of the chapel. "I received sad news from Rhode Island this morning. Joe Nunes died at his home while recuperating from an appendectomy." Stunned, we all said prayers for his repose. The next morning the first Requiem Mass ever offered in that chapel was said for Joe, the first close friend of mine to die.

Joe had just been ordained a deacon the previous month. After a routine operation, he had gone home to Bristol on October 13 to rest up for a few days. His mother's birthday was Columbus Day, but she postponed her party until the night of the thirteenth. For the first time in several years Joe was not away at school for the occasion. His father and his brother Al made the family gathering complete that night.

The next morning, as he rose for breakfast, Joe was stricken by a creeping embolism and died immediately. This was the day he was to make his final decisions on the design of his chalice.

I was one of several classmates from St. Mary's Seminary permitted to travel to the funeral. On the day before the funeral I witnessed an indelible scene at the funeral home. Into the quiet of the crowded room, an elderly relative suddenly burst, threw himself

across the casket, and, between sobs, cursed God and Mary and all
the saints.

Everyone in the room was frozen with a shock of pity for Joe's
mother, seated at one end of the room. But as soon as she realized
what was going on, she rose from her chair, walked to the casket,
and began to console the old man for the death of her son. She
spoke no word of reproof for his language or his behavior. She was
just a loving woman, sharing pain and showing compassion. On that
day of death, Michelangelo's *Pietà* came alive for me for the rest of
my days.

The next day Joe was buried in the cemetery where he had
worked at a summer job a few months previously. I had visited him
at the time, and we played a joke on the groundskeeper, a good but
simple man who bore an antipathy toward a certain local family. Joe
told his boss that a powerful monsignor was coming to visit the
burial plot of that family; in fact, he was a relative of the family.

The boss hastened to tidy up the plot before I arrived, dressed in
cassock and sporting a red monsignorial collar improvised from the
label on an oatmeal box. A candle burned in the ashtray of the car in
which another classmate chauffeured me. When I exited from the
car, my chauffeur held an umbrella to shield my prelatial head
from the summer sun.

Tom, the caretaker, was duly impressed to learn that I was the
Roman delegate in charge of all U.S. Catholic cemeteries. He allowed that he knew my local relatives, and fine people they were, indeed. He would consider it a special honor to keep their plot in tip-
top shape. Fortunately, Tom didn't recognize me at Joe's wake.

I had met Joe four years earlier and we fast became fast friends.
He was serious and humorous all at once, and a great sportsman,
like our underclassman Jack Hooper. When Joe visited Baltimore
that last summer of 1954 Jack took an automatic shutter shot of all
three of us. Their classmates might well have voted them the
likeliest to live the longest. But Joe died in his twenties and Jack in
his forties. "One shall be left and one shall be taken"—but not always the ones you might suppose.

�֍

To grow mature is to pass from passion to compassion.
                                        Albert Camus

October 15

Today was a day for experiencing severe depression. What does that mean? I don't think "normal" people can truly appreciate the power and terror of this "emotionless emotion," but my fellow sufferers will know. Your blood turns to a dull, suffocating sand. All the magnets that normally motivate you are mysteriously switched off. All the color drains out of the interests that usually intrigue you. The tide of vitality has gone out—forever?—and you feel like an empty concrete ship sinking into the mud.

When "normal" people have their down moments, they are like swimmers who have dived into the water; down, down they go, but eventually the water begins to resist more successfully and they start the upward curve of their return to normalcy. But in our kind of depression you just keep going down, down, down. The thought of any duty or chore calling you from above, in that other world, only adds to the agony and the panic.

Years ago I was struck by the similarity with which two English poets described one aspect of this experience. Wrote A. E. Housman:

> When the bells justle in the tower
> The hollow night amid,
> Then on my tongue the taste is sour
> Of all I ever did.

In one of his "terrible" sonnets, Jesuit Gerard Manley Hopkins starts by saying "I wake and feel the fell of dark not day" and concludes, "Selfyeast of spirit a dull dough sours." In another poem he wrote, "Oh the mind/mind has mountains; cliffs of fall/Frightful, no-man-fathomed./Hold them cheap/May who ne'er hung there."

After all these years I do have some suggestions for my companion sufferers. Try to head off such moments by listening to what your own heart is trying to tell you about the source of your own unhappiness and the roots of true happiness. If there seems to be a chemical cause of the depressions, try to get medical help. Seek out a friendly ear and share your worry. (Six centuries before the first psychotherapist, Dante gave the role a good job description: "I began as one in doubt who craves counsel from him who sees and rightly wills and loves [*Paradiso* XVII].")

With respect to depression it is vital to remember that although the tide comes in, it also goes out. One therapist used to ask his depressed patients what their three greatest worries were one year previously. Practically none could remember, and the point was that a year from now even the present crisis will most likely be forgotten. Another therapist had his own predictable slump every April. So he arranged to take his vacation at that time and took it easy on himself until the siege was over.

The worst thing a depressed person can do is to project into the future the burden he or she is bearing: how will I ever be able to endure this weight tomorrow and next week and next month? This kind of torture by imagination strangles hope and multiplies the crush of weariness many times over. It has been well said that he who crosses a bridge before he comes to it has to pay the toll twice . . . at least.

So it is essential to live rigorously in the present, unless thoughts of the future give you heart. Such was the wisdom of these lines written by a child in a Nazi camp:

> From tomorrow on I shall be sad,
> From tomorrow on.
> Not today. Today I shall be glad.
> And every day, no matter how bitter it may be,
> I shall say:
> From tomorrow on I shall be sad,
> Not today.

Undeniably, there are many aspects of life and of existence and of the historical situation which are genuinely depressing, but we are under no obligation to be paralyzed by them. The problem of evil has a forgotten twin—the problem of good. ("Good grows wild and wide, has shades, is nowhere none," as the poet Hopkins probably reminded himself during his depressions.) We are surely free to focus on the hopeful and the possible rather than the hopeless and the impossible.

"Thoughts produce feelings; people produce thoughts." Maybe there is some reason waiting to be smoked out as to why we are partial to our depressing thoughts. If we can discover the source of that "carrion comfort," that "rotten luxury," we may well be on our way to a triumphant moment of liberation, in the glow of which we will say that the previous pain was all worthwhile.

If, despite your best efforts—and maybe your mistake lies in "efforting" when you should really try to let go—if the blackout times still come, be kind to yourself when they do. "My own heart let me more have pity on"—Hopkins said that, too. In addition to catching up on needed rest, try to keep busy with some work that refreshes you or at least gently turns your mind away from yourself. Do not turn out all the lights to see how dark it is. Even better, remember Coventry Patmore's advice: "We should not deny in the dark what has been revealed in the light."

On the subject of "letting go," psychologist William James offered this prescription: "Give up the feeling of responsibility, let go your hold, resign the care of your destiny to higher powers, be genuinely indifferent as to what becomes of it all. It is but giving your private, compulsive self a rest, and finding that a greater Self is there."

Most important of all: hug your dragon. Accept as best you can the fact that such depressions come despite your best efforts, and that they seem endless and hopeless when they do come. Remember that you are not alone in your aloneness. Your suffering admits you into an aristocracy of pain whose members have learned some of the deepest secrets of the human heart.

And if you find it hard to hug this dragon, then let that very difficulty be your dragon, and start by hugging that. There is a law of dragon size: for every foot you walk toward it, toward hugging it, the dragon shrinks another foot.

My supreme wish for everyone who is my brother and sister in this special kind of trial is that they may discover this law of dragon size, perhaps the very day and hour they read these knowing and well-wishing words.

❧

A man who is unable to despair has no need to be alive.
Goethe

October 16

On this first anniversary of Pope John Paul II's election, the *National Catholic Reporter* arrived with a whole collection of reactions to his U.S. visit. Many commentators foresee a restoration period that will try to bring the church back to pre-Vatican II attitudes. All in all, a depressing view of the future was presented, with the prospect of further alienation among the very Catholics who are most willing and able to promote the pope's progressive social views.

I was as surprised and intrigued as anyone else last year when the bulletin came over my car radio that a Polish cardinal had been elected. (I had predicted, though, that the new man would call himself John Paul II. Regrettably, I hadn't taken any bets on the issue.) I was near my home when the word came, so I could follow the rest of the drama on TV.

By 1:30 the next morning I was able to deliver an article to the *Sun*, which appeared later that day. My title had been "From Behind Two Curtains: A New Pope." I was referring to the Iron Curtain and to the curtain behind the balcony of St. Peter's. Unfortunately, my title had to be squeezed into two columns, so it came out embarrassingly as "A Two-Curtain Pope." . . .

In midafternoon today I had a surprise visit from friend Bill Nagle, who lives near Washington, works for the Department of Agriculture, and flies all over the nation giving speeches. He happened to be passing nearby and took a chance that I'd be home. His eldest son, born the day after my friend Joe Nunes died, left home about five years ago and has disappeared from their lives. Bill recently learned that his son is in the Oregon area. He respects his son's desire for privacy, but would like to embrace him and tell him it's all right that he has done what he felt he had to do.

That's an endless story, for sure, the tension between parents and children. One of my students told me that his mother, who lived through the Depression, was bugging him lately about "wasting" his money buying plastic bags for the leaves he had raked together in her backyard. He had been hearing such sermons on thrift all his life long. That day he had had enough. He took a $10 bill from his wallet, said, "Look, Mom, it's only money," and tore it to pieces. His mother burst into tears and nearly went into shock. She got down on her knees and tried to save the pieces.

The best way to give advice to your children is to find out what they want to do, and then advise them to do it.

Harry S Truman

October 17

We must come to love even our wounds.
                                    Nietzsche

October 18

Wisdom is a comb that life provides you after you've lost your hair.

October 19

He who is married to the spirit of the age is soon a widower.

October 20

A flatterer will say to your face what he will never say behind your back.

October 21

Sentimentality is unearned emotion.

October 22

Is there a doctor in the house? Two doctors arrived at my house today, and will stay till Friday. Bill Sharpe is a pathologist in New York's Cabrini Hospital. I met him in the mid-fifties when he was a med student at Hopkins and attended Mass at the old cathedral. With him is a cardiologist friend, Heracleo Alabado, who was born in the Philippines fifty-two years ago today. They are on a two-week vacation.

As I lay me down to sleep, I thought of the brief speech Bill Sharpe once told me he plans to give when he meets his Maker:

"Well, I played with the cards You gave me, and tried not to complain."

Cuba's Premier Fidel Castro addressed the UN recently, some days after the pope did so. This day in 1962 was also a Monday, and President Kennedy took to radio and TV to announce the quarantine of Cuba after Soviet missile installations were detected there. I can recall reading in the paper two days previously that the President had returned early from Chicago "because of a cold." On Sunday there were rumors of a crisis, followed by an announcement that the President would address the nation on Monday night.

At the *Catholic Review* office on Monday, everyone was trying to guess what the crisis might be. Tom Murn, a young writer on our staff, said he thought it had something to do with China. He said he had just learned one sentence in Chinese. "What's that?" we inquired. "The Catholics are in the other room."

> Life is not a matter of holding good cards, but of playing a poor hand well.
>
> *Robert Louis Stevenson*

October 23

> When a critic complained that Bruckner's symphonies were too long, the composer replied, "It is rather you, sir, who are too short."

October 24

> I like all the classical composers except Wagner. You can't hear over him.

October 25

> Mahler was looking for God; Bruckner had found him.
>
> *Bruno Walter*

October 26

On this day in 1968 I rose about 6:20 at old St. Mary's Seminary. I was due to say 7 A.M. Mass for the five students who were going with me that day for an overnight visit to Virginia's Skyline Drive. I turned on the radio for the 6:30 news as I began shaving. "Among the victims of the crash were Dr. and Mrs. James Whedbee of Cockeysville, Maryland."

A kind of warm chill rippled through me, but I just went on shaving. I was grateful for the ninety hours I had spent in his therapeutic presence over the previous eighteen months. But I had so looked forward to drawing strength from him for at least another year. It was as though a surgeon had died while operating on my brain. How would I weather the future without him? How would his other patients cope?

Four months earlier I had jotted down my thoughts about this extraordinary man who had somehow helped me to learn, for the first time in my life, how to live peaceably and trustingly in the present moment. He had taught me how to float emotionally, so that emotionally I need no longer thrash about incessantly in dread of drowning in the world's sorrows and my own.

"I know I idealize and perhaps idolize him; I know I reverence and love him and regard him as an almost unbelievable father figure. I frequently worry that he will die or that I will somehow lose him."

When he did die, I eventually learned that I had gained just enough from him to do without him. His secretary told me that when she phoned each patient to tell of his death—and one patient had been seeing him for nineteen years—time and again patients would ask how some other patient was handling the news, often a patient whose name they didn't even know, but whom they had seen before or after their own appointment. Apparently, we had all learned something special from this loving man.

On the evening after his death, in the quiet of the Blue Ridge Mountains, I spelled out the image of him that has remained till this day: "I see him sitting there just in front of me. Neat, aristocratic white hair. Strong, handsome features, ruddy complexion. A gentle bearing, almost shy at times, especially when he would invite you quietly to his office with his eyes (blue, bright eyes). A soldierly, priestly bearing. Dignity. Manliness. Ready to laugh. No gimmicks, 'techniques,' or 'oppressive silences.'"

Dr. Whedbee was a deeply spiritual and prayerful man. Once, when a patient realized that he was having back trouble and said she would pray for his improvement, he begged her not to, "since the pain is a source of strength for me." In the year of his death he wrote a statement of his personal beliefs for his children. A key sentence was this: "As a physician, my work has revealed, at the merely human level, the astonishing powers of personal love to create and integrate." . . .

The life and death of another saintly soul were much on my mind six years earlier. In preparation for her approaching beatification (and eventual canonization), the remains of Mother Seton were exhumed at Emmitsburg, Maryland, on this day in 1962. As archdiocesan archivist, I was permitted to attend the rare procedure taking place on the grounds of St. Joseph's College, sixty miles northwest of Baltimore.

Elizabeth Ann Seton, widowed mother of five children, had died on these grounds on January 4, 1821. Twice before, her remains had been transferred to new coffins, so it was the third coffin which was to be opened that day in order that her remains could be identified for purposes of veneration and relic-making.

The small, select group, which included two pathologists from Washington, D.C., were placed under threat of excommunication if we added anything to or took anything away from the remains. The only exception was the vice-postulator for Mother Seton's cause, who was permitted to remove some of the soil and bones as relics. The remainder of what was found in the third coffin was now placed in a small fourth coffin made of solid copper with silver-plated trimmings. This was eventually lodged in a new shrine built on the property.

As the only person who had a camera, I took the only pictures made of the event. During a time of financial anemia, I sold these originals to the Daughters of Charity for a modest fee. I still possess one original item from that day, an autographed copy of a biography of the saint entitled *Mrs. Seton*, which was coincidentally published on that precise day. The author, Father Joseph Dirvin, was on hand for the exhumation.

Many people, I know, find all this business of exhumations and relics quite distasteful, if not actually ghoulish. For me, witnessing this event in the midst of the Cuban Missile Crisis was especially sobering. . . .

My two visiting doctors (including one pathologist) left for Richmond this morning. I told them I regretted not having had some sort of spell or attack while they were so freely available in my house. Bill gave me a brief but stern lecture on my presumed dietary habits and the considerable unpleasantness of a heart attack.

Attar has traveled the Seven Cities of Love, but we are still at the first corner of the first street.

Words of one Moslem mystic (Rumi) about another

October 27

"When it comes to art, I know what I like."
"Or is it rather that you like what you know?"

October 28

Between the 7:30 and 9 A.M. Sunday masses, I read that Father Charles Coughlin died yesterday. This was the man who in the thirties was arguably the most powerful man in the U.S. after President Roosevelt. At one point, his Sunday radio broadcasts reached thirty million listeners and his weekly mail approached the million-letter mark.

When I visited Detroit in 1957 I went to the Shrine of the Little Flower, which he had built. There I saw an altar dedicated to Christ the King, which had the flags of the world as part of its decoration. At the time the altar was built the German flag carried the swastika. Shocked to find that fetid flag still defiling an altar in the late fifties, I wrote to Father Coughlin but received no answer.

This day in 1966 was a landmark in my life. It was the eighth anniversary of the election of Pope John XXIII and of the new spirit he had aroused in the church. In particular, his watershed encyclical, *Pacem in Terris*, had struck another forceful blow against racial injustice. The October 28, 1966, issue of the *Catholic Review* carried an open letter from me to George Mahoney, a Catholic of the archdiocese who was running for the governorship on a racist slogan, "Your Home Is Your Castle."

His campaign had gained national attention—one of his TV ads was run as part of a network news program. The Congress of Racial Equality (CORE) had made Baltimore its target city during the previous summer and racial feelings were running high. Opposing Mahoney were a Jew, Hyman Pressman, and a Greek Orthodox, Spiro Agnew. At that time Agnew was the executive of Baltimore County and enjoyed a fairly decent reputation.

Mahoney was the only Catholic candidate, then, and as a wealthy man was known to be a heavy contributor to archdiocesan campaigns. No archdiocesan voice had spoken out against Mahoney and his racist opposition to open housing laws. I knew that this silence was giving scandal. So, I planned to devote two columns to his campaign. In the first (October 14) I stated my belief that supporters of Mahoney were not necessarily racists. Some civil rights proponents, I learned, were disturbed at the seeming noncommittal character of this first column. One government employee wrote that she didn't know whether I was naïve or incredibly uninformed, but I was clearly an "ignorant white" who had made the sickening statement that "many white people are understandably afraid that integration will mean an increase of crime and disorder in their streets."

I had decided to save my personal assessment of the Mahoney candidacy for the issue of the twenty-eight. It was a long column and I worked hard on it. (In a sense it was going to be my swan song at the *Catholic Review*, and that may explain why it had so many verses.)

On the twenty-sixth I showed it to my lawyer brother, whose only advice was that I make it as clear as possible that I was giving my own opinion and not some official stance. I accepted this advice. Then, on the afternoon of the twenty-seventh, the presses began to roll before Cardinal Shehan or any other archdiocesan official had seen my column. I left for Washington shortly thereafter, to attend a meeting of the Catholic Association for International Peace.

By coincidence, the cardinal had scheduled a press conference for the morning of the twenty-eighth to announce some building plan. I was told later that the lay editor, Mr. Wall, showed the cardinal a copy of my column shortly after it came off the press but that no attempt was made to stop the presses. By that time quite a few copies would already have been mailed out or delivered by the *Review* truck. I was also told that some of the news media, knowing that there would be a second column, quickly obtained a copy and quoted from the column in the evening news on the twenty-seventh.

During the question period of the news conference on the twenty-eighth, the cardinal pointed out that the column represented my personal opinion, that the archdiocese does not endorse candidates —nor had I, in fact—and that he had already stated his views about racial justice. But he gave no indication of any disapproval of the Mahoney stance or campaign. As one correspondent wrote me, "The cardinal left you all alone out on the high seas." Another man who took seriously the fight for social justice sent me a copy of his letter to the cardinal. "What can I say to my children who heard your comments on the news?"

Coming back from D.C. on that Friday afternoon, I heard those comments myself on the radio news. Violent phone calls were already coming into the *Review* office. There was even a telegram from a woman who said she was going to see that her grandchildren were taken out of Catholic schools. She signed herself, "A former white Catholic grandmother." I could only presume that "former" modified "Catholic."

It was going to be a rough couple of weeks for me, in which I would indeed feel quite alone and would be getting brickbats from both sides. I was blamed, for instance, for the pro-Mahoney ad which appeared in our paper just before the election and after my "Open Letter." Twelve seminarians wrote to object, finding the paper's acceptance of the ad bordering on hypocrisy.

The fact was that the *Review* policy committee overruled my vigorous objection to the ad—Mahoney having in the meantime been endorsed by the KKK. The committee also vetoed the two columns I wrote after the "Open Letter," columns in which I tried to answer some of the objections voiced in the dozens of critical letters and phone calls I had received. In view of Mr. Agnew's subsequent history, one anti-Agnew letter merits citation: "What has Mr. Agnew done for anyone except himself? He is a self-centered, articulate wind-bag of the mud-slinging variety."

(For the text of the "An Open Letter to Mr. Mahoney," see Appendix C.)

✤

He who would be a friend of God must either remain alone or make the whole world his friend.

Mahatma Gandhi

October 29

The cynic smells the flowers and looks for the coffin.

October 30

The young give all or nothing. We ask for all.
Mother Teresa of Calcutta, explaining the vigor of her order

October 31

You are such a wonderful Baedeker [guidebook] to life. All the stars are in the right place.

Elizabeth A. Bibesco

November 1, 1979

"Well, I guess I'm the hatchet man." It was All Saints' Day, 1966; Baltimore's auxiliary bishop, Austin Murphy, was aiming a preliminary hatchet at me, a sinner. My "An Open Letter to Mr. Mahoney" had appeared four days earlier. In the meantime the gubernatorial candidate had been to see Cardinal Shehan and was promised that the archdiocesan newspaper would not further criticize him.

Austin Murphy was a good-hearted man. On several previous occasions he had been the messenger to tell me of items in the *Review* which had upset the cardinal. In each case he had told me that he didn't share the cardinal's reaction. But had he told the cardinal that? I doubt it.

Earlier this morning he had told my co-editor, Ed Wall, that my opinions about Mr. Mahoney and his racist campaign "had to be said." Now he was telling me that he didn't object to what I said, but that I said it without first consulting the cardinal. Any other editor who had done such a thing would have been fired.

Dear Austin: Do you really believe that in his tumescent timidity the cardinal would have allowed me to say what "had to be said"? Would he have wanted to acknowledge that I spoke with his approval? I did him a favor by not consulting him.

I told the bishop that two readers had demanded that I print their pro-Mahoney, anti-me letters either as letters or as paid ads. The next day I attended an emergency meeting of the newly established *Review* policy committee, and was told I could print one pro-me and one anti-me letter.

Bishop Murphy asked me if I still would have published my "Open Letter" had I known the uproar it would cause. I said I would, because of the scandal of the previous silence on the part of the archdiocese. Monsignor Nelligan heatedly retorted that "we have not been silent." I presumed he was referring to the cardinal's pastoral of three years earlier. I pointed out that just recently Atlanta's Archbishop Hallinan had used his diocesan paper to disavow personally a racist Georgia candidate.

> The church: all saints, all souls, all sorts.
> *Ronald Knox*

November 2

> "Why do you keep weeping when it will do no good?"
> "That is why I keep weeping—because it will do no good."

November 3

> A martyr is someone who lives with a saint.

November 4

The assigned topic for my two Masses this Sunday morning was "Vocations," which I chose to treat in its broadest sense. I told how Buckminster Fuller was on the verge of suicide in 1927 when an inner voice spoke up, "You do not have the right to eliminate yourself. You do not belong to you. You belong to the universe."

I said that what was needed these days is planetary piety, a sacred sense of being responsible for what "Bucky" Fuller was the first to call "the Spaceship Earth." On another occasion he attributed human puzzlement to the fact that this protoplasmic experiment called life came without an instruction manual.

I hurried downtown after Mass to catch the 1:30 bus for Pittsburgh. The 250-mile trip cost me about ten cents a mile. En route I began reading Nathanson's *Aborting America*, an account of his changing attitude toward abortion by the doctor who once was the head of the busiest abortion clinic in the world. As such he presided above 75,000 abortions.

The Trailways bus arrived in the Steel City about 6:30, and my carpenter friend, John Corcoran, was waiting for me. We headed for the funeral parlor where his mother's father was laid out. "Bup-Bup" had thirty-four grandchildren and thirty-three great-grand-children. When one of the latter was taken in to see him, she asked, "Did he died in his suit?"

Back at his home, John, his wife, Nanci, and I watched on TV the end of the movie *Jaws*, which I had avoided when it was in the theaters. The late news gave more details of today's takeover of the U.S. Embassy in Teheran, the holding of sixty or so hostages, and the demand that the sick Shah be returned from the U.S. to Iran.

When I first arrived at the Corcorans' tonight, three-year-old Brenda inquired about my absent beard and thinning hair. "When you get old," I explained, "you lose your hair." "And when you get real old," she added in her soft and thoughtful way, "you die."

Learn as though you will live forever; live as though you will die tomorrow.

November 5

On this date in 1966, *America* magazine carried an article of mine entitled "The American Bishops on Modern War." I was lamenting the lack of antiwar leadership on the part of our Catholic bishops. As examples of the blinding force of patriotism, I quoted World War II statements of German bishops: "We encourage and admonish our Catholic soldiers, in obedience to the Führer, to do their duty . . . inspired by God's love, we faithfully stand behind our Führer."

Later that month, *America* published three letters endorsing my views. One praised the Jesuit magazine's "courage" for printing it. Another, signed by three persons, mockingly suggested that I be "deported" to Mexico, as had the antiwar priest Daniel Berrigan.

The union of church and state is like the union of horse and rider, and the church is usually the horse.

Tallyrand

November 6

We are all ignorant, only about different things.

November 7

The Iranians are still holding the American hostages in Teheran. Both Ramsay Clark and the Palestine Liberation Organization seem to have been rejected as mediators.

On this day in 1966 negotiations of my own were breaking down. In the late afternoon the lay editor of the *Catholic Review* and I were summoned to Cardinal Shehan's office on the seventh floor. It was the eve of the gubernatorial election, and my column against candidate Mahoney had been published some ten days earlier.

Bishop Austin Murphy was waiting in the room with the cardinal, whom I had scarcely seen since I submitted my resignation in early September. His Eminence pulled a chair over for me to sit on, then handed Mr. Wall and me a single sheet of paper each. It was the new policy statement drawn up by a special committee headed by Bishop Murphy. It stated that the *Review* was primarily a paper of news and not of opinion; that the cardinal had full confidence in the lay editor, Mr. Wall; that editorials should reflect the mind of the cardinal, and if his mind wasn't known, it should be inquired about.

The paper had been handed to us without comment. Was it a *fait accompli*, or were Ed and I being asked for our contribution, as I had hoped and requested? Since nobody was saying anything, I pointed out that an entire Catholic Press Association meeting could be devoted to the question of whether a Catholic paper's editorials should be expressing the mind of its episcopal publisher. Did the cardinal want it presumed that he was expressing himself through future editorials? How could a busy bishop properly inform himself about so many complex subjects?

I had fought for years to make a clear distinction between the archbishop's opinions and my editorial opinions. How else could I do my job, devote my mind and my time to timely and controversial subjects, and fashion honest statements of personal opinion? If a publisher cannot trust his editor, he should replace him. But he shouldn't expect a self-respecting editor to be a mindless mouth-piece.

One of the ironies of this situation was that, as the episcopal mod-erator of the Catholic Press Department of the National Catholic Welfare Conference, Cardinal Shehan had issued in his own name a much-lauded statement of the role of the Catholic press and of responsible public opinion in the church. I had written the statement for him, and this present policy statement violated both the spirit and the letter of the earlier document.

With this fact in mind, I said that I hoped this policy statement would not fall into the hands of the *National Catholic Reporter*. With a touch of humor, the cardinal said that surely neither he, Bishop Murphy, nor Mr. Wall would send it to them. When Ed and I were leaving the room, however, the bishop took the paper away from us.

Rather gently, the cardinal added that the paper shouldn't address itself to a political candidate by name, and that my "Open Letter" would probably hurt the archdiocese's upcoming financial campaign. ("It's a shame we have to think about such things.") In that letter I had referred to blind fear as "Satan's holy water"; the cardinal said that fellow-candidate Spiro Agnew probably took that idea from me when shortly afterward he called Mr. Mahoney a devil.

When I pointed out that the policy statement made no mention of the executive editor (my job), Bishop Murphy looked surprised and said to the cardinal, "I thought Mr. Wall came to the *Review* with the understanding that he would take over complete author-ity." This was news to me, but the point was not pursued. I was at-tending my own funeral, and details about the floral arrangements seemed unimportant.

Bishop Murphy rounded out the occasion by saying that my "Open Letter" would probably help Mr. Mahoney to win the elec-tion.

The enemy is north, south, east, and west of us. He shall not escape this time.

November 8

But he didn't, despite an election evening prediction of victory by a TV network computer. Spiro Agnew won by 455,000 to 373,000. The Mahoney camp said that "the Catholics" let him down, and Mr. Mahoney let it be known that in his view my "Open Letter" was the villain.

I did not lay that flattering unction to my soul with any certitude, since there was no reason why any voters had to follow my lead even if they knew of it. Besides, Mr. Mahoney had fallen into the habit of losing elections.

Am I sorry that I may have helped Spiro Agnew become Vice-President of the United States? First of all, there were three candidates plus the option of not voting, and I endorsed no one. Secondly, Agnew's public record was comparatively not all that bad at that point. Finally, had he won, Mahoney would have been a greater disaster for Maryland, I believe, than Agnew was for the nation. But I was given a personal lesson in the difference between intentions and consequences in the area of moral decision.

❦

We do not want joy and anger to neutralize each other and produce a surly contentment. We want a fiercer delight and a fiercer discontent.

G. K. Chesterton

November 9

Mankind's most precious instrument of progress is the impractical ethics of Christianity.

A. N. Whitehead

November 10

Sanctity is the poetry of ethics.

J.G.

November 11

> A young Apollo, golden-haired,
> Stands dreaming on the verge of strife,
> Magnificently unprepared
> For the long littleness of life.
>> *Frances Cornford on Rupert Brooke,*
>> *poet and World War I casualty*

November 12

> Never try to console me for dying. I would rather follow the plough as thrall to another man, one with no land allotted him and not much to live on, than be a king over all the strengthless dead.
>> *Achilles in Homer's* Odyssey, *XII, 488*

November 13

> "Why are your characters so bizarre?"
> "When you're talking to the deaf you have to shout."
>> *Flannery O'Connor*

November 14

> It is only in extreme situations that man becomes aware of what he is.
>> *Karl Jaspers*

November 15

> Dear Mr. Chekhov: You are withering without having flowered. A great pity.
>> *A letter from a drama critic to the young Russian playwright.*

November 16

In recent days the *Evening Sun* has published two letters criticizing my column assessing Pope John Paul's first year in office. "Pope John Paul Viewed as Locked in Polish Conservatism" was the paper's headline for my thoughts; inserted into my column was a cartoon showing a tear falling from the eyes of Pope John XXIII. Probably my most venturesome remark was this: "More and more observers are gaining the impression that the present pope does not do much listening, at least with the prospect of changing an opinion he already holds."

One critical response to my words called my article "sick, very unCatholic, impertinent, inane, ridiculous, and scandalous. God help such traitorous shepherds." That was from a priest in McConnellsburg, Pennsylvania.

The other was from a Redemptorist brother in Annapolis. He found my article "shocking, illogical, misconceived," and an example of my long-standing papaphobia. His letter was also published in the *Catholic Review*, which did not, however, reprint my article so that its readers could understand what the letter writer was enraged about. There is nothing like a duel with one duelist.

The changes in Catholicism over the past fifteen years have spurred some very angry letters in various publications. A classic one was sent by a local priest to the *Catholic Review* in March 1974. "Finding a nun with brains," he wrote, "is like finding a rhinoceros that can ice skate. . . . Let Protestants be Protestants and the hell with them (with their religion, anyway). . . . Let's give our kids their birthright and not a miserable mess of pottage." A man who writes like that is really hurting.

❦

> The worst condition is having enough religion to hate but not
> enough to love.

November 17

The current *Time* magazine carries a picture of some of the 120 cardinals who met in Vatican City last week. Baltimore's Cardinal

Shehan is quite distinguishable in the group as he gazes soberly at a document. Fifteen years ago at this time he was also in Rome, gazing in shock at one of my editorials in his archdiocesan newspaper. On this precise day I was gazing in my own shock at a letter he sent me in response.

Here's the background of the roughest letter I ever received from him. Paul VI gave a 1964 speech in St. Peter's, praising the draft of a Council document on the Missions. Not many days later, after a series of harsh speeches, the bishops sent it back to committee for revision. To many observers, this seemed like a rebuff to the pope. Would this diminish his enthusiasm for the concept of collegiality?

During the Council I usually wrote a wrap-up editorial each week about what had been happening at the Vatican. Referring to the incident of the Mission draft, I said, "Humorists who rely on headlines might be excused for depicting Pope Paul as now putting the torch to the De Ecclesia Chapter on Collegiality."

Soon comes a letter from the Grand Hotel in Rome: "I was shocked at the seeming disrespect, particularly toward Our Holy Father." Misquoting my first word, the cardinal continued, "I find particularly offensive the statement, 'Hundreds who rely on headlines . . . etc.' I understand that the *Review* is sent weekly to the Cardinal Secretary of State. . . . It seems to me that the editorial can be interpreted as an open insult to the Pope and the Holy See. I wish therefore that in the coming edition . . . you would include an editorial or a statement making it clear that no irreverence or disrespect was intended or that you withdraw such as seems apparent."

The cardinal ended by saying that he had been rereading Cardinal Newman's book *An Essay on the Development of Christian Doctrine.* He referred me to the section about "the reverence which should be expected of us towards the Pope and the Holy See. It should be remembered that Newman must have written that chapter a considerable time before he made his submission to the Church." (Ouch!)

I sent my reply the same day, pointing out that nothing had caused more puzzlement lately than the pope's praise of the Mission draft and the reaction of the bishops to it. "It seemed to me to be of value in terms of public relations and public opinion in the Church that a Catholic paper point out unanswered questions which have surely scandalized some Catholics."

Before my answer reached my publisher, a second letter arrived from him. "Yesterday I wrote in haste. . . . On rereading the editorial I still think that the impression it makes—which I know was not intended—is one of irreverence. . . . I hope you were not offended by my abrupt criticism. . . . To tell you the truth I was truly chagrined when I read it."

It was in this second letter that the cardinal gave me the hopeless advice that I should not "editorialize on the account of someone who was not actually at the Council, or, if he was present, did not understand what was actually happening."

A third letter was dated November 22. "Many thanks for your prompt and satisfactory response to my letter." A fourth was dated the twenty-third: "The last number of the *Review* arrived today. I think you handled the matter of last week's editorial very well indeed."

End of the affair, for the time being. It ominously underscored how different were our views about what constituted fair comment and what were grounds for scandal.

Wisdom keeps you from making mistakes, and comes from having made plenty of them.

Bernard Baruch

November 18

Wisdom is what you need from the start and might have by the end.

J.G.

November 19

My verses may be elegant and genteel, but my heart is incorrigibly vulgar.

Aleksander Puskin

November 20

The louder he talked of his honor, the faster we counted our spoons.

R. W. Emerson

November 21

Haven't I done enough by writing my poems? Let somebody else explain them.

Dylan Thomas

November 22

Sixteen years ago today President Kennedy was murdered in Dallas, Texas. At that time I was consulting editor for Baltimore's archdiocesan paper. Since the *Catholic Review* goes to press on Thursday, Friday, November 22, 1963, would ordinarily have been a relatively relaxed day for the editorial staff.

But we were just a week away from the exact fiftieth anniversary of our first issue, and we were intensely busy preparing our special ninety-six-page anniversary edition. We were due to complete work that day on one of the special issue's three sections.

I recall listening to the 7 A.M. news that morning and feeling unpleasant about the announcement that President Kennedy was going to visit Dallas that day. Adlai Stevenson had undergone a bad experience there not too long before.

Time slipped by at the busy *Review* office and I didn't go out for lunch until the President's limousine was threading its way through downtown Dallas. Since I had a 2 P.M. appointment I made a point of eying the clock as I headed for the Cove Restaurant just across the street. Managing editor Dave Maguire joined me for a routine meatless lunch. We talked about the anniversary issue and were just finishing dessert when our waitress came to the table and asked whether we had heard the report that President Kennedy had been shot. We didn't want to believe that the report was serious, or at least that the wound was serious, so we asked for the check with a kind of forced calm, and then headed back to the office.

As we approached the entrance we sped up our pace. Once inside we bounded up the stairs to the second-floor room where the teletype stood. Grimly subdued, many of the personnel, even from other departments, were clustered around the machine reading the bulletins. The first one had read: "Dallas (AP)—President Kennedy was shot today as his motorcade left downtown Dallas. Mrs. Kennedy jumped up and grabbed Mr. Kennedy. She cried, 'Oh, no!' The motorcade sped on." It was timed at 1:42 Eastern time.

"Where was he hit?"

"In the head."

That was bad news.

The radio was on, and time and again we would read a report from the AP and then hear it over the radio a few seconds later. As details grew more dismal, we all knelt and said a prayer. Somebody went to the magazine rack and reversed the current issue of *Look* magazine, which had a cover photo of young President Kennedy playing with his little son.

I knew the news sources would soon be after a statement from Bishop Murphy, who was governing the diocese during Archibishop Shehan's absence in Rome. I phoned the old cathedral to offer the *Review*'s help in transmitting a statement to the news media.

Not long afterward, the dreaded news came from the lips of a priest. There was an irony here. John Kennedy might well have lost the presidency because of his Catholicism; now, precisely because of his priesthood, Father Huber was able to give the nation its first raw certainty that it had lost a President.

Almost spontaneously, everybody knelt for a second prayer, this time of stunned resignation. What would become of the country? If the assassin was a political fanatic, would the nation be split in two? The President should never have gone to Texas. Somebody turned off the teletype machine. "Eternal rest, grant unto him . . ."

The phone rang. WJZ-TV wanted to know if there was going to be a special service at the old cathedral. A daily 5:30 P.M. Mass was already scheduled, and after checking with Monsignor Hopkins, the rector of the old cathedral, the bishop decided to make it a Requiem Mass and to offer it himself. Why not have the choir and students come over from the nearby St. Mary's Seminary?

Within minutes the decision was made to have a Solemn Pontifical Mass. The priests on the old cathedral staff were soon busy on several phones inviting prominent civil officials. Many of them, including Governor Tawes, Mayor McKeldin, and U.S. Attorney Joseph Tydings, were seated in the front pews less than three hours later. It was most likely the first such Mass offered in the United States for the slain President, whose body was still airborne from Texas.

Father Joseph Connolly, who had charge of television for the archdiocese, phoned to see whether I'd be able to serve as narrator for the Mass.

Meantime, WJZ-TV was rushing equipment and engineers to the old cathedral, making arrangements with the telephone company for clearing video and audio cables, and offering the other Baltimore channels the opportunity to pick up the broadcast. Ultimately the Mass, beautifully sung by the seminarians and attended by a packed congregation, was carried on all of Baltimore's channels and by radio. Many in Washington viewed it also, and later that night a tape of it was broadcast at least once in the Baltimore-Washington area.

I later learned that just as I was translating the *Agnus Dei* and offering the threefold prayer, "Lamb of God . . . have mercy on him . . . grant him peace," the video switched to Andrews Air Force Base, where the President's coffin was being taken from the plane. The audio continued, however, and those ancient and poignant words of the Mass served as a background to the President's final return home.

It was drizzling lightly after the Mass. The downtown streets were dark and growing deserted. Walking back to the *Review* office, I recalled the warm, bright evening three years earlier when I had seen a sun-tanned, vital senator ride up Howard Street a block away, in an open car, on his way to a campaign speech in the suburbs.

I thought of the letter he had sent to the *Review* on January 22, 1960—just a year before his inauguration—after the paper had tried to see the humorous side of some of the reasons being given as to why no Catholic could ever be trusted to be President.

"I just want to say," he had written, "that it was a welcome relief. . . . Please be assured that your editorial had a heavy readership in my office. With every good wish, I am, sincerely, Jack Kennedy."

"I am, sincerely." Now, he was no more—at least to human eyes. The sincerity was gone too, and the youthful, enthusiastic vision of a better world. Somebody had said JFK was an idealist without any illusions. There aren't enough of those on the world scene. Now there was one less, one exceedingly less.

The way he tackled problems and met adversity showed how right it is to be an idealist. The way evil had revenged itself showed how right it is to live without illusions. November 22, 1963, had much to say about the meaning of life. At least it showed what the important questions really are.

But these were thoughts that came later. At the moment it was scarcely 7:00 P.M. The thought that came spontaneously was how much a measure it was of man's genius and of his misery that less than six hours earlier President Kennedy had been alive in Texas and now the wax was cold on candles which had burned at his thronged and televised Requiem several thousand miles away.

> Cry. Cry if you must. But do not complain. The path chose you. And in the end you will say, thank you.
>
> *Dag Hammarskjöld*

November 23

I usually listen to a classical music station on FM. This morning, even before I rose, I turned on an AM station to hear the latest news about the hostages in Iran. Then I heard Nat King Cole singing "Chestnuts roasting on an open fire . . ." and I knew the holiday season was upon us, more than a month before Christmas. I thought of what the manager of a highly decorated drugstore said to me one late November day when he noted my Roman collar: "We certainly make a mess of your friend's birthday."

> Our task is not to conquer for the truth, but only to struggle for it.
>
> *Blaise Pascal*

November 24

Poet-friend Elliott Coleman said he felt punk when I phoned him, but he was agreeable to my taking him in his wheelchair to our favorite neighborhood Chinese restaurant. He said he had been planning to save up eighteen nights' worth of sleeping pills and swallow them all at once but found that he couldn't even get through one night without them.

Reverting to the theme of his funeral, he said that he thought champagne should be served afterward, not blanc-blanc wine, which a friend had suggested but which no one but a connoisseur would recognize and appreciate. I promised him I would campaign for champagne, and that as we lifted our glasses we would use them as telescopes to look up at him where he belongs, among the sparkles. . . .

This evening marks the anniversary of the night I stood in line for eight hours to pay my respect at the coffin of the assassinated President Kennedy. During the nineteen hours when it was possible to do so, more than one out of every one thousand Americans passed by his remains beneath the Capitol dome. Drawn by the magnetic power of that flag-draped casket, I left Baltimore about 9 P.M. that Sunday night with Father Joseph Gossman, the future bishop of Raleigh.

By 10:30 we arrived at St. Matthew's Cathedral. Stopping briefly at the rectory, we talked with Father Bernard Gerhardt, who would be assisting Secret Service men in checking the identity of clergymen who came for the presidential funeral. He invited us to come, but in the event we were too tired. We also talked with Father Frank Ruppert, who had gained the unexpected privilege earlier that day of saying Mass for the Kennedy family in the White House, where the President lay. Since early Saturday he and other priests from St. Matthew's had been taking turns attending the coffin with prayers. Leaving the rectory, we paid a short visit to the cathedral, where preparations for the funeral were still under way at that late hour.

Before parking on Constitution Avenue near the back of the Capitol, we drove by the White House. It was not hard to sense the sad, dramatic events taking place under the lights that blazed against the darkness from many of its rooms.

That we were able to find a parking place so near the Capitol was due to the despair of one driver who decided to pull away when he discovered that it was taking seven hours of waiting to reach the Capitol rotunda. Thinking that such a long delay and the growing lateness of the hour would cause many to leave the long line, Father Gossman and I tried to find the end of it.

When we joined it we were actually moving eastward away from the Capitol! We knew that the front of the line was moving in the opposite direction on East Capitol Street, one block to our right. When we crossed intersections we could see that line, but we had no way of knowing how many blocks we would have to walk before we reversed our direction. There were even jokes about where our particular line might really be going. As it turned out, we had to continue to Thirteenth Street, going, appropriately enough, around Lincoln Square. The pace of the crowd was fairly brisk at times—we saw one man stumble and hurt himself.

The temperature was now going down into the thirties and neared the freezing point before we reached the Capitol at 7:00 A.M. In Lincoln Square and at intersections, the open space gave the wind greater force and caused the crowd, at times fifteen or so persons wide, to huddle even more closely together.

Especially when the line halted for periods of ten or more minutes, "cheaters" from behind would walk along the outside of the line and try to push into advanced positions. At times a loud protest greeted such tactics.

"This is neither the time nor the place for pushing ahead," said one policeman sternly and repeatedly as he moved past the line. Toward the end of the procession, ropes along the street side of the crowd helped to maintain order.

Long pauses gave you plenty of time to note the bright half-moon, the steely stars, the overhead trees with their last few withered leaves. From time to time trucks stopped nearby to deliver bundles of newspapers to stores, and vendors passed by selling cigarettes and coffee.

Transistor radios brought heartening news that several persons at a time were now passing through the rotunda. Various radio stations signed off with "The Star-Spangled Banner." A few hours later, the same music reappeared on stations which were beginning their broadcast day.

As the cold, slow minutes wore on, the crowd grew increasingly silent. During long delays some would sit on curbs or lean sleepily against fences. Young children, holding a parental hand, or perched on their fathers' backs, bore up with remarkable patience.

At intersections there were sudden bursts of energy as people tried to run across the street before policemen interposed their authority again. At one crossing, about 4:00 A.M., the sole policeman seemed to despair of keeping the intersection clear. He boarded a bus and rode off as its solitary passenger.

Occasionally a flashing police car sped by, or the siren of an ambulance broke the frigid silence. Near us a teen-age girl from Winchester, Virginia, fainted away. Like General Sheridan, she was indeed "up from Winchester at the break of day."

The crowd, of course, was as diverse as could be. It seemed timely to remember Edmund Burke's remark that public calamity is a mighty leveler. The young and the old were there, the wealthy and the poor, whites and Negroes, civilians and servicemen. Groups of servicemen had been passing us on the street for some time when a person in the crowd shouted to a soldier in our midst, "Servicemen are permitted to go directly to the Capitol." "That's all right," he answered, "I'll wait in line."

About 6:00 A.M. we reached the Supreme Court Building again. A few lights went on in the Folger Shakespeare Library across the street. "Cheer up," someone announced in a friendly voice. "You're in the homestretch. You've only an hour to go." He was just about right.

Behind us the eastern sky began to brighten slowly. The gleaming white of the Capitol stood out vividly against the dawning sky. Television crewmen began to take their places again on its steps. We watched with quiet envy as policemen entered "emergency units" to get a cup of steaming coffee.

It was exactly 7:00 in the morning as we passed banks of flowers and filed by the casket in the warm rotunda. The scene was just as incredible as it had been on television. In little more than a minute we were leaving the Capitol on its opposite side. There wasn't much to say. Someday, we knew, we'd appreciate more than we did now, more than we could now, how worthwhile it had been to stand all night in the cold to see a single coffin for a single minute beneath the Stars and Stripes.

❦

One man can make a difference, and every man should try.
A favorite maxim of President Kennedy

November 25

Thirteen years ago today I made a decisive break with the Archdiocese of Baltimore. I knew that I did not care to continue working under the new (1966) policy directives of the *Catholic Review,* and I worried about threats of thousands of cancellations as a result of my column against the George Mahoney, who had lost his bid for the Maryland governorship. Just at that juncture, John Whalen, a priest-cousin in Washington, offered me the position of co-editor of the general books division of a publishing project he headed.

This was the day I went to Cardinal Shehan's office and asked to be released from the newspaper and the archdiocese to work in D.C. I told him I felt that my usefulness at the newspaper was ended, and though he mildly disagreed with my statement, he readily acceded to my request. I advised him against announcing my resignation immediately, for rumors would surely rise that I had been fired as a sacrificial lamb to the anti-black, pro-Mahoney forces.

The cardinal seemed to agree with me, so that I was surprised and somewhat aggrieved when the order came down to the *Review* a day or two later to print the announcement immediately. The cardinal whom I had closely and filially served for five years seemed to be making sure that I couldn't change my mind.

As I had foreseen, rumors and counter-rumors erupted and kept agitating for the next few months. The Jesuit weekly *America* carried a December 24th column entitled "Baltimore Blues" by Monsignor Sal Adamo, the feisty editor of the Camden Catholic paper. He spoke of the "ugly story" behind my leaving.

Father John Reedy, the editor of the weekly *Ave Maria*, devoted his January 21st column to the "confusing, if not contradictory stories" about my departure from the *Review*. John, a journalistic friend, spelled out why he thought my leaving the *Review* was a "severe loss on at least two counts . . . the loss of a first-rate priest-journalist and the feared loss of influence of a first-rate diocesan paper." (In order to tell this pivotal story adequately, I must suppress my customary and remarkable modesty.)

There were related stories in the Washington *Post* and, thanks to the National Catholic News Service, throughout the country. Locally, there was at least one front-page story in the Hearst *News-American*. Each morning from December 28th through the 30th, the *Sun* carried prominent stories, one with a photo of me looking benign and the cardinal looking severe. The headlines ran: "Msgr. Gallagher's Leaving *Review* Linked to Criticisms of Cardinal"; "*Review*'s Wall Rebuts *America*"; "Msgr. Gallagher Denies Being Pressured to Resign."

One main reason for the confusion was my desire not to hurt the cardinal by telling the whole truth as I saw it. At the same time I did not intend to lie or to deny those parts of the truth which were already in circulation. Mr. Wall, who assumed my role as executive editor, was also on a hot seat. During the month of December I was away from my desk a good bit, trying to get established in Washington. So, in one case, Mr. Wall put a statement on my desk for approval and then released it when he heard no disapproval. I didn't even see it until after it was published.

One day the Washington *Post* tracked me down in D.C. and asked me whether it was true that I had already submitted my resignation in September, before the Mahoney affair. This question bowled me over—how had the *Post* discovered that fact? It turned out that Mr. Wall had made the fact public, to take the heat off the charges that Mahoney had done me in. I was, again, on the spot trying to explain the earlier "Vietnam" resignation without injuring the cardinal.

As a newsman I knew how newsmen can put you on the spot. When, for instance, Weldon Wallace of the Baltimore *Sun* came to see me in December, he said he was already certain of his facts "from other sources," but he would give me the chance to confirm or deny or correct. When you try to correct an inaccuracy, you may very well reveal more than the newsman knew and more than you wanted known.

As I write these final words on the protracted clash between Cardinal Shehan and myself, I should perhaps stress what a blow to my ideals and to my pride this whole affair was. I cared very passionately about the manifold sufferings of human beings, and I very much wanted to embody the belief that my church cared about such things too. I was not a Catholic who happened to be a human being, but the other way around.

As editor I no doubt perpetrated some lapses in taste and good judgment, not to say prudence. But life is still the major employment for which there is nothing but on-the-job training. Nonetheless, I worked arduously over seven years to develop a journalistic reputation for intelligence, relevance, and courteous moderation in the expression of my opinions. I did not enjoy being controversial and attacked, though I came to believe Cardinal Newman's dictum that unwelcome truth is never defended except at the expense of those who defend it.

For many years I had lacked a proper sense of my own talents and efficacy, and only slowly grew to have confidence in my own insights and instincts. But just at the time when my journalistic peers were growing most supportive, my ecclesiastical superior, my "father in

God," came to judge me an expendable obstacle. Thirteen years earlier, even as a seminarian, I had helped him write for all the U.S. bishops a national pastoral on the Dignity of Man. As new archbishop of Baltimore he won international attention with his Christian Unity Commission and Unity Pastoral; I suggested the one and wrote the other. He also won widespread notice and praise for his 1965 statement on Catholic Journalism, and his 1966 Pastoral on the Vietnam War. I wrote both and suggested the latter.

As for my peers: Dan Herr, who was the publisher of the respected and tough-minded *Critic* magazine, spontaneously wrote to me in late 1966 that he thought my *Review* column was (apart from his own!) the best in the U.S. Catholic press. The son of the publisher of the *Sunpapers* told me that their Pulitzer Prize-winning editor, Price Day, considered the *Review* editorials the best in Baltimore. In 1955 they had garnered a national award from the National Conference of Christians and Jews. There had also been heartening citations from the national Catholic Press Association and from the Maryland-Delaware Press Association.

After my resignation I was offered editorial positions with two out of the three U.S. Catholic weekly magazines: *America* and *Ave Maria*. I declined in part because at the time churchy concerns had turned sour on me. Even farewell praise tasted bittersweet, as when Don Thorman, publisher of the *National Catholic Reporter*, wrote to me: "You have made so many contributions that it would be foolhardy to attempt to enumerate them, but I hope you realize they are many and important—and appreciated by all of us who still toil in the vineyard."

For several years my editorials had been widely reprinted or quoted in both the religious and the general press, whereas diocesan newspapers are often regarded as journalistic jokes, as "pumps for the episcopal bilge," and unworthy of serious notice. Whence the hoary story of the man who said in confession: "I peeked at a diocesan newspaper—but I didn't take any pleasure in it."

I like to believe that my resignation occurred when what was strongest in me (who have many weaknesses) clashed with what was weakest in the cardinal (who has many strengths). I, too, had fears about arousing opposition, but I was trying not to give in to them. He had fears and I was forced to give in to them, at least by having my position made untenable. My disillusionment was all the more deadly because my bishop was among the best and the brightest of them. Once again, a father both failed me and rejected me.

Nor did it soften the blow that I, who had dedicated my whole celibate life to the church and the cardinal "for nothing," was judged dispensable, whereas my lay, married, and lawyer brother (who was rightly well paid by the cardinal) was judged indispensable. My job had been to speak out publicly in the name of the church's spiritual mission; my brother's was to advise privately on behalf of the church's temporal concerns. And you see who survived.

For me a real world came crashing down, but also a dream world, the kind that everybody needs. In a sense I was one of the victims of the Vietnam War. In view of what others suffered and are still suffering, I had no right to complain. But neither was I able to deny what a knockout blow the whole episode inflicted on my faith, my self-esteem, and even my will to live.

From my youth I had trained and strained to serve Beauty against the Beast. Now, in time for my mid-life crisis, I had penetrated to the inner court of Beauty. And there I saw scales on her flesh, heard the scratch of claws, and caught a timid whiff of sulphur.

It is often necessary to suffer for the church, and sometimes even from it.

Cardinal Newman

November 26

There's one positive thing about self-pity—it's usually sincere.

November 27

The truth often suffers more from the heat of its defenders than from the arguments of its opposers.

William Penn

November 28

> Perhaps everything terrible is, in its deepest being, something
> helpless that needs help from us.
>
> *Rainer Maria Rilke*

November 29

Settling into bed shortly after midnight, I noticed that my eyes
were itching. So I rose, walked to the mantlepiece in the dark, located the bottle of Visine, and squirted a few drops into my left eye.
Instant fire! I switched on the lights and with my right eye discovered that I had mistakenly grabbed hold of a bottle of cleaning solution for stereo records.

I washed my eye at once with water, then dressed and drove to
the emergency ward of Mercy Hospital. The doctor examined my
eye and said he thought I had done no serious damage, but he had
it washed out with sodium chloride . . .

My column discussing the book *Aborting America* appeared today
in the *Evening Sun*. This may be an apt time to tell of an abortion
that almost happened, but didn't. I know a student who was living
awhile with his sweetheart, who became pregnant. He thought he
wasn't ready yet for marriage, so the sweetheart made plans for an
abortion. Ed was due to take her to an abortionist on a certain Saturday at noon.

Meanwhile, the student had become obsessed with the number
1111. That was the new address of his mother's apartment, it was a
friend's license plate number, and he had noticed it in several other
recent contexts. As he waited to take his sweetheart for the abortion,
he looked at the clock and it read 11:11. Ed, who had recently been
connected with a St. Luke's House, noticed a New Testament near
him, so he opened it up to St. Luke's Gospel, chapter eleven, verse
eleven. There he read, "What father among you will give his son a
snake if he asks for a fish?" A poisonous, murderous snake or a life-
nourishing fish, the ancient Christian emblem for Christ, who came
that we might have life.

Ed put down the Gospel, rose from his chair, and put his arm
around his pregnant sweetheart. "Wouldn't you rather go for a walk

in the park with your husband-to-be?" I have often seen their beautiful, vivacious child, who arrived seven months after their marriage.

❧

Almost everything comes from almost nothing.
                                                    Blaise Pascal

November 30

After supper tonight three seminarians from St. Mary's visited me for fireside beer and pretzels. Larry I knew fairly well, the other two less so. A delightful thing happened after I agreed to read some of my poems by firelight. Eric, a seminarian from Erie, looked astounded as I read the poem *Roses As Such*, which, coincidentally, mentions the Eric who is Josephine Jacobsen's husband. It turned out that at a very critical time in young Eric's youth, a friendly priest had read him that poem and later included it in a birthday card. It helped to teach him how to enjoy life and its blessings one day at a time and for themselves. Until tonight, however, he never knew who had written the poem. These are the moments that reward a writer most of all.

In the mail today came a copy of my old paper, the *Catholic Review*, the first that I have received in perhaps a decade. Someone must have taken out a gift subscription for me. It was a poetic touch honoring a special anniversary that dates back eighteen years. On this day in 1961 I was returning to the old cathedral rectory after putting the *Review* to bed for that week. As our lay editor, Dave Maguire, dropped me off, he mentioned teasingly, "Well, this is the last day for your prophecy." "What prophecy?" I had forgotten.

Earlier that year I had written the article on the Baltimore Archdiocese for the *New Catholic Encyclopedia*. In the process I had noticed two and a half curiosities: that since 1815 whenever an archbishop of Baltimore receives a coadjutor bishop with the right of succession, the archbishop dies that same year; that archbishops of Baltimore tend to die in different months (ten had died in nine different months); and if a Baltimore archbishop dies outside of Baltimore, he tends to die in Georgetown (two out of three had done so).

After Lawrence Shehan had been appointed Baltimore coadjutor in the summer of 1961, I jokingly predicted to the *Review* staff that Archbishop Keough would have to die that year, and at least by November 30, the last day of the last unused month.

Leaving Dave Maguire's car that afternoon in 1961, I played it cool. "Well, let's not be in a rush. There are still eight hours left to the day." Walking the stairs to my third-floor room, I noted that the lights were on in Archbishop Keough's second-floor suite.

About half an hour later, I heard some commotion outside my room. Monsignor White, the archbishop's secretary, was running about. "What's the matter?" "The archbishop just had a stroke." Chills ran down my spine. The chancellor, Monsignor Hopkins, dashed to the cathedral altar to bring Holy Communion to the stricken prelate. An ambulance arrived shortly afterward. We were within a few blocks of a Catholic hospital and of the world-famous Hopkins. "Where are they taking the archbishop?" I asked. "To Georgetown."

It turned out that Monsignor White was a close friend of a doctor at Georgetown Hospital who had organized a team of experts for stroke victims. Though the kindly archbishop died at that hospital eight days later, November 30 was not only his last functioning day as the head of the Baltimore archdiocese, but also his last living day in the archdiocese.

So my prediction was not letter-perfect. Neither was one of the bold captions in his obituary issue of the *Catholic Review*. We featured a large picture of the prelate, with children on his lap and at his feet. The photo had been taken for a Catholic Charities campaign. Beneath the picture were these words: "He was always a fiend to little children." (We caught the mistake, remarkably enough.)

A lighthearted memory I retain of this churchman who ordained me pertains to an *imprimatur* given in his name to a book of Christ's parables. The volume contained nothing but direct quotes from the Gospels and illustrative child-like drawings. Yet the *imprimatur* carried the customary disclaimer: "This *imprimatur* does not necessarily mean that the archbishop agrees with the opinions expressed in this book."

🌲

Prediction is very difficult, especially about the future.
Niels Bohr

December 1, 1979

The last month of the last year of the seventies arrived today, on the last day of the week. In my own life it was to be a last day of sorts, although the only clue was a painful tightening around my throat which occurred every couple of hours and lasted for a couple of minutes.

I first experienced these pains in September when I began jogging after being told that my lipid count was four times higher than it should be. (Your cholesterol count tells you how many trucks are in your bloodstream. Your lipid count tells you how many fatty passengers are aboard the trucks.) During my stress test in October I felt the tightening come on just as the test was ending. Since then I hadn't returned to jogging but took occasional energetic walks instead.

Two nights ago, as I was finishing supper I felt some throat pains and an eerieness in the head. They passed after a minute or so. Yesterday the pains returned three or four times, once after I had climbed some steps. Today the pains occurred a little more frequently, and a particularly strong throat pressure led me to take my first nitroglycerine tablet. The pill seemed to soothe away the pain.

In the evening I made a call to Katherine Anne Porter. She had phoned at 8:15 this morning to tell me that she was "really dying" this time, and I promised to phone again tonight. Her nurse told me that one of the other nurses had taken Miss Porter's phone book away from her because she wanted to phone a friend in Paris.

As I folded my laundry in the bedroom, I listened by radio to UN delegates condemning the seizure of U.S. Embassy employees in Iran. Earlier today I had learned that Mexico now refuses to let the deposed Shah return there as he completes his medical treatment in New York.

Another ailing woman was on my mind—my cousin Anne in Philadelphia. Last night when I was told that in effect the doctor had sent her home to die, I wasn't able to learn the details. So I phoned her daughter Judy tonight about 11:00. While talking with her I was sipping a cup of tea and eating a couple of oatmeal cookies. My throat began to tighten again, and I mentioned this to Judy before I hung up.

I walked downstairs to my bedroom and prepared to turn in for the night. The throat pain kept intensifying, so I took another nitroglycerine. This time the back of my tongue felt like a rope that was going to explode. There was some pressure in my chest, and darting pains down my left arm. But the throat pain was the sharpest. It felt as though someone had put into the two sides of my throat one of those metal tongs used for lugging large blocks of ice—and was trying to lift me.

The pain finally subsided a bit, but I knew I didn't want to be alone in my room when the next attack came. Nor did I want to risk walking a flight of stairs to wake my tenant, Terry. I began redressing gingerly after I decided to drive myself to Mercy Hospital—for the second time in four midnights.

I left the house shortly before twelve. As soon as the night air hit me I began to shiver so uncontrollably that I had a hard time fitting the car key into the lock.

❦

Heart's wave could not curl nor beautifully break into the foam of spirit did not the ageless, silent rock of destiny stand in its path.

Friedrich Hölderlin

December 2

As Saturday became Sunday, I was shivering in my car and driving less than two miles to the southeast, to the emergency room of the hospital where I had been born. (My record of leaving Mercy alive was long-standing and unblemished.)

The first electrocardiogram showed nothing significant. I was asked to call out when I felt the neck pains returning. This I did some time later, and the second EKG showed definite heart involvement. A second and I believe a third doctor were called in to examine me. Finally one of them said that I was probably undergoing "unstable angina"—I learned later that this is also called "pre-attack angina."

It had been decided that I should be admitted to the cardiac intensive care unit. I also learned later that my regular doctor, Nelson Sun of the Mercy staff, had been phoned. He said that, even if it meant shackling me, I should not be allowed out of the hospital.

Before long one of the Jesuit chaplains appeared on the scene to give me absolution and the anointing of the sick. It turned out to be Frank Duffy, a boyhood friend of my deceased brother. In a poem about my father's death I mention that my brother Frank stopped at Frank Duffy's home that night to wait out a rainstorm.

The hospital staff was now readying me to be wheeled up to the eleventh floor. A small heart monitor was attached to my chest just for that short trip. An IV had already been inserted into my left hand. Such thoroughness impressed me, as did the compassionate look on the face of the young doctor who accompanied me upstairs.

It was about 3:00 A.M. when I arrived in room 1125 and was transferred to the bed by the window. My roommate, a Mr. Honaker, was awakened by the commotion. Lights had to be switched on, questions asked about dentures and money in wallets; lists had to be made of each item of clothing on me—and now off of me. A new monitor which could be read in my room or at the nurses' station was attached to my chest. I was instructed to push a button if my pains returned. It was probably about 3:30 A.M. when the lights were switched off, and I sank readily into my delayed night's sleep.

Not too many hours passed before nurses appeared to take blood and blood pressure; a second IV was inserted, into my right hand this time. One of the nurses practically fed me my breakfast. I was not even allowed to "margarine" my own toast.

My regular doctor appeared, expressed ardent regret that I was there, and told me that he had received my stress-test report and was sorry to learn that it was "positive." He said that he would be back to see me later that morning.

In the meantime, Mr. Honaker and I got to know each other better. He joked about the fact that hospitals give you private rooms and semiprivate gowns. A genial man with the cultured voice of his

native Virginia, he had already weathered several heart attacks. Now
Mr. Honaker began talking to me about that afternoon's Colt football game, and did I want to listen to it with him?

I remember finding it hard to pay attention to him. The neck
pains were returning, so I rang for the nurse. She brought me a nitroglycerine and said I could have a second one in five minutes if
the pain persisted. She took my blood pressure and then, without
removing the cuff, dashed from the room. (Apparently my pressure
was sinking out of sight.) In a flash, last night's friendly doctor and
several nurses surrounded my bed.

My memories of the next minutes are hazy. I heard a voice say,
"Atropine." I heard a voice say, "Morphine." This last command I
heard four separate times. I don't remember feeling much pain—just
wooziness and weakness. A woman's voice asked, "How much saline
solution?" A male voice responded, "Full throttle." As though she
were an auctioneer, a nurse was saying, "Sixty-five . . . seventy . . .
seventy-five." She was taking my blood pressure repeatedly. I think
she stopped around 105.

It didn't seem long before Dr. Sun reappeared on the busy scene.
I asked him whether I should try to stay conscious. I had to repeat
the question. I think he replied that I needn't make the effort, but I
did so anyway.

I wondered whether I was dying. I didn't think I was, but it
pleased me to sense that the thought of dying didn't distress me
very much. I wasn't sure that I was ready to face any ultimate examination in another world, but even that thought didn't much molest
the calm I was feeling. I had long refused to believe in a God Who
wants to scare the wits out of me, though the universe which is reputedly His frequently does.

I thought about this journal. Would it gain greater interest value
from an abrupt conclusion or from a rounded account of my heart
attack and recuperation?

It didn't seem very long afterward that Dr. Sun bent over my
head from behind and said, "You have had a heart attack." Did he
add something like, "But we have things under control"? I can't
remember now.

In the midst of the excitement, I saw Sister Mary Thomas in her
blue habit appear at the edge of the curtain drawn around my bed.
Politely but firmly, the young intern requested her to leave. "Do you
know who that was?" asked a nurse. "No," said the intern. "That
was the hospital administrator." "Well, I didn't know." (At second-

hand, I was told that she considered fetching some papal document and reading it to me, by way of raising my low blood pressure.)

Later I heard the same doctor stop at Mr. Honaker's bed and speak reassuring words: "He's going to be all right, so please don't worry."

A few minutes later Archbishop Borders was standing by my left side. I remembered that he had a December heart attack five years ago while my mother was dying. "I'm imitating you," I told him. "This isn't a very good way to imitate me." "Well, you got better."

Someone said I was going to be moved to a private room. As I was wheeled past Mr. Honaker, I thought of saying good-bye to him but somehow I was too tired.

The next thing I knew, my sister-in-law Mary and my niece Mary Ellen came into the room and kissed me. The hospital had phoned their home about 7:00 A.M. but said there was no emergency. They arrived just as I was having my attack, and a nurse emphatically escorted them away from my room. Sister Mary Thomas told them, "It doesn't look good."

In my room Mary said, "For God's sake, go to sleep." Though I had four shots of morphine in me, I felt wide awake. I kept thinking of what the apostles had said when Jesus told them, "Lazarus our friend is sleeping." (Those words are engraved on my chalice.) Their response was, "If he sleeps, he will be well." I kept repeating those latter words to myself, like a mantra. The irony was that at that point Lazarus was already dead, for Jesus had spoken of the sleep of death.

Finally, a nurse injected me with Demerol. I soon submerged into a deep sleep for four or five hours. When I awoke in a darkened room, I could see my lunch and supper trays on the table next to my bed.

Later on, a nurse came in to take my blood pressure. Suddenly she darted from the room, leaving the cuff around my arm. Was I having another attack? She didn't return, so I deduced that she was responding to an emergency call elsewhere.

When she or another nurse later entered my room, I asked, "Was that for Mr. Honaker?" "Yes." "How is he doing?" "Not very well."

Sometime later I heard a woman weeping. Then a younger voice said, "His ring is on his finger."

I knew Mr. Honaker was dead, my brief friend who had been upset by my attack. I realized there was no sense in feeling guilty. The staff tried to keep me from knowing, and the doctor was quite agitated when I told him that Mr. Honaker had died. "Who told you?" he demanded. "I figured it out."

Thus ended a day which was to have taken me alone on a 260-mile car trip to Pittsburgh, and eventually to my dying cousin in Philadelphia. I asked my sister-in-law to phone the Corcorans in Pittsburgh and tell them I wouldn't be there for dinner as expected. She got their phone number from my address book. It was the only volume I had taken with me to the hospital.

> . . . I am aware of my heart: it opens and closes
> Its bowl of red blooms out of sheer love of me.
> *Sylvia Plath*

December 3

In intensive care, where I remained for five days, I could have two visitors for the first fifteen minutes of the even-numbered hours from noon to eight. I had to remain in bed constantly, except for one externalizing activity. A portable facility was placed next to my bed for that purpose.

In addition to the IV's in each hand and monitor attachments on my chest, I had an oxygen tube in my nose and nitropaste taped to my arm. (Mr. Honaker had told me that these pastes gave him the worst headaches of his life, so I wasn't surprised when my headaches came.) To prevent blood clots, white, tight-fitting stockings were pulled onto my legs.

Blood samples were taken regularly; chest X rays and EKG's occasionally. Friendly nurses would appear from time to time bearing health in little white cups, or taking temperatures and blood pressures. Dr. Sun, the compassionate intern, and Dr. Grenzer, the cardiologist, would materialize, auscultate, question, and then disappear. Various hospital nuns and Jesuit chaplains popped in to say "Hello" and "God bless you."

I've heard it said that the first seventy-two hours after a heart attack are critical. Looking back, I recall them as a hazy, sleepy, pleasant time.

It was a savored gift to realize that I had no duty now but to contract into my healing, floating self. I had no care but to let others do the caring. I was relieved of the burden of worrying about history and wondering whether I was cravenly neglecting to play some role, bear some pain, redeem some obligation in the name of conscience.

☘

It is so *very* difficult for a sick person not to be a scoundrel.
Samuel Johnson

December 4

Today Mrs. Doris Owen, the cardiac rehabilitation nurse, introduced her slim, caring, professional, and blond-headed self. I would learn later that every day after work she visits her paralyzed husband, a doctor, in a nursing home. Eventually she would show me two movies on heart attacks and recuperation, and go over two books with me on the subject. (She skillfully flipped past the pages dealing with sex.)

I learned that heart attack, coronary thrombosis, coronary occlusion, and myocardial infarction are synonyms. She told me that I have a "million and one" of the risk factors. She also told me my clot took place toward the end of my anterior lateral descending artery. This artery feeds the left part of the heart, which sends fresh blood through the body. My cardiologist said that if you're going to have a heart attack, that's a good place to have one. I take his word for it.

(When one doctor said that I had had an "inferior" attack, I protested that I had done my best and that this was, after all, my first try. He explained that he merely meant that the attack was in the bottom part of the heart.)

I even took a test from Mrs. Owen—twenty-two multiple choices and fifteen trues or falses. She returned the test with a big red heart drawn on it, and one mistake pointed out. Of the damaged area of the heart muscle I had checked the statement: it will never heal completely. She said the answer was: it will heal to form a tough scar tissue. My cardiologist happened to enter my room when she was returning the test. He looked at the mistake and agreed with me! That did my myocardium good.

One day Mrs. Owen chastised me roundly for having eaten a candy bar and for visiting my bathroom ahead of schedule. (I still don't know how she discovered these infarction infractions.) After she left, I fell asleep and had my first heart-attack anxiety dream. I was in some kind of auditorium, listening to a concert. Behind me was a friend of mine, wearing a pink gown and a round golden pin at her throat. When the concert ended, I walked into her row to speak with her. Suddenly I slumped into one of the seats. I tried to call out to her for a nitroglycerine but realized that I was deaf, dumb, and blind.

🌱

> . . . being here amounts to so much, because all
> this Here and Now, so fleeting, seems to require us and strangely
> concerns us. Us the most fleeting of all. Just once,
> everything, only for once. Once and no more. And we, too,
> once. And never again. But this
> having been once, though only once,
> having been once on earth—can it ever be canceled?
>
> *Rainer Maria Rilke*

December 5

My last full day in intensive care brought me my first get-well mail. One card insisted, "This isn't the end of the road, it's a bend in the road." (I thought of my blocked artery and the collateral circulation working to replace its function.) Another showed on its outside a sad pup and the words "Sick as a dog?" Inside was one word: "Heal!"

The prize for personal comments inscribed on a commercial card went to a former seminarian, John Kent Lewis of Coraopolis, Pennsylvania. Wrote he, "Inasmuch as the deities and/or Deity have long since failed to show you the degree of affection entailed in the rule that 'those whom the gods love die young,' and since you yourself have breached the Dostoevskian rule of etiquette—'it is bad manners to live past forty-five'—please receive my fondest wish that you live to a shockingly ripe old age."

Here was a Johnnie who can both read and write. He would have appreciated a special woman in my life who died twenty-eight years ago today. In an *America* magazine article of April 1975, I tried to suggest what she meant to me:

The national magazines that told us some time ago why
Johnnie can't read are now spelling out the reasons why
Johnnie can't write.

The whole subject sets you to thinking about that cata-
lyst of a woman who entered your life nearly forty years
ago. Things were not going well at home, and your mother
was going to have a baby around Christmastime. So you
and your brothers got farmed out to relatives and friends.

You were the one who got farmed out the most literally.
For Francis and Tommy went to the homes of relatives
who did not live very far from that gloomy apartment in a
run-down section of Calvert Street near the present location of the Baltimore *Sun*.

But you were sent out to live with Mrs. Belva Thomas
on Ethelbert Avenue in the suburbs. Mrs. Thomas had
been a neighbor of your father before he married. Though
she did not actually live on a farm, she did live in a house
that was not a row house and that had flowers around it.
In the back there was a chicken coop, and there were
plenty of trees nearby.

Besides, Mrs. Thomas had grown up on a farm and had
in her bones "the smack and tang of elemental things."
They were big bones, too, fit for a tall woman of immense
kindness. Thinking back, you are not sure whether she had
blue eyes. But you know she had one of the cleanest,
lovingest smiles you were ever to see—the kind of luminous
smile that made it ridiculously unimportant that her face
was plain and round and rather doughy, with a little lump
down by the chin on the right side.

You stayed with her for about six months (with your
own room on the second floor). Mr. Thomas was there, too
—a guard for the B & O Railroad—and her grown daughter
Katherine, who worked in a department store and drove
the old car. Her son Gilbert stopped by now and then with
his wife, Bea, who was a minister's daughter. In fact, Mrs.
Thomas went to that minister's church on Park Heights
Avenue. They were all friendly and all Protestants, and did
not seem to mind your being a Catholic.

Thank to that lady, all sorts of things happened to you
during that half year when you were eight, going on nine.
She got you to comb your hair straight back instead of

parting it. She noticed how you were washing your food down with your milk and she got you to stop that. She impressed you by telling you that human beings are born in order to die. (And lest they die ahead of time, she stressed the importance of washing your hands after you used the bathroom.) And she let a city boy have the fun of feeding the chickens and collecting the eggs, all snowy and miraculous.

But it was inside the warm, bright, and clean wooden house that three very special things occurred. First, there was a table near the living-room window that soaked in most of the sun that autumn and winter. On it, Mrs. Thomas had placed a flowering plant. Next to the plant was a pad and pencil. On the pad with the pencil, that large lady kept a record of how many tiny blossoms bloomed on that plant, and on which day. That taught you a lot about the importance of flowers.

Near that table was a Victrola and a generous supply of records in the cabinet below it. Your own home didn't have such luxuries. Now you could sit by the hour and listen to Harry Lauder sing "I Love a Lassie" or to those nameless voices that sang "My Buddy" and "I'd Love to Fall Asleep and Wake Up in My Mammie's Arms."

But the supreme revelation of all came on the day you first played a record called *Finlandia* and discovered there were sounds in this world that could take you out of this world, could stun you with a beauty both clear and dark at the same hypnotic moment. That magic treasure box next to the counted flowers taught you the importance of music.

Mrs. Thomas was more directly involved in the third priceless revelation. People who would know you later in life would find it hard to believe that there were practically no books in your childhood home. But there was a Mrs. Thomas in your childhood. Although she wasn't a learned woman in any bookish or classroom way, she had a holy respect for knowledge. You learned that the first time you ever asked her what some word meant.

"Let's go together and find out" was her answer. So you both went into the living room (where the blossoms and the music were), and she took from the shelf a big book called a dictionary, and she sat on the rocking chair, and you sat on her lap while you both looked up the meaning of the word. And that's the way it happened, time and time again.

And so it was that in the same room where music flowered in your life, and flowers flowered, words and the meaning of them flowered too. That was a living room that really earned its name.

It's not surprising to you that your earliest memory of trying to write a poem goes back to that enchanted house. All that you remember now about the poem is that "down" and "town" were two of the rhyme words. You have a hunch that the subject was snow. All sorts of things got noticed when you were around Mrs. Thomas, and you wanted to keep a record.

March came, and you went back to the city. You saw Mrs. Thomas every now and then, exchanging visits. She died when you were in the seminary, but in those days you were not permitted to attend the funeral of a mere friend. (Your mother sat by her sickbed and, even though Mrs. Thomas was a Protestant, she didn't mind your mother saying the rosary for her as she sat there.)

The enchanted house has been torn down, and the whole block has disappeared to make room for a junior high school—an apt substitute if there had to be one. So the house is gone, and Mrs. Thomas gone from sight. But her memory is still an oasis within you, and you keep drinking from the well of wonderment she tapped, especially whenever you sense afresh the mystery of flowers and music and words.

And you feel sorry for every Johnnie who cannot read— and not just words on a page, but in the book of life as well. And you wish for each of them in the desert of their deprivation the gift of a beautiful Belva who knows how to notice and how to savor and how to teach unforgettably.

❦

Is it that words are suddenly small or that we are suddenly large that they cease to suffice us to thank a friend?

Emily Dickinson

December 6

About noon today I was moved out of intensive care to a private room in the progressive care section of the eleventh floor. One of the last things I wrote before my heart attack was the "11/11" story in the November 29 entry to this journal. So I had to smile when I realized that I had been transferred to room 1111.

(When I left the hospital thirteen days later, I looked up the phone number for the emergency ambulance service. I had to smile again that special smile when the number turned out to be 396-1111.)

Mrs. Owens was explaining a heart model to me when Cardinal Shehan walked into my room on this day. He gazed at the model briefly, then said good-naturedly, "It's very interesting but not very enlightening." He sat for a short while to the right of my bed, a man born seven months after my long-dead father, a man thirty-one years older than I, a man who has never had a heart attack.

This short, neat, enduring man had once been my spiritual father and had turned out to have such a decisive influence on my life, as this journal has detailed. This was the humble man who once said to my brother, "Perhaps all those things your brother says about me are true." On another occasion, after mistakenly releasing a touchy and tabled Vatican document on Israel, he sighed, "I'll never understand how such a simple-minded person as myself ever became a cardinal."

Now we faced one another and chatted pleasantly, I prone, he sitting. I was wondering whether he had read my recent articles on the pope; I was fairly certain how negatively he would have felt about them. But now, all was courtesy . . . and brevity. As he rose to leave, I asked him whether he knew that another archdiocesan priest was in the hospital. "I'm usually the last one to learn such things," he chuckled. "I'll wait to be told officially before paying him a visit."

I regretted forgetting to ask him how *his* memoirs were coming along. . . .

Tonight John and Pat Corcoran, whom I had planned to visit this week, arrived in my room from Pennsylvania. John brought with him a cross he had made for me, decorated with stones and sea shells I had brought back from Israel in May of 1978. Where Christ's hands would have been are two machine-gun shells I had found, one at the Jordanian border, the other at the Lebanese. These days Christ is more often crucified with bullets than with nails.

❧

Absence does to love what wind does to a fire—it kills a weak one but feeds a strong one.

Comte de Bussy-Rabutin

December 7

I understand that most Americans now living don't personally "remember Pearl Harbor," as the war slogan and song once urged. But not only do I remember that day, it was one of the first specific and living calendar days to be burned into my memory. I was twelve years old at the time, and I had taken my little sister to the neighborhood movie house to see Deanna Durbin in *It Started with Eve*. (I was later to learn that this star was Winston Churchill's favorite.)

As we headed home for supper in the early darkness, I could hear newsboys yelling their "Extra! Extra!" When I reached home at 403 East Twentieth Street, I asked my older brother what the "Extra" was all about. "The Japanese have bombed Pearl Harbor." I'm fairly sure I didn't know who or what or where Pearl Harbor was.

Twenty years to the day, I was again involved with my only sister and older brother. Mary Jo had given birth to her first child, Bill, some weeks earlier. As I worked at the printshop that morning getting the *Catholic Review* ready for press, a phone call came for me. A deeply distraught woman was saying something about a dead baby. I had to ask who it was before I realized it was my own sister.

Within seconds the lay editor, Dave Maguire, was dashing with me to his car. I think we went through a dozen red lights during our thirty-five-block trip. I raced to Mary Jo's third-floor apartment and found my mother at the top of the stairs holding little Billy. Despite her weak heart, she had run the distance from her own apartment some blocks away. Dave took her and the baby to the nearby Union Memorial Hospital, while I tried to calm Mary Jo. She was in dread that somehow the baby had swallowed one of her sleeping pills.

As it turned out, the baby had died from a kind of pneumonia which shows no symptoms. There was an autopsy and, to relieve my sister's anxiety, I phoned the morgue and asked whether the process might be speeded up. I later learned that the morgue always makes note of such calls, since murderers will at times try to hasten an autopsy in the hope that clues will be overlooked.

During this same day, Archbishop Keough was dying in a Georgetown Hospital. As his lawyer and friend, my brother Frank was at his side. I didn't want to tell him over the phone about the death of Billy, so I waited until I picked him up in my car that night at Pennsylvania Station. When I said, "The baby died," he gave me a startled look and asked, "What baby?" I had overlooked the fact that his own son, Frannie, was just two years old. . . .

Four years later was another kind of day. The Second Vatican Council was having its last working session; final votes were taken on several documents which I had spent five weeks translating. Pope Paul and a black-robed representative of the ecumenical patriarch of Constantinople embraced in celebration of the cancellation of mutual excommunications issued nine centuries earlier.

As a very reverend monsignor and papal chamberlain, I was entitled to assist at this final conciliar Mass at the high altar of St. Peter's Basilica. When I stood, I stood at the bottom step of that altar; when I knelt or sat, I used the same bottom step. In order to exercise this privilege, I was required to wear a scarlet cassock and an ermine cape (or facsimile). These I borrowed from another American monsignor residing in Rome who did not attend that day's ceremonies.

It was a splendid and historic occasion, which I was able to view about twenty feet from Pope Paul. Before each of the last documents was voted on, the first few paragraphs were read aloud. Since I had been slaving away at translations of each of these, I felt a proprietary and almost paternal interest in the documents and in the applause which greeted the overwhelming yes vote given to each. The sky had been cloudy, but just at the Consecration of the Mass, the sun broke through and drenched the high altar with sunshine. I could hear thousands of throats catching their marveling breath. . . .

Nine years later, on another anniversary of Pearl Harbor, my mother was for me again at its center. For two weeks she had been a patient at the same hospital where she had taken one grandson dead and where another nearly died. Now her doctor called me aside and invited me to sit down. Tests had finally shown that she had cancer spread widely through her body. She lived for five more, mostly pain-free, weeks.

On this latest Pearl Harbor Day, I, too, am in the hospital, receiving my first three bouquets of flowers and my first fruit basket since my arrival. For the first time during this hospitalization I had this morning seen the rising sun in all its splendor, since my new eleventh-floor room faces east and gives me an unimpeded view of the city and its skyline.

December 7 was branded into my brain nearly forty years ago. Better than I could have guessed, that date would make it easier for me to remember just when some of the most wrenching days of my life occurred, as well as some memorable ones which were easier to be thankful for.

✤

Never waste a sunset, even though it's free, though it squanders day by day such public majesty; For though a billion sunsets await as many past, Tonight's is not your billioneth, and might just be your last.

J.G.

December 8

As I rounded out my first week in Mercy, all IV's were removed from me, as well as all monitor attachments. The oxygen nose-clip had already been taken away, so I had quite a sense of liberation. I was still bed-bound, though, and wouldn't be permitted to venture from the room for another week. I was thinking of the man who had ordained me, Archbishop Keough. On this day in 1961, he died in another hospital, and Lawrence Shehan automatically became my superior.

Meanwhile, I have been relishing a kind of rerun of my fiftieth birthday party. Once again there were cards and gifts and visits. Once again the special friends of my life were spending time with me. On this occasion, however, some of the friends who couldn't make the first party could and did make this one—like the Jacobsens and Dr. Zassenhaus. Moreover, space and time limitations didn't force me to restrict this second party to a minimum number of friends; other cherished friends and relatives made the trip, this time to my actual birthplace.

As a pre-teen-ager, I didn't make the trip to downtown Baltimore very often, especially alone. But this day in 1941 was special. Since it was the Feast of the Immaculate Conception, I had a holiday from St. Ann's school. I had arranged to meet a married friend of mine for lunch—she was working then about two blocks from Mercy Hospital. I used to get change for her when she worked at a High's Ice Cream Store near my home. (Once, in order to get me the fifteen cents I needed to see *Sinbad the Sailor*, she fished three "free cone" certificates from the bottom of a bunch of cones.)

In the meantime, of course, Pearl Harbor had happened. Coming downtown on the bus this next morning, I noticed how everybody was talking to everybody. There were no more strangers, just fellow Americans. We were going to come out swinging and in a few months we would defeat those sneaky Japs and knock out their buck teeth. (A decade later two former Japanese soldiers would become my seminary classmates. One is now the archbishop of Osaka.)

My friend Ruby was right on schedule, and she took me to a Walgreen's Drug Store a few blocks away. It had a large luncheonette which was crowded and noisy. Everybody, I suppose, was talking animatedly about Pearl Harbor. Suddenly, someone turned up a store radio to full volume. A voice announced, "Ladies and gentlemen, the President of the United States."

An absolute hush overtook the restaurant. In his magnificent patrician voice, Franklin Delano Roosevelt was addressing Congress, the nation, and the world. "Yesterday, December the seventh—a day that will live in infamy . . ." No one stirred during the entire speech. At the end came "The Star-Spangled Banner."

Instantly, every person in the restaurant rose and stood in awesome silence. All across this nation, Americans were standing in wordless emotion. And thousands of those who stood that moment would fall in battle before that war was won. Never in my young life had I experienced so electrifying a moment. Nor have I often since then.

✤

May the wreath they have won never wither, nor the star of their glory grow dim.

War Memorial, Cedar Rapids, Iowa

December 9

After giving the world some practice at getting along without me, I'm beginning to catch up with it through newspapers and TV news. In Iran the U.S. hostage crisis enters its sixth week. At home Archbishop Fulton Sheen died at the age of eighty-four.

In the seminary we used to refer to this spellbinding preacher as "Full-tone Sheen." We also made a variation on the poem *Lovely Lady Dressed in Blue,* changing it to *Lovely Lady Dressed in Green, Make Me Preach Like Fulton Sheen.*

In my first year of philosophy at the Catholic University, I sat in on his last class before Christmas. Traditionally he would try out in that class the Christmas sermon he planned to give at St. Patrick's Cathedral in New York. All I can now remember of the event was the way that the then Monsignor Sheen looked out the window at the sunset sky as he asked, "How does Francis Thompson put it?— 'We are born in others' pain, and perish in our own.'"

When I was archdiocesan archivist I saw the text of a Vatican decision which declared that Bishop Sheen was technically in the right when he refused to give his superior, Cardinal Spellman, certain funds connected with the Society for the Propagation of the Faith. Sheen was director of the Society at that time. The Vatican decided that because of his rank the cardinal should prevail in this dispute.

That unprepossessing churchman exercised a spell over U.S. Catholicism which I could never fathom. Once, distressed that I might have offended the New York prelate by an editorial on the movie *The Cardinal,* my own archbishop solemnly told me, "He reads everything, and he never forgets."

At the very end of Vatican II, Archbishop Philip Hannon of New Orleans, a former army chaplain, was gathering signatures from U.S. bishops against the "anti-American" quality of parts of the final text of *The Church in the Modern World.* (The text disapproved of nuclear stockpiling as well as nuclear war.) He approached Shehan in St. Peter's before one Council session, but the cardinal asked for time to think it over. Then Hannon went to the nearby Spellman, who signed at once. Hannon then returned to Shehan, pointed out that Spellman had signed, and won Shehan's signature.

Imagine how I felt. For weeks I had been slaving over the difficult translation of this 24,000-word document. Now, as I concluded my work, my own bishop was petitioning that unless a few "anti-American" words were deleted, the whole document should be scrapped. Two days or so later (after the world's bishops had already voted to accept the controversial chapter on modern warfare) the Baltimore prelate arranged for the U.S. bishops' press panel to announce that he had changed his mind. . . .

Though I was stationary today, I was quite on the move fourteen years ago. On the previous day Vatican II had formally ended with a papal Mass in St. Peter's Square. At the personal level the Council ended for me early on the morning of this calendar day when Father Bill Ganey of Chicago and I shut the door at Rome's Villa Nova house behind the Jesuit journalist Ed Duff. The Americans at this house had entertained many an interesting and late-leaving visitor during the fourth and final session of the Council. Father Duff was the last guest to leave, and the shutting door was a punctuation mark ending the Council for me.

Later that morning I took my seat on a chartered plane heading for New York and full of U.S. bishops and their advisers. Also aboard was the genial Presbyterian theologian Robert MacAfee Brown. While the Catholics dozed or watched a TV movie, Brown was hard at work writing an article about the Council. John Calvin would have been pleased . . . but not surprised.

This seems an apt place to cite an article I myself wrote about the translation work which took me to Rome and home again. It appeared in the *Evening Sun* a decade after the Council closed:

> Shaking the hand of a man who had shaken Rasputin's hand; talking to a man who had talked to Lenin: these were fringe benefits of a trip that took me to Rome as translation editor for *The Documents of Vatican II*.
>
> In April of 1965 I happened to be visiting the New York office of the Jesuit weekly magazine *America*. The editor had been asked to prepare a book of commentaries on the five council documents already released and the eleven others which were to be issued by the end of that year. The trouble was the poor quality of the translations already in circulation. Would I be willing to make or obtain better translations for the *America* book?
>
> I had taken six years of Latin in the seminary, had studied six more years of Latin in textbooks, and had read daily from Latin prayer books and missals since my ordination.

sophic attacks about the meaning of meaning. What did more than two thousand bishops from all over the world of 1965 mean by this precise Latin word of which the dictionary tells me the meaning in Caesar's and Cicero's time? Caesar and Cicero are dead. Where do meanings go when nobody happens to be meaning them? And of all the hundreds of thousands of English words, which one means precisely what non-English bishops mean when they use an ancient Latin word?

At times the old Latin had no simple equivalent for a modern word. Thus, guerrilla warfare became *bella larvata* —"masked wars." Two billion people became *vicies millies centena milia hominum*—"twenty times a thousand times a hundred units of a thousand men."

Not long after the book appeared, *Newsweek* reported *Commonweal*'s comment that since Walter Abbott, S.J., was its general editor, I its translation editor, Harry Costello its key sales promoter, and Cardinal Shehan the author of its introduction, the book was being called in the trade "the Abbott and Costello, Gallagher and Shehan act." *Deo gratias* for a touch of lightness amid the textual heaviness.

Oh yes: Rasputin and Lenin. My professional typist in Rome was an English woman with the delightful name of Pamela Charlesworth. She lived near the Spanish Steps and had English guests in for tea every Thursday afternoon. That's how I came to meet a certain Mr. Shelley, who was related to the great Romantic poet and who had met these famous Russians in his traveling youth.

He was a bright-eyed youth when he met the notorious monk who dominated the Czarina Alexandra. Contrasting the young Shelley's fresh eyes with his own rheumy eyes, Rasputin wrapped his beard around the youngster's hand and uttered these words: "The dewdrops upon the morning grass are the tears of joy; but the damp upon the evening ground is the weeping of fate."

In 1965 Mr. Shelley was working for the British Government as a Russian translator at the Geneva Arms Conference. It was especially enjoyable to meet such a fellow translator. He and his riveting stories were welcome fringe benefits in the midst of a project which was undoubtedly exhilarating but which occasionally seemed determined to push me beyond the fringe.

God is in the details.

Mies Van der Rohe

December 10

The first telegram of my confinement arrived today. It came from my first "fellow editor" at the *Catholic Review*, Gerry Sherry, who now edits the Miami Catholic paper. When my last "fellow editor," Ed Wall, who now edits the Chicago Catholic paper, heard of my heart attack, he contacted Tom Lorsung in D.C., one of the top editors at the National Catholic News Service. (Tom also worked at the *Catholic Review* in the sixties.)

Tom sent out a story over the wire service about "stricken former editor." That's how Gerry Sherry knew. That's also how the editors of the Philadelphia and Richmond Catholic papers were prompted to send me get-well notes. All these thoughtful editors were in the business thirteen years ago when I left the business. There aren't many old-timers still working in the U.S. Catholic press, and it was touching to hear from such veterans. Gone elsewhere are the heroes of my day like Sal Adamo of Camden, Thurston Davis and C. J. McNaspy of *America*, Bob Hoyt and Don Thorman of the *National Catholic Reporter*, Ed Flannery of Providence, Frank Lally of Boston, Don McDonald of Davenport, John O'Connor of San Francisco and Wilmington, and Don Quinn of St. Louis.

Among the admirable survivors are John Foley of Philadelphia, Charlie Mahon of Richmond, Jim O'Gara of *Commonweal*, and John Reedy of *Ave Maria* Press.

A priest who works with the Davenport Catholic paper resides in a rectory with my friend and seminary roommate John Hynes. That's how John heard about me on the other side of the Mississippi. Though I still wasn't allowed to receive incoming calls, John somehow got through the switchboard and became my first caller. So much for the barrier of distance and doctor's orders.

John had already booked an airplane flight in case I was in critical condition. I had long ago grown reconciled to the fact that John is one of those friends who might write you a letter only once in every five years but who would at a moment's notice volunteer to be shot in your place if the opportunity arose.

Mankind itself has such friends. One of these, Mother Teresa of Calcutta, was today presented with her Nobel Peace Prize in Stockholm. Her tiny body, wizened face, and luminous eyes were a blessed relief on the world's front pages and on the evening TV news.

🌳

"Mother Teresa, is there something that ordinary people can do to make the world better?"
"Yes. Smile at one another."

December 11

Dr. Sun is allowing me to sit in a chair for short periods a few times a day. I like to perch on the wide windowsill and watch the day "sadden into night," lights go on in buildings, neon signs activate, and cars engage in their rush-hour ritual. If it's raining, the reflection of car lights on wet asphalt streets is a bonus of beauty. As I watch pedestrians fighting the wind or the traffic, I feel like some serene divinity. I remind myself of a statement attributed to Charles de Gaulle: "I am neither left nor right; I am above."

Over there, near Baltimore's celebrated Shot Tower, a brand-new exit sign flashes on and off above the latest section of the Jones Fall Expressway to be opened up. Within me an artery is blocked up; outside of me an artery extends itself.

Jim Winders, one of my former students, tells me a curious story over the phone. His eldest daughter, Jennifer, is about seven, and a very sober-minded child. I guess I have visited her home about a half dozen times, and I last saw her less than three weeks ago. On the afternoon before I entered Mercy Hospital she was out walking with her grandmother and heard the siren of an ambulance. "I wonder," said Jennifer, "if that is Father Joe going to the hospital." Jim's wife was so upset by the remark that she urged Jim to phone me.

Tonight the friendly intern who presided over my attack stopped by for a long, refreshing chat. It turns out that his name is Jeffrey Gaber, so we bear the same initials. He is only twenty-eight, so that means he was born the year I finished college. He told me that he was covering Mr. Honaker for another doctor on the day of his death. He said he cried when he learned of the final, fatal attack.

As we talked about that death and as I voiced my thoughts about my own possible death, he said, "I feel awkward talking about Mr. Honaker's death or your own." I once heard of a study which indicated that consciously or unconsciously young people are attracted to medicine as a way of fighting back at death. The last doctor to tend to my mother finally agreed to my request that she be bothered with no further tests. "You know," he said, "we doctors hate to admit that we are licked."

Do everything as though it were the most important act in the world, but also as though you were going to die the next minute and it didn't make any difference.

St. Augustine

December 12

Life is a secret. Death is the key that opens it. But he who turns the key disappears forever into the secret.

Maurice Maeterlinck

December 13

I get all my exercise being pallbearer for my athletic friends.

December 14

My thirteenth day in the hospital was a lucky one. With a blood-pressure cuff around my arm and his finger on my pulse, Dr. Sun took me for my first walk outside of my room. So there truly was a corridor out there, and other rooms, and Christmas decorations, and a nurses' station with busy monitors!

The walk must have lasted for all of four minutes. When I returned to my room, I thought the doctor was going to say, "Well, now you can do that for ten minutes every hour." Instead he said, "That was your walk for today." "Aw, Doc, you should have told me; I would have savored it more."

He's quite a man of medicine, this Nelson Sun. He's a Chinese Filipino Presbyterian. He's short, has a beardless moon face, a beguiling smile, a staccato manner of speaking, and a fast walk emphasized by loud heels. By his own admission, he has four gray hairs.

He has been my doctor since October 1976. I was immediately struck by his keen mind, retentive memory, and observant eye and ear. He had been recommended to me by one of the nun nurses at the hospital.

He is an extremely busy and efficient man, and a number of the hospital staff told me he is their doctor too. By temperament, I'm sure, he is inclined to impatience. One day in my room he rang for the nurse and checked his watch to see how long it would take her to answer.

From the beginning he has been quite candid with me. Talking with me lately, he said quite casually, "When a man your age has had a catastrophic illness . . ."

One day he chided me for having eaten a chocolate-covered cookie (chocolate being one of the most forbidden elements in my diet). "Well, Doctor," I pleaded, "I'm like a sailor going to a bar on the last night before he goes to sea."

"Yes," he retorted, "but you also get a last meal before execution."

"I think you won that round," I conceded graciously.

I ended the day with another doctor, the friendly intern who presided over my coronary. Today being Hanukkah and he being Jewish, I sent Dr. Jeffrey Gaber an invitation to attend a quiet celebration in my room at 9:00 P.M. I ended the note with RSVP, explaining that the letters meant "Rescuers Should Visit Priests."

He couldn't get to my room until about 10:00 P.M. I offered him some Mogen David wine which Diana Roth, the typist of this journal, brought to me yesterday. He politely declined the wine, saying it puts him to sleep and he was on duty all night.

So, even without wine, this Catholic priest fell asleep once again, secure in the care of a Jewish and Presbyterian doctor.

❧

Hospital sign: "Patients should not attempt to get into bed without the attending nurse."

December 15

The purpose of an uncle is to be such a rake, roué and rapscallion that the father looks good.

Russell Baker

December 16

Some relatives are models; others are warnings.

December 17

I waited all day to have some X rays taken. I also looked forward all day to watching a TV documentary on William Faulkner tonight. You are allowed one guess as to when I was summoned to the X ray department. My official wheelchair pusher turned out to be an Iranian. When he somewhat sheepishly answered my question about his nationality, I shook his hand. Then I wondered what he thought I meant by the spontaneous gesture. Homer's *Iliad* was in my lap, since I am due to give a course in it next month.

The mention of Faulkner and Homer remind me that I belong, however tenuously, to that strange breed called writers. In my half century of life I have undoubtedly put more words on more blank sheets of paper than the average earthling. Let me increase my output by saying a few things about this writing business, starting with some flashbacks to my own tender beginnings.

Around 1940 I was a student at St. Ann's parish school when our pastor was marking some sort of anniversary. With or without provocation (my memory fails), I composed reverential verses for the occasion, and by reading them aloud at a school assembly I discovered the thrill of "going public."

A few years later a local Irish society sponsored an essay contest for eighth graders on Civil War General Philip Henry Sheridan. All I can now recall is that my entry included the text of a telegram, and with what I deemed to be devilish ingenuity I drew a box around each word and thereby simulated the look of the real thing. Well, I won the prize—$25, I think—and discovered the thrill of financial recognition.

When I was in the third high, the local Hearst paper offered a $25 war bond to the teen-ager who in fifty words or less could best set the community straight as to "What Baltimore Youth Needs." Not only did I cop the patriotic wartime prize, but my recipe appeared in the newspaper and its author was invited to the City Hall to meet Mayor Theodore R. McKeldin and to receive a certificate from his cordial hands.

All this escalation of reward was of course very heady stuff for this young dogmatist of a writer, and I had caught the virus. So I kept trying to write and publish, and by the time I graduated from college, mine eyes had seen the glory of a score or so of my verses and articles published in school papers and various Catholic journals and newspapers.

My first published poem, by the way, was on the subject of religious vocations and appeared in 1946 in *The Sacred Heart Messenger*, a national devotional monthly published by the Jesuits. My stipend was $5.00, and I couldn't get it out of my head that words printed on the check made reference to the New York Corn Exchange.

A few years later the national Catholic newspaper, *Our Sunday Visitor*, accepted an acrostic poem of mine which went to the considerable trouble of spelling "Come, Holy Spirit" sideways. The editor wrote to tell me that normally the paper did not pay for verse but that an exception was being made in my case. Enclosed was a check for $.50. That's the kind of spiritual recognition a writer likes to frame and preserve, but such were my worldly needs that I had to cash in on it.

At the end of my college years I made a discovery which was actually an effect but which became a cause. I took the traditional graduate record exam from Princeton and was hugely surprised to learn that my score on vocabulary and effectiveness of expression put me above the ninety-ninth percentile. These results gave a hefty boost to my literary morale and prompted me to take more seriously and confidently my inclinations toward writing.

During my four university years I wrote frequently for the seminary magazine. By the time I was ordained the archdiocesan authorities were aware of my interest in writing. Four years later Archbishop Keough made me an editor of the diocesan newspaper. For more than seven years that job exerted on me a constant pressure to write, to broaden my interests, deepen my knowledge, discover my convictions and test them. Since leaving the *Catholic Review* I have found in the Baltimore *Sunpapers* my chief regular outlet for writing. Both as a regular and an occasional columnist I have appeared more than one hundred times in the morning, evening, or Sunday *Sun*.

As for the craft of writing, I'd like to distinguish between the matter and the manner. On the matter of matter, I'd say a writer needs a love for knowledge and a love for communicating it. From my early childhood I have wanted and needed to know—in part, no doubt, because I had problems and felt the pain of unknowing, and the menace of it. Later I felt the exhilaration of "seeing the light," and of pushing the threatening circle of my ignorance back another millimeter or two. Since I knew what delight and relief came from discovering, I presumed that if I could be the agent of discovery for other people, they, too, would be delighted and relieved, and I would earn their gratitude and admiration and maybe even their love. Unskilled, I strove to find in successful sentences my touchdowns and home runs and baskets.

I see the effective writer as one who has something to say—information, insight—and *has* to say something—motivation, compulsion. It won't help much if his attitude is that he has to say *something*.

Now if a writer has something to say and has to say it, he or she will want to say it as lucidly as possible, as winningly as possible, and as memorably as possible. Clarity will permit the mind to grasp it, winsomeness will make the mind want to grasp it, and memorableness will aid the mind to keep on grasping it.

It is largely from reading other authors and being angry when they are obscure, bored when they are dull, and forgetful when they are shapeless that a writer best discovers what qualities he wants in his own style. So good writing is a lifelong task, both at the writing pad and away from it. Occasionally, when someone asks me how long it took to write a certain piece, I say, "My whole life."

Here are some maxims which have guided my own writing:

(1) Easy writing makes hard reading. As Samuel Johnson ob-

served, what is written without effort is generally read without pleasure. But the art is to hide the art. You must sweat in order to make your writing seem effortless.

(2) Good literature is not written but rewritten. This is the first maxim rewritten. Occasionally an excellent piece may be produced almost spontaneously—but it will probably be by a writer who has done reams of rewriting in the past, so that he practically rewrites before he writes. (Even God may require rewriting. A minister's daughter asked him where he got the ideas for his sermons. "From God," he replied. "Then why do I see you scratching things out?")

(3) A good writer must not merely see to it that he can be understood. He must ensure that he can't be misunderstood. Lincoln called this "bounding a thought on its north, south, east, and west." This task requires imagination: how will these words strike someone who is coming to them fresh, without my special background? It has been sagely advised that a writer should never underestimate the general reader's intelligence nor overestimate his information.

It will help beyond the telling if a writer is stricken with the wonder of words—by the fact that a few little squiggles of ink can mediate the oceanic distance between one person's head and another's, can even divert the course of history, or maybe only break someone's heart or revive a reader's will to live.

The great Cherokee Sequoyah was the only man in history to conceive and perfect in its entirety a whole alphabet (or, more precisely, a syllabary). He had noticed how the white man had those talking leaves called books and learned so much from them. He felt that if he could freeze ideas on paper, he would be like a man catching a wild animal and taming it.

A writer catches his tigers in words so that they can be released elsewhere. Words are the crates that ship tigers from the jungle to the zoo, or to another jungle. At least vital words do. Lackluster, threadbare, unimaginative words ship bones from one graveyard to another—if they do that much.

So Mark Twain could say that the difference between the right word and the nearly right word is the difference between lightning and a lightning bug. Approaching his task from another angle, the poet Housman said that he saw his problem less as getting the right word than as getting rid of the wrong one. (You carve an elephant, according to one sculptor, by taking a block of marble and chipping away at everything that doesn't look like an elephant.)

Make great efforts to get rid of overused adjectives, like "great." Promote fresh liaisons between nouns and adjectives. It has been said that adjectives should never be the wives of nouns, only their mistresses. Unlike God, Who, according to Edwin Arlington Robinson, had no adjectives in His vocabulary because He always had just the right noun, we mortals need well-functioning adjectives to give our nouns sharper focus.

There are, of course, various kinds of prose writing. What I've been saying applies mainly to writing which aspires to be literary instead of strictly informational (like the phone book). By literary I mean writing which is memorable in itself because it is so well expressed, and/or because it deals creatively, revealingly, with permanent aspects of human nature.

John Kennedy Hutchens was thinking of such writing when he defined his writing self as "a man alone in a room with the English language, trying to get human feelings right."

Sara Orne Jewett was thinking of such writing when she advised, "You must find your quiet center of life and write from that center to the world—and to the human heart, that great consciousness which all humanity goes to make up. Otherwise what might be strength in a writer is only crudeness, and insight only observation."

Finally, in his Nobel Prize acceptance speech, William Faulkner was describing his own best writing and the world's when he said that the writer must leave "no room in his workshop for anything but the old verities and truths of the heart, the old universal truths lacking which any story is ephemeral and doomed—love and honor and pity and pride and compassion and sacrifice."

☘

It's easy to be a writer. You just sit before a typewriter and open up a vein.

December 18

I love being a writer, but I can't stand the paperwork.

December 19

Last night was the most restless I've spent at Mercy this visit. I awoke about 1:00 A.M. and felt full of gas. In the "midnight dreary" I began to focus on the fact that I would soon be leaving all the reassuring support systems which have surrounded me since my attack. I was currently on no medication, not even the calming Triavil, which I had been taking since last January. What if I woke up in any of the nights ahead, couldn't get back to sleep, began to grow anxious, and then began to grow anxious about growing anxious?

Finally I rose from bed, did some packing, and spent more than an hour listing the people who have sent me get-well cards, Christmas cards, and gifts. Sleepiness eventually returned to me, and I to bed.

When Dr. Sun made his usual early morning visit, he consented to my taking Triavil again. He wants to see me in two weeks. In the meantime I am to ascend no steps, take no outdoor walks, not even be driven for a joy ride. These anticipated restrictions made it impossible for me to return to my own many-staired house, so I have already accepted my sister-in-law's invitation to spend the holidays with her and my three nephews.

Just before 11 A.M. a nurse wheeled me down to the business office on the main floor. In addition to doctors' fees and telephone charges (both as yet unspecified) my bill for eighteen days came to $3,916.00. (I understand the average Maryland hospital stay is eight days and costs $1,715.10 or $214 per day.) Fortunately, the archdiocesan medical plan will absorb most of this expense, which averages about $218 per day.

My sister-in-law Mary and her older sister Kitty were waiting for me at the hospital entrance. It felt good to be on the move again.

To spare me steps, Mary dropped me off in the alley behind her house. While I waited for Mary to let me in through the back door, I developed a shiver which seemed nicely symmetrical to the one I felt when I last crossed a private threshold.

My room for the next two weeks will be a kind of glassed-in porch off of the first-floor parlor. A fold-out daybed recently donated by Kitty will serve as my bed. A kitchen, dining room, and small bathroom are on the same floor. In the parlor a fragrant and full-bodied pine tree was already put up and decorations put on. The large portrait of my deceased brother continues to gaze down from above the fireplace. His eldest son will be absent in Ireland for these holiday weeks, but his own brother will fill up the empty chair around the Gallagher table.

All the Gallagher youngsters except Frank joined me for my first family meal this month. After the evening news, I began reading Garry Wills' *Confessions of a Conservative*. Mr. Wills, who lives but a few blocks from the Gallaghers, had sent me the book in the hospital and shown he was liberal with thoughtful deeds.

Thus ended the first half year of my second half century—back in the setting of my golden birthday party.

What is philosophy but a longing to be everywhere at home in the universe?

December 20

With the help of a Triavil and with the absence of nurses by dawn's early light, I slept thirteen hours my first night away from the hospital. My sister-in-law, in her unwonted role as substitute doctor and nurse, peeked in at me nervously several times, she said, as the hours wore on.

I myself am trying not to become too preoccupied with my damaged heart, lest I become a "cardiac cripple." A priest-friend of mine wrote to tell me how fearful he became after his coronary: "You, too, perhaps, have awakened to a world so totally different from the accustomed one that you fear what it will mean and do to you . . . with a damage that may never be out of your consciousness."

I believe I have an advantage in the fact that I didn't experience much chest pain. It's as though I suffered a neck attack and not a heart attack.

When the hospital doctor told me that I should gradually resume my former activities, I told him that with respect to celibacy, I planned to start by practicing five minutes the first week, ten minutes the second, and so forth.

A book I read in the hospital claimed that making love is the equivalent of walking up two flights of stairs, but I doubt that stair-climbing will ever catch on as a substitute.

✲

Look not back in anger, nor forward in fear, but around in grateful awareness.

December 21

They would have been equally horrified at hearing the Christian religion doubted and seeing it practised.

Samuel Butler

December 22

The important distinction is not between those who believe and those who do not believe, but between those who care and those who do not care.

Abbé Pire

December 23

The truly great man is not the one who can reach some extremity, but the one who can touch opposite extremes simultaneously.

Blaise Pascal

December 24

Christmas Eve: a time when many preachers are busy putting the final touches on their holiday sermons. *Time* magazine arrived today and contained a special feature on the preacher in America. This must have been the article for which Jim Bready of the *Sunpapers* asked me to submit a taped sermon several months ago.

But lo! and behold! *Time* said something to the effect that for Catholics the Mass as such is more important than the sermon and then proceeded to limit itself to a consideration of outstanding Protestant preachers in the United States. Quite a put-down, though not an entirely unjustified one.

I think of the Catholic pastor who was described as inaccessible on weekdays and incomprehensible on Sundays. Then there is the ancient story about the preacher who beamed when a parishioner told him that his sermons were reminders of the wisdom and mercy of God. Pressed for more details, the parishioner said the sermons were "beyond all understanding" and "never cometh to an end." I used to tell my students that if they couldn't hit oil in ten minutes, they should "quit boring." In other words, "Be specific, be picturesque, be seated."

Twins Jim and Pat were assigned to assist Archbishop Borders at midnight Mass at the nearby "new" cathedral (now twenty years old). So, their mother and the three boys went off to church sometime after eleven. Aunt Kitty and my niece Mary Ellen stayed home with me.

We watched the telecast of the midnight Mass from St. Peter's in Vatican City. Pope John Paul II was the celebrant and seemed to me less exuberant than usual. The Sistine choir was its usual dreary and dusty self. In fact, there seemed to be a heaviness about the whole affair, as though recent Vatican moves against theologian Küng had cast a pall over the Vatican.

I went to bed about 12:45, but bestirred myself when I heard the Gallaghers returning from Mass. It had been decided that, for the first time in this Gallagher family, gifts would be opened before bed and not before breakfast. In no time the living room was a sea of crumpled wrapping paper.

The four children gave me a new and needed watch. My cousin Judy had mailed from Philadelphia a gift "from me" for each of the Gallaghers. For the mother of five children to think of such a kindness while caring for her own dying mother was surely a classic form of thoughtfulness and an incandescent instance of what Christmas is really all about.

✣

People can't concentrate properly on blowing other people to pieces properly if their minds are poisoned by thoughts suitable to the twenty-fifth of December.

Ogden Nash

Christmas

It was my fifty-first Christmas to heaven, and at dinner I blissfully broke all the rules of my diet, celebrating with real sugar, real gravy, and real ice cream. To work up an appetite that needed no working up, I even took several afternoon strolls in the upward-tilting backyard. The day was balmy and windless, so I felt I was not violating the spirit of my doctor's indoor orders.

Though my body was confined to the Gallagher grounds, far-flung friends gifted me with the sound of their voices. Phone calls came from Al Nunes in Rhode Island, Paul Philbert in Washington, Linda Anderson in Florida, John Standafer in Iowa, and John Corcoran in Pennsylvania. I myself phoned greetings to Katherine Anne Porter, who is celebrating her ninetieth Christmas.

Representing in the flesh all the students I ever taught and all the couples I ever married, Russ and Julie Forrester from Gaithersburg, Maryland, stopped by after supper with a cache of forbidden Toll House cookies.

About 8:00 P.M. the phone rang and nephew John shouted from the kitchen, "Frank on the phone." His mother fairly leaped from her chair as she sped to the phone. Her firstborn son, the namesake of her husband, was calling from the ancestral home of all the Kellys and Gallaghers—Ireland itself. Young Frank was visiting Kelly cousins in County Limerick and had been trying for hours to get his call through. We all talked to him awhile. He said "the day hadn't felt too much like Christmas," but that was probably just as well for a twenty-year-old spending the holidays an ocean away from family and hearth.

Christmas doesn't always bring me the happiest of moods or memories. My mother used to tell me how my father would go down to the basement alone on Christmas day to weep for the mother who had died when he was nine years old.

During the first seven Christmases of my priesthood I was assigned to Baltimore's old cathedral. Those of us on the staff took turns being on duty on Christmas day. That meant eating your holiday dinner all by yourself. I remember those four little angels on the mantelpiece who spelled out the letters of "NOEL." One Christmas when I was on duty, I was impelled to rearrange the letters to spell "LONE."

There are many ways, of course, to be alone on a holiday. One year my sister (who had been born on December 26) was spending Christmas at a hospital after the trauma of losing a second child. I went out to say Mass for her in the otherwise empty chapel. Just before I started the Mass, Mary Jo said that she wouldn't be able to receive Holy Communion because she had absentmindedly broken her fast.

In those days strict Catholics viewed the Eucharistic fast as a serious matter; so, being a strict Catholic, I said, "Well, then I guess you won't be able to receive Holy Communion." In those good old days of yardstick religion, a prominent U.S. priest-theologian declared in all seriousness that chewing gum in church was probably not a serious sin unless the chewing was done "contumaciously."

As I proceeded with the Mass, I grew more and more angry about a man-made law which would prohibit a fragile and desolated person like my sister from receiving the comfort of Communion on such a Christmas day. I also became angry that such laws put me in such a bind on such an occasion.

Finally, at Communion time, I turned around and summoned my sister to come forward and receive Communion. Many people reading these words may laugh at such scrupulosity, or be dumbstruck that a thirty-six-year-old priest could have considered that he was slaying a dragon when he decided to take this sacramental matter into his own hands. But unless a reader can grasp the seriousness of my dilemma and the audacity of my decision, he won't be able to understand the kind of sacrosanct legalism from which the spirit of Vatican II helped to liberate many conscientious Catholics.

And if even a priest is finally going to be daring enough to seize the legacy of spiritual liberation which seems to have been the intention of Jesus Christ, then Christmas was as fine a day as any for the birth of such a new maturity and personal responsibility. . . .

For the Christmas following the nation's first energy crisis (1973), I composed an acrostic for my holiday card. I like the way it turned out; maybe it will grow truer as time passes by.

❦

CAROL FOR A SEASON OF SHORTAGES
(Cantique de No Oil)

L et nothing you dismay, abundant friend,
Y elp though headlines may of shortages,
I nclement months ahead and rationing—
N ever did a crisis lack its grace:
G ood hearts grow more warm by spreading warmth.

I nheritors of music, books and brains,
N ow we're spurred to travel more within,

A nd take more heedful trips to where we are.

M ay these startling luxuries be yours:
A mple wassails of water, banquets of bread,
N oticed feast of breathed-in air, of friends,
G ratitude for gratefulness itself,
E cstasies of painlessness, and clues from
R egal gifts found nesting in our straw.

December 26

I don't know everything. I am not that young.
                                        J. M. Barrie

December 27

We cannot meet enough people, and that is why we must read.
                                        T. S. Eliot

December 28

I speed-read *War and Peace* in about an hour. It's about Russia.
                                        Woody Allen

December 29

On this pre-penultimate day of the decade, my life in quarantine was once again a matter of phone calls made and received, some mail, some visitors, some reading.

An especially bright spot was the gift of a record from a former student. About five weeks ago I awoke to a spellbinding song on the radio. The announcer merely said afterward, "That was the ABBA." I meant to phone the station for further details, but my heart attack intervened.

But I did mention the song to young friend Dave Henry. On his generous own he called the station, was given a likely title, and went to a record store to buy me the song. Actually, he bought an album whose cover featured the suspected song. So I played the song right away today, and, sure enough, "Chiquitita" was the song that had transfixed my awakening ear.

Do most people have those enrapturing moments now and then when they hear a melody and fall into a kind of instant captivity, a kind of ecstasy, which makes them ravenous to hear the melody over and over again?

I've already mentioned how in the 1930s *Finlandia* triggered in me such an experience. Other such moments come easily to mind: I'm at the lonely end of the boardwalk at Wildwood, New Jersey, during World War II. Off in the distance a jukebox plays, and by moonbeams and breakers I first hear the music of "Full Moon and Empty Arms." Only later do I learn that this melody was part of Rachmaninoff's musical triumph over paralyzing despair.

(A quarter of a century later I'm in Rome one breezy August night and come across this *Second Piano Concerto* being performed inside one of the roofless ruins on the edge of the Forum. Several dozen passersby have already sat on the sidewalk to savor this unexpected feast, and my seminarian friend Pete Garthe and I join them unforgettably there beneath the stars that the Caesars saw.)

In the 1940s I'm returning alone at night to Camp Tekakwitha near Luzerne, New York. It has been my day off as a counselor, and as I walk around the lake in the pitchy black, somebody somewhere is playing Manuel de Falla's *Ritual Fire Dance*, turning the dark

into something magical and menacing beneath each glinty star—
"Down in the dim woods the diamond delves! the elves'-eyes!"

In the sixties I'm in a movie house in New York City, watching
Elvira Madigan. Surreptitiously, the background music moves to the
foreground as my ear is smitten by a theme from Mozart's *Twenty-
first Piano Concerto*. I couldn't believe I had lived so long without
having heard that entrancing gossamer melody. (Could it be that I
have yet to hear my favorite Mozart piece?)

A final instance: I'm watching the *Ice Follies* in Baltimore's Civic
Center in the seventies. All of a sudden one spotlight focuses on a
solitary skater dressed in a pink, flowing gown. As though hypno-
tized and oblivious of the audience, this young woman skates to the
bittersweetest melody I'd ever heard. Later I discover it was Judy
Collins, singing in her voice of crystalline velvet lyrics that could cut
through ice. As the final words of "Send in the Clowns" are sung,
"Well, maybe next year," the skater glides backward into the darkness. She fades away, but another ineradicable moment of beauty
has branded itself on my memory.

Happiness is more a matter of instants than of hours.

December 30

Some people live to read. Others read to live.

December 31

At last the last day of the seventies and of this journal has arrived.
It finds me in my twelfth day of convalescence at the home of my
brother's widow and their three youngest children.

I had an apt dream for my last sleep of the old year. I was a
seminarian again, packing to go home at the end of the school year.
Instead of large luggage I was using many small bags, since they
would be easier to lift. (Even in dreams must the heart be hu-
mored.) I thought of my seminary roommate John Hynes. If I

couldn't say good-bye to him personally I would leave on his desk a note of fond farewell.

The morning paper carried the latest on the U.S. hostage crisis in Iran, now in its fifty-eighth day. UN Secretary Kurt Waldheim is due to fly today to Teheran for an uncertain reception. This afternoon the UN Security Council voted to vote on economic sanctions if Iran doesn't release the hostages by January 7.

Meanwhile, the Russians continue to send shock waves into the world by sending more troops into Iran's neighbor, Afghanistan. The Vatican has reaffirmed its ban on theologian Hans Küng. . . .

Last night the celebrated Broadway composer Richard Rodgers died at seventy-seven. Many of his melodies are especial favorites of mine—"Some Enchanted Evening," "If I Loved You," "Shall We Dance?," "No Other Love Have I," and "Love, Look Away" (the celibate's song). It must be easier to die leaving such a living legacy.

The weather was genial—in the invigorating fifties, with the sky above a hearty blue. I took two brief walks in the backyard, one in the late afternoon while Archbishop Borders was walking into Mercy Hospital for a rest and extensive tests after feeling poorly for several days. (He ended up in my old room there—1111—while I am due to take over his suite soon at the archdiocesan home for the aging.)

My last letter of the decade came from Bishop Frank Murphy and contained a gift of money. A trinity of visitors graced the day: Eric Jacobsen before supper, former student Mike Bornemann just after supper, and acupuncturist Sister Charlotte about 9:00 P.M. She brought me a red flower candle for my "fire element." We toasted the New Year with fire water—she with Grand Marnier, I with crème de menthe.

Sister-in-law Mary (who hates New Year's Eves) went to an adult party. Nephew John went to a teen-age one. The twins stayed home (like their uncle), eagerly waiting for the New Year specials to appear on TV at 11:30 P.M.

A morning phone call came from Jimmy French, one of my very first altar boys, who lives north of Philadelphia. He was the first troubled youngster I befriended after my ordination, and today he followed an impulse to phone. He voiced his thanks for my part in helping him weather that disease known as adolescence.

In the last hour of the year I reminisced that during the span of the seventies I had taught six years at St. Mary's Theological Seminary, obtained a master's degree in creative writing from Johns Hopkins, published *The Christian Under Pressure* and *Painting on*

Silence, spent a summer teaching at Oxford, and inherited a house. In that same time my mother and older brother died, my eldest nephew nearly did so, and I had a heart attack but not a coronary conclusion.

A few seconds before midnight I ended a call to my friends the Corcorans, walked about twenty paces to the kitchen, and joined my two youngest nephews in watching a small TV. The illuminated ball was descending the tower over New York's Times Square and shortly turned into the number "1980." I hugged Pat and Jimmy, who were eating scrambled eggs and waffles.

This journal and its author and the hostages in Iran had all survived 1979. That year's blizzard and blossoms had come and gone, as had my friend Jack Hooper, who was hosting no customary party this festive night. Though more than "half in love with easeful Death," Katherine Anne Porter and Elliott Coleman had outlasted still another year, and, despite his cystic fibrosis, cousin Mike Doyle was well on his way to another spring.

Conquering sorrow with hope, Gina Woloszyn is expecting again. My eldest brother's eldest son was an ocean away singing "Auld Lang Syne" on the island of its birth, while with fireworks in the harbor our native Baltimore was welcoming rainily in the first New Year of its second quarter millennium, and I the first of my second half century.

Thirteen years ago, New Year's Eve was my final day as editor of the *Catholic Review*. I spent hours cleaning out my desk and filling up trash cans, almost wishing it was my life I was winding up and not just a traumatic episode of it. In a few days I would baptize the newborn twins who were spending their first New Year's Eve at this address.

Such tidy units for such an untidy life: fourteen years at home, twelve years in the seminary, eleven years working for the archdiocese, and thirteen as a vocational vagabond. Through it all, the pain has been plentiful, but so has the privilege.

Whether or not the twins and I ever reached our eighties, we had reached *the* eighties, and we—the oldest and the youngest of the Baltimore Gallaghers—had reached them together. My diet had been restricting me to herbal tea, skim milk, and saccharine. But at this pivotal moment I celebrated with genuine tea brightened with genuine milk and sweetened with genuine sugar. For, when it comes to celebrating, as when it comes to living, each and every blessed man must do the blessed best he can.

❧

I have had my conclusions for a long time, but I do not yet
know how I am to arrive at them.

Carl F. Gauss

Epilogue

My fiftieth year had come and gone,
I sat, a solitary man,
In a crowded London shop,
An open book and empty cup
On the marble table-top.

While on the shop and street I gazed
My body of a sudden blazed;
And twenty minutes more or less
It seemed, so great my happiness
That I was blessed and could bless.

William Butler Yeats
Vacillation IV

During 1980 I sold my home to cousin Danny Doyle, who came to fix the doorbell and stayed to buy the house. I stayed on as a care-free roomer. On July 14 I underwent successful quadruple coronary bypass at Johns Hopkins.

Before surgery and over Dr. Sun's cloudy frowns I visited my nephew Frank in England and finally made it to the village of Baltimore in southernmost Ireland. Also before surgery I baptized the son of the Woloszyns. The doctors have kept a close eye on him, and so far so good. John Standafer passed the Iowa bar and works for a prosecuting attorney. He and Roberta are the parents of two girls. My suspended priest-friend Bob works as a layman in health services in New York State.

My sainted cousin Anne died three weeks after this journal ended. Poet Elliott Coleman died of a stroke on Washington's birthday. Katherine Anne Porter drifted away in a nursing home near Washington on September 18.

In 1981 death came for Aunt Stasia, Dr. "Buck" Schaffer, Mary Meyer, journalist-friend Lou Azrael, who had a Baltimore by-line before I was born, and former student Cy Brunner, who had survived near-electrocution.

In the summer of that year I gave a Dante course in Davenport, Iowa, and was close enough to fulfill my dream of visiting Lincoln's home and grave in Springfield, as well as Mark Twain's Hannibal. Later that summer I paid my maiden visit to the Grand Canyon—it does not disappoint—and in a bed across from Disneyland I trembled through my first earthquake, centered off Los Angeles on its two hundredth birthday.

In early 1982 a mutual friend sent me back to Grenada to help the Jacobsens celebrate their golden wedding anniversary in the wake of the publication of Josephine's latest and highly lauded book of poems, *The Chinese Insomniacs.*

The last word is like unto the first: this volume is cordially dedicated to all the carpenters of my days—including friends made since the seventies (Rick Paolini, Steve Vicchio) and old-timers who were not mentioned in these partial pages, through no want of significance on their part nor of gratitude on mine. I can't resist a special word of dedication for my sixteen-year-old cousin Michael Doyle, who, despite his cystic fibrosis, found the energy to be excited about this book and whose stubborn survival baffles his doctors.

In the words of the Great Emancipator, I commend all of them and all my readers to Him Who can go with me and stay with them and be everywhere for good—that good which even in this often harrowing world "grows wild and wide, has shades, is nowhere none."

☘

Never lose sight of the graph of a human life, which is composed of three curving lines . . . always meeting and always diverging: what a man believed himself to be, what he wished to be, and what he was.

Marguerite Yourcenar

APPENDIX A

"An Open Letter to the U.S. Catholic Bishops"

by Monsignor Joseph Gallagher
the National Catholic Reporter, March 20, 1968

Your recent national pastoral letter was an obvious attempt at dialogue with American Catholics, an attempt marked by an unusual degree of direct response to the kind of painful and embarrassing problems which are more customarily passed over in silence when church officials speak officially.

This attempt deserves an open, candid response, or, rather, many such responses. Out of such dialogue a more balanced and creative idea of problems and solutions can be expected to emerge.

I write as a "middle-breed" priest with experience in an inner-city parish, in Catholic journalism, in an orphanage, a nuns' motherhouse and a high school seminary. Over the past year, I've had close acquaintance with senior college seminarians from thirty different dioceses. As philosophy teacher, confessor, and faculty member I've talked and listened for hundreds of hours as discussions centered on God, Christ, Christianity, the Institutional Church, the priesthood, celibacy.

From many points of view modern-day seminarians are or should be the hope of a renewed church. But many of the most talented, generous, and perceptive among them are leaving or are going to leave the seminary, and even the church. One of the key reasons is that the leadership of the church they were thinking of serving has an incredibly bad image, an uninspiring, disenchanting, alienating image.

Let me state the matter in the most extreme, unvarnished way, as they do among themselves: at worst, you seem to them repressive, reactionary, fear-ridden, un-Christian. At best (with a few exceptions) you appear as businessmen with little spiritual vision, men of religious mediocrity whose deepest loyalties, in a showdown, are to institutional values. More and more, these values "turn them off" as they and their peers in the world wrestle with more fundamental questions: does God really exist, is Jesus Christ anyone special, is the church more of a harm than a help in the quest for human fulfillment?

Mention the U.S. hierarchy, and what images come to mind? Bishop ousts energetic Paulists, southern bishop has pro-Negro priest removed, bishop disbands group seeking more meaningful liturgy, bishop fights with nuns over modernized dress, bishop disciplines seminary priests who fight fossilized worship, bishop proclaims, "My country, right or wrong," bishops frown on Dutch catechism, bishop calls leading Scripture scholar heretic and denies relevance of love to role of hierarchy, bishops flex political muscles over government aid to birth control program, over aid to Catholic schools, bishop praises U.S. war effort in Vietnam, bishop clashes with outspoken editor, bishops back expulsion of Catholic theologian who has the backing of his peers.

Many of today's best seminarians and best young Catholics are passionately concerned about human issues of war and peace (particularly Vietnam), racial strife, national and international poverty. They are trying to hold on to their faith in God, in Christ and in the church, and are trying to help others hold on to these. Yet they find you as a group either absent from the struggle, or positively complicating it, or squandering your moral prestige on issues of much lesser urgency. (Did you really have to comment negatively on the Dutch catechism? Do you realize that that book is helping to keep some people in the church?)

In a few harsh words: you seem to them almost hopelessly remote, institutional, establishment, bureaucratic, bourgeois, defensive, legalistic, real-estated, cigared, Cadillacked, mansioned. You give few compelling signs of any consuming, Christ-like concern for noninstitutional truth and justice, of open humility and penitence for past and present corporate sins, or of trust in the Spirit. You do not candidly own up to the dilemma of the birth control issue, a dilemma which clashes with your comforting words about trust in the magisterium.

No matter how eloquent your pastorals are or may be, they just won't be believed or taken seriously in the present atmosphere. As Eliza Doolittle sang, "Words, words, words, I'm so sick of words . . . don't tell me how, show me!" Many of your efforts at reform seem like polishing brass on a sinking ship. Or (to change the image) you are busy (at last) rearranging furniture on the flagship, but a large part of the fleet is just ignoring you and sailing off in its own direction.

Here are some random symptoms of what ails the hierarchy and alienates the best among the faithful:

(1) It is Christmas, 1967, birthday of the Prince of Peace who came to teach universal brotherhood. The war in Vietnam grows daily more barbarous. A presidential election year is in the offing. Many Americans, including many Catholics, are urging war actions absolutely repudiated by Vatican II. Pope Paul has asked the U.S. to cease bombing North

Vietnam. He has pleaded that New Year's Day be a special day of thought and prayer about peace and peacemaking. The local bishop issues a Christmas pastoral. *He doesn't even mention the Vietnam War.* Behold the relevant, compassionate, concerned local Church!

(2) An auxiliary bishop is to be appointed. He is to be a successor of the Apostles, a special representative of the Good Shepherd, a man of faith, a godly man fighting for eternal values. The Ordinary calls a press conference to announce the name of the new bishop and points out the special qualification of this new candidate to the fullness of the priesthood: he has had excellent experience in handling finances.

(3) It is New Year's Eve, 1967. The news announcer reports that the local Episcopal bishop refuses to resign and continues to defend the right of one of his priests to speak a critical view of the war. Says the non-Roman bishop: the church must be where the action is, where the agony is. She must get involved in the anguish of the times and give witness. Pause. The announcer continues: today the local Catholic bishop gave his annual financial report. Hearing this broadcast, a seminarian said to me with a sad shrug of the shoulder, "That's the whole story, isn't it?"

(4) A non-Roman bishop of New York announces that work will be suspended on the Cathedral of St. John the Divine in protest against the human misery existing within the environs of the edifice. Could one reasonably hope that the Catholic bishops would even consider doing the same thing with respect to the scandalously expensive National Shrine in Washington?

(5) A seminarian writes a letter of moral concern to Dow Chemical Co. about its manufacture of napalm, and receives in reply a six-page single-spaced answer to his specific questions. He is taken seriously. Another seminarian writes a three-page single-spaced letter to a bishop, raising questions about the bishop's bald declaration of support for the Vietnam War. The bishop sends a one-sentence reply regretting that the seminarian disagrees with him. No discussion of specific points, no willingness to bring out into the open the background to his thinking. The seminarian is not taken seriously.

The basic problem is not merely what seems to get the attention and the concern of institutional Catholicism in the U.S., but the priorities. Buildings and finances do have some importance, Catholic education does have some value; but what of the deeper, broader human issues? Is this not a case of the way that what we *have* to do keeps us from doing what we *ought* to do?

Is it altogether cynical to ask how long the U.S. bishops would have kept silent if U.S. planes were dropping contraceptives on Vietnam instead of 1.6 million tons of deadly and torturing explosives? Is life a Catholic concern only at the moment of conception or when abortion is considered, but not when thousands upon thousands of innocent *born* people are wounded or slain or made homeless? Is American Catholicism more American than it is Catholic? One would at least like to see these questions persistently raised and honestly faced by U.S. Catholic leadership.

If one accepts the premise that the institutional church is worth saving, what can be done? The first requirement is that the saving of the institution must not be given top priority. The institution must show that it is worth saving because it is willing to suffer and to die for Gospel values which are more important than the institution. To every bishop I would make other recommendations:

(1) Listen, listen, listen to what your people are saying, especially your young people and your seminarians.

(2) Don't be afraid to acknowledge your own confusion and sense of inadequacy as you strive to fulfill your supremely difficult role in the midst of an upheaval which is going God knows where and which will end God knows when. Such an acknowledgment will show that you are human in a way that honest people can respect and not inhuman in a way which they repudiate. Ask those who are critical or questioning to help you find the answer with them and for them and through them.

(3) Manifest more open and repeated concern about human values, whether specifically Catholic or not. Be willing to lose financial backing for your bold affirmation of Gospel values. Don't hide behind vague national statements. To make the Gospel real you must make it local.

(4) Own up to mistakes and weaknesses and failures, both personal and corporate. This will increase your credibility and be a reassuring sign of the presence of the Spirit. Such signs are what are most desperately and immediately needed.

(5) See to it that many pastoral-minded, open-minded, humanity-minded bishops and pastors are appointed as soon as possible. American Catholicism needs charismatic figures like Pope John and Bishop Bekkers who will not fear to trust the Spirit and wait for the eventual emergence of timely wisdoms from the community of believers, men who will not fear to express their values in such actions as living with the poor, renouncing the trappings of wealth and splendor, refusing to have expensive consecration photos taken of themselves, and to mark their installations with costly banquets. The younger generation is hungry for some signs that the church is more than a self-perpetuating and self-promoting big business and that the radical call of the Gospel can be heard in the institutional church.

(6) If you are emotionally, spiritually, or intellectually incapable of providing dynamic, pastoral leadership in this period of crisis, make way for men who can. The hour is already late, the need is urgent, and the possibility of massive alienation is altogether real. The church is obviously sweating blood in a new Gethsemane, but Easter is still possible.

APPENDIX B

"Pastoral Letter on Peace and Patriotism"
by Lawrence Cardinal Shehan
Archbishop of Baltimore
[*published in the* Catholic Review, *July 1, 1966*]

June 28, 1966

Dearly Beloved in Christ:

The approach of our national Independence Day provides me with an opportune occasion for suggesting some lines of thought about the patriotic duties of an American Catholic in the present hour. My desire to do so is intensified by the fact that I have just returned from Rome where, on the feast day of his patron saint, I heard our Holy Father itemize his various and unwearying efforts for world peace during the past year.

Pope Paul made specific mention of Vietnam where, in ever-increasing numbers, our fellow Americans and fellow human beings are fighting, suffering, and dying. He called it a land "tormented by a conflict and by struggles that make it suffer greatly and seem to have no end." He also spoke of the "worsening of the situation and the terrible prospect of a possible extension of the conflict."

Our Holy Father, of course, has been speaking and acting in harmony with the somber and urgent words of the Second Vatican Council on the unique dangers of war and warlike attitudes in the nuclear age. It is no secret that the immensely complicated situation in Vietnam is a source of grave concern to the whole world and also a subject of acute controversy, not only in our own country but throughout the world.

In the remarks which follow, I intend only the modest purpose of recalling some of the pertinent principles formulated by the Vatican Council concerning modern warfare. It devolves on each Catholic citizen in every country to weigh political situations in terms of such principles and to exert whatever moral and civic influences seem dictated by his conscience.

Christians of equal sincerity and equal devotion to the Gospel may honorably differ in their conclusions, especially when the problems are gigantic and important facts are themselves a matter of dispute. But certainly no Catholic who claims to find in the living teaching of the church a source of moral guidance can be indifferent to his duty to care about the overriding moral issues of modern warfare, as well as his duty to know and to follow the pronouncements of the church on the moral limitations even of lawful self-defense.

Because America is militarily the strongest nation in the world, because her policies can influence literally every human being on earth, and because numerically Catholics are the largest organized religious body in the United States, American Catholics have a particularly grave and binding obligation to follow the lead of the church and to exert their share of moral influence on the councils of government.

Let it first be said that the Vatican Council recognized the legitimate role of patriotism: "Citizens should develop a generous and loyal devotion to their country, but without any narrowing of mind. In other words, they should always look simultaneously to the welfare of the whole human family, which is tied together by the manifold bonds linking races, peoples, and nations." (*The Church in the Modern World,* ✠75)

Again, "The Christian faithful should live for God and Christ by following the honorable customs of their own nations. As good citizens, they should practice true and effective patriotism. At the same time, let them altogether avoid racial prejudice and bitter nationalism, fostering instead a universal love for mankind." (*Missionary Activity of the Church,* ✠15)

Though this approval of patriotism is qualified, the Council did not rule out, as Pope Paul did not rule out in his speech to the United Nations, a country's right to legitimate self-defense: "As long as the danger of war remains and there is no competent and sufficiently powerful authority at the international level, governments cannot be denied the right to legitimate defense once every means of peaceful settlement has been exhausted." (*The Church in the Modern World,* ✠79) Neither did the Council rule out what love of neighbor itself might demand, namely that one nation help another in its struggle against aggression.

The work of self-defense is normally carried out by the military personnel of a nation. Speaking of such, the Council affirmed that "those who are pledged to the service of their country as members of its armed forces should regard themselves as agents of security and freedom on behalf of their people. As long as they fulfill this role properly, they are making a genuine contribution to the establishment of peace." (*The Church in the Modern World,* #79)

Surely it is not blindly nationalistic for us to believe that most of the American servicemen involved in the Vietnam conflict are not acting and do not wish to act against their consciences. Hence, their valor is in itself worthy of praise, and their spirit of sacrifice worthy of more intense imitation on the part of their fellow citizens who are spared the perils and rigors of the battlefield.

At the same time, especially since modern warfare bears within it the seeds of global holocaust, the viewpoint of the sincere conscientious objector merits careful consideration: "It seems right that laws make humane provisions for the case of those who for reasons of conscience refuse to bear arms provided, however, that they accept some other form of service to the human community." (*The Church in the Modern World,* #79)

The Catholic citizen who can conscientiously support his government in a struggle against aggression, whether direct or indirect, must do all that he can to see that this struggle is carried on in morally acceptable ways. Such a citizen will, for instance, be guided by the Council's words: "Nor does the possession of war potential make every military or political use of it lawful. Neither does the mere fact that war has unhappily begun mean that all is fair between the warring parties." (*The Church in the Modern World,* #79)

In particular, the Council gave its "unequivocal and unhesitating condemnation" to "any act of war aimed indiscriminately at the destruction of entire cities or of extensive areas along with their population." (*The Church in the Modern World,* #79) It is clear how contrary to Catholic teaching are some of the suggestions occasionally made about the degree and kind of violence our nation should inflict on its enemies. The Council emphasized what modern popes have repeatedly affirmed—that all is not permissible in even a presumably lawful war of self-defense.

Because citizens who enjoy representative government are especially answerable for the decisions of their leaders, these citizens have a moral right to know, insofar as national security permits, the truth about government decisions and operations which implicate the general public: "There exists within human society a right to information about affairs which affect men individually or collectively, and according to the circumstances of each." (*The Instruments of Social Communication,* #5)

This right entails a corresponding duty of the citizenry to seek out the facts about government policy, especially in time of war, when human beings suffer injury and death in the name of one's own country. The Vatican Council was not speaking only of government leaders when it insisted: "The men of our time must realize that they will have to give a somber reckoning for their deeds of war, for the course of the future will depend largely on the decisions they make today." (*The Church in the Modern World*, ✠80)

It is difficult for a nation to wage war with restraint and to nourish sentiments of peace at the same time. This is true particularly when its own casualties begin to mount and the conflict threatens to grow in duration and intensity. In such circumstances, those who argue against restraint and against keeping a nation's war-making acts within moral bounds are likely to win an ever-greater hearing. Within our nation it seems that such harsh voices are growing stronger and are attempting to pressure our leaders into decisions which the Christian conscience could not endorse.

If we are to resist such lethal appeals to our understandable impatience, we must constantly recall that only on moral grounds can our cause in Vietnam be just. If our means become immoral, our cause will have been betrayed. Let us also avoid the narrowness of supposing that all the vice and bad will lie on one side of any major conflict and that all the virtue and good will lie on the other.

Assuming that our cause in Vietnam is just, our duties to mankind as a whole forbid us to indulge in passions of hatred and aggression. Indeed, viewing the world as a whole, the Council insisted: "Those who mold public opinion should regard as their most weighty task the effort to instruct all in fresh sentiments of peace." (*The Church in the Modern World*, ✠82)

Even though our hands are embattled, then, our hearts must remain steadfastly peace-loving. Otherwise, at the peril of an escalation which could end in mutual annihilation, we may fail to be responsive to the possibilities of reasonable and honorable negotiations.

That our President has earnestly sought such negotiations in the past, we do not doubt. That he and our other national leaders would gladly enter into such negotiations now we firmly believe. All of us have the duty to beg God fervently that He in His wisdom may quickly provide the occasion of such negotiations, and that they will be fruitful in lasting justice and peace.

✠ Lawrence Cardinal Shehan

"*An Open Letter to Mr. Mahoney*"
by Monsignor Joseph Gallagher
the Catholic Review, *October 28, 1966*

Dear Mr. Mahoney:

Two weeks ago in this column I expressed my belief that neither you nor all your supporters are necessarily racists. As your campaign draws to a close, however, it is necessary for the conscientious Catholic voter to evaluate the over-all meaning of your candidacy—a meaning which has serious religious implications.

That is why I am addressing this open letter to you and telling you why I personally cannot in conscience vote for you to be my highest political representative under the President himself.

Like yourself, I am an American, a Baltimorean, a Catholic, a Democrat, and a descendant of those Irish immigrants who knew the meaning of oppression. These common bonds might ordinarily have inclined me to a special sympathy with you.

I am sadly convinced, however, that your election would mean a victory for forces which are hostile to everything honorable which being Catholic, American, Democrat, and Irish should mean. I believe your election would harm the true interests of Baltimore as well as of Maryland, and would be a disaster for human relations within our already troubled community.

Whatever your own intentions, your campaign has inescapably made you the racist candidate, the candidate of blind fear—"Satan's holy water." As of this moment you have said or done nothing to suggest that you have a realistic grasp of the profound problems and dangers facing Maryland, nor that you have a serious program for solving these problems according to the best interests of this state's 2,954,490 whites and 596,910 non-whites.

Your slogan is a prime example of the mental and moral deficiencies of your candidacy. What do you really mean by saying, "Your Home Is Your Castle. Protect It"? What proof does it offer, for instance, that you have any sensible solution for the critical housing problems afflicting the nation's sixth largest city, in whose metropolitan area one half of all Marylanders live?

If your slogan means that you are against any law which would compel me to sell my house to any particular person or race, then I have no objection to it. But the typical fair-housing law does not require this. Rather, it merely specifies that when a house is placed on the open market, a potential buyer may not be excluded from the possibility of purchase solely on the grounds of race, religion, or national origin—an exclusion which would have to be proven.

Seventeen states and the District of Columbia already have such a law. No major upheavals have occurred, no one has gone to jail and fines have been extremely rare, even though the area covered contains 52 percent of the total U.S. population and 61 percent of its non-white population.

A few weeks ago a Catholic family moved into a non-Catholic section of Belfast, Ireland, but neighborhood bigotry forced them out. No doubt the family suffered from the charge that Irish Catholics are dirty, shiftless, uncouth, alcoholic, superstitious, and disloyal. (Irish Catholics in America long suffered from the same prejudices; even as prejudice called all Polish Catholics stupid and pugnacious, and all Italian Catholics malodorous, lustful, and criminally inclined.)

Now, a fair housing law in Belfast would not force Protestants to sell to Catholics. But it would keep bigoted people from discriminating against Catholic home-seekers solely on religious grounds. How would you feel about such a law, Mr. Mahoney, if housing discrimination in Belfast compelled several hundred thousand Catholics to live in decayed, ill-heated, rat-infested, disease-ridden, fire-prone, and crime-spawning ghettos in the city?

What if Catholics like your mother, wife, and children wanted to improve their lot and to escape from the ghetto but were kept from doing so by the threats and prejudices of the surrounding non-Catholic population? What would you think, Mr. Mahoney, of a Protestant candidate for high office in Northern Ireland whose slogan was "Your non-Catholic home is your castle, even when you are ready to sell it. Protect it from Catholics who might be seeking a decent castle of their own"?

Things look different, don't they, when we apply our Lord's words: "Do unto others as you would have them do unto you"? (This is the Lord Who, you say, wants you to win this time.) Were you not truer to your faith and your ancestry when you spoke out last November in favor of fair housing?

If your slogan means that a man has absolute lordship over his property and can use and dispose of it without consideration for the common good, then you are backing up the white man who unscrupulously uses his home for block-busting purposes. (Why can't he do what he wants with his own property?) If a Negro family legitimately buys into a bigoted white neighborhood, would you as governor call out the National Guard to protect that family's castle from hostility and harassment?

Your slogan leads many people to believe that property rights are absolute. Yet, for the sake of the common good, such rights have long been limited by zoning laws, health laws, building codes, and other legislation. Because God created the earth for all people and gave each person the right to decent living conditions, it is a key part of the common good that everyone should have equal access to needed housing. Those who frustrate that right are asking for disorder and violence.

Housing discrimination means that the Negro housing market is severely limited and competitive, so that the average Negro pays from 25 to 35 percent of his below-standard income on housing, while whites pay from 10 to 20 percent. Moreover, the "white noose" around the ghetto puts almost all the Negro housing pressure on areas just outside the ghetto, so that panic easily overtakes those areas and many nearby whites sell at a loss.

Reliable studies show, however, that where the market is truly open and where neighborhood integration is widespread and naturally gradual, property values do not decrease, but can actually increase. What panic means, on the other hand, was illustrated recently in Baltimore when a dealer bought a white home for $8,000 and sold it a few weeks later to a Negro family for $12,000. It is this same senseless kind of panic which causes stock markets to crash and banks to go under.

Most panicky whites can move, but where can a panicky Negro go who wants to get out of the ghetto? (A recent survey of Watts and Harlem suggests that Negroes fear the lack of police protection more than police brutality. Over an eleven-year period in Baltimore, four times as many non-white men were murdered as white, twice as many non-white women as white.)

As a harassed Negro father said in Philadelphia earlier this month, "We got out of a ghetto apartment that had no heat. It was cold, cold. My brother Jerry is with the Marines. What is he fighting for?" A few blocks away from where this family was being terrorized by white gangs, a fifteen-year-old white girl was raped and killed by a white teen-ager.

Everybody knows about the large and rising amount of crime committed by a small percentage of teen-agers. (Remember the wild white youths in Ocean City, Maryland and their annual Labor Day riots?) Suppose, Mr. Mahoney, that all Baltimore teen-agers were forced to live in the slum area of the city? No doubt their rebelliousness would grow, swollen by the anger of the innocent ones who were made to suffer for the sins of the few.

Would you be against "open occupancy" for such teen-agers on the ground that it would lead to the spread of immorality, irresponsibility, and criminality into "respectable" all-adult neighborhoods? If the resentful and desperate teen-agers began to demonstrate and riot, would you cite their behavior as proof of how right the anti-teen-agers were? . . .

The fact is, Mr. Mahoney, that American society, especially the large urban areas, is in serious trouble from the results of 250 years of history's cruelest system of slavery, of one century of racial discrimination, and of the galloping technological revolution which is making America's unskilled and undereducated poor increasingly worse off.

Unlike our Irish immigrant ancestors, the Negro of today can find no free land, does not find muscle power at a premium, finds no champion in labor unions, and cannot mask his minority status by a change of name or of clothes. In fact, Negro unemployment today equals the general degree of unemployment during the Great Depression.

Meanwhile, in a time of titanic struggle between democracy and communism, the world's 2 billion 70 million non-whites are watching the behavior of its 930 million whites. White America says it cares enough about the human dignity of 17 million South Vietnamese people to ask our black soldiers to die 10,000 miles away from home. But our own nation's 20 million Negroes are suffering from mounting despair at their human plight in the matter of housing, schooling, employment, and opportunity.

Like all the poor, of course, the Negro is invisible. We can see the miseries of the South Vietnamese, but we are blind to the human tragedies downtown.

In this critical situation, wise and intelligent leadership is needed in America as perhaps never before. Needed too are moral courage, deep human understanding, and a passionate belief in the brotherhood of all under God. Christians especially must realize that if they do not see God in their neighbor, they may never see Him at all.

But while the ship of state is leaking and burning, Mr. Mahoney, you are asking the first-class passengers to choose you as captain with the promise that you won't let the other passengers interfere with their pleasures and privileges. Meantime the whole ship is in peril of disintegrating.

You should not be surprised if the passengers trapped below protest and riot. When the draft laws were put into effect in the midst of the Civil War, thousands of hard-pressed Irish Catholics rioted in New York City for five days. Troops had to be deployed from Gettysburg that July of 1863 in order to quell the burning, looting, and killing which turned the city into a nightmare. Estimates of the death toll go as high as 1,200. (In Watts, thirty-four died.) Property damage was estimated at $1.5 million—in a day when money values were much higher.

In their frenzy, our Irish Catholic ancestors even burned down a Negro orphanage sheltering two hundred children, and set a number of innocent blacks on fire after lynching them on the streets of New York. The logic of their fury was simple: drafts were caused by the war, the war was caused by slavery, slavery existed because of Negroes.

Prejudice is a terrible thing, Mr. Mahoney, and human beings may do the most atrocious things when they tire of being the victims of it. The peril of the Civil Rights Movement is that revolution has led to hope, hope has led to frustration, and frustration is leading to fury. Maryland today needs a governor of unusual stature, intelligence, humanity. But you, Mr. Mahoney, are unfortunately the candidate of the prejudiced. You have given no signs of an ability to lead the ship of state through the perilous storms which may lie ahead.

I do not say that you realize all these facts. Indeed your seeming lack of realization is one of the most frightening aspects of your candidacy, even apart from the question of your competence to administer a billion dollar annual state budget and to formulate imaginative and courageous programs. You can't even keep your promise to block fair housing, since you can't veto federal laws, county laws, or city laws, and state laws can overcome your veto.

When comedian Dick Gregory's young son died, a woman from Atlanta called him long-distance to say that she had heard the news on the radio, and was glad of it. It served Gregory right for his work in Civil Rights. The grief-stricken Gregory paused a moment, and then answered, "I'm glad too. I had five million bucks insurance on that kid."

There was silence on the other end of the line for half a minute. Then the woman said, "I'm sorry. Forgive me."

Most of us will be sorry when, in God's presence, we realize what our prejudices did to other human beings, our brothers and sisters in Christ. Hatred is a failure of the imagination, and we would almost always know what fairness demands of us if we imagined ourselves in our neighbors' situation and pictured them as having the same human feelings and needs that we do. Eventually injustice boomerangs against even the selfish interests of the unjust person.

There will be no peace in America nor in the world until people realize that this is a time for moral greatness. But it is painfully clear, sir, that you are not gifted with the greatness required of a Maryland governor today. In a brotherly spirit I wish you every success—except in your aspirations for high office in a time of crisis.

Alas, how few books there are
of which one can ever
possibly arrive at the
last page.

Samuel Johnson